Consuming Empire in US Fiction, 1865–1930

Edinburgh Critical Studies in Atlantic Literatures and Cultures
Series Editors: Laura Doyle, Colleen Glenney Boggs, and
Maria Cristina Fumagalli

Available titles
*Sensational Internationalism:
The Paris Commune and the
Remapping of American Memory
in the Long Nineteenth Century*
J. Michelle Coghlan

*American Travel Literature,
Gendered Aesthetics, and the
Italian Tour, 1824–1862*
Brigitte Bailey

*American Snobs: Transatlantic
Novelists, Liberal Culture and the
Genteel Tradition*
Emily Coit

*Scottish Colonial Literature:
Writing the Atlantic, 1603–1707*
Kirsten Sandrock

*Yankee Yarns: Storytelling and the
Invention of the National Body
in Nineteenth-Century American
Culture*
Stefanie Schäfer

*Reverberations of Revolution:
Transnational Perspectives,
1770–1850*
Edited by Elizabeth Amann and
Michael Boyden

*Consuming Empire in US Fiction,
1865–1930*
Heather Diane Wayne

Forthcoming titles
*Emily Dickinson and Her British
Contemporaries: Victorian Poetry
in Nineteenth-Century America*
Páraic Finnerty

*Following the Middle Passage:
Currents in Literature Since 1945*
Carl Plasa

*The Atlantic Dilemma: Reform
or Revolution Across the Long
Nineteenth Century*
Kelvin Black

Derek Walcott: A Life in Pictures
Maria Cristina Fumagalli

Visit the series website at: www.edinburghuniversitypress.com/series/
ECSALC

Consuming Empire in US Fiction, 1865–1930

Heather Diane Wayne

University Press

Edinburgh University Press is one of the leading university presses in the UK. We publish academic books and journals in our selected subject areas across the humanities and social sciences, combining cutting-edge scholarship with high editorial and production values to produce academic works of lasting importance. For more information visit our website: edinburghuniversitypress.com

© Heather Diane Wayne 2023, 2024

Edinburgh University Press Ltd
13 Infirmary Street,
Edinburgh, EH1 1LT

First published in hardback by Edinburgh University Press 2023

Typeset in 11/13 Adobe Sabon
by Manila Typesetting Company

A CIP record for this book is available from the British Library

ISBN 978 1 3995 0571 0 (hardback)
ISBN 978 1 3995 0572 7 (paperback)
ISBN 978 1 3995 0573 4 (webready PDF)
ISBN 978 1 3995 0574 1 (epub)

The right of Heather Diane Wayne to be identified as the author of this work has been asserted in accordance with the Copyright, Designs and Patents Act 1988, and the Copyright and Related Rights Regulations 2003 (SI No. 2498).

Contents

Series Editors' Preface vii
Acknowledgments viii

Introduction: Getting to Know the Inter-Imperial
   "Lineages" of Domestic Commodities in US Fiction,
   1865–1930 1
   Methodology: Nation, Gender, Race, and Taste in
      Inter-Imperial Commodities 7
   "Geography in a Cup of Coffee": Nineteenth-Century
      Commodity Lessons 20
   Overview of Chapters 26

1. Cotton, Carmine, Coal, and Flour: The Ethics and
   Aesthetics of Domestic Consumption in Alcott and Phelps 40
   Jo's Imperial-Inspired "Prosing Away" in *Little Women* 44
   Avoiding "Oppressive but Extremely Distant Facts" in
      The Story of Avis 55
   Confronting Avis's Orientalist Gaze 60
   The "Inarticulate Passion" of Cochineal Beetles and
      Carmine Dye 66
   Conquering Florida's Oranges with a "Little Northern
      Pluck" 73

2. Maneuvering through Centuries of Inter-Imperial
   Fur Trading and Gold Speculation in Woolson and
   Ruiz de Burton 86
   Fur Trade Nostalgia in *Anne* 88
   Manipulating the Anglo-Saxon Goddess 98
   Anne's Consolidation of Power 105
   "A Great Acquisition" in *Who Would Have Thought It?* 114

	Imperial Extraction of New World Gold, Fifteenth Century–Nineteenth Century	117
	Layers of History in Lola's Shifting Skin Color	124
3.	**Bouguereau is Best: Disentangling Economic and Aesthetic Values in Norris and Du Bois**	135
	Global Wheat and Cotton Dramas	141
	Bouguereau as Cultural, Economic, and Political Capital	149
	Artistic Intrigues	164
	Concluding Studies in Contrast	170
4.	**Orientalist Consumption of Pearls and Blue Chinese Porcelain in Wharton and Larsen**	184
	Violent Desires for Pearls in *The Custom of the Country*	190
	The "Real Thing" and the Copy	200
	Undine's Royal Pearls and Global Vision of Conquest	211
	Shuttling Toward Orientalist "Things" in Larsen's *Quicksand*	215
	The Inter-Imperial Hybridity of "Blue Chinese" Porcelain	219
	Weaving an Integrated Selfhood	228

Conclusion   235

Bibliography   244
Index   266

Series Editors' Preface

Modern global culture makes it clear that literary study can no longer operate on nation-based or exceptionalist models. In practice, American literatures have always been understood and defined in relation to the literatures of Europe and Asia. The books in this series work within a broad comparative framework to question place-based identities and monocular visions, in historical contexts from the earliest European settlements to contemporary affairs, and across all literary genres. They explore the multiple ways in which ideas, texts, objects, and bodies travel across spatial and temporal borders, generating powerful forms of contrast and affinity. The Edinburgh Critical Studies in Atlantic Literatures and Cultures series fosters new paradigms of exchange, circulation, and transformation for Atlantic literary studies, expanding the critical and theoretical work of this rapidly developing field.

Laura Doyle, Colleen Glenney Boggs, and
Maria Cristina Fumagalli

Acknowledgments

This research project began with two deceptively simple questions: what is carmine, and why might a nineteenth-century writer of domestic fiction mention it repeatedly? Words are inadequate—though I will attempt it here—to express the depth of my gratitude to the remarkable Laura Doyle for creating the conditions that led me to ask these novel questions about a text I had read many times before and for urging me to share my findings with the wider world. With curiosity, intellectual rigor, and warmth, Laura has challenged and encouraged me at every iteration of this project. I likewise thank Laura for her own ambitious and provocative research to which my own is heavily indebted. I extend my thanks both to her and to the other series editors of *Edinburgh Critical Studies in Atlantic Literatures and Cultures*, Colleen Glenney Boggs and Maria Cristina Fumagalli; I am humbled by your support of my work. I thank the anonymous reviewers of my book proposal for their eager engagement with my argument and their astute insights about how it might be strengthened; this final manuscript is certainly all the better for it. Thank you to everyone at Edinburgh University Press, past and present, for working to bring my book into the world, including (but I'm sure not limited to) Susannah Butler, Michelle Houston, Fiona Conn, Caitlin Murphy, and Emily Sharp. I also owe a tremendous debt of gratitude to the meticulous Fiona Screen for her keen copy-editing eye.

Many others have read versions of this work while it was in progress, and I thank Randall Knoper, Asha Nadkarni, Marla Miller, Nick Bromell, and Suzanne Daly for their incisive feedback. The broad and at times dizzyingly ambitious conversations during the World Studies Interdisciplinary Project's 2015–16 Mellon Sawyer Seminar challenged me to think over a longer *durée* and over a wider geography. I appreciate those who have listened to and raised questions about chapters-in-progress at conferences, including those organized by the MLA, C19, the Society for the Study of American Women

Writers, the Nineteenth-Century Studies Association, the Constance Fenimore Woolson Society, and the Futures of American Studies Institute.

I am also thankful for my colleagues, students, and advisees over the years for teaching me the pedagogical implications of my research. I will never forget my students' rousing celebration of my dissertation defense, and I have learned so much in discussing the international contexts of *Quicksand* with them. My writing group made the completion of this manuscript possible, and I am especially grateful to Carly Houston Overfelt and Faune Albert for their constructive comments, companionship, commiseration, and camaraderie. Deepest thanks to all of my family for their constant support over many years of study, and to my parents John and Dale Wayne for the childhood trip to Orchard House that made me want to be a writer like Louisa May Alcott. My grandmother Viki Meyrick encouraged me to love reading from a young age, and I wouldn't be the reader I am today without her. I am in awe of the terrifyingly gorgeous cover image of cochineal dye created by my sister Danielle Dravenstadt, an artist and visionary. And most of all, I thank Rich, a true partner in work, in life, and in love, whose faith in my abilities has always far outstripped my own, and who has made sacrifices both big and small to ensure that I would be able to fulfill my vision for this project.

Introduction: Getting to Know the Inter-Imperial "Lineages" of Domestic Commodities in US Fiction, 1865–1930

In her 1841 poem "To a Fragment of Cotton," Lydia Sigourney apostrophizes the commodity whose volatile economic and political history would come to define much of the nineteenth century. With a curiosity and ambivalence about the circumnavigatory history of the scrap of cotton that sneaks its way into her home, the speaker of Sigourney's poem raises questions about the cotton cloth's origin that would be echoed by US writers for decades to follow about many goods beyond cotton. She implores, "If thou hast aught to say, / I'll be a listener. Tell me of thy birth, / And all thy strange mutations, since the dow / Of infancy was on thee, to thine hour / Of finish'd beauty 'neath the shuttle's skill" (9–13). Though the cotton does not literally speak to answer the question of its "birth" and "strange mutations," its physical presence in her home causes the speaker to imagine how the cotton's progeny has "sown themselves in every sunny zone / Of both the hemispheres" (21–2), how "Commerce loves thee well" (26), how "thou dost make / Much clamour in the world" (26–7), and how difficult it is to count the cotton's "many transmigrations" (36).

The speaker travels with the cotton across the globe, from "the vessel's hold" (38) where it sleeps "in ponderous bales" (39), to its transformation into "many-colour'd chints" worn by "the country-dame in Sunday-gown" (45–6), or its "slow emerg[ence] from the Indian loom" (47). Sigourney's fanciful engagement with this humble scrap of household cloth expands into a vision of the multidirectional nineteenth-century system of global trade, in which raw cotton was cultivated in the US and shipped across the Atlantic Ocean to supply material for England's cotton-spinning industry, with India also supplying inexpensive colorfully printed chintz cotton textiles to England and beyond. Awareness of this vexed international history fills Sigourney's speaker, like many of her fictional successors, with consternation about her responsibility given this knowledge, as she exclaims, "Mysterious Guest! / I seem to fear thee. Would that I had known / Thy lineage better, and been less remiss / In the good grace of hospitality" (58–61). Given cotton's "lineage" as a commodity harvested by the labor of enslaved people working under tortuous conditions, a commodity that would also later lead to the US Civil War and greater colonial and imperial expansion, Sigourney's speaker is perhaps prescient to fear this "Mysterious Guest."[1]

In a metafictional turn that closes the poem, the speaker wonders "what form / Thou next may'st wear?" (66–7), envisioning the globe-circling cotton finding its final form as "the pictured page" of a child's book (67), or as "the tablet of the sage" (72), or as bearing "some message from the Book of Life" (74).[2] With this conclusion that transforms the cotton cloth into the material upon which artists and writers form their fictional worlds, Sigourney reflects on the entanglement of cultural production with global flows of commodities. She deconstructs the process by which material goods trigger an imaginative journey to the geographically disparate points along its path of production and trade, awestruck at the slippery way in which such visions of economic conquest can make their way into the work that writers and artists produce.

Sigourney's poem thus poses a series of inquiries that would be investigated with greater urgency by the generations of US writers to follow her: what happens when you listen to what the objects in your home have to say? What should you do with the fearsome knowledge gained when following a commodity's many "transmigrations" across the globe? And what are an artist's ethical responsibilities once they have full knowledge of a commodity's "lineage"? *Consuming Empire in US Fiction, 1865–1930* examines the range of responses that late nineteenth- and early twentieth-century US writers developed to these questions. For writers from Louisa May Alcott to W. E. B. Du Bois, commodities like cotton were not mere *mise-en-scène* for their novels, but rather a symbol of the intimate connections between the domestic home and a globally connected economy shaped by inter-imperial conflict, exploitation, and extraction of natural resources.[3] Such connections became increasingly visible in the years during and following the US Civil War, as the Northern blockade on Southern cotton exports disrupted the British cotton-spinning economy, dependent as it was on a steady supply of raw cotton from the US, a disruption that was the impetus for further British colonial expansion to locate a source for cotton elsewhere, especially in India and Egypt.[4]

Consuming Empire pairs close readings of commodities depicted in fiction with these goods' global economic histories in order to shed new light on the strategies that both well-known and under-studied authors used to critique US economic expansionism at the turn of the twentieth century. I draw connections between texts as apparently dissimilar as *Little Women* and *The Quest of the Silver Fleece*, presenting possibilities for reconsidering traditional periodizations of US literature by identifying a common concern with the origins, paths, and destinations of imported and exported goods among these authors who depict commodities. Examining authors' strategic allusions to contested goods like cochineal, cotton, coal, oranges, fur, gold, pearls, porcelain, and wheat, *Consuming Empire* reveals a linked global imagination among authors who were often directly or indirectly critical of US imperial ambitions. Through analysis of a range of primary texts—mainly novels, but also poems, short stories, domestic handbooks, women's magazines, and geography textbooks—*Consuming Empire* identifies nineteenth-century precedents for twenty-first-century concerns such as ethical consumption, shopping locally, farm-to-table dining, single-origin coffee, buying goods "Made in America," and tariff policies. As *Consuming Empire* demonstrates, literary and cultural texts have long trained consumers to imagine their relationship to the world through the things they own.

In the late nineteenth and early twentieth centuries, debates about foreign trade policies entered the home and infiltrated literature in the form of internationally traded commodities. As Arjun Appadurai has convincingly argued, the circulation of goods can shed light on human relationships, and in order to unearth the truths about those relationships, "we have to follow the things themselves, for their meanings are inscribed in their forms, their uses, their trajectories. It is only through the analysis of these trajectories that we can interpret the human transactions and calculations that enliven things" (5).[5] This material history reveals the larger international maneuvers that these goods might have represented for the writers and readers of late nineteenth- and early twentieth-century US literature. Emphasizing the competitive, dialectical relationship between empires over the *longue durée*, Laura Doyle's framework of inter-imperiality helps to parse these fraught political and economic connections between empires that inhere in commodity representations. In Doyle's conception—developed in a series of articles and most recently and comprehensively in her book *Inter-Imperiality: Vying Empires, Gendered Labor, and the Literary Arts of Alliance*—inter-imperiality is "a long-historical, dialectical theory of relationality and power that integrates feminist-intersectional, economic, materialist, literary, and geopolitical thought" (*Inter-Imperiality* 1). This framework "names a political and historical set of conditions created by the violent histories of plural interacting empires and by interacting persons moving between and against empires" ("Inter-Imperiality: Dialectics" 160).[6] The interdependent relationality between empires raises urgent ethical questions, according to Doyle, because "the fundamentally co-constituting, labor-intensive conditions of existence install a dynamic interdependency and in turn an ethical call at the heart of relations. Empire builders eschew that call when they exploit productive labor and simultaneously disavow their dependence on its world-shaping efforts" (11). The nineteenth- and twentieth-century writers I discuss were likewise moved and troubled by the "ethical call at the heart of relations" that Doyle names, uneasily pondering over household commodities as emblems of inter-imperial relationality. Inter-imperiality is especially revelatory for interpreting literature, according to Doyle, because it "opens up new backstories about the sedimented political conditions of culture. Critical vocabularies of expropriation, creolization, and commodification, for instance, can now help us to name the longer history of these processes" ("Inter-Imperiality and Literary Studies" 337). In their fanciful, critical, and curious renderings of internationally traded goods, American writers of late nineteenth and early twentieth-century literature register the "longer history" of inter-imperial commodification that Doyle mentions here.

Consuming Empire locates the inter-imperial conditions that Doyle describes in the histories of the commodities that *fin-de-siècle* authors depict, combining a Marxist attention to capitalist economic structures, feminist analysis of domestic discourses, and postcolonial interrogation of imperialism, to interpret the ways in which late nineteenth- and early twentieth-century American novels "enliven" things and sometimes critique the interactions that create them. Commodities can serve as metonyms for the long chains of production and exchange that cross oceans and national borders—at times projecting US economic power, at others manifesting anxiety about the exploitative conditions under which such goods were produced and traded, and at others still registering uncertainty about the interdependent international trade relationships they represent. Drawing on Amy Kaplan's understanding of the word "domestic" as evoking both the home and the nation, I identify how discourses of domesticity contribute to an understanding of home, family, and selfhood in a global consumer market. In the novels I discuss, writers allude to foreign commodities to meditate on, efface, or disavow the uncomfortable realities of the United States' aggressive economic expansion.[7] Art objects in particular present opportunities for authors to provide metacommentary on national aesthetic values and cultural production. Thus, I consider the commodification of art itself, interpreting writers' allusions to paintings, sculptures, and artists as self-reflexive gestures to their own complicity in global capitalism.

By focusing on commodity representations in US fiction from approximately 1865–1930, I engage with a period of national turmoil, international expansion, and imperial ambition. The international commodities in late nineteenth- and early twentieth-century US novels materialize historical instabilities such as the Civil War and the global economic dependence on slavery that its fractures made ever more obvious; questions about rights, citizenship, labor, and the economy raised by the abolition of slavery; expansion of national boundaries and colonization of territories; rapid industrialization; population shifts to urban centers; and an increasingly globalizing economy.[8] Furthermore, global trade increased rapidly at this time; in the latter half of the nineteenth century, American imports of foreign goods more than doubled, and US exports to the rest of the globe quadrupled (Pletcher 9). With the dramatic rise in foreign imports so Americans' imagined participation in empire grew, as the consumption of imported goods functioned, in Kristin Hoganson's words, as "an act of imperial buy-in" (11). The United States' early connections to British mercantilism meant that Americans long had access to luxuries from across the globe. According to Carroll Smith-Rosenberg, "as a result of the trade, the riches of the world increasingly found their way onto the wharves of Philadelphia, Boston, and New York—Chinese silks and porcelains, Caribbean sugar, Brazilian chocolate, Indian calicoes, and British manufactures" (*This Violent Empire* 8).[9] Americans "bought into" empire at this time not only through their purchases but also through their policies, as the US sought consolidation of its status as a world power through territorial conquest and commercial expansionism. The larger history of expansion that took place in the nineteenth century provides an important context for the inter-imperial plot lines in the novels I will discuss, including the Louisiana Purchase, the War of 1812, the Mexican–American War of 1846–1848, the conflict over and eventual purchase of Florida from Spain, and the removal of Native American tribes from their land in Florida and elsewhere (Kaplan 26). By 1853, the newly emerging US empire had acquired territories from France, Spain, Britain, and Mexico, reaching the Pacific Ocean and continuing its imperial efforts in commercial forms of expansionism before turning overseas to Puerto Rico and the Philippines by the end of the century, and then participating in the massive clash of empires that was World War I.[10] In the decades after the Civil War, the US also experienced a period of dramatic economic growth, fueling both domestic production and international trade, and making the United States' imperial rise economic as well as territorial.[11] As the United States emerged as a global power competing for status in an inter-imperial field, writers crafted fictional commodities as metonyms for the United States' increasingly unsettled international economic relations.

In their depictions of cotton, wheat, pearls, and more, novels written between 1865 and 1930 unearth the often hidden web of connections between domestic consumption and imperial power. As Doyle suggests, "for millennia, aesthetic culture has been an effect and a witnessing voice of imperial dynamics" ("Inter-Imperiality: Dialectics" 182), and the writers I discuss here witness those imperial dynamics from a variety of subject positions. Some writers, like Louisa May Alcott and Elizabeth Stuart Phelps, warn against blindly avoiding the uncomfortable and often exploitative realities of imperial economies that are represented through commodities like cotton. Others, like Constance Fenimore Woolson and María Amparo Ruiz de Burton, excavate the "sedimented political conditions of culture" (Doyle, "Inter Imperiality and Literary Studies" 337) embedded in coveted commodities—those hidden conflicts that can script interpersonal relationships centuries later. Conscious of the determinative power of narrative, W. E. B. Du Bois and Frank Norris juxtapose commodity-driven dramas with moments of aesthetic acquisition to capture the symbiotic relationship between cultural and economic capital. Still others, like Edith Wharton and Nella Larsen, represent foreign luxury commodities as a means for women to access proximate imperial power in protest at their limited economic capital. Together, these writers establish commodities as a potent imaginative entry point for dramatizing Americans' varied and shifting attitudes toward US economic imperialism in the latter half of the nineteenth century.

In this introduction, I sketch out the theoretical methodology that guides *Consuming Empire*, which draws on transnational and postcolonial examinations of US economic imperialism in history and literature, historical and cultural analyses of global commodity chains, art historical interpretations of aesthetics in a global context, and American Studies' exploration of the intersection between consumerism and nineteenth-century definitions of selfhood. I then cull from nonfiction primary sources to demonstrate how thoroughly conscious nineteenth-century Americans were about how their consumption entangled them in a global, inter-imperial economy. Finally, I conclude with an outline of this book's chapter organization.

Methodology: Nation, Gender, Race, and Taste in Inter-Imperial Commodities

Interdisciplinary in scope, *Consuming Empire* brings together methods from history, art, economics, sociology, gender studies, cultural studies, and literary studies to assemble an integrated geopolitical analysis of Americans' material, gendered, affective, and aesthetic experiences of empire. Though the authors I discuss here write in a variety of genres and modes—sentimental, realist, naturalist, modernist; bildungsroman, epic, historical fiction, romance—they are united by their interest in the ethical, economic, and imperial implications of consuming globe-crossing commodities. Because such goods were so ubiquitous at the turn of the twentieth century, and because knowledge of the related rise of the US as an economic world power was almost unavoidable, attention to international commodities opens up an unusual constellation of authors and texts united around the issue of inter-imperial trade. Sentimental reform fiction by Phelps and sociological economic critique by Du Bois are brought together by their common awareness of the global injustices wrought by the cultivation of cotton. Children's literature by Alcott and naturalist drama by Norris join in their concern over the fluctuating prices of wheat and flour.

Consuming Empire reconstellates these authors and, in effect, re-narrates US literary history by drawing on recent scholarship that has reframed American history and culture in a more global context. My discussion in this section both situates *Consuming Empire* in relation to current scholarship and spells its further contribution in investigating the commodities that spurred US imperial ambitions internationally. Amy Kaplan and Don Pease's seminal 1993 volume *Cultures of United States Imperialism* has been hugely influential in reigniting American Studies' interest in and critique of US empire, sparking such strong interest that Susan Gillman asked in 2005 if American Studies had "gone imperial." Many scholars have described and contributed to the "transnational turn" in American Studies, including Laura Doyle, Paul Jay, John Muthyala, Shelley Fisher Fishkin, Paul Giles, Paul Gilroy, Françoise Lionnet and Shu-mei Shih, Caroline Levander and Robert Levine, Nicole Tonkovich, and Stephen Shapiro, among others. Of course, as Robin D. G. Kelley has persuasively detailed, Black historians developed transnational frameworks for interpreting diasporic African American experiences decades before transnationalism was in vogue in American Studies more widely.

The publication of *Cultures of United States Imperialism* sparked a field of anti-imperialist critique among Americanists and literary scholars that currently persists, with some more recent scholarship offering comparative methods as an important corrective in order to avoid simply reinforcing US exceptionalism through exclusive study of American imperialism in isolation. For instance, in a response to Gillman's 2005 article, Raúl Coronado stresses that a true critique of US imperialism must "learn and listen to those from outside the US" (214), while Hsuan Hsu highlights "the importance of developing comparative methods of analysis that would cut across multiple sites of colonialism and resistance without re-centering the US" (5).[12] Ann Laura Stoler likewise argues for comparative methods for studying colonialism because they can "help identify unexpected points of congruence and similarities of discourse in seemingly disparate sites ... Not least, such an exercise may challenge cherished distinctions between American empire and European overseas ones—or undo those distinctions altogether" (40). Though these particular comparative methods are beyond the scope of this book, they do underscore the value of widening one's interpretive lens to encompass a greater field of vision than is typically captured by traditional chronologies and geographies of literary study. Indeed, Christopher Hager and Cody Marrs link the work of transnationalism to the work of re-periodization, arguing that although the "remapping" work undergone through transnational analysis "is often construed as a problem of geography, we would argue that periodization is an unavoidable horizon and consequence of the field's spatiotemporal reimagining" (261) because "the literature of the nineteenth century is an archive not of progressive displacements but of coeval mixtures, piebald genealogies, promiscuous exchanges, and uncanny retrievals and durations" (266). The commodities that populate the novels I discuss here certainly bear witness to these "promiscuous exchanges," telescoping backward and forward in time as they tell the stories of the international paths they traveled and the inter-imperial struggles fought over them.

Globally oriented accounts of the many manifestations of US imperialism helpfully draw attention to the international jockeying for power that has nearly always, in some way, shaped US literary production. For decades, historians, cultural critics, and literary scholars have argued that the imperialist overseas territorial expansion of 1898 was not an anomaly in the United States' history, but rather part of a longer pattern.[13] Sharing this assumption about a long history of US empire, I focus specifically on the economic manifestations of US imperialism, which appear at various points in American history and culture, from the eighteenth-century eagerness for direct trade with China to the twentieth-century pride about the international reaches of US agricultural exports like cotton and wheat.[14] Though I address novels from the turn of the twentieth century, a longer, earlier imperial economic history looms within these texts through their indirect and direct references to the battles waged over the commodities they depict.[15] Literary texts like these, I argue, both reflected and affected readers' thinking about the fraught relations between empires figured in the goods they consumed, encouraging readers to navigate their roles as willing or unwilling participants in the United States' imperial economic mission more consciously. Looking closely at the commodities depicted in late nineteenth- and early twentieth-century novels can give literary critics a more expansive appreciation of the range of questions readers and writers confronted about their ethical entanglements, consumer choices, aesthetic judgments, and gendered participation in the economy.

Because literary texts often link their stories to imperial commercial endeavors, representations of commodities act as a synecdoche for international economic maneuvering among and between empires.[16] Many have noted the economic reaches of US imperialist efforts, terming them "capitalist imperialism" (Harvey), efforts of a "market empire" (De Grazia), or "commercial expansionism" (Pletcher).[17] By simultaneously "sustaining and exploiting whatever asymmetrical and resource endowment advantages can be assembled by way of state power" (Harvey 33), securing advantageous trade relationships, and exporting "the practices and values of laissez-faire capitalism to convert people into consumers and thereby expand markets" (Rowe xi), US economic imperialism establishes commercial relationships with other nations while sustaining US status as a world power.[18] As I elaborate later in this introduction, scholars of oil cultures explore how such economic imperialism becomes even more perilous when it perpetuates planetary disaster, and they examine how the aesthetic allure of fast cars or modern conveniences obscures the consequent environmental ravages.[19] If inter-imperiality, as Laura Doyle contends, "allows us to consider how aesthetic forms have arisen in part to negotiate in-between positions, amid the fluctuating, violent contests and economies of large states and within politically, ethnically or religiously layered traditions" ("Inter-Imperiality: Dialectics" 191), then depictions of commodities in fiction can offer an entry point for unpacking the inter-imperial entanglements they represent and the rhetorical maneuvers used to manage those entanglements.[20]

Fictional representations of commodities also seek to make sense of the United States' contradictory self-conception as a nation and an empire. Internationally traded commodities present a physical manifestation of the paradoxical nature of US imperialism, which has relied on discourses of exceptionalism to distinguish itself from older empires like Britain while simultaneously engaging in commercial practices that exploit geopolitical imbalances in power.[21] The inconsistencies in American national identity were evident from its early years as a nation, according to Carroll Smith-Rosenberg:

> Contradictions and ironies marked the birth of the new nation, contradictions and ironies that continue to this day. Is the United States the world's first postcolonial nation, the bold defender of democracy and self-determination around the world, or is it the world's most powerful empire? Which identity would be—is—dominant? (*This Violent Empire* 5).[22]

The contradictions in American identity were not limited to its anti-imperial origins and imperial ambitions, however; as Cathy Davidson contends, the early American novel addressed the "gaps in independence" presented by the uneven distribution of the promises of freedom articulated in the Declaration of Independence. The liberation of women and African Americans, rather than being secured "on the level of the political and legal system," was instead imagined "within a fictive world of words" (*Revolution and the Word* vii). A commodity like cotton tangles together all of the thorny threads described above: it invokes the labor of the enslaved African people who harvested it, the women's needles that sewed their way through it, the empires across the globe that depended upon a supply of it from the US, and the tension between economic self-sufficiency and expansion that it signified for the US.

In depicting the fetishized consumption of commodities from far-off lands, American novels at the turn of the twentieth century also dramatize the process of racial marginalization that US imperialism relied upon. Indeed, by 1906 W. E. B. Du Bois well understood the relationship between empire and race, writing in an article titled "The Color Line Belts the World" that "The policy of expansion, then, simply means world problems of the Color Line. The color question enters into European imperial politics and floods our continents from Alaska to Patagonia" (30). As Jonathan Arac and Harriet Ritvo observe, "in the nineteenth century, imperialism . . . names a historically crucial process by which an 'other' conceived as exotic is represented and subordinated for the purpose of strengthening the worldly place of a metropolitan nation-state" (3).[23] Buying Chinese porcelain or Persian Gulf pearls because of their seemingly exotic provenance was a way of "subordinating" the nations that produced these goods into an "other" whose sole purpose was to fulfill American consumer fantasies of a luxurious Orient. While Edward Said has detailed at great length the formation and deployment of Orientalist discourses in European culture, Malini Schueller argues that the United States' own imperial ambitions resulted in distinctive forms of Orientalist American literature, including three she observes in writing from 1790–1890: "literature of the 'Barbary' Orient," "Near Eastern Orientalist literature," and "Indic Orientalism" (3–4). Nineteenth-century national instabilities in the US precipitated racist discourses that attempted both to resolve these fractures and bolster imperial power; according to Schueller,

> a naturalized discourse of empire, predicated on oppositions, was interrupted by a violent destabilization of these oppositions, usually revealed in moments when questions of national incoherence surfaced. The Orient served the dual purpose of containing national schisms and constructing an imperial nationhood (3).[24]

Orientalist discourses around commodities reveal how this racial logic worked to solidify Americans' conception of home, to manage the reminders of foreign economic power brought on by imported goods, and to justify along racial lines who could participate in "free trade" or have the freedom to buy rather than be bought.

Racial constructions of difference were deployed not only to imagine imperial American dominance over the Orient, but also to maintain domestic hierarchies, and scholars of African American history have long recognized the harm done to Black Americans at the turn of the twentieth century by the interlocking forces of nationalism and imperialism. At the same time, African American writers, leaders, and historians have constructed transnational conceptions of Black identity as a form of communal resistance to the hegemony of empire.[25] Robin D. G. Kelley explains how Black intellectual transnationalism long preceded the more recent "transnational turn" in American Studies because of the unique displacement faced by African Americans throughout history:

> Black historians had to write the history of a "homeless" people, a people who resided in a country that was largely hostile to them—indeed, an entire global system that was both hostile and a central catalyst for their dispersal. In such a context, how could anyone not write histories that are transnational? (1077).[26]

At the end of the nineteenth century, as John Cullen Gruesser discusses, Black writers like W. E. B. Du Bois and Pauline Hopkins actively contributed to movements critiquing US imperial expansion and were more attuned to issues of race and empire than their white counterparts, perhaps because of their keener awareness and experiences of the contradictions in American identity that I outlined in the paragraphs above. Gruesser explains that

> in their responses to expansion African Americans differed profoundly from their white counterparts because they rejected racist assumptions and insisted on the salience of the country's founding documents, which whites, in embracing the negrophobia and xenophobia of the era, considered null and void in connection with U.S. blacks, Chinese immigrants, Puerto Ricans, Hawaiians, and Filipinos (4).[27]

For African Americans, the stakes of consumption and property ownership were likely different than for white Americans, as novels by W. E. B. Du Bois and Nella Larsen will illustrate in Chapters 3 and 4. African American consumption of commodities in an interimperial context is vexed and ambivalent both because of the history of Black intellectual resistance to imperialism and because of the historical commodification of African American people. According to Anna Arabindan-Kesson, this historical commodification was naturalized through nineteenth-century visual art that established "a kind of visual parity" between "Black bodies and white cotton," and Arabindan-Kesson "excavat[es] the ways this relationship emerged from economies of exchange in which cotton and Blackness enhanced each other's 'appearance of value' as commodity forms" in order to "propose a method for uncovering an ontology of the surface, crucial to such economies of exchange, in which things come to appear as they are" (27). As Sandy Alexandre further suggests,

> The interpellated thingness of blacks and the humanity of whites have been dialectically connected since the very formation of the republic ... One can well imagine the kind of identity crisis Americans must have undergone and simultaneously attempted fiercely to suppress or deny when blacks were transmogrified from objects of property into property-owning subjects (76).[28]

Literary representations of commodities can come to represent a conflict between the anti-imperial sentiment that would abstain from the spoils of capitalist expansion on the one hand, and the needs and desires fulfilled by having access to possession that had so long been denied to Black Americans on the other. As intertextual responses to their contemporaries, Du Bois's and Larsen's representations of commodities in particular reveal the racial stakes of consumption that white writers often ignore or avoid.

The investigation of a single object can lead one on unexpected journeys across time and space, as the recent work of historians, journalists, and scholars of American culture has shown. My study uses this method to reveal authors' meditations on the often disturbing histories of the labor expended and imperial power exerted in the production and trade of goods. In a 2005 *PMLA* article, Bruce Robbins terms the commodity history "a suddenly ubiquitous genre of popular nonfiction" (454) that answers "the question of how much sense ordinary Americans are making of the United States' ties with the rest of the world" (459). In this sense, contemporary histories of coal, cotton, pearls, or oranges perhaps perform for twenty-first-century readers similar cultural work as did geography textbooks for nineteenth-century Americans—though some contemporary texts encourage a more critical eye toward problems of capitalism, colonization, and imperialism. Classics of the commodity history genre, such as Harold Innis's *The Fur Trade in Canada*, Sidney Mintz's *Sweetness and Power*, and Mark Kurlansky's *Cod: A Biography of the Fish that Changed the World*, demonstrate the macroscopic insights to be gained through microscopic focus on objects like fur, sugar, and cod.

The period- and genre-busting recent work on "petrofiction," energy epochs, and "oil cultures" exemplifies how the cultural analysis of a single commodity—in this case, oil—can reconfigure existing paradigms of literary and cultural study. As scholars of oil cultures have shown, attention to the material conditions invoked in literature can likewise reveal how writers and artists register, critique, or even elide the material conditions within which their art is produced.[29] In their editorial introduction to the 2012 special issue of the *Journal of American Studies* on oil cultures, Ross Barrett and Daniel Worden identify how oil "complicates not only historical periodization but also the national boundaries that conventionally limit scholarly inquiry ... The global economics and politics of oil demand that we reevaluate the temporal and spatial boundaries of American Studies, as well as the 'natural' resources that we have neglected as historians and critics of American culture" (271). The 2011 Editor's Column in *PMLA* on "Literature in the Ages of Wood, Tallow, Coal, Whale Oil, Gasoline, Atomic Power, and Other Energy Sources" further pursues the question of how following commodities like oil might disrupt traditional literary periodization, wondering, in Patricia Yaeger's words, "what happens if we sort texts according to the energy sources that made them possible?" (305). The editors provisionally answer this question by situating authors as geographically and chronologically diverse as William Shakespeare, John Milton, William Blake, and Upton Sinclair within their respective energy eras to explore how idioms of wood, coal, oil, and other energy sources infiltrate their language and epistemologies, and other scholars have likewise probed the lexicon of energy and oil evident in work by Edith Wharton and Frank Norris.[30]

If commodities bring to the surface the inter-imperial struggles undergone to secure them, then oil is a particularly fraught commodity; as Amitav Ghosh speculates in his much-cited essay on "Petrofiction," oil's ugly history perhaps contributes to the glaring lack of literature about the "oil encounter" because

> To a great many Americans, oil smells bad. It reeks of unavoidable overseas entanglements, a worrisome foreign dependency, economic uncertainty, risky and expensive military enterprises; of thousands of dead civilians and children and all the troublesome questions that lie buried in their graves. (30)

Here, with his observations about the ineluctable "entanglements" and "dependencies" that oil creates, Ghosh seems in part to anticipate Laura Doyle's later argument about the interdependency and dialectical relations between empires, often forged through trade, and the resulting disavowal of such dependencies that emerge as an assertion of dominance.[31] As with the more ornamental commodities of carmine and pearls, oil can also be aesthetically seductive, as

Stephanie LeMenager discusses in her chapter of *Living Oil* on "The Aesthetics of Petroleum." LeMenager takes a metafictional turn to consider the media that is materially made possible by oil:

> Loving oil has a great deal to do with loving media dependent on fossil fuels or petroleum feedstock from the early to mid-twentieth century, when oil became an expressive form, although often hidden as such, in plain sight ... Literature and film have recorded sensory and emotional values associated with the oil cultures of the twentieth century. To explore how social affects might be shifted toward a different-looking and -feeling post-petroleum future, I read physical infrastructure against artistic forms such as the novel, keeping in mind that almost every media available to us today is materially and even philosophically indebted to oil. (66–8)

Writers and artists are themselves always enmeshed in the material worlds and economic systems that they depict or critique, at times calling into question how such complicity limits the capacity of their critical perspectives. LeMenager models self-reflexivity as one response to this critical problem, including an appendix to her book that analyzes and calculates the energy expended to produce and distribute her very own monograph. The nineteenth- and twentieth-century writers I discuss offer another self-referential tactic in their depictions of cotton, wheat, and pearls, indexing their own aesthetic labor in their portraits of visual artists who are various degrees of morally compromised within a violent *fin-de-siècle* world-system. In sum, here I have surveyed this scholarship in oil cultures in order to underscore the wider horizons made available through the study of a single commodity; as these scholars have demonstrated, and as I aim to suggest in this book, a single commodity has the potential to launch an entire subfield of study, to reconfigure existing literary periodizations and geographies, and to re-narrate the story of US imperialism.

Further study of fictional commodities is warranted because of the global context they provide for US-centric texts. The narrow lens of commodity studies makes the global connections between product, consumer, laborer, producer, capitalist, merchant, state, and empire clearer than a more wide-ranging economic analysis might allow. Sandip Hazareesingh and Jonathan Curry-Machado assess the descriptive power of commodities for studying global history, observing,

> Historically, commodities had multiple social lives, partaking both in imperial endeavours and in local resistance to them. The varied movements embarked upon in the course of these life cycles—local,

regional, across oceans and continents, within and beyond empires—make commodities a particularly apt mode of exploring global history (2).[32]

Sven Beckert's *Empire of Cotton* exemplifies the way in which an individual commodity can lead researchers along these "multiple social lives" across the globe, transforming variously into a tool of imperial power or economic resistance. Beckert's study explains why the cost of cotton is something one ought to care about, as Elizabeth Stuart Phelps argues in her 1877 novel *The Story of Avis*, and Beckert explicates the global exploitation of labor that was predicated on racial subjugation, a topic taken up by W. E. B. Du Bois in his 1911 novel *The Quest of the Silver Fleece*.[33] Linking together the divergent parts of the world that have touched these objects, commodity histories reveal the global traces that are typically obscured once an object makes its way to a shelf in the kitchen.

Though literary critics have usefully discussed the ways in which nineteenth-century US fiction trained readers to respond to the emerging consumer culture, in delimiting their focus to regional and national contexts, these critics at times overlook the larger geopolitical conditions of production and trade that many writers register, and that the global histories of commodities listed above illuminate.[34] Bill Brown observes in his discussion of the "things" in nineteenth-century novels that American literature reflects a "slippage between *having* (possessing a particular object) and *being* (the identification of one's self with that object)" (13). If, as I suggest, the "things" in US novels have global resonances, then this slippage discussed by Brown presents an important formulation for considering how objects have been collected, depicted, and mystified as a means of claiming a stake in the world economy through the power of consumption. Adapted for an American context, scholarship on commodities in Victorian literature by Suzanne Daly, Elaine Freedgood, and Andrew H. Miller reveals that American discourses around nineteenth-century commodities and consumerism were likewise concerned with national sovereignty, international interconnectedness, and the US's recent rise as an empire.[35]

Reframing nineteenth-century constructions of selfhood within an inter-imperial context offers another layer to the triangulation of US identity in relationship to the home and the marketplace, a triangulation that was often mediated through the possession of commodities, and navigated in literature.[36] Understanding and accounting for the global and imperial dimensions of this market economy, I suggest, lends further ethical complexity to the already fraught conception of self in a capitalist system that C. B. Macpherson terms "possessive individualism." According to Macpherson, the tradition of seventeenth-century liberal thought that persisted into the nineteenth century relied on a definition of freedom as self-possession or self-ownership. Because of this assumption, society thus "exists of relations of exchange between proprietors" (3). The problem with this ideology, as Macpherson observes, is that it results in a lack of collective political will, because "a possessive market society is a series of competitive and invasive relations between all men, regardless of class: it puts every man on his own" (271). As critics following Macpherson have illustrated, nineteenth-century Americans reacted to the entrenchment of their subjectivity in capitalist systems of exchange through a retreat to antimodernism (Lears), a renewed desire for authenticity in the face of increasing mechanical reproduction (Orvell), the naturalist fiction that internalizes the logic of capitalism (Michaels), or the ideology of domesticity (G. Brown).[37]

As important to the ideology of individualism as it was to the logic of empire, domesticity worked to construct the home as an insulated retreat from the unpredictability of the marketplace. While I focus here on the postbellum era, feminist scholarship on early American literature and empire has helpfully worked to center women's experiences in the nation's ideological formation, analyzing how early nineteenth-century women's political activity, economic consumption, and writing dismantled separate spheres ideology in the decades during and following the American Revolution.[38] Furthermore, as Gillian Brown and others have argued, in its idealization of "values of interiority, privacy, and psychology" (1), domesticity shored up the very same masculine individualism that it imagined itself in opposition to.[39] Because women's agency was precluded by nineteenth-century politics—even as liberal ideology depended on the withdrawal into self that domesticity figured—women exerted agency in their authority over the home, in their affective consumption of goods, and in their writing. Domestic fiction accordingly produced a form of "sentimental identification," as Lori Merish describes, working to "construct equivalences between material and subjective 'refinement'—between commodity and psychological forms—while suppressing the marketplace orientation of 'private' life, often by advertising a distinction between home and market" (*Sentimental Materialism* 2). If the complex integration of the home and marketplace was a philosophical problem that nineteenth-century culture worked in various ways to repress, then women's active participation in the literary marketplace and the money they made from the sale of sentimental images of the domestic space was rendered all the more suspect.⁴⁰ Sharing the longstanding awareness of the limitations of the separate spheres model, voiced by these critics as well as those of later nineteenth-century literature, I offer an alternative framework that draws on global history to better understand the ways in which women writers contended with the gendered, classed, and raced conditions of their unavoidable participation in an inter-imperially contested economy.⁴¹ As Ann Laura Stoler posits, studying the "intimacies of empire" allows scholars "not to turn away from structures of dominance but to relocate their conditions of possibility and relations and forces of production" (13).⁴²

An ever more complex range of moral questions come into view when it is not only the "marketplace orientation" of the home that must be suppressed, but also the exploitative labor conditions and imperial battles waged in the process of cultivating the commodities with which one develops such "sentimental identification." To follow commodities' global paths and to see literature's grappling with these paths enhances our sense of the ethical work of literature. Many late nineteenth- and early twentieth-century authors implicitly engage with commodities as "vibrant matter," in the way Jane Bennett urges. Bennett imagines a "vibrant materiality" that takes seriously the "capacity of things—edibles, commodities, storms, metals—not only to impede or block the will and designs of humans but also to act as quasi agents or forces with trajectories, propensities, or tendencies of their own" (viii).⁴³ Though postbellum writers would likely not have attributed the same degree of agency to objects as Bennett argues for here, the fact that the title character of *The Story of Avis* imagines that carmine textiles "throb" with the lives of the cochineal beetles that have "been yielded to make them" suggests that writers like Phelps did indeed appreciate—and struggle with—the vitality of the objects around them (133).

In tracing tropes of material culture within fictional homes we can follow two levels in which imperial structures of dominance can become embedded and questioned: the physical home and the literary text. The figurative language of literature also marks strategic absences or silences about colonial commodities. As Lisa Lowe points out, "Literature and literary language may offer us instruction in how to read for the presence of colonial goods and the absence of colonial labor and imperial trade in the history, politics, and economics of the modern world" (97). Such absences, according to Simon Gikandi, mark an unspoken discomfort about histories that consumers would rather repress, noting that in the case of slavery, "The culture of taste contains few overt traces of the violence of slavery, but this absence tells us a lot about the extent to which the agents of modernity and the civilizing process were willing to go to repress or contain what was considered to be unmodern" (87). In the American novels I examine, we find a diversity of responses to the suppressed history of exploited labor and inter-imperial competition that always bubbles beneath the surface of fictional commodities.

Finally, examining paintings and other art objects as a particular category of commodity reveals how turn-of-the-century US novels dramatize the naturalization of inter-imperial aesthetics. Questions about art's role in America's national and imperial identity are particularly relevant for this historical period because American high culture was in the process of being formed, institutionalized, and "sacralized" (Lawrence Levine 136).[44] Developing alongside these hierarchies of aesthetic taste was a culture of "conspicuous consumption" and "conspicuous leisure" centered around the performance of bourgeois identity, detailed in Thorstein Veblen's influential 1899 text *The Theory of the Leisure Class*. When taste is a signifier of class, artists become implicated in the market's exploitations because their aesthetic work participates in shaping prevailing norms of taste. I suggest that the late nineteenth- and early twentieth-century US writers discussed in this book nod to the complexities of such involvement through their self-referential depictions of visual artists.[45] As Edward Said has demonstrated, cultural production is also a battleground for imperial power. While he notes that imperialism's primary battle is "over land, of course," Said adds that

> when it came to who owned the land, who had the right to settle and work on it, who kept it going, who won it back, and who now plans its future—these issues were reflected, contested, and even for a time decided in narrative . . . The power to narrate, or to block other narratives from forming and emerging, is very important to culture and imperialism (xiii).[46]

Discourses of aesthetic taste exert this "power to narrate" in determining which stories are elevated and which are repressed. Such discourses are in turn naturalized to conceal the hierarchical cultural work they perform, which was, beginning in the seventeenth and eighteenth centuries according to Simon Gikandi, "the need or desire to quarantine one aspect of social life—the tasteful, the beautiful, and the civil—from a public domain saturated by diverse forms of commerce, including the sale of black bodies in the modern marketplace" (20). Fictional representations of art and artists in literature draw our attention to aesthetics' role in imperial assertions of cultural and economic power.

Writing in a variety of literary modes for a range of audiences and purposes, the authors I discuss use narrative techniques to critique, ironize, express ambivalence about, or encourage empathy for their characters' consumption of international commodities.[47] Each writer's response to commodities and US economic imperialism is inflected by their gender, race, and class position: a white woman writer like Louisa May Alcott is especially attentive to women's often complicated roles as consumers of domestic goods, while an African American male writer and sociologist like W. E. B. Du Bois is more attuned to colonization's effect on racial minorities' access to capital. A self-supporting writer like Constance Fenimore Woolson has a more critical relationship with the consumption of luxury goods than an affluent writer like Edith Wharton does. Furthermore, the evidence we have of these writers' political awareness—from María Amparo Ruiz de Burton's anti-imperialist proclivities, to Elizabeth Stuart Phelps's writings on a variety of progressive reform causes—helps us to understand their strategies for depicting internationally traded commodities. To help establish the pervasive degree to which these and other nineteenth- and twentieth-century Americans were conscious of the global paths their possessions traveled, in the following section I gather a range of primary sources that share an interest in the international origins of the goods in their homes. This assortment of geography textbooks, ladies' magazine articles, and newspaper columns attests to the range of economic and ethical questions that internationally traded goods raised for consumers during this era.

"Geography in a Cup of Coffee": Nineteenth-Century Commodity Lessons

Like the speaker of Lydia Sigourney's poem that opened this introduction, nineteenth-century consumers knew the origins of the commodities in their homes, and they thought about those origins in terms of empire and economic expansion. In children's geography textbooks, women's magazines, home decorating guides, consumer boycotts, and congressional debates about tariffs on imported goods, US consumers at the turn of the twentieth century expressed ample awareness of the international flows of production and trade that brought objects like cotton cloth into their households and out to the rest of the world.

From the early decades of American independence, geography textbooks instructed children on the United States' climate, topography, and major exports, as well as the geographic, political, and economic characteristics of the major countries of the world. In early America, Jenny Heil notes, these geography textbooks were "best-sellers second only to the Bible and Noah Webster's spellers" (626). Susanna Rowson, the British-American author most well known for her novel *Charlotte Temple* (1790), taught with a geography textbook she wrote herself, titled *Abridgment of Universal Geography* (1805). As Heil's analysis of this text reveals, geography books were not neutral transmitters of information, but rather they imparted ideological positions about the relationship between the US and the rest of the world.[48] Nineteenth-century geography textbooks took a variety of forms: an 1801 text by Nathaniel Dwight, for example, uses a catechism-inspired format to encourage memorization and recitation of questions and answers such as, "Q. What are the productions of Old Mexico? A. Gold and silver in vast quantities, sugar, indigo, cotton, cocoa, cochineal, and all kinds of tropical fruits in perfection" (195).[49] An 1875 volume by William Swinton even begins with an object lesson titled "Geography in a Cup of Coffee," a short story in which the children's merchant ship captain uncle visits and recounts the geographic origin of the coffee he drinks.[50] The uncle remarks mysteriously about the cup of coffee at the start of Swinton's story, quipping, "there is a good deal more in *that* than you suppose" (1). He continues in a playful Socratic-style dialogue with his niece and nephew to explain that the coffee likely came from Rio de Janeiro, where he recently sailed. He then inquires about the other items that make up his cup of coffee: the sugar from Cuba, the spoon made of silver mined in the western territories of the US, and the delicate cup from China. At the conclusion of the story, the uncle marvels at the "great multitude" of hands at work preparing the cup of coffee, including "the agriculturist, the navigator, the miner, the artisan, the merchant," before declaring, "Now, children, isn't there more geography in the cup of coffee than you had any idea of?" (3).

Books like Swinton's *Elementary Course in Geography* trained young children in the mode of geographic and economic inquiry that I propose twenty-first-century readers should adopt when approaching the objects in *fin-de-siècle* novels. Yet the novels I discuss also encourage inquiry that is often much more critical than the attitude of amused curiosity modeled by Swinton. If nineteenth-century schoolchildren learned to recite facts such as that the United States' leading exports are "cotton, tobacco, beef and pork, petroleum, gold and silver" (Swinton 57), or that the Chinese "manufacture all kinds of silks and cotton; the China ware is known among all civilized nations on earth" (Dwight 98), then those same objects, when represented in literature, must have called to mind "a good deal more ... than you suppose" (Swinton 1). Some texts even explicitly instruct on the material benefits of colonization; one 1919 text published after the Spanish–American War era of US territorial expansion explains, with a matter-of-factness likely jarring to the twenty-first-century decolonial ear:

> Many nations possess lands in foreign countries, called colonies. The Philippines and Porto Rico are colonies of the United States. Colonies are of great value to the mother country in various ways. Nearly all colonies are cheap producers of raw materials, such as tobacco, rubber, ivory, and spices, a large part of which are sent to the mother country; the colonies usually buy more manufactures from the mother country than any other nation. (Adams 36)

This framework initiates an early imperial mindset by teaching students to see colonies as sources of raw goods, without a full acknowledgment of the people who live in these colonies or the labor expended to extract these resources.

Women's magazines and domestic guides of the time similarly oriented their readers to the rest of the world through their knowledge of commodities. A perusal of the *Godey's Lady's Book* archives reveals that these magazines consistently educated their readers about the international origins of the objects in their homes, implicitly guiding readers to see their consumer purchases as an expansion of the domestic empire described by Amy Kaplan in her similar work on *Godey's*.[51] Such articles on the origins of commodities included treatises on "The Manufacture of Silk" (Hinckley), "Tea for the Ladies, and Where It Comes From," "India Rubber; or, Caoutchouc," and a months-long series in 1855 on "Furs for the Ladies, and Where They Come From." The latter article remarks on the particular draw of goods that come from afar:

> almost every country or city which produces or exports furs, imports and consumes the fur of some other place, often the most distant. An article is rarely consumed in the country producing it, but is eagerly sought by another quarter of the globe. A suit of English silver-gray rabbit is seldom witnessed in England, and when exhibited is far from being admired, as in China.

Women also displayed their knowledge of the nineteenth-century global economy in the decoration of their homes, which became a stage for performing their adherence to elite norms of taste through their selective juxtaposition of objects from different regions of the world. For instance, Harriet Prescott Spofford's 1877 home furnishing guide *Art Decoration Applied to Furniture* conceives of the nineteenth-century home in terms of ideals about nation and empire. Spofford makes a startling pivot from detailing the preferred styles of hand-carved chairs, the many elaborate ways to drape curtains, and the proper assortment of bric-a-brac to the geopolitical implications of this decor. She writes that the study of furnishing "is as important, in some respects, as the study of politics; for the private home is at the foundation of the public state, subtle and unimagined influences moulding the men who mould the state; and the history of furniture itself, indeed, involves the history of nations" (232). Illuminating the entanglement of domestic discourses and consumerism with the project of US empire, Spofford draws a direct connection between bourgeois acquisition and the nineteenth-century world-system. Spofford moralizes the aesthetic values that inhere in home decor, fantasizing that these values will transfer to the men who live among these signifying objects. Likewise, Edith Wharton's 1897 guide *The Decoration of Houses* draws a similar line between aesthetics and geopolitics, as I will discuss in Chapter 4.[52]

Yet many Americans during this era were sobered by the geopolitical implications of their consumption beyond the space of the home, and some even modified their consumer habits to effect political change. Quakers and abolitionists organized the "free produce" movement, a transatlantic effort to boycott goods produced by slave labor. Prominent nineteenth-century writers and activists participated in and supported the movement, including Lucretia Mott, Lydia Maria Child, William Wells Brown, Frances Harper, and Harriet Beecher Stowe (Glickman 890). A vision of the economy as globally interconnected gave this movement its force, as Lawrence Glickman explains: "In this interconnected world, every purchase affected other links of the chain; the manufacturers, distributors, and, especially, the laborers, whose jobs were all initiated by the first cause of consumer demand" (897). Elias Hicks, a Quaker minister and early proponent of the free produce movement, expresses his understanding of the connection between consumer and supply chain, asserting in an 1811 essay, "If we purchase the commodity, we participate in the crime" (15). Hicks imagines the consequences of a widespread international boycott of slave-produced goods, writing,

Should the people of the United States, and the inhabitants of Great Britain, withdraw from a commerce in, and the use of the produce of slavery, it would greatly lessen the price of those articles, and be a very great and immediate relief to the poor, injured and oppressed slaves, whose blood is continually crying from the ground for justice (16).[53]

Nineteenth-century women also debated the merits of buying American products instead of imported goods as a symbol of patriotism and economic "independence."[54] In an 1865 letter to the editor, a woman writing to *Godey's Lady's Book* mentions the recent efforts of the "New England Women's League for diminishing the use of luxuries during the war" to substitute American manufactured goods for imported ones as a means of lessening dependence on foreign goods. In this context, the author praises the merits of "Holyoke cotton" and "Portsmouth cotton spools," raising a rhetorical question about the possibility of American independence from foreign imports: "With all the necessaries, and, so many of the luxuries of the wardrobe already furnished here, shall we depend on foreign aid to complete the amount, or shall we so encourage our own artisans that nothing shall be wanting?" ("American Manufactures").[55] The United States' interdependence with its international partners in trade was debated not just in the pages of *Godey's*, but also on the floors of Congress.[56] Although tariffs were raised significantly to help finance the Civil War, they—controversially—remained at high levels once the war was over, so tariffs became a contentious political topic in the decades following the war, with tariff reform "a dominant issue in the elections of 1884, 1888, and 1892" (Eckes 37).[57] Whether motivated by the ethical urgency of boycotting slave labor, by the patriotic desire to demonstrate wartime self-sufficiency, or by a pragmatic wish to pay lower excise taxes, these Americans were well versed in the implications of foreign and domestic trade.

When considering these varied questions that commodities may have evoked for readers at the turn of the twentieth century, it is telling that most of the goods I will discuss in this book are "domestic" ones produced, harvested, or cultivated in the US and exported across the world. In the case of cotton, coal, and wheat, these commodities played particularly substantial roles in the United States' rise as an empire, since the US was one of the top global exporters of cotton and wheat in the nineteenth century, and the large reserves of coal in the US facilitated its independence from England.[58] An 1861 article in the *New York Times* takes pride in this economic self-sufficiency, much like the author of the *Godey's* letter praises domestic artisans.

The author tallies the shifting balance of trade during the Civil War and notes that while the US increased its reliance on domestic production rather than on imported goods, US export levels remained steady. The author opines that this data reveals that

> foreign nations do not bear the same relations toward us, for the good reason that we are self-sustaining, while they are more or less dependent ... The superiority of the United States over all other nations, in its commercial position or strength, is now fully demonstrated ("Our Civil War").[59]

By affirming the "superiority of the United States over all other nations," this article equates power in trade with imperial power, but this formulation also presents a paradox for understanding the United States' identity as an empire. While the author (along with many other Americans) celebrates the fact that the US is "self-sustaining," their conception of power in an inter-imperial economy simultaneously means that the US is not entirely independent because other nations find themselves "more or less dependent" on US exports. In framing this competition for economic status as a battle between "nations," the author obscures the imperialism that drives the economic desire for dominance over all other nations. Again, Doyle's conception of inter-imperiality is instructive here: she notes that inter-imperiality

> rests on the observation that, like persons, polities are co-constituted and thereafter coformed, despite all disavowals to the contrary. We might recall that a state's claim to sovereignty must be recognized by other states to exist or have force. Moreover, most empires, nations, kingdoms, and villages depend materially on trade, a relational activity. Even an embargo expresses a negative relation. (*Inter-Imperiality* 2)

In insisting that the United States is "self-sustaining" while other nations are "more or less dependent," the author of the 1861 article evinces precisely the kind of "disavowal" of relationality through trade that Doyle describes. Such disavowals no doubt contributed to the United States' self-conception as an empire, in part because, as Doyle contends, "Imperialist narratives of history rest on the denial of interdependence" (35).[60] The economic rivalry envisioned by the author of "Our Civil War" formulates an American national identity that is implicitly shaped by inter-imperial competition. Though the author lauds the reduction in consumption of imports "to one-half of their accustomed volume," the American importation of foreign goods throughout the nineteenth century was part of the American imperial imaginary, helping consumers envision their ownership over geographically distant lands.[61] Yet many Americans either repressed or dismissed any notion that nations and empires like England, Spain, Russia, Japan, or France might similarly imagine imperial control over the US when they purchased American goods.

Ultimately, in light of the varied political and cultural contexts I have described above, representations of contested commodity chains in literature may have called to mind for readers the many paradoxes of inter-imperial trade relations, including: the desire to compete for independent control versus the need to cooperate in interdependent commercial relationships, the draw of protectionist tariff policies versus the rhetoric of free trade, and the appeal of reciprocal trade agreements versus an unwillingness to adhere to equitable terms. Readers may have also felt the twinge of ethical questions about the impact that their purchases could have in perpetuating exploitative systems, or in signifying their status as patriotic American citizens. In my chapters, which I outline below, I attend to the novels' structure and narrative devices to explore how authors deploy language of conquest, rivalry, maneuvering, Orientalist mystification, and geographical distance in their representations of commodities as they attempt to make sense of the United States' emerging position as an economic and imperial world power.

Overview of Chapters

Consuming Empire maps fictional representations of commodities thematically and chronologically. Each chapter focuses on a specific set of commodities while also identifying certain kinds of critique (or "limits of critique") in the texts' treatment of them. At times my analysis indeed relies on the spatial metaphors of "digging down and standing back" (52) that Rita Felski names as endemic of "suspicious" literary critique that is "always 'on the lookout'–scrutinizing, scanning, searching, surveying, observing, gazing, examining. This looking is not a yielding gaze of pleasure, absorption, or entrancement but a sharp-eyed and diligent hunt for information, as we press beyond appearances to ferret out hidden dangers" (37–8). Yet, as I aim to show, the global lives of commodities in US fiction often do not require much "ferreting," but rather occupy the surface of these texts' concerns. Furthermore, following the lives of these commodities can indeed cultivate a "gaze of pleasure, absorption, or entrancement": I invite readers to linger and relish the material worlds of the novels I discuss, as I myself have done, and to allow these commodities to spark an imaginative (and at times critical) journey much in the way they did for the authors who wrote these novels.

Consuming Empire's chapters are organized around commodities' formal manifestations in the text—from calculated allusion, to allegorical drama, to strategic juxtaposition, to thematic motif. My chapter arrangement also attends to various categories of art references, including visual artists, collections of paintings and sculptures, the iconography of women's bodies, and artists' models. When paired with depictions of commodities, these artistic allusions knowingly nod toward the writer's perceived role in the literary marketplace. Meanwhile, in moving from the late nineteenth century to the early twentieth century, I track authors' responses to the United States' evolving global position, as the US emerged as a powerful agricultural exporter beginning in the 1860s and accelerating in the 1870s, and as it expanded its economic vision through increasingly aggressive territorial expansion at the turn of the twentieth century.

Chapter 1 traces allusions to cotton, carmine, oranges, coal, and flour in Elizabeth Stuart Phelps's *The Story of Avis* (1877) and Louisa May Alcott's *Little Women* (1868–1869). I argue that Phelps and Alcott explore the surprising intimacies between material objects in the home and transnational flows of capital and trade. By signaling toward the economic networks connecting India, Egypt, Mexico, Spain, and the US, these authors invite readers to become more attuned to the workings of the global landscape in which domestic dramas take place, and acknowledge their own complicity in international economic systems through their artist characters. In Chapter 2, I address the ways in which inter-imperial contests between French, Dutch, British, Russian, Spanish, Aztec, and American empires provide a script for characters' domestic rivalries in novels by Constance Fenimore Woolson and María Amparo Ruiz de Burton. By adorning their female protagonists with the detritus of inter-imperial trade in the form of fur garments and gold jewelry, Woolson and Ruiz de Burton meditate on the ideological and iconographic weight that images of women bear in the work of empire.

Chapter 3 discusses how Frank Norris and W. E. B. Du Bois juxtapose fictional art acquisitions with the instability of commodities markets to elucidate the arbitrary nature of economic and aesthetic value. Du Bois recenters Black people's experiences of global capitalism in what I interpret as an intertextual response to Norris's erasure of these realities. In *The Pit* (1903), Norris follows the wheat barons who profit from speculation on global markets, while in *The*

Quest of the Silver Fleece (1911), Du Bois depicts those who have been taken advantage of through the inequities of the global cotton trade. Using these authors' allusions to French painter William-Adolphe Bouguereau as a pivot point for comparison, I demonstrate how Norris and Du Bois dramatize the seductions and dangers of aestheticizing imperial economic ambition. In my fourth chapter, I compare the parallel paths of female protagonists in novels by Edith Wharton and Nella Larsen as they consume foreign goods like pearls and "China blue" porcelain in their attempts to triangulate access to imperial power. In Wharton's *The Custom of the Country* (1913) and Larsen's *Quicksand* (1928), Undine Spragg and Helga Crane attempt to buy their way into American dominance in inter-imperial trade, and they strive to perform a stable gendered identity when they pose for portraits by fictional painters. Serving as Larsen's critical homage to the class- and gender-bound struggles of Wharton's white heroines, *Quicksand* demonstrates how much more vulnerable women of color are to commodification and exoticization as they navigate a capitalist, imperialist, global economy. I follow this fourth chapter with a brief conclusion that considers the contemporary implications of studying literature as a prism that refracts writers' concerns about globalization and imperialism through their representations of internationally traded commodities.

These American novels are written within a specific historical period, yet they take us on a much longer and wider journey. They transport us to the gold-laden territory of the Aztec empire where Cortés first encountered Montezuma in the sixteenth century, to the frozen North American hinterlands where fur-bearing creatures were hunted in the seventeenth century, and to the rich pearl beds of the nineteenth-century Persian Gulf where native divers fished for oysters in treacherous conditions. If the historical journeys this book travels are consequently wide-ranging and, at times, eclectic, it is because of the symbolic density of the commodities depicted in these novels. Tug ever so slightly at the frayed edges of a scrap of cotton, and far-reaching threads will gradually unravel: threads of gendered consumption, racial exploitation of labor, intractable hierarchies of class and taste, questions about artistic production, inter-imperial competition, and historical paths of production and trade weaving ties transnationally over a *longue durée*. Phelps's *The Story of Avis* bears out a tale of international espionage over a coveted red dye, the production of which was kept secret by the Spanish empire, leading to at times absurd speculation that the dye was made from worms, or berries, or perhaps a worm-berry hybrid.[62] Digging a little into

Alcott's uncontextualized reference to a "Belzoni" reveals the story of Venetian archaeological explorer Giovanni Battista Belzoni, who had a checkered reputation for his mercenary and Orientalist plundering of ancient Egyptian sites.

These are just two of the many stories that have unfurled in the process of following my hunches about the histories embedded in American novels at the turn of the twentieth century; you will hear many such stories as *Consuming Empire* proceeds. I hope to show, as the uncle in Swinton's *Elementary Course in Geography* proved, that with novels written at the moment of the United States' consolidation of its power as an empire, there is always "a good deal more in *that* than you suppose" (1). These authors knew the truth in Swinton's remark. Their depictions of artists reflect a widespread self-consciousness among late nineteenth-century authors about their works' aesthetic merits and economic entanglement in a system of global capitalism. Ultimately, *Consuming Empire* illustrates the crucial cultural work literature performed in navigating the questions raised by the gendered geopolitical economy at the turn of the twentieth century.

Notes

1 On the colonial expansion driven by the cotton market, see Sven Beckert's *Empire of Cotton* and Ricky-Dale Calhoun.
2 See Joan R. Wry on Sigourney's poem about another household commodity, "To A Shred of Linen." Wry argues that Sigourney transforms the linen into an "expression of literary genius" (403) through her invocation of the sublime.
3 Laura Doyle has defined inter-imperiality as a framework for understanding the "dialectical accretions, convulsions and transformations" created by the "multi-directional interactions" between empires "over a very *longue durée*: dynamic and uneven, yet systemic and accretive and formative for 'modern' history" ("Inter-Imperiality: Dialectics" 160). Making a persuasive case for applying world historical methods to the analysis of literature, Doyle argues that inter-imperiality can allow scholars of culture to better see or understand "art's foundational entanglement in a multilateral and sedimented geopolitics, specifically as shaped by interacting states and empires, past and present" ("Inter-Imperiality: Dialectics" 183). Doyle develops her case for a dialectical, *longue durée* analysis of macropolitical relationality in her ambitious and wide-ranging 2020 book *Inter-imperiality: Vying Empires, Gendered Labor, and the Literary Arts of Alliance*.
4 See Beckert, "Emancipation and Empire."

5 A note on terminology: whereas a strict Marxist definition of "commodity" limits the term to a product of labor that has both use-value and exchange-value, I am not concerned here with a rigid delineation of the term, instead invoking it somewhat profligately throughout this book to refer to a wide array of physical goods that can be bought, sold, and exchanged across national boundaries—including works of art. Marx provides a much longer discussion of commodities in his chapter on the subject in *Capital* (125–77). However, Appadurai's discussion of the social function of commodities more closely captures my usage of the term. For further discussion of the social relations around commodity exchange, see Igor Kopytoff. For further discussion of recent commodities research, see Jennifer Bair.
6 Doyle elaborates her theory of inter-imperiality elsewhere as well, including in "Inter-imperiality and Literary Studies in the Longer *Durée*" and "Inter-imperiality: An Introduction."
7 As Kaplan elucidates, "To understand this spatial and political interdependence of home and empire, it is necessary to consider rhetorically how the meaning of the domestic relies structurally on its intimate opposition to the notion of the foreign. *Domestic* has a double meaning that links the space of the familial household to that of the nation, by imagining both in opposition to everything outside the geographic and conceptual borders of the home" (*Anarchy of Empire* 25).
8 These kinds of national instabilities often find their way into literary texts, as Stephen Shapiro points out, crediting the development of the early American novel to writers' anxieties about the United States' role as a "re-export republic" (5).
9 See also Patricia Johnston and Caroline Frank for the history and symbolism of US trade with Asia. They note that early Americans were eager for direct trade with China: "Intense desire for Asian commodities, particularly porcelain, silk, and tea, led to direct Asian trade immediately after independence. In the colonial period, trans-shipment through London had been the only legal means to obtain these expensive luxuries; smuggling them hidden among legal products from the Caribbean was a less costly avenue. No sooner was peace with Britain concluded than American ships embarked for China and other ports in Asia and around the Indian and Pacific Oceans . . . Within only six years of American independence, U.S. ships made fifty-two *recorded* voyages (probably more unrecorded ones) beyond the Atlantic basin" (5).
10 For a fuller history of these territorial acquisitions, see Walter Nugent. While Frederick Jackson Turner's presentation of his influential "frontier thesis" at the 1893 Chicago World's Fair attributed the rise of American democracy to these nineteenth-century westward conquests, critiques of Turner's thesis written as early as the 1920s indicate that his celebration of US territorial expansion was far from unanimous.

For further discussion of Turner's thesis and its subsequent critiques, see George Rogers Taylor.

11 As historian John Steele Gordon points out, in spite of the devastation wrought by the Civil War earlier in the century, the war also created a manufacturing boom because of the necessity to produce weaponry and supplies—a boom that continued well after the war (200). According to David Pletcher, "Between 1865 and 1900 the United States underwent an economic revolution. Its population more than doubled, and its gross national product (measured in terms of 1958 prices) nearly trebled" (9). Exponential growth in railroads, steel, and other manufacturing meant that wealth accumulated rapidly in the hands of the nouveaux riches (Gordon 260); however, the end of the century was met with increasing uncertainty, with a series of financial panics and depressions from the 1870s to the 1890s that temporarily stabilized before crashing again dramatically in 1929 (Pletcher 9).

12 See also Winfried Fluck, who expresses skepticism about transnational studies' ability to cover new ground in analyzing US identity formation: "The longterm prospect of transnational American studies may be to enhance our knowledge and capture the full complexity of America's international entanglement, but the short-term goal seems to take up the question of identity-formation again and extend it to elusive transnational identities" (380).

13 See Richard Slotkin, Reginald Horsman, Francis Jennings, William Appleman Williams, Walter LaFeber, Michael Hardt and Antonio Negri, and David Harvey. Assumptions of a long history of empire are reflected in historical approaches like that of Thomas Bender, and in literary and cultural approaches by John Carlos Rowe, Amy Kaplan, and Laura Doyle. Doyle's *Freedom's Empire* is particularly ambitious in the scope of its literary analysis, identifying a racialized narrative of freedom in Atlantic modernity in Anglo-Atlantic texts from the seventeenth century to the twentieth century.

14 David Harvey notes that while either a capitalist or territorial logic of empire may dominate at any one time, the two logics are difficult to untangle: they "intertwine in complex and sometimes contradictory ways. The literature on imperialism and empire too often assumes an easy accord between them: that political-economic processes are guided by the strategies of state and empire and that states and empires always operate out of capitalistic motivations. In practice the two logics frequently tug against each other, sometimes to the point of outright antagonism" (29).

15 Of the novels I discuss, Constance Fenimore Woolson's *Anne* deals perhaps most explicitly with inter-imperial trade through her dramatization of the former fur-trading epicenter of Mackinac Island, as I elaborate in Chapter 2.

16 While my approach is certainly indebted to critics like Walter Benn Michaels who have explicated the capitalist underpinnings of many nineteenth-century texts, I am more concerned with the ways in which US economic policies were conceived of in terms of imperial power. For more on the economic contexts of American literature and culture, see Hildegard Hoeller, David Zimmerman, and Alan Trachtenberg.

17 Thomas Bender also describes the often aggressive tactics used by the US to protect commercial interests across the globe, while Malini Schueller cites trade with Asia as an especially contested site of imperial scrambling (28).

18 Indeed, economists Kris James Mitchener and Marc Weidenmier analyze thousands of bilateral trade agreements from 1870–1913 and draw the conclusion that "being in an empire roughly doubled trade relative to those countries that were not part of an empire" (1806).

19 See, for instance, the work of Stephanie LeMenager, Imre Szeman, Amitav Ghosh, and Patricia Yaeger.

20 In his well-known "frontier thesis," Frederick Jackson Turner acknowledges this tension when he praises US westward expansion for limiting the necessity of trade with England and increasing the importance of domestic manufacturing, which would be able to reach the western regions of the US more readily, suggesting that "the advance of the frontier decreased our dependence on England" (Taylor 17).

21 See, for instance, Teemu Ruskola's discussion of US enforcement of extraterritorial jurisdiction in China beginning in the 1840s. Essays in Kaplan and Pease's volume *Cultures of United States Imperialism* elaborate on the employment of exceptionalist discourses to mask or deny US imperialism.

22 Daniel Immerwahr's engaging history of this "hidden" empire suggests that "One of the truly distinctive features of the United States' empire is how persistently ignored it has been . . . It is only the United States that has suffered from chronic confusion about its own borders. The reason isn't hard to guess. The country perceives itself to be a republic and not an empire. It was born in an anti-imperialist revolt and has fought empires ever since . . . This self-image of the United States as a republic is consoling, but it's also costly. Most of the cost has been paid by those living in the colonies, in the occupation zones, and around the military bases" (19).

23 Carroll Smith-Rosenberg notes that the construction of "fabricated others" has been a strategy since the beginning of the United States' history for rendering "insignificant the divergences and contradictions that divide us as national subjects. They mark the boundaries of our belonging" (*This Violent Empire* 21). But of course this idea of unification around shared national subjecthood is vexed because of the internal contradictions in American identity, which excluded Native and African-descended peoples.

24 Furthermore, as Laura Doyle elucidates, Anglo-Atlantic discourses of empire relied on a discourse of freedom that naturalized racial inequalities, and thus "race articulated a genealogy for the nation ... which in turn ennobled its imperial projects, profits, invasions, and enslavements as part of a people's world-historical freedom struggle" (*Freedom's Empire* 15).

25 See Robin D. G. Kelley, Paul Gilroy, and Michelle Ann Stephens.

26 See also Paul Gilroy's discussion of the "Black Atlantic," in which he suggests we consider the matrix of the entire Atlantic region and the ways in which it facilitates a diasporic Black cultural identity, taking the ship as his "organizing symbol" (4).

27 Kelley likewise points to the "problem of citizenship" as motivating African American transnational identification, writing that "the experiences of free African Americans during the antebellum era demonstrated that citizenship was beyond their grasp, and the Fugitive Slave Law of 1850 and the *Dred Scott* decision in 1857 denying black people citizenship rights cleared up any ambiguity on the matter" (1048), pushing early twentieth-century Black leaders toward "a point of profound pessimism" that made them "question their allegiance to and identification with the United States" (Kelley 1048).

28 Simon Gikandi argues that the institution of slavery troubled the notion of modern identity and the culture that attempted to mediate these contradictions because of modernity's emphasis on self-possession: "Modern identity was premised on the supremacy of a self functioning within a social sphere defined by humane values; indeed, the distinctiveness of this moment in the history of the Western world has been predicated on the existence of free and self-reflective subjects, not bodies in bondage" (18). This context, too, might add to the "identity crisis" that Alexandre speculates about, as early twentieth-century Black Americans became increasingly active participants in the culture that once sought to repress or erase them.

29 Amitav Ghosh's 1992 essay on "petrofiction" has been an influential inspiration, impetus, and call to action for this burgeoning field, arguing that the "oil encounter" is "a story that evokes horror, sympathy, guilt, rage, and a great deal else, depending on the listener's situation. The one thing that can be said of it with absolute certainty is that no one anywhere who has any thought either for his conscience or his self-preservation can afford to ignore it. So why, when there is so much to write about, has this encounter proved so imaginatively sterile?" (30). On energy epochs, see Laurie Shannon et al. Stephanie LeMenager explores the ubiquity of "oil cultures" in her book *Living Oil: Petroleum Culture in the American Century*, claiming, "compelling oil media are everywhere. Films, books, cars, foods, museums, even towns are oil media. The world itself writes oil, you and I write it. Petrofiction provides one route to understanding our entanglement . . .

This is a short cultural history of, essentially, destructive attachment, bad love" (11). See also Imre Szeman and Sheena Wilson et al.
30 On Wharton, see Alan Ackerman. On Norris, see Jeff Diamanti.
31 Saree Makdisi identifies similar themes of empire, interdependence, and disavowal in the work of William Blake, writing, "The great theme running through Blake's work is his engagement with the ontological capacity of empire, its drive to organize time and space and to situate human bodies in relation to them in order to most productively tap into and devour human energy—and, of course, he engages with the resistance to that power, the refusal of those forms of organization, temporality, subjectivity, and indeed, history" (319).
32 One such text that exemplifies the way in which commodities facilitate the study of global history is *The Global Lives of Things: The Material Culture of Connections in the Early Modern World*, eds. Anne Gerritsen and Giorgio Riello.
33 See also Amy Butler Greenfield's lively account of carmine dye, John McPhee's classic extended nonfiction essay on oranges, and Stephen Bloom's thoroughly reported deep dive into historical and contemporary pearl trades. Frank Trentmann's *Empire of Things* takes a more expansive view, aiming to tell a global history of consumption of all kinds, from the fifteenth century to the twenty-first.
34 See Miles Orvell, T. J. Jackson Lears, Gillian Brown, and Lori Merish.
35 For further critical theorization of the concept of entanglement, see Rey Chow, who describes entanglements as "the linkages and enmeshments that keep things apart; the voidings and uncoverings that hold things together" (12).
36 For a detailed historical discussion of various aspects of American material culture (including front hallways, dining rooms, embroidered mottoes, parlor organs, and seating furniture) and its meanings for Victorian consumers, see Kenneth Ames.
37 See also Mark Seltzer, who explores how the rise of technology and machine culture gave birth to a form of "disciplinary individualism" that stood in tension with possessive individualism. This nineteenth-century desire for authenticity was reflected in Mark Twain's performative tendencies, according to Randall Knoper, who suggests that Twain's "grasping for the 'genuine'" and "persistent sense that it was out of reach" is evidence for the realism of his oeuvre (2).
38 See Eve Tavor Bannet, Cathy Davidson, Elizabeth Maddock Dillon, Jenny Heil, Carroll Smith-Rosenberg, and Marion Rust. Bannet and Dillon have also contributed to the transnational turn in American literary studies, identifying the transatlantic region as an important object of study for material and cultural exchange.
39 According to Brown, "the account of market manhood to which domestic reformers object images a self by definition already domesticated, insofar as its character is secured and authenticated by the

domestic ideology of the home. Conceived as withdrawn to himself, the individual shares the definitive principle of domesticity: its withdrawal from the marketplace. While women's deployment of domestic ideology directs it to genuinely reformist ends and counters prevailing dispositions of power that disenfranchise women, their domestic reforms, instead of projecting an antithetical model of selfhood, further domesticate an already domesticated selfhood" (7).

40 The well-known debate initiated by Ann Douglas and Jane Tompkins in the 1970s and 1980s continues to help frame the stakes of such wariness toward women's popular fiction. While Douglas dismissed the artistic merits of sentimental fiction because of its apparently crass pandering to nineteenth-century emotional appetites, Tompkins argued for the merits of understanding sentimental fiction within its cultural moment and on its own terms, as "a blueprint for survival under a specific set of political, economic, social, or religious conditions" (16).

41 This skepticism was voiced influentially in Cathy Davidson's preface to the 1998 special issue of *American Literature* on "No More Separate Spheres." Of course, nineteenth-century women themselves demonstrated that the idea of "separate spheres" was a fiction: the boundaries of women's political power were challenged through the activism of women reformers (including Elizabeth Stuart Phelps) who agitated for a variety of progressive causes, including abolition, temperance, labor conditions, birth control accessibility, and suffrage. The 1848 Seneca Falls convention brought women's rights into wider public discourse, leading to the formation of women's suffrage groups, and to the eventual passage of the Nineteenth Amendment in 1919. By proposing the Equal Rights Amendment in 1923, the Woman's Party recognized that despite the achievement of women's suffrage, the battle for women's rights was far from over. See Deborah Madsen for a fuller history of feminist discourses.

42 For more on domesticity and women's cultural production within global and imperial contexts, see Nicole Tonkovich, Kristin Hoganson, and Laura Wexler. Asha Nadkarni demonstrates the nationalist and imperial stakes of women's bodies and reproduction, revealing just how "intimate" empire can become with her analysis of "eugenic feminism." For more on Anglo-American racialized logics of freedom, see Laura Doyle, *Freedom's Empire*.

43 In Stephanie LeMenager's analysis of Upton Sinclair's *Oil!*, she suggests that the oil itself takes on this kind of life and agency: "In the novel *Oil!*, oil itself returns, with almost every representation of its discovery, as an excessively embodied figure, the viscous medium of unregulated play. It is apparently more alive than its human witnesses" (93).

44 Although there were art galleries and academies before the Civil War, according to Alan Wallach there were no institutions that could be considered national museums until after the war, when the Metropolitan

Museum of Art in New York, the Museum of Fine Arts in Boston, and the Corcoran Gallery in Washington, DC were established. See also Randall Knoper, who tracks the influence of the emerging middle-class theater culture on nineteenth-century literature, focusing specifically on Mark Twain's performative strategies.

45 See David C. Miller, who uses evidence from literary and visual texts to argue that "artists and writers increasingly responded to and also helped to direct the opportunities opened up by expansion across the continent and into global financial markets. They interacted closely with such processes of the developing market economy as consumerism and commodification" (3). Russ Castronovo also comments on the global stakes of art and aesthetics. As Laura Doyle argues, inter-imperiality can be useful for understanding "the labours of art-making within a trans-hemispheric political force-field and economic system, and in turn may allow new insight into some artists' self-consciousness about their positions" (191).

46 As Elizabeth Maddock Dillon has illustrated, aesthetic judgment can also serve as grounds for resistance or dissensus. In "Atlantic Aesthesis," she argues that in an early American context, the process of "shared sensation and meaning making" (367) that she terms "aesthesis" has "the capacity to challenge the structural regime of imperial knowledge at the scene of the imposition of that violence—in the very face of books, guns, and compasses—insofar as aesthesis enables dissensus and the 'represencing' and repurposing of sensation and perception." (387)

47 For further discussion of nineteenth-century narratological strategies and the distance writers construct between their imagined readers and actual readers, see Robyn Warhol.

48 Heil highlights Rowson's invocation of Christopher Columbus as central to the cultural work her textbook performed, writing that she represents Columbus in such a way that it "serves to maintain a link between it and the British colonial past. Rowson does not neatly divide world geography into Old and New Hemispheres but rather puts Spain and South America at a distance from England and North America in an effort to project an Anglo future onto the continent" (628).

49 See also Cyrus Adams's 1919 text, which aims to "call special attention to the great trade routes that are followed by those commodities which are most prominent in international commerce" (v), following an expository structure, with chapters on countries around the world, subdivided into sections on the country's animal products, vegetable products, mineral products, manufactures, and commerce.

50 Many thanks to Karen Sánchez-Eppler for suggesting I investigate nineteenth-century geography textbooks, and for recommending William Swinton's book in particular.

51 In examining Sarah Josepha Hale's editorial work for *Godey's Lady's Book* and Catharine Beecher's *A Treatise on Domestic Economy*, Amy Kaplan identifies a discursive pattern of applying "the language of empire to the home and even to women's emotional lives" (28), examining the ideological function of symbolically imagining women as ruling over the "highly ordered space of the home" (30).

52 This sententious attitude toward home furnishings was prevalent among the nineteenth-century bourgeoisie, as Patricia West observes: "the single-family suburban home . . . began to take on mythical dimensions as the potential savior of American morality" (54). For further historical context on nineteenth-century home decorating, see Kristin Hoganson and Dianne Sachko Macleod.

53 For more on the free produce movement, see Elizabeth O'Donnell, who details the movement's British iteration. O'Donnell's article also helpfully drew my attention to the writings of Elias Hicks. See also Charlotte Sussman, who examines British anticolonial and antislavery consumer protests in the eighteenth and early nineteenth centuries.

54 Such consumer boycotts can be traced back prior to American independence, when Patriot men enlisted their wives and daughters in the boycott of British goods and encouraged them to sign nonimportation agreements (Smith-Rosenberg, *This Violent Empire* 137). While patriotism might have been one motivation for eschewing imported goods, community might have been another, according to Marla Miller. Early American women formed communal ties around quilting, according to Miller: "Women of the rural gentry certainly could afford to purchase the stylish, imported quilted petticoats made in London workshops . . . So why, we might ask, did they devote so much time and energy to the production of fine quilted petticoats? Quality, in part, provides an answer . . . But also worth noting is the degree to which collaborative quilting itself was valued by women of the rural gentry" (106).

55 An 1851 article by Kate Berry expresses the opposite sentiment about imported goods, writing that despite accusations of "an unpatriotic preference for foreign fabrics, customs, and manners," women need not give up imported goods to be patriotic. The author argues that women should instead use their influence in the home and their social circles in order to show patriotism. As historian Joanna Cohen demonstrates, these conflicting values of self-denial and self-indulgence eventually cohered into an ideology of the "modern citizen-consumer" (2), defined by the idea that "American citizens are free to consume without being asked to restrict their choice or alter their desires, that indulging in the world of goods is a positive civic good. It is the certainty that the liberty to consume has defined the meaning of American democracy and fueled the success of the modern American nation. It is the conviction that these same freedoms and rights should spread across the globe" (3).

56 According to Alfred Eckes, nineteenth-century politicians expressed two competing views on tariff policies: "Economic nationalists, or protectionists, argued for advancing the wealth and safety of the American nation through development of the domestic market ... Economic internationalists, or free traders, focused on improving the economic welfare of individuals and maximizing wealth in the cosmopolitical system" (29).

57 David Pletcher suggests that the ideological divide in Congress stoked the ferocity of these debates, observing that "despite the complexity of the tariff question, it, more than any other issue, was the touchstone of American politics during the two decades between the mid-1870s and the mid-1890s when the two parties were nearly balanced" (39). For more on nineteenth-century tariff debates, see Cynthia Hody, Douglas Irwin, and Joanne Reitano.

58 On cotton, see Beckert, Riello, and Schoen; on wheat, see Hunter and Perren; on coal, see Adams and Freese. Despite the United States' agricultural strengths, it was a net importer of goods until the 1870s, when it began a decades-long pattern of exporting more than it imported. See Robert E. Lipsey for more on the United States' historical balance of trade. Frederick Buell argues that "energy history is significantly entwined with cultural history" (273), and that understanding the movement from the coal era to the oil era illuminates how imaginative works internalized this shifting paradigm: "In considering oil history and ultimately culture, then, we need to consider the previous energy system it disrupted and transformed: we need to orient oil in relation to the energy system it emerged within and also disrupted, the system Deleir and colleagues call 'coal capitalism.' Coal capitalism deployed the steam engine, humanity's first converter capable of turning thermal into mechanical power; coal, thus converted, extended itself far beyond its extensive precapitalist uses (for heating and medieval industry once firewood became scarce), transforming the previous medieval energy system into the more modern coal-capitalist one" (277).

59 In case studies of nineteenth-century manufactured exports by companies such as Singer, Heinz, Kodak, New York Life Insurance, and McCormick, Mona Domosh identifies a similar discourse associating the United States' export of goods with its economic and cultural domination of other regions. Domosh suggests that "Western products were seen as active agents in the 'civilizing' process and proof that one had achieved the stage of civilization. Correct consumption, then, was not simply a social necessity but was a national imperative" (14).

60 For further discussion of the complicated co-formation of ideas of nation and empire, see Amy Kaplan, who points out that "imperialism does not emanate from the solid center of a fully formed nation; rather, the meaning of the nation itself is both questioned and redefined through the outward reach of empire" (12). John Carlos Rowe likewise

argues for the importance of examining "the complex relation between U.S. imperialism as it worked to expand national territory and functioned within its territory to consolidate the idea of the nation" (5).
61 This is certainly the case in Wharton's representation of pearls and Larsen's depiction of Chinese blue porcelain, as I will discuss in Chapter 4.
62 See Greenfield 125–42.

Chapter 1

Cotton, Carmine, Coal, and Flour: The Ethics and Aesthetics of Domestic Consumption in Alcott and Phelps

> "They adopted Jo's plan of dividing the long seams into four parts, and calling the quarters Europe, Asia, Africa, and America, and in that way they got on capitally, especially when they talked about the different countries as they stitched their way through them" (Alcott, *Little Women* 18).

Whether through competition with European powers over trade with Asia, or through debates about tariff policies, or through consumption of imported goods, nineteenth-century Americans could indeed imagine how "capitally" they got on through the economic ties they stitched between different parts of the world.[1] Such globally interconnected economic conditions surface through the commodities represented in postbellum domestic novels by women writers—including the goods I will discuss in this chapter: cotton, carmine dye, coal, wheat, and oranges. By punctuating their novels with allusions to the internationally traded commodities filling their characters' homes, women writers grapple with the imperial and ethical implications of their consumption, and use allusions to art and artists to self-reflexively consider their own place as writers selling their work in a global marketplace. Looking at Louisa May Alcott's *Little Women* (1868) and Elizabeth Stuart Phelps's *The Story of Avis* (1877) as illustrative examples, in this chapter I resituate nineteenth-century domestic fiction in a larger geopolitical context in order to examine how women writers reckon with the surprising and sometimes disturbing intimacies between material objects in the home and transnational flows of capital and trade.[2] Authors like Alcott and Phelps meditate on the United States' place in a global economy, not through depictions of the men who produce, monopolize, and speculate on commodities such as cotton and wheat (as I will explore in Chapter 3), but rather through the women and households who consume these commodities. Writing through the perspective of artistic heroines—Alcott's writer Jo March and Phelps's painter Avis Dobell—these authors raise questions about the relationship between artistic production and economic consumption, wondering how it is possible to call for reform through one's art when that art is part of the very systems that need reforming.

If nineteenth-century domesticity, as Amy Kaplan has argued, encouraged Americans to perceive the United States as "home" in opposition to a "foreign" outside world, these novels engage with the intrusion of the foreign and geopolitical through the management of household goods—goods that inevitably traversed contested international paths in the process of production, trade, and consumption. Purchasing objects from around the world involved nineteenth-century American consumers in "the formal empire of U.S. political control, the informal empire of U.S. commercial power, and the secondhand empire of European imperialism through shopping for trifles and savories" (11), as historian Kristin Hoganson puts it. In its preoccupation with the material workings of the household, sentimental domestic literature is particularly poised to engage with the imaginative consequences of consuming goods that signify imperial conquest. This chapter explores how Alcott and Phelps strategically deploy this genre's conventions to confront readers with the terms of their participation in the global economy through the internationally traded commodities that infringe upon the ostensible geographic isolation of women's households.

The excerpt from Louisa May Alcott's *Little Women* (1868–1869) quoted in the epigraph presents one such way in which nineteenth-century women writers responded to the question of the United States' place in the world economy through their representations of material objects. A novel set squarely in the space of the home, *Little Women* nonetheless reflects an awareness of the potential international reaches of US empire. The quintessentially "domestic" task of hemming sheets allows the novel's four sisters to indulge inter-imperial imaginings that later find their analogue in the girls' various misadventures. The sisters' impulse to figure the globe in their household textiles by "calling the quarters Europe, Asia, Africa, and America" draws on a longer European iconographic tradition of allegorically rendering the four continents in order to picture their relationship to one another.³ Symbolically reenacting the nineteenth-century inter-imperial scrambling for territorial and economic expansion in their sewing, the sisters negotiate the implications of such conquest through their peripatetic conversation. While Alcott's description of how "capitally" the girls got on obviously draws on nineteenth-century slang, a close reading of a range of women writers suggests that it may also be intended as a pun that hints at the symbolic capital accumulation accomplished by the girls as they conquer the continents through their stitches.

Elizabeth Stuart Phelps's 1877 novel *The Story of Avis* likewise features a scene in which cotton sheets tie the apparently domestic space of the home to a larger international economic context. The title character asks, seemingly bewildered,

> What is it . . . that *has* happened lately in the cotton-market? Aunt Chloe keeps telling me how cheap unbleached cotton is. I think it is twenty-five cents,—or really, perhaps it was five. Is that a fact so vital to the interests of the country, that I ought to care about it? (122)

Avis poses her naïve inquiry during the height of the US Civil War, as she assembles her trousseau with her friend Coy in preparation for Avis's marriage to college professor Philip Ostrander. In asking this question, the aspiring painter Avis performatively emphasizes her identity as an artist and her fundamental difference from other women who know about such mundane household matters—elsewhere in the novel Avis is even described as "undomestic" (77). At the same time, Avis's question also demonstrates her obliviousness about one of the most hotly contested and valuable US exports during the Civil War era, and Coy smugly responds to Avis's cluelessness with "her most matronly smile" (123). Tellingly, Coy condescends not to Avis's lack of political awareness, but to her lack of housewifery skills, as she informs Avis that her aunt is interested in the price of cotton because of her need to purchase sheets for her servants (123). Avis scrambles to establish further distance between her artistic aspirations and the unsettling realities of contemporary international economics when we are told that she "listened to the household chatter of women, with a kind of gentle indifference, such as one feels about the habits of the Fee-jeeans. Unbleached cotton, like x in the algebra, represented an unknown quantity of oppressive but extremely distant facts" (123).

Alcott's and Phelps's characters thus situate a common domestic good—cotton sheets—on an international horizon. Avis's choice of Fiji as a signifier of foreignness becomes more relevant to US cotton prices when understood in the context of the Pacific island's history: in the mid-nineteenth century, British and US settlers seeking to compete with the southern United States' near-monopoly on the production of cotton identified Fiji as a potential location for its cultivation. The difficulty of securing labor to work the cotton in Fiji led to the coercive practice of "blackbirding," which forced tens of thousands of Melanesians and Polynesians into indentured servitude from 1863–1904, and to the eventual annexation of Fiji by Britain in 1874.[4] The "oppressive" facts conjured up in Avis's mind by the unbleached cotton can thus be read to represent not simply the mysteries of housekeeping, but also the oppression of enslaved laborers in the US and indentured workers in Fiji who harvested the cotton in service of the brutal international competition over cotton production.[5]

Throughout the novel, Phelps reveals that Avis's "gentle indifference" is not gentle at all, but instead violently effaces the history of inter-imperial economic competition and abusive labor practices behind the production and circulation of cotton and other commodities. Phelps distances herself from her protagonist through Avis's utter ignorance of the cost of domestic goods. When we look to historical cotton prices, we discover that Avis has her facts very wrong: the conversation in question takes place sometime during the winter of 1862–1863, when cotton prices were comparatively high because of the interruption in exports from the US South, according to a report by the Boston Board of Trade. By the report's measure, the price of cotton rose as high as seventy-three cents a pound—much higher than Avis's imprecise estimate of somewhere between five and twenty-five cents (44).[6] Given Phelps's meticulous and often sanctimonious listing of the prices of consumer goods in her dress reform writings, it seems unlikely that Avis's ignorance is a symptom of Phelps's.[7] Contra Avis's opinion, the cost of cotton *is* a fact vital to the interests of the nineteenth-century United States; disruptions in the international cotton supply instigated by blockades during the Civil War led to increased exertion of imperial power to promote cotton cultivation in locations such as Fiji, Egypt, and India in order to guarantee a continuous supply of cotton for the global market.[8]

Both Avis's uninformed comments about the cost of cotton and the transcontinental sheets depicted in *Little Women* thus engage international economic contexts in ways that dramatically revise the typical profile of nineteenth-century women writers. These cotton-fueled fantasies encapsulate the different but related warnings that Alcott and Phelps present to their readers about the imperial imaginings ushered into the home through globally traded commodities like cotton. Consume such goods too fancifully or uncritically and the logic of empire and conquest might sneak unawares into your imagination, as is the case with the March sisters' transcontinental stitching expedition, and as will be the case with Jo March's literary career, upon which I will elaborate later in this chapter. Conversely, consuming such goods with obstinate refusal to face the conditions that produced them leaves you unprepared to face the realities of an economically interconnected world and unable to call out injustice in your art, as is the case with Avis both in this scene and throughout Phelps's novel.

Alcott and Phelps urge their readers to pay closer attention to the surprising intimacies between material objects in the home and international flows of capital and trade in order to become more attuned to the global landscape in which domestic dramas take place.[9] Alcott and Phelps also grapple with the heightened responsibility women artists face to ethically navigate their involvement in often exploitative economic systems. Because an inter-imperial method of analysis "lays a certain kind of stress on art's foundational entanglement in a multilateral and sedimented geopolitics," Laura Doyle argues that it "tracks the signs of that political history in texts not to reduce them to political treatises but rather to reveal the dynamic onto-political conditions of their production and circulation, as expressed, often beautifully, in distinctive genres, vernacular voicings or hybridities of form" ("Inter-Imperiality: Dialectics" 183). As I will elucidate in this chapter—focusing first on Jo March's literary mishaps in *Little Women*, then on Avis's conflicted painterly project in *The Story of Avis*—nineteenth-century women strove to understand their "foundational entanglement in a multilateral and sedimented geopolitics" as writers making a living through their art. Alcott and Phelps cannily take advantage of the instructive possibilities of sentimental fiction to educate their readers about their similar entanglement in the global economy.

Jo's Imperial-Inspired "Prosing Away" in *Little Women*

While *Little Women*'s character of Jo March is often conflated with Alcott herself, Jo has not yet learned the lessons her savvy creator imparts. Closely reading the chapter titled "Literary Lessons" with a keen eye toward Alcott's allusions to global economic circumstances illuminates the critical distance Alcott establishes between herself and her loveable but fallible character. "Literary Lessons," an episode that first celebrates Jo's foray into published authorship and then later punishes her for being too indiscriminate and mercenary in her writing, exemplifies the apparent contradictions in Louisa May Alcott's work that scholars have long sought to understand. Alcott's critics have struggled to reconcile her feminist activism with her affectionate depiction of domestic life, contrasting her apparently insular image of the home with her deconstruction of separate spheres mythology through her female artist characters and through her own labor in the literary marketplace.[10] Furthermore, Alcott's feminism does not always fit easily into binary, heteronormative, and cisnormative nineteenth-century ideas of gender; as Ivy Schweitzer suggests, through Jo's frequent protests over not being a boy, "Jo gives voice to transgender desire" (21). Erin Hendel summarizes the interpretive tension Alcott scholars have faced in parsing her feminist politics, explaining that "despite generations of feminist readings of Alcott's work, her fiction refuses to reveal definitive feminist statements calling for the expansion of women's rights into the public sphere or for the dismantling of separate spheres ideology" (159). The elusiveness of Alcott's feminist ethos that Hendel describes here can be attributed in part, I propose, to her ability to speculate about the complicated reality of egalitarian ideals put into practice in a competitive capitalist economy.[11] She weighs the possibility of expanded vocations for women against the potential exploitation of their labor, and considers the increased political capital women would gain with suffrage in light of their subsequent political complicity in the project of US empire. Tracking Alcott's references to the global economy, I propose, complicates the text's ambivalences further: in *Little Women*, Alcott depicts the March family's insulated environment in an attempt to construct a utopian vision of domestic space free from international entanglements, but she ultimately demonstrates that in a globalizing economy, this is an impossible ideal.[12] Through the internationally traded objects she represents in her fiction, Alcott urges readers to become aware of the convoluted international paths of production and trade that potentially implicate women in the very exploitative labor practices from which they themselves are trying to break free.[13] By acknowledging the global stakes of women's participation in the marketplace, we can imagine how domestic reforms and expanded vocations for women could simultaneously and troublingly promise feminist self-actualization while also threatening involvement in the work of US expansionism.

As evidence from her journals attests, Alcott recognized the geopolitical consequences of unchecked or unethical consumption, keeping a close eye on the economic circumstances of her family and of the nation. During the Alcott family's ill-fated experiment in communal living in 1843, they wore exclusively linen rather than cotton garments to avoid participating in the exploitation of enslaved people's labor.[14] In Louisa's early life, the Alcotts lived in a near-constant state of financial precarity due to Bronson's impractical and idealistic economic decisions.[15] Eventually becoming the breadwinner of the family through her literary success, Alcott painstakingly detailed her income and expenditures in her journals for nearly forty years.[16] She held the United States to the same standard of budgeting she practiced, denigrating the US centennial celebration by writing that "America ought to pay her debts before she gives parties" (200). In this comment, Alcott taps into contemporary fears about how to curtail the rapid increases in the national debt in the 1870s.[17]

Few critics have devoted significant attention to the imperial and international economic contexts that *Little Women* engages, although Louisa Jayne Hodgson discusses the novel's transatlantic intertextual references.[18] Such contexts allow us to see this American "domestic" text in light of the complex economic and political entanglements that informed nineteenth-century culture. Alcott infuses *Little Women*'s mode of moral instruction with a sardonic sense of humor in order to goad readers into becoming more attuned to the workings of the global landscape in which domestic dramas take place. In *Little Women*'s "paradigm of maturation" (Douglas 61), Alcott's characters progress not only from girls to women, but also from naïve consumers of material goods to savvy participants in the global economy, and from mindless reproducers of sensational literary clichés to thoughtful critics of fiction and its place in the world.[19]

Alcott reflects most clearly on the integration between the home and the global economy in a chapter from *Little Women* titled "Literary Lessons," in which Jo attends a public lecture and has a burst of artistic inspiration. Offering insights on "the Pyramids," the lecture Jo attends caters to nineteenth-century US Orientalist tastes, and a related fascination with Egypt so ubiquitous that it has come to be known as "Egyptomania."[20] As Jo prepares to listen to this "People's Course" lecture, she comments on the apparent incongruence between the topic at hand and the domestic worries of the audience: she "rather wondered at the choice of such a subject for such an audience, but took it for granted that some great social evil would be remedied or some great want supplied by unfolding the glories of the Pharaohs to an audience whose thoughts were busy with the price of coal and flour, and whose lives were spent in trying to solve harder riddles than that of the Sphinx" (211). Jo's assessment of the lecture ribs nineteenth-century Egyptomania, repeating the phrase "some great" for ironic effect when conjecturing about what "great" evil or want might be resolved with knowledge about this seemingly distant land and culture.[21]

In part, Jo's mockery here enables Alcott to voice her disdain for detached intellectualism that neglects to consider the practical realities of life, a tendency with which Alcott was well acquainted. Her father, although a recognized Transcendentalist scholar, failed to make a living that would sustain his family, coming home after one especially disastrous lecture tour with only a dollar in his pocket.[22] By juxtaposing the domestic industries of coal and flour with the Egyptian lecture, Alcott leads readers to see the false dichotomy Jo has unthinkingly constructed. To a casual observer like Jo the price of coal and flour may seem to be entirely separate from the history of Egypt. However, an informed reader like Alcott recognizes the interconnections between commodity prices and worldwide shifts in supply and demand, which are often affected by technological innovations, foreign investments, or political conflicts in places like Egypt and the US alike.

Understood within the context of nineteenth-century economic history, Jo's comments reveal her shortsighted disavowal of the relationship between the prices of household goods and the contemporary Egyptian economy, which were intertwined through global commodities markets. An especially dramatic example of the United States and Egypt's economic connection is their shared participation in the nineteenth-century cotton trade, united in competition between the British, French, American, and Ottoman empires. As Sven Beckert explains, when the supply of cotton from the American South was disrupted during the US Civil War, global cotton shortages were eventually met by increased production funded by investments from British and Ottoman imperial powers in countries such as Egypt and India—investments that ultimately transformed the Egyptian economy (256).[23] The United States and Egypt also competed as suppliers in the global wheat market; Brooke Hunter notes that in one instance, the US met demands in the Iberian Peninsula when a bad harvest in 1813 left Egypt unable to supply wheat to the region (518). Flour and wheat, like cotton, were domestic commodities that were crucial in establishing US power in the world economy in the eighteenth and nineteenth centuries, as the newly formed American nation jockeyed for influence by supplying wheat to empires in the midst of inter-imperial conflicts.[24] Because of agricultural resources and innovations, US wheat and flour exports expanded rapidly, achieving market dominance by the end of the nineteenth century, while nonetheless competing with suppliers in India, Canada, Argentina, and Australia.[25]

Just as wheat and cotton exports granted the United States leverage in international trade from its early history forward, the discovery of reserves of coal in US territories also presented a path to economic independence from England and became instrumental in the expansion of railroads across the US.[26] According to Sean Patrick Adams, while the US initially imported its coal supply from Britain, "the underlying assumption among most Americans was that their young nation's infant coal industry should eventually supplant the transatlantic trade" (22).[27] At the same time that coal enabled US economic power to expand, it allowed Britain to reap the benefits of industrialization in ways that other nations and empires could not; as Kenneth Pomeranz argues, the ready availability of coal in England was one of the conditions, along with resources from the colonies, that enabled the European economy's "great divergence" from China (218). While Alcott may have been aware of the fraught transnational paths of production and trade that commodities followed, given her family's eschewal of cotton garments because of the textiles' ties to slavery, Jo is either unconscious of or oblivious to the global interdependencies that contribute to price fluctuations.

Thus, Alcott directs her irony here both toward ascetic philosophers and the dismissive Jo, whose pragmatism prevents her from seeing the relationship between her domestic burdens and the larger world around her. Alcott's wry sense of humor likewise identifies her own youthful missteps. As Julie Wilhelm articulates, Alcott's use of humor grants her a subversive power to deconstruct norms of gender, class, and genre.[28] The self-consciousness of Alcott's wit sharpens further into focus through her journal entries, which are filled with cynical commentary written by her older self. For instance, Alcott ironizes her initial conception of *Little Women* in a May 1868 entry, where she notes,

> Mr. N. wants a *girls'* story, and I begin "Little Women." Marmee, Anna, and May all approve my plan. So I plod away, though I don't enjoy this sort of thing. Never liked girls or knew many, except my sisters; but our queer plays and experiences may prove interesting, though I doubt it.

Marginalia written presumably from the view of *Little Women*'s later wild success remarks, "Good joke" (165). The same sardonic sensibility that we see in Alcott's journal entries, I argue, is also at play in her rendering of Jo's "Literary Lessons." In this chapter, Alcott satirizes her own earlier attempts at literary success and thereby criticizes writers and readers for ignoring literature's entanglement in the wider world.

In a further ironic recasting of her own writing history, Alcott looks askance at Jo's seduction by lucrative forms of writing, her unthinking adoption of the Orientalist literary tropes that sensationalist fiction traffics in, and her ignorance of the international origins of her literary inspiration. With subtle repetitions in language, Alcott makes the relationship between the mysteries of Egypt and the prices of coal and flour evident as the rest of this episode unfolds. Jo's literary imagination follows an imperialist logic similar to that of the lecture, eventually enabling her to earn money that alleviates her anxieties about how to buy household necessities. Significantly, Jo's first foray into the literary marketplace is indirectly inspired by the events of this lecture on Egypt. Sitting next to someone reading an illustrated newspaper, Jo notices one of the images, and finds herself

> idly wondering what unfortuitous concatenation of circumstances needed the melodramatic illustration of an Indian in full war costume, tumbling over a precipice with a wolf at his throat, while two infuriated young gentlemen, with unnaturally small feet and big eyes, were stabbing each other close by, and a disheveled female was flying away in the background, with her mouth wide open. (213)

Just as Jo "rather wondered" about the subject matter of the lecture, so here does she find herself "idly wondering" about the literary impetus for this illustration.

In repeating this language of "wondering," Alcott draws readers' attention to the similar thought patterns underlying the Egyptian lecture and the sensational story: the same imaginative impulse that envisions Egypt as foreign, exotic, and outside of contemporary time also depicts exaggerated images of "Indians in full war costume" to justify ideologies of Manifest Destiny, westward expansionism, and the violent removal of Native populations. Alcott shows the slippage between Jo's wondering about Egypt and her wondering about the sensation stories to illustrate the insidious ways in which imperialist modes of representation can infiltrate one's imagination. By imagining racialized hierarchies and colonial violence to be a mere "unfortuitous concatenation of circumstances," uncritical writers help naturalize uneven global distributions of power and wealth, and Alcott implies that they need to be more attuned to the systemic biases that lead to those apparent "concatenations."

Through the affinities she identifies between the lecture on Egypt and the sensation story, Alcott establishes that her criticism of such "lowbrow" fiction is not simply because of its comparatively low generic status in an increasingly hierarchized literary market, but also because of the expansionist imagination it subconsciously cultivates. The newspaper illustration, as Jo discovers, accompanies a story by "Mrs. S.L.A.N.G. Northbury"—Alcott's parody of the popular nineteenth-century writer E.D.E.N. Southworth—and as the reader of the newspaper in *Little Women* attests, "she knows just what folks like and gets paid well for writing it" (213). While the reader of the newspaper and Jo see Northbury's generous compensation as a boon, Alcott's ironic distancing strategies allow us to see the distasteful pandering of these stories and establish a distinction between Alcott and Jo. Richard Brodhead sees the contrast between the "story-paper" genre and *Little Women* itself as an intentional contrast that Alcott sets up in order to differentiate her own writing and class status, asking, "what is Alcott's rejection of story-paper writing but a repudiation of a form she fears will declass her?" (104). However, given the parallels that Alcott draws between the intellectual lecture and this fantasy story, Alcott's critique here can be understood to eschew this story for both its déclassé genre and the troubling orientation to the world it fosters in its readers. Furthermore, with this character in the act of reading, Alcott knowingly winks at her own readers, inviting us to examine the ethical implications of our reading practices.

Alcott's embedded warning hangs in the air as we read on about Jo's literary endeavors: inspired by hearing how much money Mrs. Northbury makes writing stories, Jo starts coming up with her own plan. The narrator describes Jo's creative frenzy:

> Here the lecture began, but Jo heard very little of it, for while Professor Sands was prosing away about Belzoni, Cheops, scarabei, and hieroglyphics, she was covertly taking down the address of the paper, and boldly resolving to try for the hundred dollar prize offered in its columns for a sensational story. By the time the lecture ended, and the audience awoke, she had built up a splendid fortune for herself (not the first founded upon paper), and was already deep in the concoction of her story, being unable to decide whether the duel should come before the elopement or after the murder. (213)

The arch aside that Jo's fortune was "not the first founded upon paper" references the flimsy foundation of Jo's ambitions and links the spinning of her fantastical tales to other acts of financial speculation, perhaps even making a deprecating allusion to the introduction of greenbacks as currency during the Civil War.[29] Additionally, although we are told that Jo "heard very little" of the lecture, her imaginative construction of a "splendid fortune" for herself is not dissimilar to the likely motivations of nineteenth-century Venetian archaeological explorer Giovanni Battista Belzoni—the Belzoni named in Professor Sands's lecture—who plundered ancient Egyptian ruins for artifacts.[30] In seeming to ignore the lecturer, Jo is unable to recognize her similarly geographically oriented imagination, yet Alcott signals toward the similarity through her strategic language. Jo, too, is "prosing away" to exoticize subjects seemingly distant from her own experiences for profit.

Through the content, themes, and setting of the story Jo concocts after this lecture, Alcott exposes the slippery ways in which unconscious literary impulses perpetuate problematic modes of representation. In choosing the climax of her story, Jo reflexively turns to the well-trodden ground of the historical 1755 Lisbon earthquake without examining the existential implications it had for her literary antecedents. The narrator's description of Jo's inspiration emphasizes the apparently haphazard nature of her creative choices: "Her story was as full of desperation and despair as her limited acquaintance with those uncomfortable emotions enabled her to make it, and, having located it in Lisbon, she wound up with an earthquake, as a striking and appropriate denouement" (214). Jo's adopted sensationalist literary posture seems to get away from her, as the narrator's deflecting language implies: Jo does not actively write a melodramatic earthquake, but rather "wound up with" this geological rupture as her finale. Just as Mrs. Northbury's sensation story appeared to Jo to be an "unfortuitous concatenation of circumstances," so does Jo's literary climax *seem* to come to her by happenstance.

However, as Alcott implied previously, many literary impulses are no mere "concatenation," but can be traced to subconscious attitudes about the world. Thus, if we are the careful readers Alcott asks us to be, we should be suspicious about how Jo "wound up" with an earthquake in her story. The fictional earthquake Jo writes draws inspiration not only from the conventions of sensational stories—which, the narrator wryly comments, typically conclude when a "grand catastrophe clears the stage" (213)—but also from an actual earthquake that killed tens of thousands of people. The 1755

Lisbon earthquake caused damages that cost between 32 and 48% of Portugal's GDP, destabilized the price of staples (including wheat) in the years after the quake, weakened Portugal's military power at the height of its era of imperial dominance, and delimited the nation's capacity to ally itself with either France or Britain in the impending Seven Years' War.[31] The earthquake also had a profound metaphysical effect on many writers and thinkers; Voltaire, for example, features the seismic event in *Candide* (1759) to refute the philosophical notion that we live in the "best of all possible worlds" (18).[32] Unlike Voltaire's informed, intentional, and satirical invocation of the Lisbon earthquake, Jo's almost accidental inclusion of the disaster in her writing evinces a lack of purpose that Alcott discourages.

Alcott thus unveils Jo's lazy trafficking in geopolitical tropes, using the narrator's sardonic characterization of the "grand catastrophes" that bring sensation stories to a climax to comment on Jo's entanglement in the global marketplace as a result of her financially precarious circumstances. While the Lisbon earthquake resulted in a nationwide spike in the price of wheat, the fictional reappropriation of this disaster enables Jo to more readily buy flour for her family.[33] Through Jo's fictionalizing of this cataclysmic event that had serious repercussions for Portugal's imperial and economic trajectory, Alcott places Jo's own domestic circumstances in play with global geopolitics, just as she hinted at the relation between the costs of coal and flour and the history of Egypt. In doing so, Alcott undermines the idea that artistic vocations are removed enough from the forces of global capitalism to be able to present ideological critique. A February 1865 journal entry exemplifies Alcott's dependence on the literary marketplace. In it, she compares her progress on her semi-autobiographical novel *Work* (then called "Success") to her efforts writing sensation stories:

> Wrote a new Novelette for Elliott "A Marble Woman" & got $75 for it with which I made things comfortable at home with wood, coal, flour, clothes &c ... Wrote a little on poor old "Success" but being tired of novels I soon dropped it & fell back on rubbishy tales, for they pay best & I cant afford to starve on praise, when sensation stories are written in half the time & keep the family cosy. (139)

Like Jo, Alcott was well aware of the price of coal and flour. Unlike her protagonist, however, Alcott accounts for the many complex global economic circumstances that affect commodity prices, and invokes geopolitical circumstances to make a purposeful statement about the artist's role in the world.[34] With the self-deprecating humor that

"Literary Lessons" directs at her youthful literary endeavors, Alcott strives to point out her own complicity in an often exploitative system.

Although Jo is able to improve her domestic circumstances by selling her sensation stories, Alcott reminds readers that Jo is in essence bringing the spoils of her international literary plundering into the March home. After submitting her Lisbon earthquake story to the magazine the *Spread Eagle,* Jo wins a hundred-dollar prize, sends her mother and sister Beth to the seaside, and becomes "bent on earning more of those delightful checks" (215). Her newly found earning capabilities cause her to begin "to feel herself a power in the house," as her subsequent assortment of publications funds a variety of household purchases: "'The Duke's Daughter' paid the butcher's bill, 'A Phantom Hand' put down a new carpet, and 'The Curse of the Coventrys' proved the blessing of the Marches in the way of groceries and gowns" (215).[35] By juxtaposing the titles of Jo's stories with the purchases they finance, Alcott toys with the intimate ties between world historical events, the sensational and geographically oriented literary tropes they inspire, and the material circumstances they enable. Holly Blackford reads Jo's purchases as acts of familial bonding through which her literary labor "can be reinvested in the 'blessed' objects of home" (31); however, Alcott's subtle repetition of language from earlier in the chapter complicates our reading of Jo's economic success. Jo's fantasy of financial self-sufficiency alludes once again to the lecture on Egypt she attended, as she now takes "great comfort in the fact that she could supply her own wants, and need ask no one for a penny" (215). Whereas she once jokingly assumed that "some great want" would be supplied by the lecturer's "unfolding the glories of the Pharaohs," here she is happy to "supply her own wants" by describing as merely sensational the real-world conditions that allow her to support her family.

While Alcott initially seems to reward Jo's latent imperialist urges through her financial success, the mixed critical reception of Jo's fiction further undermines her ambitions. After writing a novel for purely mercenary reasons and selling it for three hundred dollars, Jo finds herself perplexed by the contradictory reviews of her book. The reviewers variously declare Jo's book "one of the best American novels," decry it as "full of morbid fantasies," or denounce it as a "dangerous book," perhaps implicitly voicing Alcott's own critique of the dangers of indulging in "morbid fantasies" about faraway lands (217). Jo comments on reviewers' desires to extract hidden meanings from the novel, noting that she wrote it not because she had "some deep theory to expound," but rather "for the pleasure and the money," observing with exasperation, "I do hate to be so horridly misjudged" (217). Later, when Jo hears her future husband Professor Bhaer criticize sensation stories as "bad trash" that damages the minds of young readers, she reforms her ways; her "hard-earned money" lies "rather heavily on her conscience," and she gives up writing sensation stories altogether (280).

Typically this conclusion is read as a cautionary tale through which Alcott shores up bourgeois norms by disciplining Jo for a variety of wrongs—for sacrificing her integrity for a paycheck, partaking in a low-class literary genre, poisoning her imagination, or transgressing gender norms.[36] However, because of the self-referential nature of this chapter, Alcott's message is perhaps a little more unwieldy. Taking on a metafictional resonance, Jo's writerly misadventures simultaneously index Alcott's participation in the sensation genre early in her career and ironize readers' responses to the very novel in front of their eyes, enabling Alcott to gesture to her own mercenary reasons for writing that necessarily entangle her in imperialist economic systems. Alcott herself once succumbed to readers' salacious tastes with a racist depiction of a Hindu assassin in an early anonymously published story titled "The Fate of the Forrests," which Alcott privately called "rubbish."[37] Whether a symptom of youthful ignorance or of nineteenth-century bias, the Orientalism of this story mirrors the troubling attitudes that Alcott chastises Jo for perpetuating.

Jo's experiences with the literary marketplace during the publication of her novel also reimagine Alcott's own efforts with her first novel *Moods* (1864). The ambivalent reviews of the novel led Alcott to express regret about the ambitious commentary her book presented on the nature of love, friendship, and women's place in the world; Alcott asserted in her journal, "My next book shall have no *ideas* in it, only facts, & the people shall be as ordinary as possible, then critics will say its all right" (140). Susan Naomi Bernstein doubts the ingenuousness of Alcott's purported lack of "ideas" and Jo's similar claim that she had no "deep theory to expound," contending that "the denial of 'theory' or 'doctrine' seems to point to the likelihood of its presence ... Such protest inserts the idea of theory into the text, drawing attention to itself as an attribute that finally cannot be denied" (24). Concurring with Bernstein's skepticism about Alcott's reluctance to theorize, I would argue that Alcott invokes the concrete realities of material objects to point to the important abstractions about economy and empire that they represent. Understood in light of Alcott's stubborn insistence that her next book will have "only facts" in it, *Little Women* explores the depths that the "facts" of daily life and the activities of people who are "as ordinary as possible" can reveal. As the chapter about "Literary Lessons" indicates, quotidian household duties, economic stresses, and domestic purchases cannot in practice be extricated from larger ideas about wealth, power, nation, and empire.

Alcott's canny depiction of the entanglement of domestic and global economies in other moments throughout *Little Women* provides further evidence of her interest in the international paths of material objects. For instance, as a young girl Amy delights in "an Indian cabinet full of queer drawers, little pigeon-holes, and secret places in which were kept all sorts of ornaments" (153), a relic that metonymically represents nineteenth-century imperialist curiosity, exploration, and colonization of "exotic" lands in India and elsewhere. Later, Alcott illustrates the blurring of the domestic and the political quite literally when Meg's thoughts wander "from the state of the nation to the state of her bonnet" (312) while chatting with her husband. Meg's children Daisy and Demi interrupt her husband's reading of the newspaper so much that "Demi's colic got into the shipping-list, and Daisy's fall affected the price of stocks" (305). Alcott's hyperbole here not only jokes about the oversized presence that Meg's children have in their household, but also dryly observes how readily the rhythms of family life can be interrupted by global economic fluctuations, and in turn, how the workings of the world economy can be shaped by the consumer choices of domestic households. Often characters treat these incursions of global geopolitics with glib dismissiveness, as evidenced by Jo's favorite slang exclamation, "Christopher Columbus!" (26), or by Jo's threat to pose as a boy and run away with Laurie "among the ships bound for India" (170), or Laurie's reluctance to join his grandfather's Indian trade business because he hates "tea and silk and spices, and every sort of rubbish his old ships bring" (119). Such glibness expresses Alcott's characters' uncomfortable avoidance of the coercive, violent, and exploitative realities of nineteenth-century American economic imperialism—realities that Alcott encourages readers to face.

Avoiding "Oppressive but Extremely Distant Facts" in *The Story of Avis*

A New England writer of sentimental literature similarly concerned with women artists' participation in the global economy, Elizabeth Stuart Phelps features a painter, rather than a writer like Jo March, to present a cautionary tale about the dangers of ignoring the exploitations of the global economy. Phelps and Alcott were contemporaries, and there is also evidence that they were familiar with one another's writing. In a letter, Alcott wrote that she hoped her artist sister's marriage would "prove Avis in the wrong" (qtd. in Boyd, *Immortality* 64), fearing that her sister's marriage might eventually supersede her artistic career, as was the case with Phelps's fictional painter Avis. Alcott's offhand comment speaks to the powerful example Phelps's heroine set for artistically ambitious women in the nineteenth century and demonstrates the degree to which Phelps and Alcott were similarly attuned to the sacrifices nineteenth-century women were forced to make when balancing career aspirations and domestic duties. Both Phelps and Alcott earned a living through their writing, and the urgency of supporting their families through this work made them aware of the compromises that arise when offering one's art as a commodity in a global economy, whether that involves pandering to audiences' baser instincts like Jo, or, as will be the case with Avis, selling one's art before it is fully formed and developed. Phelps acknowledged the empowerment that came from making a living through her writing, observing in her autobiography *Chapters of a Life*,

> It is impossible to forget the sense of dignity which marks the hour when one becomes a wage-earner ... I felt that I had suddenly acquired value—to myself, to my family, and to the world. Probably all people who write "for a living" would agree with me in recalling the first check as the largest and most luxurious of life. (22)

While Phelps revels in the fact that she had "suddenly acquired value" when she received "the first check" for her writing, putting a price on one's worth can also leave female artists vulnerable to moral compromises, enmeshed in unethical capitalist systems, and complicit in imperialist ideology—a theory Phelps elaborates in *The Story of Avis*.

The novel follows the courtship and marriage of aspiring painter Avis, critiquing the limitations of nineteenth-century gender roles through Avis's failed marriage and abandoned artistic career. Perhaps because of Phelps's vociferous condemnation of women's circumscribed career opportunities, existing scholarship on *The Story of Avis* has tended to focus on the novel's feminist and artistic ambitions, reading Avis's efforts to reconcile her vocation as a painter with socially prescribed gender roles as emblematic of the difficulties many nineteenth-century women writers themselves faced.[38] Because

Avis is a compelling character, many of Phelps's female readers likely found her protests against patriarchal strictures cathartic; even today, Avis's feminist anger proves strikingly resonant. However, the distance Phelps constructs from her protagonist undermines such identification with Avis, ironizing Avis's avoidance of global economic realities—an avoidance evident in Avis's ignorance of cotton prices, as discussed in the introduction of this chapter.[39] The ethical commitment that separates Phelps from Avis is evident in her autobiography, where she writes, "the province of the artist is to portray life as it is; and life *is* moral responsibility" (263). In *The Story of Avis*, Phelps illuminates the difficulty of maintaining that sense of moral responsibility when attempting to represent the United States' place in the global economy while simultaneously entangled in that very economy through the sale of one's art.

Phelps's moral and ethical concerns encompassed a wide array of contemporary issues that she explored in both her fiction and nonfiction. Her bestselling novel *The Gates Ajar* (1868) had a fundamentally palliative aim: to provide comfort to the thousands of people who lost loved ones in the Civil War by offering them a more expansive vision of heaven in which the dead live on as fully embodied spirits. Other causes that Phelps embraced include women's rights, antivivisectionism, dress reform, and better working conditions for factory laborers.[40] Although Avis forcefully defends a woman's right to a career, her unexamined privilege distinguishes her from other Phelps heroines who are more overtly politically active—such as Perley Kelso of *The Silent Partner*, who confronts the need for labor reform when she takes charge of her father's cotton mill after his death; or Zaidee Atalanta Lloyd of *Dr. Zay*, who ardently defends her career as a doctor in rural Maine; or Nixy Trent of *Hedged In*, who demonstrates the unfair cultural attitudes toward unmarried women who bear children. Though Avis's defense of her career as an artist aligns her with the progressive values expressed by other Phelps heroines, her ignorance of the implications of international trade and her thoughtless consumerism indicate to readers that she is not a character Phelps would unreservedly valorize. Avis's feminist ambitions have caused readers to overlook this aspect of Phelps's critique, and closer attention to the international commodities referenced in the novel brings to light Phelps's pointed view of her heroine's uncritical consumption.

Through Avis's devotion to the costly color carmine, which I will discuss at length later in this chapter, Phelps signals that Avis is an imperfect heroine struggling with an avoidant acquisitiveness that clouds her artistic vision. Avis's casual consumption of foreign commodities such as richly dyed textiles (133), Fayal lace (7), and fine china (130) presents a sharp contrast to the conscience-stricken eschewal of such luxuries voiced by Perley Kelso. Confronted by the poverty of the laborers who work in her father's factory, Perley exclaims to her fiancé, "do you see that shawl on the arm of the *tête à tête*? It cost me three thousand dollars ... And there's lace up stairs in my bureau drawer for which I paid fifty dollars a yard. And, Maverick! I believe the contents of any single jewel-case in that same drawer would found a free bed in a hospital" (132). Perley's costly shawl seems to provide a calculated parallel to a carmine crape shawl that Avis wears. Likewise, Perley very likely knows the cost of cotton, since she decides she will inspect the raw cotton that comes into the factory (65), whereas Avis claims total ignorance of the price of cotton sheets as a means of distancing herself from these domestic concerns and tawdry, uncomfortable economic realities. The fact that Avis's attitude and actions conflict with the values expressed in other novels by Phelps suggests that as sympathetic a character as she is, Avis should also be seen as a caution against a celebratory consumption of aesthetically pleasing but vexed commodities. Reading Phelps's fiction in the context of her dress reform writings, Roxanne Harde suggests that Phelps uses her characters' clothing choices to indicate their values, but then argues that the novel "punishes [Avis] for her preoccupation with fashion" by bombarding her with marital strife, infidelity, the loss of a child, and the waning of her artistic talents (177). While Harde is right to note the symbolic significance of Phelps's characters' fashion choices, the language of punishing does not fully capture Phelps's strategic balance of sympathy for Avis's entanglement and critique of her disregard for the conditions inflicted on others in the production of the commodities she consumes.

Furthermore, there is convincing textual evidence that Phelps's progressive vision expanded to geopolitical affairs, revealing that her ethical orientation was both domestic and global. Phelps saw foreign diplomatic and trade relations culminate violently in the latter decades of the nineteenth century and sought to argue against US expansionism in a letter she wrote in December 1895 and published in *The Advocate of Peace* in January 1896. Protesting US intervention in South America through enforcement of the Monroe Doctrine during a period in which the US was also trying to expand its economic influence in the region, Phelps writes, "The whole of South America is not worth one day of war in the United States. An aggressive and entangling policy is not worth one week of the ruin, the death, the torture, the lifelong heartbreak involved in the slaughter of battle" ("Greatest Crime" 16).[41] Phelps's comments were provoked by the 1895 Venezuelan Crisis, during which the US arbitrated boundary disputes between Venezuela and Britain, and thereby ensured expanded influence in the hemisphere.[42] Although Phelps's emphasis on American casualties in this possible confrontation clearly draws on her memories of the ravages of the Civil War and not necessarily on anti-imperialist sentiments, her letter nonetheless voices the dangers of increasingly interventionist foreign policies motivated by commercial ends. Phelps understood how "entangling" such an endeavor could be because she recognized that South America was not some empty void to be conquered, but rather a region with its own priorities that the US would be forced to reckon with. Phelps's 1895 letter was not an isolated outburst of anti-war fervor; she wrote for the *Boston Herald* in 1892 against the possibility of a potentially "ridiculous" and "terrible" war against Chile ("Protest"), she contributed to a collection of editorials by women around the question, "Is War Ever Justifiable from a Woman's Perspective?", and, as a column in *The United Opinion* attests, she apparently wrote a critique of the press coverage of the 1898 sinking of the *Maine* for stoking fears and war-mongering ("The Guilty Press").

Despite recent scholarship on *The Story of Avis*'s transatlantic contexts and Orientalist tropes, critics have yet to fully untangle the threads of inter-imperial economic competition, gender liberation, and artistic inspiration that connect the domestic plot of *The Story of Avis* to the geopolitical conditions Phelps engages more directly in these later anti-war essays.[43] In her fiction and nonfiction, Phelps frames a gendered response to geopolitical conflict, opening her 1895 letter, for example, by affirming that "I am sure that I am expressing the voice of every woman," and calling the president to think of "the women whom war would bereave." In her 1892 letter, she presents a similarly gendered call, exhorting, "Lift your voices, women whose life-long anguish has filled an abyss" (52). Elsewhere, Phelps eviscerates the tendency to romanticize war, identifying the way the military's material trappings glamorize its violent mission: "War is murder legalized on a large scale. Strip it of its gold lace, silence its drumbeats, hush its martial songs, remove its bunting, reduce its romance to the terms of fact, and battle is nothing but civil or international murder" ("Is War Ever Justifiable?"). Deeply aware of the distinctive pain women experience with the loss of their sons and husbands in military conflict, and perhaps conscious of women's limited economic and political power to effect change, Phelps urges women to make use of the tools they do have—their voices, emotions, and choices within domestic and artistic economies.

While Phelps makes her case more urgently and explicitly in these later editorial pieces, I propose that *The Story of Avis* is a precursor to this globally oriented advocacy. In the novel, she warns women of the price of geopolitical and economic indifference through the fictional example of Avis, an artist who resorts to shallow Orientalist modes of representation in avoidance of the injustices that Phelps herself represents in her work. Relatedly, by turning to her art, Avis attempts to escape the economic realities behind the commodities she consumes—cotton, carmine dye, and oranges in particular. Resistant to marriage because of the threat it poses to her artistic vocation, Avis seems instinctively aware that marriage necessarily entangles her in the global economy: metaphorically as a woman on the "marriage market," and literally through the goods purchased to sustain her domestic household. In representing the unequal division of labor that Avis and women like her experience in their domestic lives, Phelps implies that there is a similar logic underlying the exploitative capitalist, imperialist practices that make goods like cotton, carmine, and oranges available in consumers' homes.

Confronting Avis's Orientalist Gaze

With Avis's formative moment of artistic inspiration, Phelps dramatizes the temptation to shy away from morally uncomfortable truths about women's vexed position in the global economy. In this scene, Avis cloisters herself in her studio to paint, trying to ignore the tragedies of the Civil War as news of the bloody battle of Bull Run reaches her New England town.[44] Avis's artistic project aims to establish distance from violent geopolitics, but Phelps brings Avis's art to life in order to confront Avis with her shortcomings. Here, commodities infuse Avis's consciousness literally. First, she ingests a "cautious dose" of "*Eau de Fleurs d'Oranger*"—a French liqueur made from oranges, a commodity laden with inter-imperial encounters, from oranges' introduction in Spain through Islamic traders and rulers who brought the fruit from North Africa and Asia, to their arrival in the New World with Spanish conquistadors, to their export across the US from Floridian orange groves that were forcibly taken from the Seminoles (McPhee 6, 89, 91). As Avis imbibes the orange blossom liqueur, she lapses into a hallucinatory state and reflects on her role as an American woman artist, musing, "the wine of a flower has carried many a pretty Parisian to an intrigue or a convent. Could it carry a Yankee girl to glory?" (80). The French liqueur primes Avis's inter-imperial imagination, as she pits her emphatically Yankee self against her hypothetical French rivals while consuming the fruits of imperial conquest—positioning herself in opposition to a country that until recently she depended upon for her artistic training.[45]

Consuming the French orange blossom liqueur sends Avis into a dissociative haze that allows her to temporarily push aside the competitive pressures of a globally interconnected economy, the violence of the war, and the unpredictable fluctuations in the cost of cotton and other commodities that accompany such geopolitical disruptions. However, as this scene progresses, it becomes clear that Phelps is not advocating for this kind of dissociative detachment from real-world concerns, but rather that she is castigating women who would choose to blur their artistic vision in this way. Facing artist's block, Avis finds "the lips of her visions muttering in a foreign tongue," the foreignness here a precursor to her later international inspiration for her art (76). After having drunk the liqueur, Avis replaces thoughts of national conflict with visions that represent potentially romantic artistic projects: Egyptian pottery, sublime landscapes, people in poverty, and religious iconography (80). In yet another moment that separates Avis from the reform-minded Phelps, Avis immediately rejects the images of poverty as subjects for her art upon imagining "an old man sowing sparse seed in a chill place; the lantern-flash on a miner's stooping face; the brow and smile of a starving child; sailors abandoned in a frozen sea; a group of factory women huddling in the wind" (82). Finding herself unable to tackle an artistic project that represents the struggles of the laboring class, Avis cries, "I am yet too happy, too young, too sheltered to understand. How dare I be the apostle of want and woe?" (82). Because Phelps represented the "want and woe" faced by "factory women" at great length in her 1871 novel *The Silent Partner*, her oeuvre presents an implicit rebuke to Avis's rejection of such themes. Just as Avis's privilege blinds her to the cost of cotton that is harvested by unpaid and abused slave laborers, so here does she choose to ignore the human costs of a capitalist division of labor—a system upon which US economic expansion depended.

Instead, Avis looks to Egypt as a foreign land ripe for economic and artistic conquest upon which she can project her fantasies of artistic self-actualization, just as Jo March was inspired during the lecture on the pyramids and turned her eye toward Lisbon for literary material. Alcott and Phelps implicitly expose the colonialism inherent in white authors' "Egyptomania," a trend analyzed by Scott Trafton in his book *Egypt Land*. Trafton argues,

> There is perhaps no better analytic frame for the violent crucible of race and nation that was the nineteenth-century United States than the figure of ancient Egypt: a land that represented the origins of race and nations, the power of empires and their inevitable falls, and the stories of despots holding people in bondage and of the exodus of the saved from the land of slavery (4).[46]

The mysterious gaze of the sphinx that appears in Avis's vision embodies this "violent crucible of race and nation" and "the power of empires" that Trafton describes, making it impossible for Avis to fully detach herself from the disturbing realities of a turbulent inter-imperial economy. As her vision proceeds, Avis sees a series of women: first historical figures enmeshed in mythologies of inter-imperial conflict like Cleopatra, Helen, and Joan of Arc, then a "silent army of the unknown," (82) and finally, the Egyptian sphinx, which becomes her muse. The sphinx's "mutilated face patiently took on the forms and the hues of life; the wide eyes met her own; the dumb lips parted; the solemn brow unbent. The riddle of ages whispered to her. The mystery of womanhood stood before her, and said, 'Speak for me'" (83).

In conjuring a vision of a mysterious sphinx that invites Avis the artist to speak for her, Phelps deftly captures the mode of eighteenth- and nineteenth-century discourse later named by Edward Said as Orientalism. The sphinx's request mirrors almost exactly the discursive power dynamics between the "Orient" and the "Occident" that Said describes; he writes that "Orientalism is premised upon exteriority, that is, on the fact that the Orientalist, poet or scholar, makes the Orient speak, describes the Orient, renders its mysteries plain for and to the West. He is never concerned with the Orient except as the first cause of what he says" (*Orientalism* 20).[47] The sphinx's beckoning presents a dilemma for Avis as a burgeoning artist: either participate in popular but problematic Orientalist modes of representation, or struggle for viable, ethically driven material that might be less commercially successful or even derided as didactic. The potential artistic triumph Avis might achieve through painting this mythical subject matter heightens the stakes of answering this question: when Avis's former painting teacher later comes to visit, he describes her painting-in-progress in nationalistic terms, praising the originality of the sphinx by exclaiming, "You must create: you cannot copy.

That is what we lack in this country. We have no imagination. The sphinx is a creation" (205). Avis's artistic identity is yet again framed on an international horizon, as her chance to become a unique American artist requires her to implicate herself in Orientalist imaginings.

Despite the painting teacher's laudatory assessment of Avis's sphinx as a unique "creation," the Egyptian sphinx was a popular subject for European painters for decades prior to Avis's version. Jeffrey Cass lists examples such as, "Jean-Auguste-Dominique Ingres, *Oedipus Solving the Riddle of the Sphinx* (1827); William Holman Hunt, *The Sphinx, Giza, Looking toward the Pyramids of Sakhara* (1854); Thomas Seddon, *The Great Sphinx of the Pyramids of Giza* (1856); Gustave Moreau, *Oedipus and the Sphinx* (1864); and Jean-Leon Gérôme, *Bonaparte Before the Sphinx* (1867–68)" (55). Several critics have also pointed to American painter Elihu Vedder's *The Questioner of the Sphinx* (1863) as the likely source material for Avis's painting.[48] Given these art historical precedents, Phelps treats the painting teacher's view of Avis's sphinx as a true original and not a copy with a touch of irony, communicating a subtle critique that American artists should look for subject matter that is closer to home.

Whereas contemporary American and European paintings taking the sphinx as a subject either celebrate the perceived exoticism of the Middle East or telegraph imperial conquest, Phelps troubles this sub-genre of Orientalist representation through the resistance of Avis's painting, which comes to life in order to confront Avis with the necessity of recognizing one's place in the world and the interdependencies of global economic relationships. Initially casting her heroine as an archaeologist unearthing and constructing a mysterious Orient, Phelps first of all hints at her critique by lacing her descriptions of Avis in the process of painting with language of control and domination, writing, "the crude Nubian features she had rechiseled, the mutilated outline she had restored; the soul of it she had created" (143). The parallel structure of the three clauses creates a neat pronouncement of mastery—almost recalling Julius Caesar's famous *veni vidi vici*—and Avis animates her painting with a soul that she envisions submitting to her restorative measures.

Phelps then further challenges Avis's participation in contemporaneous Orientalist regimes of representation by enabling Avis's painting to resist her mastery. The sphinx's returned gaze undermines Avis's uneasy avoidance of inter-imperial relations; as she works on the painting, Avis admits "the eyes baffle me," and finds herself frustrated with the sphinx because "in its deep eyes flitted an expectant look that did not satisfy her; meanings were in them which she had not mastered; questions troubled them, to which her imagination had found no controlling reply" (143). Here, Avis works to assert her vision as a painter, which seems to her a liberatory struggle for her equal right as a woman to have a career as a painter without having to wade into a messy geopolitical quagmire. Through Avis's subject matter of the uncontrollable sphinx, however, Phelps questions visual and literary narratives of imperial economic domination, reminding Avis and her readers of the entanglement of artistic practices in larger workings of power, and of the ethical imperative for artists to look injustices squarely in the eye.

Given nineteenth-century economic history, Avis's confrontation with the sphinx also grapples with the uncertainty of being an artist tasked with representing the volatilities of an economy in which Egypt participated in an inter-imperial scramble with England, France, the United States, and others in a global cotton crisis. The "cotton famine" that resulted from the embargo on exports from the US South during the American Civil War made cotton "a matter of state," according to Sven Beckert, who documents the international search for raw cotton sources outside the US from a wide variety of interests, but "especially the two European powers that had both substantial cotton industries and large colonial holdings, Britain and France" (*Empire of Cotton* 250). According to Beckert, "The French Ministry of Colonies commissioned reports on cotton growing prospects in such diverse places as Guyana, Siam, Algeria, Egypt, and Senegal" (251), while Britain focused its cotton production investments on its colonies in India (251–5). The Ottoman empire also accelerated its decades-long project "of modernizing Egypt through the sale of cotton on world markets," which included building "new railroads, new canals, new cotton gins, and new cotton presses" (Beckert 256), as well as changing Egyptian property rights (297), converting land into cotton farms (256), coercing Egyptian laborers (168), and importing enslaved workers from Sudan (256). Eager to assuage European leaders' concerns about the cotton supply and to discourage them from intervening on behalf of the Confederacy, American diplomats like William Thayer, the consul to Alexandria, urged cotton production in regions across the globe, including Egypt.[49] As a result of these Ottoman investments, "By 1864, 40 percent of all fertile land in Lower Egypt had been converted to cotton," and "Egyptian rural cultivators, the fellaheen, quintupled their cotton production between 1860 and 1865 from 50.1 million to 250.7 million pounds" (Beckert 256). Despite its modernizing effects, this metamorphosis in the economy was not entirely beneficial for Egyptians. Egypt faced food shortages in the 1860s as farms were converted to cotton crops instead of subsistence farming (Beckert 334), and it became unable to service the debts it took out to fund its infrastructure improvements when cotton prices dropped after the Civil War, subsequently going bankrupt and succumbing to British control in 1882 (Beckert 299). In sum, while nineteenth-century Americans and Europeans like Avis Dobell and Jo March were constructing images of Egypt as an exotic and mysterious other, the Egyptian economy was undergoing radical and complex transformations as a result of imperial investment in local cotton cultivation.

Thus, even as Avis attempts to master the Egyptian sphinx through her painting, it eludes her because it represents a nation with its own interests, including a dramatically evolving national economy. While Avis's encounter with the sphinx is often—quite rightly—read as a reclamation of women's traditional role as the artistic muse, such interpretations risk overlooking the role the sphinx's "expectant," "baffl[ing]," and "question[ing]" gaze plays in forcing Avis to recognize the shortcomings of her aesthetically ambitious but morally vacuous artistic project.[50] An "overdetermined figure" (79), as Deborah Barker observes, the image of the sphinx brings together associations with ancient history, the Oedipus myth, nineteenth-century Egyptomania, and the gendered implications of the female sphinx's mysterious silence. Although critics correctly identify the Orientalist tropes that Avis's painting engages in, these readings, I suggest, imply an elision between Avis the character and Phelps the writer, minimizing Phelps's authorial distance from her protagonist—typified earlier by her mockery of Avis's ignorance of cotton prices, and evidenced in this scene through her interference in Avis's attempted domination of the sphinx. While Barker contends that such varied associations make the sphinx both "a symbol that allows Phelps to represent women as a group in terms of what they have in common" and a signifier that "no single set of attributes can define women" (93), I suggest that the sphinx also serves as a potent embodiment of the inter-imperial tensions that threaten to dismantle Avis's individual, gendered, national, and artistic identities—tensions exemplified by the competitive cotton market, the threat Egyptian cotton production presented to the US's near-monopoly on cotton production, and the multiple imperial actors that vied for cotton ascendancy in the nineteenth century. The sphinx's defiance of Avis's determining gaze—presenting meanings "which she had not mastered" and questions for which she has "no controlling reply" (143)—unsettles her attempt to build an artistic identity that is predicated on empty aesthetics, devoid of purpose, and ignorant of the global economy around her.

The sphinx thus models a form of gendered resistance that Avis could but does not assimilate in her fraught domestic relationship with her husband. The fact that Phelps characterizes the sphinx as the "mystery of womanhood" suggests that the sphinx's message for Avis, at this moment of artistic revelation before her later marriage to Philip Ostrander, contains a riddle about the inherently unequal premises upon which nineteenth-century womanhood was based. Perhaps, Phelps implies, the same logic that constructs the "Orient" as mysterious and other as a means of extracting wealth from it also mystifies women's desires and sublimates them into domestic labor in order to perpetuate an uneven distribution of labor in the household.[51] Avis later attempts to manage the anxieties of her marriage through her aesthetic affinity for rich red textiles, as I will elaborate upon in the next section. However, like the sphinx, these textiles have a life of their own, betraying a history of inter-imperial competition, exploitation of labor, and harm to living creatures that comes back to ensnare Avis herself.

The "Inarticulate Passion" of Cochineal Beetles and Carmine Dye

Throughout the novel Avis expresses her artistic and "undomestic" (77) persona not only through her commitment to her time in the studio and her depiction of the mysterious sphinx, but also through her almost instinctive attraction to the color carmine, a deep, expensive red. Harnessing carmine-dyed textiles as both backdrop and adornment, Avis disregards the exorbitant price of the dye in another example of her avoidance of international economic realities. Phelps employs the carmine shawl that Avis dons repeatedly in the novel as a multivalent symbol. First, the shawl symbolizes Avis's commitment to aesthetic beauty while trying to keep the exploitation that produced that beauty at arm's length. Second, the shawl symbolizes Avis's ambivalence in putting on the mantle of marriage and motherhood. Although the carmine shawl heightens Avis's value on the marriage market because its lush hue complements her appearance, it also entangles her in inter-imperial economies, whose logic will inform the division of labor within her eventual marriage. In the opening scene of the novel, for example, Avis has recently returned to New England from her Parisian artistic training, and, intent on making a dramatic appearance, deliberately sets herself against the bright backdrop of a curtain when attending a poetry club. The narrator specifies that the curtain is the color "called variously and lawlessly by upholsterers cranberry, garnet, or ponso; known to artists as carmine" (6), a color with which Avis feels a "fierce kinship" (7).

Phelps positions Avis as distinctive both in her ability to correctly identify the precise name of the color and in her willingness to silhouette her profile against the bright hue; while "Coy or Barbara would have known better than to have ventured their complexions against this trying background," Avis "knew perfectly well that the curtain became her" (7).[52] Given that the novel is set during the US Civil War, Avis's fervent interest in the luxury cloth seems out of touch with the contemporary hardships.[53] Yet Avis's affinity for the color carmine allows her to perform her status as a woman whose complexion can stand up to such an aggressively colored backdrop, as an artist who loves vibrant colors so much that she sidles up to bright textiles during poetry discussions, and as a consumer who is concerned about the aesthetic value of goods without regard to their material origin or cost. As the history of the color carmine will reveal, however, no amount of holding herself aloof from other women or from the economic realities of housekeeping can disentangle Avis from the inter-imperial history that the carmine shawl represents.[54] Trafficking in the currency of her own image, heightened as its beauty is when put in relief against the stark red curtain, Avis ignores the way in which the commodification of her beauty leaves her susceptible to the cruelties of a marriage market that treats Avis and women like her as not fully autonomous human beings.

By juxtaposing the "fierce kinship" Avis feels for carmine with an empire-inspired topic of discussion for the poetry club, Phelps, like Alcott, hints at the way narratives of imperial plunder quietly infiltrate the minds of uncritical readers. The topic treated by the Harmouth poetry club that Avis attends in this opening scene is Edmund Spenser's *The Faerie Queene*, as editor Carol Farley Kessler identifies in her footnotes, based on brief excerpts from Spenser's poem quoted throughout the chapter. Kessler comments that Spenser's epic poem "was dedicated to the fame of Elizabeth I" (251). A monarch who oversaw British expansion, exploration, and imperial jockeying with Spain, Elizabeth also commissioned piracy against Spanish fleets with the express purpose of absconding with their stockpiles of cochineal—otherwise known as carmine—extracted from the New World colonies.[55] Tens of thousands of pounds of cochineal were seized from Spanish ships by British pirates in the late sixteenth century, according to Amy Greenfield (116). One raid in 1597, led by the earl of Essex, Robert Devereux, captured 55,000 pounds of cochineal dye, and was "the largest cochineal prize of the century—enough, proclaimed the queen, 'to serve this realm for many years'" (Greenfield 111). Just as the Orientalist logic of the lecture on the pyramids slipped unawares into Jo's literary imagination, so here does the celebration of imperial power that is Spenser's *Faerie Queene* subconsciously make its way into Avis's artistic imagination. At the poetry club, Avis shares a charcoal sketch of Spenser's character Una that bears "the mark of the artist's peculiar style" (9), revealing how she has assimilated Spenser's lessons into her artistic practice. With Avis's almost compulsive return to the carmine textiles she loves mere paragraphs after describing her charcoal sketch, Phelps signals toward the shared impulses of the privateering British monarch honored by Spenser's poem and the New England artist drawn incessantly by the exotic allure of carmine.

As she leaves the Spenserian reading club, Avis imagines her distance from typical New Englanders through a geographic metaphor that previews the global paths of circulation that carmine dye traverses: "her mind was pre-occupied in ways to which the little inner life of a Harmouth reading-club was as foreign as—ah, well!—as foreign as the carmine curtain to the cold north star" (13). Casting the carmine curtain as foreign, Avis symbolically orients herself geographically in relation to the "cold north star" in order to once again emphasize her unique perspective of the world. Yet, as the economic and social history of carmine dye illuminates, Avis's artistic identity is not unique but is reflexively constructed in relationship to historical and ongoing global configurations of power.

A rich red pigment coveted for its brilliance and its capacity for creating colorfast textiles, carmine was produced from the desiccated bodies of cochineal beetles and primarily used for dyeing valuable fabrics because of its high price in the eighteenth and nineteenth centuries.[56] The complicated history of the circulation of carmine reveals a centuries-long inter-imperial struggle for control over trade of the dye, of which Queen Elizabeth's British piracy was only one small part. These inter-imperial trade battles serve as a synecdoche for the competition for global status between the empires that were involved in the carmine trade—including the Spanish, British, French, Dutch, Portuguese, and eventually the newly emerging US empire. Formerly the exclusive province of Aztec imperial producers, cochineal cultivation was exposed to the Spanish when explorers entered Mexico in the sixteenth century, and carmine dye was introduced to Europe.[57]

Although European empires dominated the competition for a monopoly on the dye, once the United States emerged as a nation in its own right, it sought to stake a claim in the carmine trade, perhaps as a way of signaling its status as an economically powerful empire. When the United States acquired territories in Florida and Texas in the early nineteenth century, settlers discussed attempting to cultivate cochineal in these warmer climates as a means of entering the international carmine trade (Greenfield 207).[58] The United States' eagerness to prove itself on a world stage, presented through this microcosmic example of the carmine trade, thus provides an important context for Avis's struggle to establish herself as a US artist through her affinity with carmine textiles.

Reading carmine as a symbol of inter-imperial economic competition together with Avis's domestic and artistic failure presents the possibility that Phelps's references to carmine textiles slice with a keen critical edge—especially since these references coincide with key plot points, including Avis's artistic debut, her marriage, and her discovery of her husband's infidelity. This long history of global competition over carmine production and trade reframes Avis's "fierce kinship" with carmine fabrics as evidence of the stealthy way in which imperial desires sneak unconsciously into the imaginations of uncritical consumers, readers, and artists. Like Jo March, Avis fetishizes the glamorous aspects of imperial conquest without caring to counteract the insidious discourses that perpetuate global inequality.

While Avis turns her gaze toward the beauty of the foreign textiles to dissociate from the unsettling implications of her participation in the marriage market and in the global economy, Phelps problematizes Avis's actions by imbuing the fabric with life, signifying the reciprocity of global economic and cultural relationships that Avis has difficulty confronting. The carmine cloth radiates with the silent forces expended for its production, as the narrator notes the curtain "seemed to throb as if it held some inarticulate passion, like that of a subject soul" (6). Just as the sphinx silently subverts Avis's controlling gaze through its inscrutable expression, so, too, does the carmine fabric burst forth with repressed life to undermine Avis's aesthetic detachment. If, as Amy Kaplan suggests, domesticity works to construct a process of domestication, through which "the home contains within itself those wild or foreign elements that must be tamed" (25), here, the novel demonstrates that Avis can't fully "domesticate" the foreignness that the carmine represents: as it turns out, the carmine has a life of its own, just as empires competing with the US on a global stage also have their own trajectories and interests.

An awareness of the destructive process of carmine production—which involves the desiccation of thousands of insects and the efforts of untold numbers of peasant laborers—renders new, troubling meaning to this sense of "inarticulate passion, like that of a subject soul" invoked by the carmine cloth. Manufactured in Mexico and parts of Central America, carmine dye was produced by harvesting hundreds of thousands of cochineal beetles from nopal plants. The beetles were then baked in the sun and pulverized to create the dye powder.[59] Avis displays her awareness of this brutal process of production in a discussion with her husband Philip. When Philip compliments a carmine-colored shawl she wears by marveling, "it looks like a live thing," Avis alludes to the process by which the red dye is produced, explaining: "it is one of the colors made from the cochineal . . . I have always fancied that they throb with the life that has been yielded to make them" (133). Repeating the language of vitality used to describe the carmine curtain in the earlier scene, Avis's image of the "throbbing" textiles emphasizes the life forces expended to produce both the curtain and the shawl. Though Avis's observation about the cochineal beetles may seem like a strangely specific piece of trivia knowledge, the process of carmine production was detailed in children's geography books of the period, with one 1875 text elaborating in a section on Mexican products of commerce about the "cochineal cactus," which "is much cultivated for the sake of the cochineal insect which feeds upon its leaves. These insects are scraped from the plants into bags, killed by boiling water, and then dried in the sun. Their tiny bodies, when rubbed to powder, yield a brilliant crimson dye called cochineal" (Swinton 46).[60] Though this evidence makes it not entirely surprising that Avis would know how carmine dye was made, her knowledge here does further underline her apparent ignorance about other commodities, like cotton.

Phelps's strong sense of moral obligation, her later antivivisection activism exemplified by her 1904 novel *Trixy*, and her concern for labor conditions in her other writings suggest that she does not share Avis's sentimental view of the production of carmine textiles.[61] Lori Duin Kelly characterizes the sense of conscience that motivated Phelps for her entire career, writing that "Phelps functioned at the end of her career much as she had throughout it, that is, as a writer less concerned with commercial success than with a clear desire to effect changes in powerful institutions and practices she found intolerable. In the case of vivisection, her goal was nothing short of an end to animal suffering and a transformation in the way doctors would be taught to care for their patients" (76). Reading the "life that has been yielded to make them" in light of Phelps's lifelong commitment to reducing harm to animals and people alike, we can understand the phrase as an allusion to both the cochineal beetles and the laborers who harvested this dye. No clear-eyed moralist like Phelps, Avis creates a rose-colored transformation of the pulverized bodies of the beetles and the back-breaking labor of Mexican Indian peasants into a romanticized vision of an exceptionally vibrant color. If the meanings of things, as Arjun Appadurai suggests, are "inscribed in their forms, their uses, their trajectories," here, Avis deliberately revises the violent meanings inscribed in carmine's form (5). Constructing a romantic vision of labor relations wherein the beetles—and implicitly, the laborers and empires competing over control of this commodity— "yield" to the US, Avis obscures the exploitation inherent in the cultivation and global exchange of carmine and commodities like it by imagining those disadvantaged by this system to voluntarily cede their rights. As the novel progresses, Phelps reveals the shortsightedness of Avis's attitude toward the world as reflected here, reminding readers that art necessitates an acknowledgment of one's own position in global systems of power: one must meet the gaze of the sphinx without projecting oneself onto it.

As a symbol of the labor exploitation and inter-imperial economic volatility that Avis attempts to evade, the carmine shawl loses its vivacity when Avis's marriage encounters obstacles, fading in color as if Avis's own life force has been wrung from it. In a scene of marital discord when Philip commits an infidelity, the novel establishes a parallel between the competitive jockeying over monopolistic control over carmine dye and the rivalry that Avis herself engages in with another woman vying for her husband's affection. Through this parallel, Phelps illuminates the impossibility of fully disentangling from the imperial economies that structure the nineteenth-century world because domestic dramas are scripted through the same logic. Once the beauty has faded from alluring luxuries like carmine textiles, it becomes more difficult to ignore the violent systems that produce and circulate such luxuries. Formerly a color against which Avis posed because she thought it "became her" (7), the carmine now signifies the gradual deterioration of her relationship with Philip and her concomitant uncertainty about her artistic vocation and economic circumstances.

The flirtation between Philip and Barbara Allen in the latter half of the novel presents a competitive threat to Avis's attempted sovereignty over her domestic household in an allegorical enactment of the inter-imperial battles fought over the commodities in Avis's home. Avis creates an unsettling silhouette against the carmine shawl when she encounters Philip and Barbara in a moment of inappropriate tenderness. As Philip and Barbara realize that Avis has been watching them holding hands, the narrator transmits Philip's impression of Avis's daunting appearance: "she was paler, perhaps, than need be, in that red drapery. She gathered it, for it had fallen almost to her knee, in one hand. The other was thrust into the empty air" (185). The formerly flattering carmine textiles now overwhelm Avis, suggesting that she is not at all able to "tame" the wildness represented by the foreign dye—nor is she able to manage the threat of a disruption to her household represented by Barbara, whom she once defeated in the battle for Philip's hand. Thus she gathers the falling red cloth, as if grasping for the beauty she once saw in the carmine, pale with the recognition of the combative history it is imbued with, and the allegorical fight over her domain it scripts before her. Later Avis again attempts to resuscitate the aesthetic allure of the carmine shawl and sweep away its combative connotations, asking her husband, "Philip, this poor old carmine shawl that you used to like so much is pretty well faded out. Do you remember the night when we first came home, when I had it on?" When Philip responds that yes, he remembers that night, Avis remarks in a rather maudlin tone that "we were very happy, Philip—then . . . Sometimes I wonder . . . if nothing in this world can ever make us feel so again." Philip's cold response indicates the degree to which their relationship has disintegrated, as he replies with "cool, distant eyes": "that . . . is entirely out of the question" (200).

When Avis is forced to sell her painting of the sphinx after her husband is asked to resign from his position as a professor, it becomes Avis's soul, not the sphinx's, or the cochineal beetles', that is for sale on the global marketplace. When a collector comes to extract payment for Philip's college debts, Avis finds herself "grieved and shamed, and vaguely in need of money," and thus quickly dispenses with her painting, striking "the great sphinx dumb with the uplifted finger of a child," and sending it "desperately from her before the cool of her frenzy fell" (205). A far cry from the early chapters of the novel when Avis could not be bothered with the price of cotton, this moment leaves her amply aware of her involvement in the global marketplace. After the rapid sale of the painting in a New York gallery, Avis's friend Coy mentions the purchase casually before recognizing the sting of her own words: "'And of course, you've heard,' said Coy absently, 'that Stratford bought your sphinx last winter?' Coy spoke lightly; but her own voice sounded to her as if she had said, 'He bought your soul.' She rather wished she had said nothing about the sphinx" (248). The sale of Avis's painting represents the complete entanglement of her art in the global economy—the realm of wild swings in cotton prices and violent obliteration of cochineal beetles, a realm Avis long attempted to keep separate from her aesthetic concerns. Adding insult to injury, it is Avis's marriage to Philip that exposes her to this entanglement, as she is left to support their family when Philip loses his job. Because Phelps maintained the clarity of her moral vision all while being a prolific, bestselling author, she questions Avis's decision to succumb to her desire to give a "controlling reply" to the sphinx's "expectant look" instead of working through the difficult inter-imperial economic entanglements her artwork represents (143).[62]

Conquering Florida's Oranges with a "Little Northern Pluck"

The messily intertwined narrative threads of gender liberation, economic uncertainty, domestic discord, imperial domination, and artistic ethics culminate in Avis's miniature reenactment of the Manifest Destiny-driven expansion of the first half of the nineteenth century. When the couple travels to Florida for Philip's health, they displace their problems by transforming themselves into veritable conquistadors upon their arrival in the southern state: "they seemed to themselves now to have become the discoverers of the State of Florida. Above them widened new heavens; below them a new earth leaped" (233). This language of exploration recalls Florida's recent history as a contested territory that was inhabited by Native Americans, claimed by Spain, and incrementally taken over by the United States.[63] In this reimagined narrative of territorial expansion that coincides with the unraveling of Avis and Philip's marriage, Phelps's mock-heroic language draws readers' attention to the insidious discourses of imperial conquest that make their way from consumer purchases, to artistic imaginations, to domestic relationships.

As this episode unfurls, Phelps makes it apparent that Avis is as eager as ever to keep the ugly realities of the international economy at arm's length, in spite of Philip's best efforts to further ensnare her. Philip harbors dreams of economic expansion by going west, or starting his own orange business: "he was convinced that there was room for a large orange-grove even here; and, farther up the river, a little Northern pluck would work a miracle any day" (234). A fruit originating in Asia and gradually making its way westward across the globe over centuries of trade and imperial encounters, oranges were first introduced to Florida by Spanish colonizers in the sixteenth century (McPhee 89). In the years following 1821 when Florida became a US territory, orange groves were expanded, and 160 acres of land was promised to "anyone who could fight off the Seminoles and hold his ground for seven years" (McPhee 91). Growing oranges in Florida came to be seen by northerners as a lucrative pursuit, and literary star Harriet Beecher Stowe (an acquaintance of Phelps's) even purchased thirty acres of Floridian land in 1868, establishing a successful citrus business that shipped oranges north (McPhee 95–6). Art historian Shana Klein analyzes Stowe's paintings of oranges and references to oranges in her fiction and nonfiction, suggesting that for Stowe—and perhaps, I would add, for Phelps—oranges signified the promise of exporting Northern politics to the Southern region of the United States.[64] At the turn of the twentieth century, oranges were a commodity that continued to serve as an impetus for imperial conflict. Amy Kaplan uses the 1901 territorial incorporation of Puerto Rico in the case *Downes v. Bidwell* as evidence of the tension inherent in the United States' understanding of itself as a nation and empire—a case related to the taxation of imported oranges (2). While Phelps could not have known the imperial implications that the production and trade of oranges would eventually have, her depiction of Philip's fantasy of orange cultivation here is suggestive of the commercial expansionist desires that would later lead to the territorial incorporation of Puerto Rico.

Through Philip's vision of an orange grove nurtured through "a little Northern pluck," Phelps reinserts the specter of imperial economic practices that Avis fled to Florida to forget. The complete deterioration of the couple's relationship and Philip's death in the Florida swampland illustrates that marriage—in its white, middle-class, heteronormative, nineteenth-century iteration—is incompatible with economic justice and the art that advocates for such justice. Thus, Avis seems to feel a strange sense of relief when her would-be orange capitalist husband succumbs to his illness. After Philip is dead, Avis casts a warm glow over his memory, conveniently forgetting any domestic conflicts they had. On her journey back to Massachusetts, Avis reflects:

> Philip seemed quite near,—nearer than when it had been possible to be conscious of any imperfection in himself or in their union. Only his ideal visited her heart. She was not without a strange, exultant

sense that now she never could see a weakness or a flaw in him again ... She thought of him with something of the proud and peculiar triumph of the widowed girl, who kneels to the vision of the man whose wife she never was, to learn to reverence him by one blind thrill the less. (242)

In clinging to Philip's "ideal" with the thrilling sense that she will never "see a weakness or a flaw in him again," Avis's language denotes mastery and domination, reminiscent of American discourses that idealize the nation as innocent and free from flaws.[65] Avis ultimately chooses a narrative of her marriage that effaces the allegorical imperial battles between her, Philip, and romantic rival Barbara Allen, just as the United States has long sought to obscure its imperial actions and ambitions.

Perhaps not coincidentally, as Avis persists in disavowing the international economic conflicts that inhere in her household commodities and are allegorized through her domestic relations, she becomes further detached from her work as a painter and the call implicit in her art to recognize the gaze of others. She eventually concludes that her "style is gone" and gives up her work as an artist (244). Avis's rejection of her art career reflects her inability (or unwillingness) to face the reciprocal relationship between self and other, between aesthetic and moral ideals, and between the US and the world.[66] Phelps reiterates the importance of this reciprocity as Avis reflects on the future before her:

> Horizons with which her own youth was unacquainted, beckoned before her; the hills looked at her with a foreign face; the wind told her that which she had not heard; in the air strange melodies rang out; uninterpreted colors gathered about the rising of the sun: her own chastised aspiration looked humbly out upon the day whose story she should never read. (246)

Just as the sphinx once "baffled" Avis and disrupted her artistic attempts at mastery, so here does the future become animated in its resistance of Avis's "controlling gaze." Personifying the landscape that looks at Avis "with a foreign face" that she cannot translate and presenting Avis with "uninterpreted colors" that, like carmine, she cannot fully tame, Phelps confronts Avis with the limitations of her vision. By incorporating one final allusion to the sphinx, Phelps connects Avis's "chastised ambition" to her Orientalist imaginings, as the narrator ponders, "Were there subtle readings of the eternal riddle astir upon the desert? Had the stone lips of the sphinx begun to mutter? God knew; and the desert knew—and the dumb mouth" (247). Attributing knowledge to the sphinx that Avis is prevented from accessing, Phelps implies that US artists like Avis must examine their own complicity in capitalist, imperialist structures, and allow for a multiplicity of voices in the ever-shifting dynamics of the world economy.

Ultimately, in *The Story of Avis*, Phelps forwards a moral imperative that women indeed "ought to care about" the price of cotton, the origin of carmine dye, the colonial expansionism involved in securing affordable oranges, and the labor expended to make these goods available to consumers, because these questions are in fact "vital to the interests of the country"—and to the interests of women who are implicated in these systems through their consumption and domestic labor. According to Phelps, artists have a particular obligation to combat injustice in what they choose to portray, even if that moral vision becomes clouded by their participation, through the sale of their art, in the global capitalist systems they seek to critique. The distance Avis constructs between herself as an artist and the quotidian realities of household life deflates the power of her artistic project, leaving it toothless. This failure of Avis's art in turn leaves her vulnerable to the very economic vagaries that she so strenuously seeks to disregard. Seen through the structuring device of commodities like cotton, carmine dye, and oranges, which appear at key plot points, the novel unfolds as Phelps's complex, conflicted meditation on the difficulty of presenting critique and pushing for reform when entangled in imperialist capitalist structures.

By way of conclusion, I would like to return briefly to *Little Women* to highlight a piece of advice from Mrs. March, the moral center of the novel—advice offered to Meg that might well extend to Alcott's and Phelps's readers. After Meg's confession that she has difficulties connecting with her husband's political interests, Mrs. March chides Meg for her disengagement and wholesale acceptance of nineteenth-century ideologies of "separate spheres," instructing: "Don't shut yourself up in a bandbox because you are a woman, but understand what is going on, and educate yourself to take your part in the world's work, for it all affects you and yours" (308). Mrs. March warns Meg of both the dangers of political disengagement and of identifying too closely with the material objects in one's life: care too uncritically about things like hats and gloves, and you yourself will become an accessory, shut up in a bandbox and cut off from the world. Alcott invites her readers to pay attention to both the pyramids and the prices of coal and flour; to both the state of the nation and the state of one's bonnet; to both the seams of sheets and the borders of continents, because, as Mrs. March points out, "it all affects you and yours." Avis learns all too well that apparent trivialities like the price of cotton and the origin of carmine "all affect you and yours," and Phelps, like Alcott, encourages readers to "educate yourself to take your part in the world's work." As writers who depended on the sale of their art to support themselves, Alcott and Phelps understood the difficulties of navigating competing aesthetic, ethical, and economic obligations. Over a hundred years ago when the newly reunified United States was striving to establish its place as a global economic power, seemingly "domestic" texts like *Little Women* and *The Story of Avis* were in fact looking outward to grapple with the implications of US economic expansionism. As critics of American literature, we may see that we have yet more work to do in expanding the geopolitical scope of our analysis if we are to avoid shutting up nineteenth-century women writers in the bandboxes of national domesticity.

Notes

1. On tariffs, see David Pletcher. On competition for control over Asian trade, see Malini Schueller. On consumption of imported goods, see Kristin Hoganson.
2. My use of the language of intimacy here is indebted to Ann Laura Stoler's conception of the "intimacies of empire," as well as Lisa Lowe's articulation of the "intimacies of four continents." Both Stoler and Lowe identify the surprising relations forged between nations and peoples that occur with imperialism and colonialism.
3. See, for instance, Jean Jacques François Le Barbier's series of eighteenth-century tapestries (Peck 271).
4. Gerald Horne notes that "according to one study, blackbirding, as this practice of luring Melanesians and Polynesians to toil for next to nothing was called, occurred between 1863–1904 and involved 61,610 people, mostly men but also some women and children. Another study estimates that 62,000 Pacific Islanders went to Queensland and at least 22,000 to Fiji—though others see these figures as rather low" (2). For more on imperial intervention and nineteenth-century cotton production in Fiji, see Jane Samson and Ricky-Dale Calhoun.
5. For more on the global reaches, repercussions, and representations of the nineteenth-century cotton market, see Brian Schoen, Sven Beckert, Suzanne Daly, and Ricky-Dale Calhoun.

6. The Boston Board of Trade reported that at the end of 1862, raw cotton prices were "quite fluctuating from day to day, but have reached a higher point the past two months than the most sanguine in the trade expected. Last year the article was forced up to what was then considered extraordinary high prices, but the rates lately current have been nearly double the highest prices obtained in 1861" (48). Sven Beckert elaborates on the global crisis brought on by these high prices, noting that by early 1862, "cotton prices had quadrupled from their prewar levels and, consequently, manufacturers closed shops and tens of thousands of operatives found themselves out of work" (247).
7. See *What to Wear?* (48–56). For further discussion of Phelps's dress reform writings, see Roxanne Harde.
8. See Beckert 242–73. See also Giorgio Riello for more on the global history of cotton.
9. See Lisa Lowe, *The Intimacies of Four Continents*.
10. For more on the ambiguity of Alcott's feminism in *Little Women*, see Ann B. Murphy, Susan Naomi Bernstein, and Janice M. Alberghene and Beverly Lyon Clark. On questions of domesticity, labor, and separate spheres ideology, see Tara Fitzpatrick and Caroline Chamberlin Hellman. On Alcott's depictions of creative vocations, see Deborah Barker, Anne Boyd, Naomi Sofer, and Erin Hendel.
11. In "Love's Labor's Reward," Tara Fitzpatrick likewise observes Alcott's critique of the inevitable inequalities of a capitalist economy, and suggests that she constructs an alternative "sentimental economy" in her novel *Work*.
12. The afterlife of Alcott's fiction in the restoration of Orchard House as a museum, documented exhaustively by Patricia West, illustrates the later nationalistic politicization of Alcott's portrait of domesticity.
13. For a discussion of Alcott's attitudes toward household labor and domestic service, see Caroline Chamberlin Hellman and Carolyn Maibor.
14. Madeleine Stern describes the Alcott girls' life at the commune Fruitlands, noting the influence of Bronson Alcott's fellow architects of the experimental living situation: "The girls did dress a little differently from the way they had done at home, for linen tunics were the only permissible raiment for the Consociate Brothers. Mr. Lane designed the garments for the girls, along with broad-brimmed linen hats, since cotton would encourage slavery and wool would deprive the sheep of its natural clothing" (32).
15. For a detailed account of the Alcotts' financial difficulties, see Sarah Elbert's biography, *A Hunger for Home: Louisa May Alcott and Little Women*. As Elbert explains, Bronson refused to charge set fees for his frequent lectures for fear of compromising his anti-commercial ideals (41). Furthermore, although Abba May came from a well-to-do family, she was unable to use her inheritance to pay Bronson's debts because of restrictions her father included in his will (43).

16. Even her final entry written before her death, when she was a very wealthy woman, notes the bills that she paid that day (*Journals* 334).
17. See the 1877 *Proceedings of the Convention of the American Bankers' Association*. One attendee of the Convention commented on the problem of the national debt, proclaiming, "the debt exists—so the question now before us is, shall it be paid? For one, sir, I say it must be paid, and we all, as good patriots, as good citizens, as good bankers, should put our shoulders to the wheel, put our efforts together, mass them, and pay off this national debt as fast and as soon as we can" (59). During this convention, the members argued over the form of legal tender to be used to pay the debt and compared the US system of banking to those of other nations to answer how to proceed.
18. Though she does not discuss *Little Women*, Lorinda B. Cohoon examines another novel by Alcott, *Eight Cousins*, to elucidate the Orientalism of a chapter in which a character tours a merchant ship recently arrived from China.
19. Douglas elaborates: "The March girls grow up, as all of us would like to, realistic enough to redefine childish dreams, and fortunate enough to actualize them. They simultaneously inhabit the realms of myth and mimesis: they are ideally full American citizens. In a charmed creative act, Alcott documented, in her finest novel, the promised moment when democracy works" (61). For further discussion of Alcott's conflicted attitude toward aging and maturation, see Sari Edelstein.
20. On Egyptomania, see Malini Schueller and Scott Trafton.
21. Alcott similarly poked fun at philosophers visiting Concord in her journal, remarking, "If they were philanthropists I *should* enjoy it, but speculation seems like a waste of time when there is so much real work crying to be done. Why discuss the Unknowable till our poor are fed & the wicked saved?" (216).
22. In February 1854, Alcott notes in a journal entry that when her father arrived home, she and her sisters "fed and warmed and brooded over him, longing to ask if he had made any money, but no one did till little May said, after he had told all the pleasant things, 'Well, did people pay you?' Then, with a queer look, he opened his pocketbook and showed one dollar, saying with a smile that made our eyes fill, 'Only that! My overcoat was stolen, and I had to buy a shawl. Many promises were not kept, and travelling is costly; but I have opened the way, and another year shall do better'" (71).
23. Beckert explains that production increased so dramatically and the value of cotton exports rose so high that this moment marked "a permanent economic change of such significance that historians of Egypt rank the American Civil War among the most crucial events in that country's nineteenth-century history" (256).
24. Hunter documents the US's wheat-supplying strategies in the Seven Years', French Revolutionary, and Napoleonic Wars (506).

25. On the global wheat and flour trade, see Richard Perren, Paul Sharp and Jacob Weisdorf, Mette Ejrnæs, Karl Gunnar Persson, and Søren Rich, as well as Hunter. Perren attributes the increase in US exports to Britain to an early adoption of roller milling technology, and Hunter suggests that inter-imperial conflict had a role in the United States' adoption of these new wheat-milling technologies. Ejrnæs et al. note that "wheat from the Americas and India gained an increasing share of the market, crowding out most of the European wheat by the end of the nineteenth century. The United States was the largest overseas supplier, but lost a significant part of its market share to new market entrants such as Canada, India, Argentina, and Australia shortly before and after the turn of the century" (146).
26. Michael Ziser explicates the discursive impact of coal in the nineteenth century: "The mining of coal, which must be brought by brute force from seams buried far below the ground, epitomizes the zero degree of labor that so fascinated many nineteenth-century intellectuals and underscores the ultimate dependence of even an advanced industrial society on the input of *human* energy" (321).
27. For more on the history of the coal industry, see Barbara Freese, *Coal: A Human History*.
28. Wilhelm writes, "Humorous instances throughout *Little Women* draw attention to the difficult process whereby the little women learn to be wives and mothers; later in the novel, once their performances are naturalized, humor intervenes to recall earlier incarnations of the characters and remind readers of the labor these identities require" (63).
29. For further discussion of the disparate effects paper currency had on Northern and Southern US economics during and following the Civil War, see John Steele Gordon.
30. For more on Belzoni's spotted reputation among contemporary archaeologists and perceived mercenary reasons for excavating Egyptian sites, see Ivor Noël Hume.
31. For more on the political implications of the Lisbon earthquake, see Ana Cristina Araújo. On the economic costs of the disaster, see David Chester and Olivia Chester, and Alvaro Pereira.
32. While the skeptical Candide declares upon the event of the earthquake that "this is the end of the world!" the fatally optimistic philosopher Pangloss asks, "What can be the sufficient reason for this phenomenon?" (29). The fact that Pangloss is hanged shortly after in an act of religious attrition to prevent future earthquakes shows how useful Voltaire believes his rationalization of horrific events to be.
33. Pereira notes that "one major consequence of the 1755 earthquake was a dramatic change in prices, both at the national and regional level ... This was especially true for staples, such as wheat, in regions such as Lisbon and the Algarve" (478).

34. Sarah Lahey sees the demands of the literary marketplace as complementary to Alcott's artistic ethos, arguing that Alcott's journals "question whether it is even desirable to work simply for the improvement of one's soul" (151). However, I would posit that Alcott simultaneously unveils the ethical compromises such mercenary work entails.
35. The title "A Phantom Hand" seems to be a literary and an economic allusion, referencing both E.D.E.N. Southworth's popular 1859 novel *The Hidden Hand* and Adam Smith's description of the "invisible hand" of the marketplace.
36. See, respectively, Sarah Way Sherman, Stephanie Foote, Ann Douglas, and Ann B. Murphy. Alternatively, see Ivy Schweitzer, who takes pleasure in a "perverse" reading of the novel, embracing her own "readerly refusal to accept the feminine conditioning and constriction that the last part of the novel imposes on Jo" (19).
37. For more about Alcott's anonymously published sensation stories, see Madeleine Stern's introduction to *A Double Life: Newly Discovered Thrillers of Louisa May Alcott*, a volume that also includes "The Fate of the Forrests" (73–124).
38. For example, while Deborah Barker suggests writers like Phelps depict female artists to project the "aesthetic seriousness" of their own work (11), Anne Boyd and Naomi Sofer situate Phelps among other postbellum writers interested in claiming a place for women within the United States' emerging high culture by revising existing models of (male) authorship and honing "self-consciously literary" styles (Sofer 11). Others, such as Susan Donaldson and Lisa Long, have focused on the novel's radical questioning of nineteenth-century gender roles and its parallel unsettling of the period's literary categories of sentimental and realist fiction.
39. For more on engaging and ironizing narrative techniques, see Robyn Warhol.
40. See Lori Duin Kelly, Roxanne Harde, Lisa Long, and Laura Smith.
41. See David Pletcher for a more complete history of the United States' commercial efforts in South America.
42. See R. A. Humphreys, T. Boyle, and Srdjan Vucetic for further history of this diplomatic crisis.
43. See, for example, George Griffith and Jennifer Cognard-Black on Eliot's influence on Phelps. On Phelps's allusions to Browning, see Becky Wingard Lewis and Maria Dolores Narbona Carrión. On the novel's Orientalist tropes, see Jeffrey Cass and Scott Trafton.
44. Naomi Sofer reads this scene as an example of Phelps's disdain for the rhetoric of war; however, such an interpretation does not fully account for Phelps's simultaneous critique of imperialist modes of representation, and of European and American tendencies to use imperial exertion to resolve contradictions in national identity.
45. For more on nineteenth-century Americans' artistic training in Europe, see Bailey Van Hook.

46. Trafton discusses one of Alcott's sensation stories titled, "Lost in a Pyramid, or, The Mummy's Curse," suggesting that "her tale demonstrates the extent to which authors by midcentury had become accustomed to the automatic relays between mummies and revenge and had begun taking liberties with, as well as capitalizing on, the trope" (126). Likewise, he claims that in *The Story of Avis*, "Avis's historical identity, as a woman as well as a feminist, is dependent on her ability to enlist the signs of race" (204).

47. Said includes Egypt specifically as central in his history of Orientalism, claiming that "Although it was almost immediately preceded by at least two major Orientalist projects, Napoleon's invasion of Egypt in 1798 and his foray into Syria have had by far the greater consequence for the modern history of Orientalism" (*Orientalism* 76). He elaborates on the imperial significance of Egypt for Napoleon (and for those who came after him): "Because Egypt was saturated with meaning for the arts, sciences, and government, its role was to be the stage on which actions of a world-historical importance would take place. By taking Egypt, then, a modern power would naturally demonstrate its strength and justify history; Egypt's own destiny was to be annexed, to Europe preferably. In addition, this power would also enter a history whose common element was defined by figures no less great than Homer, Alexander, Caesar, Plato, Solon, and Pythagoras, who graced the Orient with their prior presence there" (85).

48. In her notes to her edited edition of *The Story of Avis*, Carol Farley Kessler cites Vedder's painting as Phelps's possible source material (255); Scott Trafton comments that Avis's painting is "obviously reminiscent of Elihu Vedder" (203); and Jeffrey Cass agrees that Vedder's painting is the "principal iconographic source for Phelps's Sphinx referencing" (56).

49. During the Civil War, Thayer "met regularly with the viceroy to discuss cotton production and eventually hired a confidant of the viceroy, Ayoub Bey Trabulsi, to examine 'the cottons of Egypt,'" later remarking favorably on the "great agricultural revolution" that was taking place under the influence of viceroy Muhammad Sa'id Pasha (Beckert 264).

50. Naomi Sofer, for instance, suggests that in this scene, Avis, like the sphinx, becomes a "speaking subject of her own art" (39), and Deborah Barker emphasizes how the sphinx unites women under their shared experience of patriarchal oppression (93). Scott Trafton accuses Avis's painting of constructing an image of white womanhood that is "predicated on the colonization of the Other" (204), while Jeffrey Cass argues that Phelps identifies "the progress of women to the cult of true womanhood and then connects this feminine manifest destiny to the mythological presence of the Sphinx" (53).

51. Indeed, Said comments on the intrinsically misogynist nature of Orientalism, writing that "Orientalism itself, furthermore, was an

exclusively male province; like so many professional guilds during the modern period, it viewed itself and its subject matter with sexist blinders. This is especially evident in the writing of travelers and novelists: women are usually the creatures of a male power-fantasy. They express unlimited sensuality, they are more or less stupid, and above all they are willing" (207).

52. Later in the novel, Philip fancies that Avis "breathed color as other women breathed pale air" (132), again underscoring her difference from other women.

53. Dorothy and James Volo explain that women were forced to become resourceful with their attire because of the exorbitant prices of textiles and other goods during the war. Additionally, they write that women donned more sedate colors than the vibrant red Avis is attracted to: "although some showy young women in the North did wear [vibrant colors], proper ladies did not. *Peterson's* [a nineteenth-century ladies' magazine that often advised on fashion trends] counseled against the use of bright colors: 'Though they may gratify the savage, [they] will not please the educated eye'" (242). Avis's conspicuous attachment to the expensive fabric, then, implicates Avis as a "showy" young woman.

54. Naomi Sofer sees Avis's exceptionalism as a negative quality because it singles out Avis as "unnatural" because of her art, instead of imagining a broader range of artistic identities for women. However, I would suggest that Avis's emphasis on her unique artistic identity is instead a symptom of her resistance to her imbrication in a complex geopolitical and economic landscape—which Phelps chides her for avoiding.

55. See Greenfield 110–24.

56. The brilliance of carmine's hue in fabrics like wool and silk made the cost well worth it to many nineteenth-century consumers, as evidenced by Harriet Prescott Spofford's discussion of its effect in home decorating. She comments: "We have known a person to leave a room, where the prevailing tone was neutral, with an idea that the whole room was brilliant with carmine, because the eye had been caught by one very distinct and beautiful piece of carmine blazing out of all the ashes tints like a coal of fire" (235). Here, Spofford attests to carmine's potent resonances in the nineteenth-century imagination. For more on the use of dye on expensive fabrics, see Susan Fairlie (491). On the process of cochineal cultivation and production, see Carlos Marichal, "Mexican Cochineal."

57. Amy Greenfield follows carmine dye from its production in sixteenth-century Mexico, to its exportation by Spanish colonizers, to seventeenth-century British attempts to steal the valuable dye, to eighteenth-century French espionage used to abscond with heavily guarded live cochineal specimens from Mexico, to nineteenth-century production of synthetic dyes that eventually made cochineal obsolete.

58. While the climates did not turn out to be conducive to cochineal cultivation, this attempt by the United States to participate in this contested

inter-imperial carmine market marks a key transition for the US from newly formed nation to burgeoning empire.

59. Carlos Marichal explains the painstaking labor involved in the process of producing carmine dye, as well as the brutal ways in which the beetles themselves were killed: "The cochineal insects were cultivated with extraordinary care by Mexican Indian peasants on the nopal plants and later killed directly by hot water and then dried (red-brown). Alternatively, they were baked slowly in the hot sun, which gave them a silver color, or in hot pans or ovens, which made the final color of the grains black" ("Mexican Cochineal" 85).

60. As further evidence that women like Avis might have known the full details of carmine production, Catharine Beecher's 1869 housekeeping guide includes an entry about carmine that reads: "Carmine: A crimson color, the most beautiful of all the reds. It is prepared from a decoction of the powdered cochineal insect, to which alum and other substances are added" (476).

61. For more on Phelps's anti-vivisection activism, see Lori Duin Kelly. In Kelly's conception, Phelps's support for ethical treatment of animals in her novel *Trixy* implies that the care one has for animals reflects the way one will treat human beings—so the fact that Avis romanticizes the beetles' sacrifice suggests a parallel potential for her to be cruel to people, as well. Discussing Phelps's attention to labor issues, Laura A. Smith suggests that Phelps uses *The Silent Partner* to display "the brutalizing alienated labor behind the textiles on which middle-class domesticity and textile refinement are predicated" (186) and to exact "a conscientious response to textile consumption; textile consumers should, at the very least, rail against the contexts of production" (190).

62. In her autobiography *Chapters From a Life*, Phelps reflects on writers who "do not write for money" by speculating, "It must be a pleasant experience to be able to cultivate so delicate a class of motives for the privilege of doing one's best to express one's thoughts to people who care for them. Personally, I have yet to breathe the ether of such a transcendent sphere" (79). Phelps's soft condescension toward those who have the "privilege" of "cultivat[ing] so delicate a class of motives" for their writing makes it clear she believes that being cognizant of economic necessities can be beneficial to one's art.

63. See Walter Nugent for further explication of Florida's colonial history. Similarly, Jamie Winders characterizes the US South as a kind of "postcolonial site" during the Reconstruction era because of the role Northern occupying forces had in facilitating the Reconstruction.

64. See also Kathryn Cornell Dolan's *Beyond the Fruited Plain*, which argues that "Stowe's orange-based writings perform the domestic side of the national mission put into question by the Civil War. Stowe focuses on the production and consumption of regional foods as an integral element of her larger domestic reform work" (104).

65. Amy Kaplan describes her project in *Anarchy of Empire* as part of an effort "to counter the denial of empire that structures the discourse of American exceptionalism" (17). Shelley Streeby identifies denialist strategies employed by US continentalists, writing that "by claiming that contiguous lands were part of the continental 'domestic' space rather than foreign territory, U.S. continentalists promoted an exceptionalist understanding of the United States as a nonimperial nation" (10). In *Freedom's Empire*, Laura Doyle traces early American historiography's borrowing from earlier British discourses of racialized Anglo-Saxon liberty that were widespread during the English Civil War (63, 73–9), a context that she argues helps to dismantle "the pattern of American exceptionalist historiography and literary study that forgets this history whenever it takes the period of the American Revolution as the first institutionalization of the liberty discourse" (61).
66. Reciprocity agreements were much debated in nineteenth-century discussions about foreign trade policies. Such agreements proposed "modest bilateral agreements by which the United States and some other country would reduce or abolish duties on certain of each other's products so as to promote trade and economic development" (Pletcher 37). Although Phelps is not necessarily making direct allusions to such agreements, it is important to note that nineteenth-century readers were conscious of the give-and-take of global economic interconnections.

Chapter 2

Maneuvering through Centuries of Inter-Imperial Fur Trading and Gold Speculation in Woolson and Ruiz de Burton

In the opening of his history of John Jacob Astor's fur company titled *Astoria; Or, Anecdotes of an Enterprise Beyond the Rocky Mountains* (1836), Washington Irving declares the centrality of two commodities to American economic success: fur and gold. He writes:

> Two leading objects of commercial gain have given birth to wide and daring enterprise in the early history of the Americas; the precious metals of the South, and the rich peltries of the North. While the fiery and magnificent Spaniard, inflamed with the mania for gold, has extended his discoveries and conquests over those brilliant countries scorched by the ardent sun of the tropics, the adroit and buoyant Frenchman, and the cool and calculating Briton, have pursued the less splendid, but no less lucrative, traffic in furs amidst the hyperborean regions of the Canadas, until they have advanced even within the Arctic Circle. These two pursuits have thus in a manner been the pioneers and precursors of civilization. Without pausing on the borders, they have penetrated at once, in defiance of difficulties and dangers, to the heart of savage countries: laying open the hidden secrets of the wilderness; leading the way to remote regions of beauty and fertility that might have remained unexplored for ages, and beckoning after them the slow and pausing steps of agriculture and civilization. (1)

Irving's florid language here wildly stereotypes the national characteristics of the various imperial invaders who were motivated by the New World's lucre, including the Spanish, the French, and the British. Irving also equates the "wide and daring enterprise" of America with the spread of "civilization," anticipating the Manifest Destiny ethos that would drive American western expansion during much of the nineteenth century, and connecting that expansionism to economic advancement. Pinpointing the apparent permeability of national borders when commodities like fur and gold are at stake, Irving celebrates in sexually suggestive terms the way these "pioneers and precursors of civilization" have "penetrated" these territories to lay "open the hidden secrets of the wilderness" that is lush with "beauty and fertility."[1]

Decades after Irving's account of the fur trade was published, two fictional treatments of the commodities he lauds present a more cautious perspective on the impact of imperial economic conquest. Constance Fenimore Woolson's novel *Anne* (1882) takes place in the Northern region of Michigan that was once contested territory because of French, British, Anglo-American, and Indigenous peoples' interest in the lucrative fur trade centered there. Set for part of the novel in a similarly liminal area of North America, María Amparo Ruiz de Burton's *Who Would Have Thought It?* (1872) grapples with the extraction of gold from territories that were once inhabited by Indigenous Mexicans, then colonized by the Spanish, and finally annexed by the US in the Mexican–American War. Ruiz de Burton is more explicitly critical of the United States' expansionist efforts than any other author discussed in this book, perhaps because of her positionality as someone who became a US citizen as a result of mid-nineteenth-century territorial conquest, which forced her to live through the damaging effects of imperialism first hand. Whereas the economic and inter-imperial histories of cotton, carmine, flour, and coal operate as carefully crafted subtexts in Phelps's *The Story of Avis* and Alcott's *Little Women* (as discussed in the previous chapter), the imperial pasts of Northern Michigan and the Southwestern border of the United States rise to the surface of these texts by Woolson and Ruiz de Burton because their landscapes are so inextricably linked to inter-imperial conflict and trade. Haunted by centuries of historical trauma, these locations are sites of expansion whose liminal position between the US and the expanding borders of its empire makes an indelible impression on the bodies of those who live there.

These texts' allusions to the past, through references to the now-extinct fur trade in *Anne*, and through the geological exploits of one of the main characters in *Who Would Have Thought It?*, draw attention to the layered histories of imperial conflict at the northern and southwestern borders of the US. We can better see these traces of older imperial networks through the framework of inter-imperiality, which articulates the ways in which texts register "the embedded legacies of successive empires *and* the pressures created by contemporaneous empires" (Doyle, "Inter-Imperiality and Literary Studies" 337). In the following sections—the first focused on the fur trade in Woolson's *Anne*, the second focused on the extraction of gold in Ruiz de Burton's *Who Would Have Thought It?*—I argue that these "embedded legacies of successive empires" are made visible through the material evidence of economic conflicts: fur garments and gold jewelry. Woolson and Ruiz de Burton transpose the historical dynamics between competing imperial powers onto the interpersonal lives of their characters, who allegorically stand in for America, France, the Netherlands, Spain, and Mexico. Through these domestic dramas that echo geopolitical theater, Woolson and Ruiz de Burton investigate how imperial ventures can create a logic that remains long after the actual territorial contest is over. In these inter-imperial reenactments, women's bodies become the nexus of conflict because of the way they can signify futurity and the potential for national and imperial reproduction.[2]

Fur Trade Nostalgia in *Anne*

Constance Fenimore Woolson's 1882 novel *Anne* recalls the history of Michigan's Mackinac Island as a thriving outpost for the nineteenth-century North American fur trade through its characters' nostalgia for the former "merry fur-making times" (7), and through their fur garments, such as the title character's "fur boots, fur gloves, and a little fur cap" (46). *Anne* follows its eponymous protagonist as she loses her father, struggles to support her four younger siblings, travels to New York to train to be a teacher, manages romantic entanglements with various suitors, faces the outbreak of the Civil War, and, in a surprising twist, turns detective to solve a murder mystery before marrying and moving back to Mackinac. Preserved as an American national park by the time of *Anne*'s publication and later made a state park in 1895, Mackinac Island and the surrounding region was initially populated by Ottawa, Huron, and other Native peoples before being taken over by French explorers as a strategic location for the fur trade, then controlled by the British, acquired by the US after the Revolutionary War, and contested again during the War of 1812.[3] A consideration of the novel's many references to fur within the longer history of this commodity chain links the domestic spaces of the novel to Mackinac Island's violent history of territorial and economic competition.

Woolson frequently acknowledges the history of rivalry in Mackinac that is symbolized by the inactive fort at the center of the Island. For example, as Anne overlooks the expanse of Mackinac from the highest point of the Island, the narrator comments on the region's economic history, noting that the land she peruses consists of

> the great wild northland called British America, traversed by the hunters and trappers of the Hudson Bay Company—vast empire ruled by private hands, a government within a government, its line of forts and posts extending from James Bay to the Little Slave, from the Saskatchewan northward to the Polar Sea. (81)

Describing the uneasy tension between private economic interests (like the British Hudson Bay Company and the American Fur Company) and between national governments with imperial aspirations (like France, Great Britain, and the US), the narrator points to Northern Michigan's contested past as a strategic site for economic expansionism. Woolson positions Anne literally above this violently competitive economic past and depicts her "gazing off" (81) at it, as if to visually render the distance Anne imagines between her present moment and the volatile history of the island she inhabits—a distance Woolson later undermines by demonstrating how much these past inter-imperial rivalries continue to narrate Americans' lives. Immediately following her observation of this "great wild northland," Anne declares, "How delightful it is!" (81), a comment that dramatizes the pleasures to be found in expansionist visions of the frontier. Yet as Woolson explores later in the novel, it is easy to see this "vast empire" as "delightful" when viewing it from a distance as Anne does here. It is much more challenging to find such delight when the violence of imperial expansion that this land represents infiltrates your life.

In short, internationally traded commodities structure the domestic plot of Woolson's novel. Once critically neglected and pigeonholed as a "regional fiction," Woolson's work was recovered by feminist critics in the 1970s and 1980s, and the recovery work still continues decades later, as is evident by the recent publication of Anne Boyd Rioux's 2016 biography *Constance Fenimore Woolson: Portrait of a Lady Novelist* and the enthusiastic ongoing work of the Constance Fenimore Woolson Society. Even so, as Victoria Brehm explains, Woolson has been unfairly "marginalized as a minor writer because the tag of 'local color' has often been one of disapprobation," in spite of the fact that "Woolson used regional settings to critique national issues" (8). Recent transnational and postcolonial readings recognize that Woolson dissects the local in order to extrapolate lessons about the global.[4] For instance, John Lowe explores how "history becomes a palimpsest" in her fiction because varied national identities are layered within individuals with hybrid ancestries (42). Anne Boyd Rioux similarly identifies Woolson's interest in cultural amalgamation, tying it to her "discomfort with the effects of imperialism" that becomes expressed in a "form of hybridity predicated on an inequality that blurs cultural and racial distinctions" ("Tourism, Imperialism, and Hybridity" 56). While Rioux and Lowe focus on Woolson's Southern fiction, I show here that her Great Lakes fiction is similarly concerned with the mélange of racial and cultural identities brought together by imperial jockeying. In *Anne* specifically, Mackinac Island is populated by the ancestors of Anglo-Americans who were posted at the fort as well as French fur traders and Indigenous peoples who traded and intermarried with European and American settlers.

Woolson supported progressive political issues—she once called herself a "red hot abolitionist" (qtd. in Rioux, *Portrait* 40)—yet she was also susceptible to the prejudices of her era and her white Eurocentric education, as she later admitted in an 1890 letter written upon her travels to Egypt. Woolson reflected on her encounters with Arab people, writing that because she "was greatly struck by the intelligence & dignity of the oriental character," she "can't look down upon them as I used to,—from a superior Anglo-Saxon standpoint. That is the trouble of traveling widely over the world, and living for years in foreign countries; one inevitably loses one's standards, and comfortable fixed prejudices and opinions" (qtd. in Rioux, *Portrait* 247). Though still drawing on her era's Orientalist language, Woolson here creates critical distance from her former "superior Anglo-Saxon standpoint." In *Anne* there is a hint of such circumspection about "Anglo-Saxon" biases, though much more inchoate and ambivalent than what Woolson expresses in this later letter. Further, as Anne Boyd Rioux observes, Woolson saw herself as a realist first and foremost, and was "adamant that realism must trump moral concerns in her own art" (*Portrait* 150). Thus, Woolson's vision in *Anne* is global in scope to capture the realities of the internationally intertwined world that she experienced, identifying geopolitical tensions and power imbalances yet reserving overt judgment of them.

Woolson's geopolitical imagination takes form in her representation of the competitive, inter-imperial economic rivalries that have characterized the United States' history. In *Anne*, this framework attunes readers to the language of rivalry that goes beyond Mackinac and the North American fur trade, infiltrating characters' intimate relationships. Just as Mackinac Island served as an embattled location for inter-imperial trade, so does Anne, with her "clear Saxon eyes," (12) become a contested territory over which her French and Dutch friends compete—all the while remaining as "unconscious of these manoeuvres" (177) as she is distant from the "vast empire" she gazes at from the Island. Anne's initial naïveté about such manipulations, I suggest, allegorizes the United States' construction of a national self-image that effaces its violent history of territorial and commercial imperialism. Early in the novel, Woolson depicts the quintessentially American Anne as oblivious to her fellow characters' machinations. By writing a conclusion that reveals Anne's selective ignorance and gradual education, Woolson ironizes readers' assumptions about her, thereby mirroring the learned innocence of the American mythos that Anne represents.

The fur garments that proliferate in the section of *Anne* set on Mackinac Island reveal Woolson's engagement with contemporaneous questions of US economic imperialism. The priest Père Michaux, for instance, wears "a furred mantle, [with] a black silk cap crowning his silver hair" (37), while Anne's sister Tita nestles in a corner of their home that "she had lined and carpeted with furs" (9), and the prototypical customer of the Island's stores is always "enveloped in furs or a blanket" (7). Anne's fur garments flatter her, especially in the eyes of the opinionated local army wives, as the narrator's description of Anne's cloak and other accessories attests:

> The cloak was of strong dark blue woolen cloth . . . it reached from her throat to her ankles, and was met and completed by fur boots, fur gloves, and a little fur cap. The rough plain costume was becoming to the vigorous girl. "It tones her down," thought the lieutenant's wife; "she really looks quite well." (46)

Long before the publication of Woolson's novel, the sort of fur that Anne is draped in had nationalist resonances, playing a key role in US mythology and international diplomacy by communicating a uniquely American identity to the rest of the world. During the American Revolution, Benjamin Franklin traveled to Paris to lobby for French support for the rebelling colonies, wearing, famously, a distinctive fur cap. Deliberately constructing an image as a rugged frontiersman, Franklin wore the cap at all social gatherings, and was depicted in portraits and commemorative medallions donning the recognizable cap. Franklin's choice to wear this cap, as Walter Isaacson points out,

> was partly a pose, the clever creation of America's first great image-maker and public relations master . . . It helped him play the part that Paris imagined for him: that of the noble frontier philosopher and simple backwoods sage—even though he had lived most of his life on Market Street and Craven Street. (328)

This tale of American self-fashioning at the very moment of the nation's formation speaks to the power of fur as a signifier.

Beyond its role in Franklin's diplomatic maneuvering, fur conjures up a longer history of inter-imperial conflict, particularly in the region of Northern Michigan where *Anne* is set. The history of the fur trade on Mackinac Island and in the surrounding area gives a more concrete sense of the intimate ties between imperial conquest and economic expansion that surface in the militaristic language of competition throughout Woolson's novel. Developing after explorers' failed attempts to find a northeast passage by water to Asia, the North American fur trade from its inception was a consequence of inter-imperial competition and conquest (Brandão xxiii). Explorers saw economic potential in North America's natural resources, leading the French, English, Russian, Dutch, and various Indigenous groups to jostle for control over territories where fur-bearing animals were plentiful.[5] As a 1919 history of the Michigan fur trade attests,

> from the beginning of the fur trade regime to its close a bitter warfare was waged for the possession of this 'golden fleece' of the New World; monopolizing companies competed with coureurs de bois, Indian tribe with Indian tribe, French with English, English with American, independent traders with trading companies, and vice versa. It was a competition that lasted until the forest was stripped of its rich supply of peltries. (Johnson 17)

Harold Innis's well-known 1930 account of the North American fur trade similarly depicts its ruthlessly competitive nature, and a more contemporary history of the fur trade agrees that "the fur trade determined the course of empire" (Dolin xvi).[6]

The area near the Straits of Mackinac became an epicenter of economic activity for the fur trade, and consequently, a contested military site because of its important location connecting Lakes Huron and Michigan (Widder 299).[7] While sables, martens, and ermines were highly sought after early in the fur trade's global history, beaver dominated the trade from the late sixteenth century to the early nineteenth century (Dolin 13), until overhunting led traders to turn to other fur sources like deer, raccoon, bear, and muskrat (White 124, 135, 489). Upon establishing a fort near Mackinac in the 1680s, the French sought to secure their dominance in the region by establishing allegiances with Native Americans, and the fur trade was crucial to creating and maintaining these alliances (Brandão xxvi). According to Richard White, the Algonquians leveraged these strategic alliances to jockey between the French and the British for more favorable valuations for the fur they traded for European goods (119). The French and Indian War eventually ended the French semi-monopoly over the region's fur trade as they were forced to relinquish the territory to the British in 1760.[8] The territory of Mackinac was granted to the US at the end of the Revolutionary War in 1783, but the British later recaptured the fort there during the War of 1812.[9] While the fort's military significance declined after it was returned to US possession at the end of the War of 1812, it remained important as an outpost for the American fur trade until the 1850s. By the 1820s and 1830s, overhunting caused the North American beaver population to sharply decline to the point of near extinction, the beaver fur that was once so plentiful in Northern Michigan fell out of style, and in 1834 Astor's American Fur Company was sold.[10] By 1854, the fur trade in Michigan was effectively over, and Fort Mackinac became a relic of past military and economic ventures (Johnson 153).

Read within this volatile economic history, Woolson's characters' garments take on a different valence. Anne's "rough plain costume" trimmed with fur apparently casts her as the sort of frank, independent, frontier spirit that Benjamin Franklin sought to project to the French. This history also reframes Anne's previous gaze at the "delightful" northwestern frontier in an even more inter-imperial context. By adorning Anne with such a fraught commodity, Woolson symbolically covers her with the detritus of empire, implicitly suggesting a symbiotic relationship between national identity and imperial violence. That it is a lieutenant's wife who finds Anne's ensemble so "becoming to the vigorous girl" underscores her garments' connection to Mackinac's strategic military position (46). This characterization of Anne's attire as "becoming" both suggests that this imperial posture looks good on Anne and—if we read the adjective as a pun—implies that Anne is *becoming* the embodiment of empire.

The Island's economic and military past reverberates across all aspects of its inhabitants' lives, as many of the residents used to work for the Fur Company that flourished there, made their wealth through fur trading, and think back to those times happily, using the formerly affluent era of the Fur Company's success as the "island standard of comparison" (29) for assessing the current times of deprivation. The army fort at the center of the Island bears signs of decay that belie its military history; despite its former strategic role in the War of 1812 and its function as an outpost for the fur trade, it now "could hardly have withstood a bombardment" (50). Sketching the economic downturn Mackinac has experienced since the decline of the fur trade, the narrator describes the "irregular old buildings of the once-powerful fur company" that rise "like gallows ready for the old traders to hang themselves upon, if they came back and saw the degeneracy of the furless times" (7). The narrator's comments here mark the passing of one era to the next with a bit of morbid exaggeration that imagines the fur company's former buildings as "gallows," perhaps a slightly tongue-in-cheek reference to the island's past and ongoing violence.

Suggesting that the Islanders might have made something of these abandoned buildings if they had "looked upon them with progressive American eyes," the narrator laments that they

> were not progressive; they were hardly American. If they had any glory, it was of that very past, the days when those buildings were full of life ... Those were gay days, they said; they should never look upon their like again: unless, indeed, the past should come back—a possibility which did not seem so unlikely on the island as it does elsewhere, since the people were plainly retrograding, and who knows but that they might some time even catch up with the past? (7)

The narrator's characterization of the Island's inhabitants as "hardly American" refers to Mackinac's multi-ethnic French and Native population, expressing a dismissive attitude toward them that mimics ideologies of racial hierarchy common among white Americans during that time. Because of the narrative-distancing strategies that Woolson employs throughout the novel, it is unclear here if Woolson herself is voicing this attitude from her own "Anglo-Saxon superior standpoint" that she later renounced, or if she is critiquing the racist attitudes of her time. Later narration focalized through the French priest Père Michaux lends further ambivalence to this passage, if read metafictionally. After Père Michaux expresses his criticism of the United States, the narrator notes, "The priest generally placed America as a nation in the hands of possessive pronouns of the third person plural; it was a safe way of avoiding responsibility, and of being as scornful, without offending any one, as he pleased. One must have some outlet" (98). If we apply the priest's logic about "possessive pronouns of the third person plural" to this earlier passage describing Mackinac residents, it attunes us to Woolson's self-consciousness about the simultaneous deflection and judgment made available through the use of "their," or here in the non-possessive form, "they." Reading these two passages together suggests that Woolson, too, might be "avoiding responsibility" even as her narrator expresses these "scornful" sentiments.

Further, with her narrator's contrast between the "past," present, and the potentially "progressive" vision of the future of the region, Woolson also seems to engage in the kind of "metahistorical discourse" (180) that Jeffrey Insko identifies in an earlier American novel, Catharine Maria Sedgwick's *Hope Leslie* (1827). Insko argues that Sedgwick disrupts the "unidirectional course of history" (188) and demonstrates history's "fictive qualities" (185) by "ask[ing] the reader to imagine a kind of cross-temporal community, a simultaneity among historical periods" (190). One such passage Insko cites is a moment not unlike this scene in Woolson's novel, when Sedgwick's narrator steps outside of the plot to present a subjective commentary on how far nineteenth-century Americans had come from the earliest days of their history:

> how far is the present age in advance of that which drove reformers to a dreary wilderness!—of that which hanged quakers!—of that which condemned to death, as witches, innocent, unoffending, old women! But it is unnecessary to heighten the glory of our risen day by comparing it with the preceding twilight. (Sedgwick 15)

Woolson echoes Sedgwick's narrator with her commentary on whether or not Mackinac residents "had any glory," and on their regression to "that very past" when the fur trade was at its height. Rather than comparing the "glory of our risen day" to the "preceding twilight" (Sedgwick 15), Woolson reverses Sedgwick's account of historical progress with her narrator's observation that the Mackinac residents were "plainly retrograding." Thus, Woolson's narrator both wryly critiques the islanders' nostalgia for the past and establishes an "awareness of the *present-within-history*," as Insko puts it (192)—through the multinational makeup of the former fur trade that directly contributed to the diversity of the current population, through the past establishment of territorial boundaries that determines present national identities, and through the nation's formative imperial ambitions that might at any point reignite in contemporary violence.

The Fur Company's lingering influence and the Island's military past are especially visible in the family history of Anne's childhood friend Rast Pronando. Rast's father "liked the wild life of the border, and even went off on one or two long expeditions to the Red River of the North and the Upper Missouri after furs with the hunters of the Company" (48), evincing an unconventionality and "wildness" that portends Rast's later unpredictability. The narrator explains Rast's father's alienation from his family in terms that liken the ubiquitous Fur Company to an army regiment. By marrying the daughter of a clerk whose position is "only a grade above the hunters themselves," Rast's father undermines the company's hierarchy: "a person from the rank and file of their own Fur Company—it was as though a colonel should marry the daughter of a common soldier in his own regiment: yes, worse, for nothing can equal the Pronando pride" (49). Rendering the dynamics of the Fur Company in combative language, Woolson highlights the domestic conflict engendered by imperialistic trade practices.

In the face of the multitude of evidence that the Island's geopolitically fraught past coexists with its inhabitants' present-day lived experiences, Woolson's narrator imitates and ironizes historiography that denies the connections between past and present imperial violence.[11] As Anne and Rast look down on the town together from a high cliff, their physical distance metaphorically suggests their temporal distance from the Island's embattled past:

> They were now on the second plateau, the level proper of the island above the cliffs, which, high and precipitous on three sides, sank down gradually to the southwestern shore, so that one might land there, and drag a cannon up to the old earth work on the summit—a feat once performed by British soldiers in the days when the powers of the Old World were still fighting with each other for the New. (84)

Implying that the "Old" and "New" worlds no longer vie for global dominance, the narrator injects commentary that, in another echo of

Sedgwick, disrupts the "unidirectional course of history" (Insko 188) by voicing and undermining the distance that many perceive between the imperial past and present. The narrator opines:

> How quaint they now seem, those ancient proclamations and documents with which a Spanish king grandly meted out this country from Maine to Florida, an English queen divided the same with sweeping patents from East to West, and a French monarch, following after, regranted the whole virgin soil on which the banners of France were to be planted with solemn Christian ceremony! They all took possession; they all planted banners. Some of the brass plates they buried are turned up occasionally at the present day by the farmer's plough, and, wiping his forehead, he stops to spell out their high-sounding words, while his sunburned boys look curiously over his shoulder. A place in the country museum is all they are worth now. (85)

In an analogous moment in *Hope Leslie* that Laura Doyle calls "the story of Hope's initiation into a certain sort of imperial seeing" (*Freedom's Empire* 294), the title character gazes from the summit of a Massachusetts mountain down to the valley below, imagining the "invisible intelligences" filling the forests, and wondering,

> Have these beautiful vallies of our Connecticut, which we saw from the mountain, looking like a smile on nature's rugged face, and stretching as far as our vision extended, till the broad river diminished in the shadowy distance, to a silver thread; have they been seen and enjoyed only by those savages, who have their summer home in them? (104)

Through these intertextual reverberations with Sedgwick's novel, Woolson draws attention to the Indigenous occupants of New England and the Great Lakes region—who are imaginatively erased by Hope Leslie, by the European imperial powers invading these territories, and eventually by Anne Douglas herself later in Woolson's novel.[12] Yet these Native peoples have not been completely erased by Woolson, whose narrator later raises an eyebrow at the sanctimonious New England attitudes about the norms of a "border population" like Mackinac, given the fact that New England "long ago chased out, shot down, and exterminated all her own Indians" (54). When describing the "regranting" of the nominally "virgin soil" that has been claimed by various empires in succession, the narrator in the passage above seems to reduce seventeenth-, eighteenth-, and nineteenth-century battles for control over US territory to a distant, "ancient" game of chess, a "quaint" relic of the past that only has relevance to the present as a kind of curiosity. However, because the novel is set during a time when the US had recently battled Mexico for control of Southwestern territories and was still engaged (as Woolson acknowledges) in the internal colonization of Native Americans and African-descended enslaved people, and published during a time when Northern troops had until recently occupied the US South, the narrator's arch tone subtly draws attention to the United States' own participation in persisting imperial attempts to "take possession" and "plant banners" in seemingly "virgin soil."[13] Woolson thus dramatizes Americans' nostalgic reconstruction of national history, wherein people like Anne construe the US's violent past as "quaint" in order to minimize its ongoing significance.

Manipulating the Anglo-Saxon Goddess

The fur trade's competitive relationships likewise provide a discursive framework for *Anne*'s sentimental plot. Throughout the latter half of the novel, past inter-imperial tensions are displaced onto characters' domestic rivalries and relationships to suggest the influence of the ever-present imperial past, and to explore Americans' attempts to create more distance from the country's violent history than actually exists. Woolson accomplishes this displacement through three related rhetorical maneuvers: first, by exaggerating Anne's white Americanness and related naïveté; second, by positioning her as a pawn for others to manipulate; and third, by rendering her unconscious of the many ways in which she is manipulated by other characters. Through these narrative moves, Woolson pieces together a messy geopolitical allegory in which Anne acts as the American terrain over which her international cast of friends competes for control—an allegory Woolson constructs in order to dramatize gendered and racialized processes of US identity formation within a global, inter-imperial context.

As part of her strategy in depicting Anne as a symbol of white American identity, Woolson consistently characterizes her as "tall and straight," with a "nobly poised head and clear Saxon eyes" (12), and a "fine, frank young Saxon" (104).[14] Anne's whiteness is frequently compared to the darkness of her half-siblings, whose mother was part French, part Native American; the four children appear "more Indian than their mother" (17) and are described as "odd children, with black eyes, coal-black hair, dark skins, and bold eagle outlines" (9). Though Anne's father cautions her that she should "not expect too much" of Tita and that she must "remember always her—her Indian blood" (20), Anne stands fiercely by her half-siblings throughout the novel in the face of such racist insinuations from her father and others.[15] In contrast to her siblings, Anne is cast as a sort of Anglo-Saxon goddess, as we see in the novel's first description of its titular character as she climbs a ladder to hang a wreath:

> Viewed from the floor, this was a young Diana, or a Greek maiden, as we imagine Greek maidens to have been. The rounded arms, visible through the close sleeves of the dark woolen dress, the finely moulded wrists below the heavy wreath, the lithe, natural waist, all belonged to a young goddess. But when Anne Douglas came down from her height, and turned toward you, the idea vanished. Here was no goddess, no Greek; only an American girl, with a skin like a peach. (2)

Characterizing Anne as both a peachy American girl and a classical Greek goddess, the narrator draws on traditional iconographic depictions of America that personify the nation as a female figure. E. McClung Fleming discusses the development of the goddess Columbia as an iconic personification of America, explaining that this figure "was a poetic personification of the United States derived from the name of Christopher Columbus" (59).[16] In the early nineteenth century, Fleming explains, these personified images of America took on a distinctly neoclassical appearance, with artists "borrowing from Greek and Roman mythology to adapt old figures or create new ones to represent the United States. Some favored Hercules and Minerva, many the Goddess of Liberty, almost everyone a new deity, Columbia" (46). Here and elsewhere, Anne serves as a Columbia figure through which Woolson reimagines the United States' imperial past and future.[17]

The almost sculptural description of Anne's "rounded arms" and "finely moulded wrists" figures her within this neoclassical representational tradition, evoking the softly curving limbs in Jacques-Louis David's 1800 painting *Portrait of Madame Récamier* (a painting to which Elizabeth Stuart Phelps's Avis Dobell is also compared), while simultaneously reflecting a later artistic impulse to categorize women into visual "types." As Martha Banta elucidates, a perceived muddying of racial, ethnic, religious, class, and gender boundaries led to anxieties about identity among nineteenth-century Americans and resulted in an increased fascination with images and categorization, with the typological American Girl becoming "the visual and literary form to represent the values of the nation and codify the fears and desires of its citizens" (2). Through Anne, Woolson demonstrates the destructive consequences of both the earlier tradition of personifying the nation in a neoclassical female form, and of the later urge to categorize actual women into these traditional types. Rast, for example, overtly engages in these simplistic typologies in attempting to understand Anne. Often accused of being old-fashioned, Anne asks Rast, "Is it unpleasant to be old-fashioned? I should think the old fashions would be sure to be the good ones" (44). Rast's reply emphasizes Anne's traditional beauty and goddess-like qualities, comparing her, just as the narrator does, to Diana: "Well, perhaps; but we don't mind it in women. All the goddesses were old-fashioned, especially Diana. *You* are Diana" (44). Anne responds with details quoted "from her school-girl mythology," commenting, "Diana, a huntress. She loved Endymion, who was always asleep" (44). Anne's old-fashioned values again mark her as an emblem of US nostalgia for a pure, wholesome past. However, the fact that both Rast and the narrator associate Anne with Diana, the goddess of the hunt, complicates typical depictions of the American goddess as a triumphant beauty by inserting an explicit symbol of violence that hearkens back to the profitable hunting of the many fur-bearing animals of Michigan.

If the narrator's language and Rast's comments were not suggestive enough, Anne's later performance as "the Goddess of Liberty" in a tableau vivant solidifies readers' vision of her as an American icon (253). At a social gathering, Anne poses among a group of "allegorical personages" dressed as Liberty, "looking like a goddess indeed (although a very young one), her white-robed form outlined against a dark background, one arm extended, her head thrown back, and her eyes fixed upon the outspread flag" (253). When the curtains rise to reveal the tableau, the weight of this allegorical association quite literally becomes too much for Anne to bear, as the support that raises her "fifteen feet above the stage" begins to give out beneath her, and she freezes: "a chill ran over her; she tried not to breathe" (253). Rescued just in time to escape a tumbling fall, Anne is nonetheless rattled when she reaches stable ground, as the narrator notes that "Liberty . . . was trembling" (253). In this playful commentary on nineteenth-century allegorical representations of America, Woolson literalizes the shakiness of the foundation upon which the US image of liberty is built.

Both the narrator and other characters equate Anne's white, Anglo-Saxon appearance with her naïveté, a characteristic Woolson exaggerates in order to foreshadow Anne's later ignorance of others' competitive plotting, and to establish a bildungsroman structure wherein Anne will eventually be educated in some of the ways of the world. Anne's naïve disposition becomes apparent in the narrator's initial description of her:

> Anne Douglas's eyes were violet-blue, wide open, and frank. She had not yet learned that there was any reason why she should not look at everything with the calm directness of childhood. Equally like a child was the unconsciousness of her mouth, but the full lips were exquisitely curved. Her brown hair was braided in a heavy knot at the back of her head; but little rings and roughened curly ends stood up round her forehead and on her temples, as though defying restraint. This unwritten face, with its direct gaze, so far neutralized the effect of the Diana-like form that the girl missed beauty on both sides. The usual ideal of pretty, slender, unformed maidenhood was not realized, and yet Anne Douglas's face was more like what is called a baby face than that of any other girl on the island. (2–3)

Sixteen at the start of the novel, Anne apparently has "not yet learned that there was any reason why she should not look at everything with the calm directness of childhood," but the use of the word "yet" here suggests that she will one day wise up to the allegorical battles waged around her. However, at this point in Anne's development, the novel often ascribes a certain vacancy to her, evidenced by the "unconsciousness of her mouth" and her "unwritten face." Together with the characterizations of Anne as an Anglo-Saxon goddess, these descriptions of her as "unwritten" and "unformed" (36) further encourage an allegorical interpretation: Anne is a blank slate beckoning readers to project a story onto her, much like the ostensibly "blank" space of the western American frontier that imperial rivals sought to conquer. However, as the novel eventually reveals, Anne is not truly a blank slate, nor are these territories simply empty for the taking.

In Anne's symbolic unconsciousness, Woolson embodies nineteenth-century constructions of an American mythos that is willfully ignorant of US practices of internal colonization and imperial ambitions. John Carlos Rowe describes the contradiction inherent in American constructions of national identity, observing that "Americans' interpretations of themselves as a people are shaped by a powerful imperial desire and a profound anti-colonial temper" (3).[18] By heightening Anne's supposed innocence, Woolson characterizes her as emblematic of this ignorance (or disavowal) of the nation's history of imperial ambitions dating back to the foundation of the country.

Anne's openness makes her especially susceptible to manipulation by others, as we see in an early example of her maneuverability in her relationship with her sister Tita. This moment of manipulation initiates a longer pattern of rivalry for control over Anne's fate that discursively mimics the historical inter-imperial rivalries alluded to in the early sections of the novel. The thirteen-year-old Tita, upon surreptitiously rifling through her Christmas presents and discovering she is not going to receive the ribbons she wanted, writes her father a seemingly innocent letter describing how desperately she wants hair ribbons as a gift. Woolson's narrator describes Tita's ploy like a military strategy, noting that after "having accomplished her little manoeuvre," Tita "fell asleep with the satisfaction of a successful diplomatist" (23). Falling right into the trap set by Tita's conniving diplomatic "manoeuvre," Anne finds her letter, is moved by its pathetic tone, and sacrifices some of her own ribbons so that Tita will find this coveted gift in her stocking. Well-intentioned Anne expresses her satisfaction, while the narrator's parenthetical aside immediately following Anne's comment pokes fun at her naïveté; Anne determines, about the ribbons, "That will be the very thing for Tita; she has not even seen it," while the narrator retorts, "(But has she not, thou unsuspicious elder sister?)" (25). Addressing Anne as "thou," the narrator's formal register mocks Anne's gullibility, and undermines her ability or willingness to fully understand her siblings' needs, desires, and machinations. There is enough available information for Anne to see through Tita's game: Lois insists to Anne that Tita is "sly," yet Anne refuses to examine her sister's actions more closely, responding "with heat": "I do not think she is sly" (27). Anglo-Saxon Anne's willful denial of Tita's maneuvering calls to mind the United States' corresponding claims of innocence of its own involvement in inter-imperial jockeying. Anne's engagement to Rast is announced with similarly militaristic language. As Anne prepares to move to New York for school so she can support her siblings, Rast secures Anne's promise to marry him upon her return to Mackinac. He announces the coup of their engagement to their teacher Dr. Gaston and Anne's family with "the tone and manner of a young conqueror" (133).

These competitive rivalries for control over Anne foreshadow even more blatant manipulations that take place when she moves to the cosmopolitan New York. These manipulations remind readers that New York, like Mackinac, was established and shaped through inter-imperial competition and maneuvering. The disdain of Anne's aristocratic great-aunt Katherine Vanhorn presents one such battle to be fought; prejudiced against Anne because of her mother's rebellion against family wishes, Miss Vanhorn only agrees to take in Anne and fund her schooling out of a vague sense of obligation. The savvy Frenchwoman Madame Moreau—Anne's teacher, who also goes by "Tante"—helps put Anne in her aunt's good graces:

> She knew all the old Dutch names, and remembered their intermarriages; she was acquainted with the peculiar flavor of Huguenot descent; she comprehended the especial aristocracy of Tory families, whose original property had been confiscated by a raw republic under George Washington. (154)

Tante, whom the narrator later calls the "Napoleon of teachers" (158), flatters Miss Vanhorn's "Knickerbocker blood," and her successful wiles prompt a comparison of her machinations to a military battle, as the narrator effuses, "Ah! skillful old Tante, what a general you would have made!" (154).

Anne's personal relationships continue to be cast in militaristic terms for much of the novel, as Anne's Dutch aunt Miss Vanhorn, her French teacher Tante, and her Spanish-Dutch friend Helen Lorrington all compete, unbeknownst to Anne, to secure a bright future for her. Given these characters' diverse national heritages, Woolson seems to play with historical competitions between Dutch, French, and Spanish powers over control of American territories in a slippery geopolitical allegory.[19] When Anne's aunt hears of her newfound friendship with Helen, she remarks disdainfully,

> What a friend for Helen Lorrington! No wonder she has pounced upon you! You would never see one of her manoeuvres, although done within an inch of you. With your believing eyes, and your sincerity, you are worth your weight in silver to that straw-faced mermaid. (176)

Drawing on the same language of "maneuvering" that was used to describe Tita's manipulation of Anne, Miss Vanhorn's admonishment also renders Anne's relationship in combative terms that emphasize her economic value, and further reinforces readers' perception of Anne's naïveté through her comment on Anne's "believing eyes."

Anne and Helen's close friendship fuels Miss Vanhorn's spite toward Helen and her jealousy for her niece's time, a fact that Helen and Tante exploit to Anne's advantage. As "two friendly conspirators" (177), they covertly encourage Miss Vanhorn's notion that she might fully embrace Anne and make her a star of her social circles, and yet again, Anne "remained unconscious of these manoeuvres" (177). Once Miss Vanhorn sets her sights on making Anne a success—partly to flatter her own powers of influence—she regiments Anne's activities to the point of telling her where to stand at a dance to best highlight her youthful appearance:

> Miss Vanhorn, raising her eye-glass, had selected her position on entering, like a general on the field: Anne was placed next to Isabel on the wooden bench that ran round the room. And immediately Miss Varce seemed to have grown suddenly old. In addition, her blonde beauty was now seen to be heightened by art. (221)

Usurping Tante's former role as a "general on the field," Miss Vanhorn shrewdly determines where Anne should sit, ironically engaging in a form of artifice in order to make Anne's rival Isabel Varce look artificial, and illuminating that Anne's ingénue persona is in some ways just as constructed as the seemingly more affected appearances of other girls. Miss Vanhorn's calculations likewise seem to parallel the amount of careful fashioning involved in constructing the United States' self-image as an innocent and benevolent "city upon a hill."

In the midst of these varied "manoeuvres" plotted to vie for control over Anne, the contested prize herself is always said to be "unconscious" of the machinations. Understood in the context of Anne's role as a goddess-like symbolic personification of America and the nation's volatile past that we are asked to remember throughout the novel, we can read this repeated underscoring of Anne's unconsciousness as Woolson's parodic reenactment of American identity construction—an identity built on a refusal to acknowledge or reckon with the ugly side of the United States' rise to prominence as a nation. Anne does not seem to see her friends' maneuvers—just as she once missed Tita's manipulations—because this would require her to realize that her success is not due to any kind of exceptional beauty or talent on her part, but rather dependent on petty, destructive rivalries, just as discourses of American exceptionalism disavow the imperial violence and dependence on international economic relationships that enabled the country to reach its status as a world power. Yet as the conclusion of the novel will reveal, Anne's supposed unconsciousness of such rivalries is more a symptom of her disavowal of reality than her innocence.

Anne's Consolidation of Power

The conclusion of *Anne* takes so many wildly melodramatic turns that it is almost impossible to summarize here: Anne falls in love with a moneyed man named Ward Heathcote; runs away from him, her friends, and family when she feels guilt over her betrayal of her fiancé Rast; volunteers as a nurse in the Civil War where she briefly reunites with Heathcote; and, in a bizarre twist, serves as the star witness in a murder trial before playing detective and solving the murder herself. The ending of the novel becomes a dizzying blend of genres—historical romance, courtroom drama, detective mystery. Such unexpected genre mixing underscores the confusion readers feel when the novel reveals that Anne is no longer as "unconscious" or naïve as she appeared to be throughout the majority of the novel. Through the bildungsroman structure that underlies the novel's generic experimentations, Anne matures and grows more conscious of the world around her; however, she still does not seek out knowledge of realities she would rather ignore.

Anne's love affair with Heathcote provides the first sign that she might be maturing and gaining greater consciousness, and it seems to be her first foray into conscious competition with her rivals. The narrator introduces Heathcote by explaining that he

> was one of a small and unimportant class in the United States, which would be very offensive to citizens at large if it came in contact with them; but it seldom does ... Money is necessary, and ought to be provided in some way; and generally it is, since without it this class could not exist in a purely democratic land. But it is inherited, not made. (200)

In Woolson's taxonomy of characters' nationalities, while Heathcote is undoubtedly American, his multi-generational inherited wealth signals he is no Horatio Alger type. Furthermore, Heathcote's name bears a striking resemblance to "Heathcliff," the famous antihero of Emily Brontë's *Wuthering Heights*, hinting at his possible British ancestry, and also portending his later capricious behavior. In spite of the fact that Anne is engaged to Rast, and in spite of the fact that her friend Helen Lorrington is also enamored with Heathcote, Anne falls in love with Heathcote, at first "unconsciously," but eventually realizing that "now she loved him consciously ... she was false to Rast, she loved Heathcote, and hated Helen, yet could not bring herself to ask that any of these feelings should be otherwise" (262). The use of the word "consciously" here marks a shift from Anne's previous "unconsciousness" and disavowal of rivalries to her present awareness of her entanglement in such contests. Conscience stricken, Anne runs away from all friends and family and becomes a teacher.

When Anne runs away to escape her conflicted feelings, her rivals fall away in a *deus-ex-machina* resolution that metaphorically signals Anne's consolidation of power, analogous to the United States' conquest of Spanish, French, and Native American forces during various nineteenth-century inter-imperial contests. First, the conflict with Rast is ameliorated when he and Tita run away together to live out west. Breaking the news in a letter, Anne's mother-figure Lois Hinsdale writes indignantly,

> What *can* I say to you? There is no use in trying to *prepare* you for it, since you would never *conceive* such *double-dyed* blackness of heart! Tita has *run away*. She slipped off clandestinely, and they think she has followed *Rast*, who left yesterday on his way back to St. Louis and the West. (343)

Lois's description of Tita's "*double-dyed* blackness of heart" once again marks her as racially "other," and the couple's destination in the west echoes the continuation of western expansion throughout the nineteenth century. This impetuous action recalls Rast's father, who likewise loved the "wild life of the border" (48). Presented here as a neat resolution to Anne's internal conflict, Rast and Tita's departure out west sentimentalizes the displacement of Indigenous peoples due to American settler colonialism. Relieved rather than scorned, Anne relishes the romantic freedom granted by her former fiancé's abandonment.

Anne's other rival is vanquished in much more convoluted fashion in a violent turn of events that leaves Anne ascendant while retrospectively smoothing over their rivalry—much in the way that Elizabeth Stuart Phelps's Avis shut out negative memories of her husband's dalliance with another woman so that "only his ideal visited her heart" (242). Perhaps not coincidentally, the Civil War breaks out at this moment of Anne's internal conflict over her love for Heathcote and her loyalty to Helen. Again evincing similarities to Avis, who was ignorant of cotton prices at the height of scarcity during the Civil War, Anne is unaware of the political and geopolitical impetus for the war: "Anne, brought up as she had been in a remote little community, isolated and half foreign, was in a measure ignorant of the causes and questions of the great struggle which began in America in April, 1861" (355). By tying Anne's interpersonal schism to the national schism between North and South, Woolson perpetuates her allegory of Anne as symbolic of the United States. Anne's utter naïveté here shows how easy it is to avoid ugliness if you fail to seek knowledge of the world around you.

However, eventually the Battle of Bull Run proves to be a galvanizing event for Anne—just as it was for Avis—and she signs up to serve as an army nurse. Anne is immediately met with praise for her participation in the conflict as if she is enlisting as a soldier, with one woman declaring, "It is so sweet, and so—so martial!" (363), and another affirming that her action is "the real downright article of patriotism, I guess" (366). In the eyes of other characters, Anne's actions signal her participation in the violent work of consolidating national identity at the very moment she is seeking to consolidate power over her domestic rivals. Their celebration of Anne's heroism is likewise undercut by the insight we are given into Anne's motivations, which stem from homesickness, loneliness, and heartache. A narrative interjection thus inserts a sly critique:

> She was weary and sad: where were now the resolution and the patience with which she had meant to crown her life? You did not know, poor Anne, when you framed those lofty purposes, that suffering is just as hard to bear whether one is noble or ignoble, good or bad. In the face of danger the heart is roused, and in the exaltation of determination forgets its pain; it is the long monotony of dangerless days that tries the spirit hardest. (361)

In the same tonal register previously used to call out Anne as "thou unsuspicious elder sister," the narrator here draws attention to Anne's less-than-altruistic motives for enlisting as an army nurse, as if she, like so many soldiers and generals before her, is driven by the "exaltation of determination" rather than any righteous calling.

As if instigated by her enlistment as an army nurse, Anne also reenters the domestic battles she once fled when she faces an unexpected romantic confrontation on the front lines. Anne hears that a soldier named "Captain Ward Heathcote" has been gravely injured, and she rushes to his side for a reunion that turns romantic. When Heathcote tells Anne that Helen has been married and thus her rival is no longer a barrier to her romantic conquest, Anne chooses not to question his story and succumbs to his flirtatious overtures. The narrator introduces undertones of conquest through the combative terms used to describe Anne's surrender: "And she, at first resisting love's sweet violence, at last yielded to it; for, she loved him" (389). The paradoxical characterization of "love's sweet violence" reminds readers of the symbolic battles waged to secure control over Anne. Heathcote's advances symbolize the seductive lure of wealthy, old-money elites, descended implicitly from the all-reaching British empire, and here, Anne is being drawn into that web. Quickly the text reveals that Anne has yielded to Heathcote's forces too soon: Heathcote guiltily admits that Helen is indeed married—but to him. The alleged rivalry with Helen still intact, Anne flees once again, unprepared for the literal violence that will soon follow.

In the final act of the novel, the inter-imperial violence that structures Anne's domestic rivalries is brought to its logical conclusion: the downfall of one of these "empires" and the ascendance of another. Initiating this chain of events is the false report of Heathcote's death. Unaware that Heathcote is still alive and grieving for her friend who is now Heathcote's apparent widow, Anne rushes to Helen's side. Any tensions between them dissolve in their shared sorrow: "at that moment she pitied the stricken wife so intensely that she forgot the rival, or rather made herself one with her; for in death there is no rivalry, only a common grief" (437). Twice invoking the word "rival" here, the narration, focalized through Anne, acknowledges the competition that once drove these women's domestic dramas, again suggesting that Anne did indeed grow to be "conscious" of their former dynamic as veritable warring nations, now united in loss.

This armistice is quickly interrupted with the news that Heathcote is still alive, and Helen departs to reunite with her husband, where she meets her final violent demise: she is murdered. As readers, we do not witness the crime, but rather read the report:

> On the 11th of June the world of New York was startled ... Mrs. Heathcote, wife of Captain Ward Heathcote,—New York Volunteers, while on her way homeward with her husband, who was wounded in the Shenandoah Valley, had been found murdered in her room in the country inn at Timloesville, where they were passing the night. And the evidence pointed so strongly toward Captain Heathcote that he had been arrested upon suspicion. (439)

A sensational case, rumors fly that Heathcote and Helen argued when Helen discovered evidence of a romantic rival, and the argument turned deadly. So ubiquitous are these whispers that they raise the suspicions of Anne's friend and one-time suitor Dexter, who confronts her by asking, "Is it possible—can it be possible, Anne, that *you* are the person implicated, the so-called rival?" Claiming innocence (or perhaps feigning it), Anne replies, "I do not know; and it is because I do not know that I am so much afraid" (461). In using the word "rival," Dexter echoes the very word that Anne herself recently employed to describe her relationship with Helen. This reverberation casts doubt on Anne's claim that she "do[es] not know" if she is the "so-called rival." If she was indeed "unconscious" before, she is not now, and she must determine how to move forward with her knowledge of her involvement in combative rivalries.

Anne's testimony at Heathcote's trial and her subsequent solving of Helen's murder show her progression from her former naïveté, supporting the possibility that she has matured to a point where she is savvier about the world around her, though she often seeks out knowledge only when it serves her purposes. Anne's appearance at the trial creates a stir, and the observers in the courtroom single out her youthfulness and beauty, reiterating the pattern from earlier in the novel of Anne being perceived as naïve: "When Anne Douglas appeared on the witness-stand in the Heathcote murder trial, a buzz of curiosity and surprise ran round the crowded court-room. 'A young girl!' was the first whisper. Then, 'Pretty, rather,' from the women, and 'Beautiful!' from the men" (479). The innocence of Anne's appearance is undercut by her thorough and knowledgeable testimony in which she provides evidence, in the form of letters and her own testimony, that she and Helen were in fact not on acrimonious terms at the end of Helen's life, and thus there was no rivalry for Helen and Heathcote to quarrel over. The narrator's account of Anne's countenance at the moment of her crucial revelations emphasizes her whiteness, which stands in marked contrast to Tita's "black eyes" and "coal-black hair" (9), and Helen's Spanish-inflected eyes that were a "dark unexpected brown" (159). The narrator recounts,

> her face, which, while the lawyer read, had been white and still as marble, was now, though still colorless, so transfigured, so uplifted, so beautiful in its pure sacrifice, that men leaned forward to see her more closely, to print, as it were, that exquisite image upon their memories forever. (481)

Whereas previously Woolson called attention to Anne's neoclassically "rounded arms" and "finely moulded wrists" (2), here she emphasizes her face that is "white and still as marble," once more invoking archetypal images of the Goddess of Liberty: carved in marble, and emphatically white. Here, Anne is not only a symbol of America, she is a symbol of white America, whose innocence and purity shine through her "colorless" face as it radiates with its "pure sacrifice."

So great is the power of Anne's external purity and internal knowledge of what she claims to be the truth that her testimony sways the outcome of the trial. The narrator, again hinging the determination of the trial on the supposed rivalry between Anne and Helen, summarizes the conclusion of the trial:

> The testimony of Anne Douglas had destroyed the theory which had seemed to fill out so well the missing parts of the story; it had proved that the supposed rival was a friend of the wife's, and that the wife loved her; it had proved that Mrs. Heathcote was devoted to her husband, and happy with him, up to the last hour of her life. This was much. But the circumstantial evidence regarding the movements of the prisoner at Timloesville remained unchanged. (486)

When the trial ends in a hung jury with a retrial scheduled, Anne determines to take matters into her own hands and solve the murder herself, commenting to her fellow amateur detective Lois Hinsdale, "it is said that women divine a truth sometimes by intuition, and against all probability. It is to this instinct—if such there be—that we must trust now" (491). Anne's comments here metafictionally draw attention to her lack of credibility in the eyes of the reader. The idea that Anne—innocent, unconscious, pure, Anne—would prove that Heathcote did not in fact murder his wife, when all the evidence we have been presented with suggests otherwise, certainly seems "against all probability." Every detail in the novel leading up to this point tells us to believe that Anne is naïvely misguided: her friends and family manipulated her at every turn, apparently without her knowledge. Heathcote fulfills the classic villain archetype: he cheats on his wife, deceives Anne about his romantic entanglements, and very nearly shares a name with the vengeful antihero of *Wuthering Heights*. And yet, Woolson subverts these expectations when Anne and her pragmatic New Englander caregiver Lois Hinsdale track down Helen's true murderer and convince him to confess to his crimes. Woolson thus contrasts the young "unconscious" Anne who was unwilling to look too hard into uncomfortable truths with the currently maturing Anne who is willing to dig in and investigate, even if it entails her further involvement in rivalries and maneuvers she would rather avoid.

Traipsing down to the remote village of Timloesville where Helen was killed, Anne and Lois follow a series of at first unreliable-seeming tips, searching for a suspicious man who is left-handed and whose accent causes him to say "cold" instead of "gold." A newspaper account of Anne's unexpected success as a detective mirrors the surprise readers experience at the fact that Anne's hunches are proven correct:

> Even the story of the last great battle was eclipsed in interest in certain circles of this city yesterday by the tidings which were flashed over the wires from a remote little village in Pennsylvania. Our readers will easily recall the trial of Captain Ward Heathcote on the charge of murder, the murder of his own wife. The evidence against the accused was close, though purely circumstantial... The accused, though not convicted, has not had the sympathy of the public. Probably eight out of ten among those who read the evidence have believed him guilty. But yesterday brought the startling intelligence that human judgment has again been proven widely at fault, that the real murderer is in custody. (529)

Juxtaposing Anne's discovery with Civil War battles, the newspaper echoes earlier passages that conveyed characters' actions in militaristic terms. Woolson's inclusion of this newspaper article serves as another self-consciously literary gesture, through which the text identifies how readerly expectations are established and subverted. The article again emphasizes how surprising Anne's resolution is, recounting the evidence against Heathcote, but also the fact that he "has not had the sympathy of the public." These words resound on a metafictional level to recognize the way that readers were perhaps prepared to find Heathcote guilty. With the newspaper's pronouncement that "human judgment has again been proven widely at fault," Woolson calls into question our ability as readers to discern the truth—especially amid shifting geopolitical borders, loyalties, and economic ties.

Anne is not the only text in which Woolson undermines readers' expectations. Grace McEntee argues that in her short story "Jeannette," Woolson manipulates novelistic conventions in order to take readers by surprise and make them aware of the limits of their own knowledge. In discussing the unusual conclusion of "Jeannette," in which the title character defies the typical plot trajectory of a story like this to declare that she is in love with a character that readers have not heard of, McEntee writes,

> Woolson was perhaps willing to risk the ambiguity and subtlety of this ending because she counted on her audience to be, in Stanley Fish's lexicon, not just "informed readers" but an "interpretive community," that is, regular consumers of literature, especially regional fiction and travel articles found in periodicals such as *Scribner's* and *Atlantic Monthly*. (165)

Dorri Beam similarly argues that Woolson takes advantage of literary types in order to skewer reductive tropes, especially those around gender. Analyzing the parallels between Woolson's short story "Miss Grief" and Henry James's story "The Figure in the Carpet," Beam contends that Woolson presents a parodic critique of James's sentimentalized image of the woman artist through her character of "Miss Crief," which mocks, "sometimes savagely, suppositions about the woman writer as naïve, natural, and unselfconscious" (143).[20] Especially since Anne is characterized in ways similar to the "naïve, natural, and unselfconscious" stereotype of women artists that Beam maintains Woolson mocks, I would argue that Woolson employs a narrative technique in *Anne* that is similar to the subversive plotting McEntee and Beam identify in "Jeannette" and "Miss Grief." The novel trains readers to see Anne as naïve and easily manipulated, and to see Heathcote as a villainous manipulator who would be exactly the type of person to kill his wife. Contrary to these expectations, however, Anne is eventually the only one who can see the truth, and Heathcote, in spite of his moral failings, did not in fact kill his wife.

If we return to Woolson's running allegory in which Anne represents the shining beacon of America amid inter-imperial contests between Spanish, Native American, French, and Dutch rivals, the novel's gradual development and revelation of Anne's savviness introduces the possibility that perhaps the US was not an innocent bystander in conflicts like the War of 1812, or in expansionist commercial efforts to extend the fur trade further west, which depleted natural resources and exploited relationships with Native American hunters. If Anne was eventually able to stop ignoring the internecine conflicts fought over her, perhaps the US could likewise take greater responsibility for its role in the inter-imperial jockeying that shaped its borders during the nineteenth century. Woolson's metafictional awareness of her twist of an ending invites readers to question their ability to judge who is the real murderer—in the case of Heathcote's trial, but also in the case of these inter-imperial contests.

The novel closes back at Mackinac Island, Anne once again gazing over the domain once traversed by intrepid fur traders, this time with her new husband Heathcote by her side. Woolson draws parallels between the recently concluded Civil War and the resolution of Anne's domestic conflict:

> The war was over at last; peace was declared. The last review had been held; and the last volunteer gone home. Two persons were standing on the old observatory floor, at the highest point of the

island, looking at the little village below, the sparkling Straits, and the blue line of land in the distant north. At least Anne was looking at them. But her lover was looking at her. (537)

Just as Anne once stood "gazing off" at this "vast empire" (81), so now does she perch at the top of the Island, "looking at the little village below" and at the Straits that were once populated with the international traders hunting, purchasing, and exporting furs from west to east. In a final intertextual recognition of the shared imperial imaginations of her heroine and Catharine Maria Sedgwick's, Woolson recalls the moment when Hope Leslie "gazed on the beautiful summits of this mountain, that, in this transparent October atmosphere, were as blue and bright as the heavens themselves" (Sedgwick 103). If, as Laura Doyle contends, Hope "barters her acquiescence to [the] erasure of Indian values in exchange for a position of discursive power" (*Freedom's Empire* 296), here Anne likewise participates in a kind of imperial compact, joining the dubious partner of Heathcote in their reign over "the little village below, the sparkling Straits, and the blue line of land in the distant north."

The novel ultimately reveals that Anne is capable of solving a crime by seeking knowledge about it, yet she still fails to seek knowledge about the murders that have created the nation because such ignorance allows her to believe that "the war was over at last" and that she might reign peacefully over this North American expanse. The remains of the lucrative and violent fur trade haunt the novel to the very end, as Anne receives a wedding gift of "Diamonds, sables, and an India shawl" (539). United in conquest, Anne and Heathcote stand veritably enthroned over this formerly liminal territory, lavished with luxurious international commodities—not only sables, but also diamonds and an "India shawl," as if perhaps there are still more lands left to conquer. In her discussion of the cultural work Indian commodities perform in Victorian domestic novels, Suzanne Daly notes how "ubiquitous" (13) India shawls are in mid-nineteenth-century British texts, and observes that these shawls were often

> a coveted gift that men returning from colonial service in India bestow upon their mothers and sisters in a move that symbolizes the fitting and desired conclusion to a man's career in India: coming home wealthy, bearing the spoils of the East even as he reenters the domestic space. (13)

Considered in this context—of which nineteenth-century readers were likely well aware—Anne's final acquisition of an India shawl together with the sable fur could be read as an allusion to her "colonial" career. Whereas Heathcote looks at Anne whom he has symbolically conquered by winning her hand in marriage, Anne looks out onto the territories before her, continuing to expand her imperial vision. The narrator's distancing language in describing Anne and Heathcote as "two persons" recalls Père Michaux's strategies for "avoiding responsibility," and the only hint of a critique we get from Woolson is the violent path the couple traveled to get to this point, Heathcote's known character flaws, and the recurrence of the fur's symbolism. Through this conventional ending to a decidedly unconventional novel, Woolson initially allows readers to settle back into a more familiar plot arc: a conclusion that ends in marriage. However, the reappearance of inter-imperially contested commodities alludes to the violence buried beneath the ostensibly happy union. The consolidation of power, signified by the marriage of Anne and Heathcote, may not in fact be a union to celebrate, but rather the foreboding of further inter-imperial jockeying to come. As I will discuss in the following section on María Amparo Ruiz de Burton's *Who Would Have Thought It?*, these novels invite readers to see that the repercussions of imperial conquest continue to echo even centuries after they are past, for both the aggressors and for those who are exploited by imperial aggression.

"A Great Acquisition" in *Who Would Have Thought It?*

Like Constance Fenimore Woolson, María Amparo Ruiz de Burton similarly explores how centuries of inter-imperial contests provide a script for characters' intimate rivalries, underscoring how marginalized women and those marked as racially "other" are especially vulnerable to the domestic repercussions of imperial conquest. Ruiz de Burton's 1872 novel *Who Would Have Thought It?*, which I will focus on in this section, opens with the arrival of the enterprising Dr. Norval back home in Massachusetts from a geological exploration in California. He appears after a four-year absence, carrying a cargo of two full wagons of spoils. When his surprised wife asks, "what on earth is he bringing now?", his daughter Ruth, accustomed no doubt to his geological findings and the "well-known idiosyncrasy of the doctor for collecting all sorts of rocks," (16) surmises, "more rocks and pebbles of course. But I don't know where he is to put them: the garret is full now" (13). Pragmatic Lavinia, Dr. Norval's sister-in-law, suggests, "He will store them away in the barn loft, where he keeps his bones and petrified woods. He brings quite a load." As we soon discover, Dr. Norval's load contains not only a massive collection of raw gold and gems, but also a young Mexican girl of Spanish descent, named Lola, who owns all of this wealth. Whereas Anne allegorically represented American terrain, Lola represents the liminal land outside the United States' expanding border, flush with natural resources to be conquered and extracted.

The novel dramatizes the mystery of Lola's heritage, the Norvals' efforts to profit from the gold that belongs to her, the outbreak of the Civil War, and the national and international ruptures the war precipitates. Although the American Civil War is typically thought of as a national conflict, novels like those by Ruiz de Burton, Woolson, and Phelps reveal the war's inter-imperial entanglements, as the North and South lobbied foreign powers for support while exerting economic pressures.[21] Furthermore, literary critics have elucidated Ruiz de Burton's parodic strategies for eviscerating nineteenth-century expansionism—an effort Ruiz de Burton experienced rather directly as a Californiana who became a US citizen as a result of the Guadalupe-Hidalgo Treaty at the end of the Mexican–American War, and who, in a further biographical complication, also married an American Captain who served in the Mexican–American War.[22] Ruiz de Burton's biography may contribute to the complicated attitudes about race and imperial hegemony expressed in the novel. Critics agree that Ruiz de Burton's critique of American imperialism and white supremacy is not univocal, but rather, at times indicts American racial hierarchies, and at other times buys into these hierarchies in order to claim the privileges of whiteness for herself and Spanish-descended people like her. José Aranda, for instance, argues that Ruiz de Burton saw herself "as part of a white, educated elite—aristocratic in its origins and with a history in Alta California as colonizers—not as colonized" (558).[23] Because she saw race as shifting and context-dependent, Ruiz de Burton uses the conflict in *Who Would Have Thought It?* to demonstrate the "unstable nature of racial categories in the late nineteenth century" (213), according to Margaret Jacobs. The intersection of race with gender further destabilizes these categories, and Beth Fisher suggests that Ruiz de Burton exploits this intersection to argue for the superiority of elite Mexican and Californiana women over white Anglo-American women who are driven only by profit.[24] As the work of these literary scholars attests, the complexity of Ruiz de Burton's responses to expansionist discourses and actions requires an intersectional analysis to fully account for the various positions from which her critique extends.

Focusing on the novel's images of gold—a commodity that is a signifier of status, formed over centuries, and extracted and exchanged by competing imperial powers—enables a full acknowledgment of the polyvocal nature of the problems that Ruiz de Burton tackles in *Who Would Have Thought It?* In the novel, gold bullion and gold jewelry metonymically represent the economic motivations behind the United States' territorial expansion in the nineteenth century, as well as the longer history of inter-imperial competition that predates the existence of the US, just as gold itself predates those who extract it. Pablo Ramirez argues that the gold in the novel figures anxieties about shifting systems of economic and racial value that allowed the US to enact an imperial instead of contractual relationship with Mexico.[25] Whereas Ramirez suggests that Ruiz de Burton negotiates the implications of a new kind of economic and political formation predicated on the implicit promises of contractual relations instigated by the Civil War, I would argue that she reflects on longer-standing structures and the ways in which commodities can call to mind inter-imperial dynamics. In particular, Dr. Norval's occupation as a geologist serves as an apt metaphor for the centuries-long accumulations of inter-imperial competition embedded beneath the surface of the novel. Ruiz de Burton gradually extracts these geological deposits through her characters' intimate relations and through the layers of trauma made visible on Lola's face. In his well-known text *The Principles of Geology* (1830–1833), Charles Lyell writes,

> As the present condition of nations is the result of many antecedent changes, some extremely remote, and others recent, some gradual, others sudden and violent; so the state of the natural world is the result of a long succession of events; and if we would enlarge our experience of the present economy of nature, we must investigate the effects of her operations in former epochs. (1)

Lyell's comparison between history and natural science invites us to see nature's "operations in former epochs," the formations of power that are embedded in Ruiz de Burton's text and brought to the surface through Dr. Norval's extraction of wealth from Lola.

Like *Anne, Who Would Have Thought It?* reflects on the present effects of past empires, focusing on Aztec, Spanish, and American powers.[26] The material detritus of Dr. Norval's excavations allows us to see the relationship between the fifteenth-century Aztec empire's control over Mexican territories, sixteenth-century Spanish colonization of Mexico and conquest of the Aztecs, and the United States' nineteenth-century colonization of the territories that became Texas and California. Understood in this light, the "bones and petrified wood" that Dr. Norval collects come to represent "dialectical accretions" of imperial violence and decay (Doyle, "Inter-Imperiality: Dialectics" 160). Lavinia's comment that Dr. Norval has "quite a load" is suggestive of the burden of history weighing down upon his actions. In my reading of *Who Would Have Thought It?*, I draw on the long history of the global gold trade to argue that María Amparo Ruiz de Burton illuminates similarities between the nineteenth-century United States and older imperial powers. Further, Ruiz de Burton explores how this imperial violence is experienced in embodied, gendered, racialized ways. In their introduction to the novel, Rosaura Sánchez and Beatrice Pita observe that the novel discusses "a more primitive type of accumulation that is more akin to the conquest, plunder and piracy practiced by European colonizers in the Americas" (xxii). While Sánchez and Pita attempt to temporally differentiate between fifteenth- and nineteenth-century forms of plunder through their use of the word "primitive" here, Ruiz de Burton, I contend, makes no such distinction. Rather, she insists on the continuity of imperial exploitation, whose violence accumulates over centuries and bubbles up in unexpected ways. In the following paragraphs, I will elaborate on the historical trajectory of imperial plundering at the US–Mexico border to more fully elucidate how Ruiz de Burton makes visible the process by which older imperial forms get reenacted in intimate contexts.

Imperial Extraction of New World Gold, Fifteenth Century–Nineteenth Century

While the material and economic history of gold could be traced back much further, I focus here on the Pre-Columbian era of Aztec gold panning and collection, the late fifteenth-century period of Spanish exportation from the New World, and the mid-nineteenth-century California gold rush, in order to link the Mexican and Southwestern territories described by the novel to their Spanish colonial history and the more contemporaneous period of US commercial expansionism. Evidence of sophisticated gold mining and panning techniques long predates the arrival of European colonizers, according to Heidi King.[27] John TePaske elaborates on some of these techniques that were implemented by Native Americans and later used by the Spanish, including "diverting gold-rich stream beds using dams, canals, and ditches; digging pits in stream terraces with significant gold accumulations; grubbing surfaces with heavy concentrations of gold nuggets; and exploiting veins in the side of hills where they found gold" (23). While some regions were naturally rich in gold ore, others relied on trade to acquire their riches; for example, the Aztecs "obtained all their gold through tribute and trade, probably from what are today the Mexican states of Guerrero and Oaxaca" (King 6). Although the "primary use of gold in Precolumbian America was for personal adornment" (King 5), this gold artisanry became an important negotiating tool when Europeans arrived in the Americas, and also made the Aztecs and other Indigenous peoples the target of imperial exploitation. One of Columbus's main missives when voyaging to the Americas was to bring back gold for the Spanish crown (along with pearls, as I will discuss in Chapter 4), a demand he and others met with great success. Gold was sought by Spanish colonizers because it was "easily transportable" and "would allow the explorer/speculator quickly to pay off the investors who financed the quest" (Hartmann 9). It was not only Columbus who was drawn by the lure of gold, but also Hernán Cortés, who landed at the Mayan coast in 1519, moved further and further inland because he "began to hear tales of a wealthy, gold-splashed empire somewhere inland" (Hartmann 16), eventually raided Montezuma's treasure room (Hartmann 49), and ran off with a great deal of Aztec gold, much of which was later reclaimed by the Aztecs (Hartmann 56).[28]

Spanish conquest of territories in the Americas enabled the Spanish monarchy to accumulate massive wealth that would then finance economic and imperial ventures in Europe.[29] Despite facing piracy by Britain, France, and Holland, Spain dominated the export of gold and silver from the Americas, but it exhausted its stockpile of wealth paying for wars against the French, Turks, German, and Dutch (Peter Bernstein 137).[30] The gold Spain extracted not only contributed to increased jockeying with European imperial powers, but also fueled trade across the globe, a fact that again illustrates the international ripples that a gold nugget in Mexico can have. TePaske enumerates some of these global reverberations:

> Even though the major portion of American bullion exports went first to Sevilla (and after 1717 to Cádiz), much of the treasure was subsequently shipped to other destinations. Ships of the Dutch East India Company, for example, carried American silver around the Cape of Good Hope to India and the Dutch East Indies. There they traded American bullion for tea, jade, damask, spices, and other commodities. British, French, and Flemish vessels plied the North Sea to the

Baltic to Russia where American ingots and pesos were exchanged for furs and lumber. Genoese and Venetian traders carried gold and silver from Sevilla and Cádiz to the eastern end of the Mediterranean. Some of this wealth remained in Turkey where it purchased luxury goods; the rest was shipped farther east to India and beyond. (305)[31]

Thus, Spanish colonialism propelled international and inter-imperial trade relationships from the fifteenth to the nineteenth centuries.

Jumping forward to the nineteenth century, the gold strike in California far surpassed the output of Spanish exports centuries earlier and similarly inspired expansionist ambitions among states and individual actors alike. Bernstein explains the scale of the strike by comparing it to Columbus-era history, noting that during the 1850s, "the amount of gold produced in ten years matched the production from all sources over the entire 356 years from Columbus to 1848" (220). The gold strike had a wide-ranging impact beyond economic concerns; widespread migration to California and other parts of the western US in response to the strike resulted in greater racial and ethnic diversity than in other regions of the US, which "quickly emphasized the presence of many different races and ethnic groups, for California, originally home to Native Americans and the Californios of Spanish and Mexican heritage, soon became the destination of peoples from across this hemisphere, Europe, and Asia" (Rohrbough 3).[32] These population shifts were only further exaggerated by the aftermath of the Mexican–American War, which left swaths of California temporarily "open access" to gold speculators because of the gradual transition in power from the Mexican to US governments (Rohrbough 12).[33] The recently shifted borders and contested territories raised the question of who rightfully had a claim to this wealth of natural resources, and why—a question that is taken up allegorically through the character of Lola in *Who Would Have Thought It?* Commercial ventures in California offered not only the promise of wealth, but also the possibility of redefining determinants of status and class.

Both this nineteenth-century history and earlier imperial histories, I argue, are invoked through Ruiz de Burton's references to gold throughout *Who Would Have Thought It?* The parallels drawn between Lola and the supply of gold she owns suggest similarly layered histories contained within them: just as the mineral formations of gold predate national borders, so does Lola's body bear witness to centuries of shifting imperial formations. Ruiz de Burton hints at this similarity through Mrs. Norval's mockery of Lola when she first enters the Norval household, and Mrs. Norval equates her with an item in her husband's scientific collection: "The doctor is not content with bringing four boxes more, full of stones, but now he, I fear, having exhausted the mineral kingdom, is about to begin with animal, and this is our first specimen" (16). Ruiz de Burton implies that for the Norvals, Lola serves as an object of inquiry, just as Dr. Norval's collections of rocks present him with specimens of study for what Lyell calls the "long succession of events" that led to current geological formations. Additionally, with the derogatory implications of categorizing Lola as an "animal," Ruiz de Burton critiques Mrs. Norval's sense of racialized superiority over Lola. Dr. Norval's retort to his wife seems to confirm his interest in her as a kind of curiosity, as he comments, "She is only ten years old, but her history is already more romantic than that of half of the heroines of your trashy novels" (17). Dr. Norval's romanticization of Lola's history reflects the same kind of uncritical nostalgia for the past that Woolson dramatized through her Mackinac Island residents in *Anne*.

As Dr. Norval explains the circumstances through which Lola acquired the gold and made her way to Massachusetts, his language again implies an equivocation between Lola's body and her wealth. He details for Mrs. Norval how he encountered Lola and her mother Doña Teresa near the Colorado River with a group of Native Americans. Doña Teresa managed to catch his attention, explained how they were kidnapped by an Apache tribe and sold to the Mohave, and quickly promised Dr. Norval stockpiles of gold she had stumbled upon and collected from the river's tributaries to rescue Lola from captivity. Dr. Norval recounts the story that Doña Teresa told him about how she accumulated her collection of gold and gems:

> Accidentally, whilst bathing in a small stream which is a tributary to the Colorado River, she saw a very bright, shining pebble. She picked it up, and, as she had some knowledge of precious stones, she saw it was a large diamond, though only partly divested of its rough coating. Then she looked about for similar pebbles, and found many more ... Afterwards the Indians brought her emeralds and rubies, seeing that she liked pretty pebbles. Thus she made a fine collection, for she took only the largest and those which seemed to her most perfect. (28–9)

Minimizing the gemstones' value by calling them mere "pretty pebbles," Doña Teresa takes advantage of the Mohave people, just as the Norvals attempt to profit from Lola.

Ruiz de Burton's depiction of the Indians' apparent ignorance of the value of the gold and gems is contradicted by historical evidence, which attests that Native Americans developed sophisticated mining and panning techniques long before their first contact with Europeans.[34] In particular, Doña Teresa's strategy for gathering treasures from the stream was one commonly employed by Indigenous Americans, and Heidi King observes that Spanish explorers took especial note of these methods: "Descriptions of native mining at the time of the conquest state that the most common method of obtaining gold was panning (placer mining), in which river gravel is washed in a pan, causing the flakes, nuggets, and grains (which have a high specific gravity) to settle at the bottom" (6). By attributing this metallurgical savvy to the Spanish-descended Doña Teresa rather than the Native Americans who hold her captive, Ruiz de Burton seems to participate in the very racial hierarchies that she eschews in the Norvals, implying that the Native Americans are not sophisticated enough to recognize the hidden wealth before them.[35] This representation of Doña Teresa's Native American captors points back to the complex and at times contradictory nature of Ruiz de Burton's critique of imperial greed. While she may indict the violence of US expansionism through her almost cartoonish picture of the Norvals' villainy, she is less critical of the same imperial impulses that drove the Spanish to kill and plunder Indigenous Mexicans. Yet it is clear that the Norvals are the primary target of Ruiz de Burton's ire because after recounting Doña Teresa's story of gold acquisition, Ruiz de Burton refocuses her lens on the Norvals' greed and exploitation of Doña Teresa's daughter Lola. As Dr. Norval is relating this tale, Mrs. Norval asks her husband how it is that he "came across the child and her gold," and Dr. Norval replies that "Her mother deposited both under my care" (27), as if Lola, like the gold, were currency to be deposited in a bank, safeguarded, invested, and speculated upon.

Although the racist and xenophobic Mrs. Norval initially balks at her husband's decision to adopt the orphaned Lola, once she hears about the girl's gold, she immediately becomes mesmerized by it: "her soul was floating over to those yellow, shining lumps of cold, unfeeling metal . . . she knelt by the chest, and with childlike simplicity began to take pieces of gold and examine them attentively and toss them up playfully" (25). Seeing his wife's delight, Dr. Norval confesses his mercenary motivations, commenting, "I think that Lola, instead of being a *burden* to us, will be a great acquisition. Don't you think so?" (25). Dr. Norval quantifies the scope of Lola's wealth, noting that the six boxes of gold are worth about a million dollars, and that the interest from investing the gold will bring in sixty thousand dollars a year—a revelation that leaves Mrs. Norval worshipful toward the gold, "so subdued, so humbled, before the yellow god!" (26). Mrs. Norval's reverential, almost religious posture toward the gold echoes the attitude of earlier empires that laid claim to North American gold before the Spanish arrived. According to Heidi King, people in the Pre-Columbian Americas revered gold in the same way that Mrs. Norval does here:

> For the peoples of ancient America gold was endowed with spiritual and symbolic meaning. The Inka of Peru thought of gold as the rain of the sun, a major deity; and the word for gold in Nahuatl, the language of the Aztecs of Mexico, is *teocuitlatl* (excrement of the gods). (5)

In the fifteenth century, as in the nineteenth century (and even the twenty-first century), gold was "associated with worldly power, status, and wealth" (King 5). Here, Mrs. Norval is implicitly the product of centuries of worshipful imperial greed; she is not unlike the people of Indigenous empires who lived centuries before her, or the Spanish colonizers who came after them, or the greed-driven American speculators of the California gold strike. Just as Anne's friends and relatives jockey for power over her in a symbolic reenactment of inter-imperial conquest in Woolson's novel, so do the Norvals seek to extract wealth from Lola in an allegorical reworking of centuries of imperial battles.

However, Lola is even more openly exploited than Anne because of her racially ambiguous appearance; through this, Ruiz de Burton condemns the colonial violence targeted disproportionately at people of color, and simultaneously explores the tensions inherent in Lola's Spanish and Mexican heritage. Lola exemplifies the way that women in liminal territories have to navigate the intersecting means by which imperial violence has both injured and empowered them. Because of Ruiz de Burton's own shifting identity—having become a US citizen as a consequence of US territorial acquisition from Mexico at the end of the Mexican–American War—her critique of the Norvals' acquisitive attitude toward Lola here is particularly pointed. Although Dr. Norval responsibly invests Lola's wealth and takes only small percentage for himself, once he leaves the US for Africa on another geological trip with some "gentlemen from England" (83), Mrs. Norval takes full advantage of Lola's wealth and uses the investment income to buy elaborate wardrobes for her and her daughters, and eventually a fancy house in New York. Early in their arrangement with Lola, Dr. Norval explains to his wife that they can benefit from the interest gained by investing Lola's millions: "in using Lola's money, of course, we can derive a great many advantages, for I don't mean to stint the income, only I shall take mighty good care of the principal" (32). He has most of Lola's gems set handsomely for her to retain when she comes of age, but Dr. Norval "thought he could conscientiously take a few of the smallest and have some pins and earrings made for his girls. He would also have a handsome breastpin and earrings for his wife, though he knew she would not wear diamonds" (47).

After Dr. Norval departs for Africa, however, Mrs. Norval faces greater temptation to spend Lola's money on herself. Upon reports (eventually proven to be false) of her husband's death in Ethiopia, Mrs. Norval feels no compunction at all about her and her daughters benefiting from Lola's treasure:

> Mrs. Norval stinted no one now, for she thought that if the money they were spending was Lola's, there was no need for her to economize. On the contrary, the more money they put to use, the more would be left in their hands when Lola was twenty-one. Therefore, even poor Lavvy had *carte-blanche* now with New York milliners, and jewelers, and shoemakers, and no end of pin-money. (104)

Thus, Mrs. Norval extracts wealth from Lola in a twisted reenactment of Spain's extraction of wealth from Mexico. Mrs. Norval's exploitation of Lola's wealth, according to Pablo Ramirez, illustrates the "failure of 'manifest domesticity'" because in "joining the domestic space with imperialist expansion, Mrs. Norval drives out all feelings of familial affection and allows the baser passions of greed and lust to invade her home" (150). Beth Fisher likewise characterizes Mrs. Norval's greed as her "involvement in the expansionist project of domestic consumption that is the focus of the author's political critique" (62). If, as these critics affirm, Mrs. Norval calls into question the sanctity of the domestic space through her consumption of the spoils of imperial conquest, then perhaps other white women in domestic novels of the time are also rendered suspect by association. Mrs. Norval's example potentially sullies the integrity of characters like Woolson's Anne and Phelps's Avis—white women who seem less overtly villainous than Mrs. Norval, but who similarly benefit from the proximate power that their access to global trade (in furs and carmine dye) provides.

Layers of History in Lola's Shifting Skin Color

Underscoring the imperial exploitation of Mrs. Norval's actions is the indeterminate but racially "other" color of Lola's skin, which stands in distinct contrast to the unrelenting whiteness of Woolson's Anne. Ruiz de Burton marks Lola's body with a lived imperial history through her changing skin color. Dyed "black" by her Native American captors to discourage escape efforts, Lola's skin gradually fades throughout the novel to an unusual spotted complexion, before turning completely white—changing from one color to the next like so many successive empires who controlled territories in Mexico, from Aztec, to Spanish, to American. This transformation causes much confusion among the novel's white characters who, in speculating about Lola's ambiguous ethnicity, reveal their anxieties about shifting geopolitical power relations. These characters initially perceive Lola to be a "little girl very black indeed," (16) or a "mixture of Indian and negro" (20). Mrs. Norval's frequent use of vile racial slurs to describe Lola indicates how racially marginalized she is, and how Mrs. Norval attempts to leverage that perceived racial difference as a means of justifying Lola's exploitation. Conversely, one character speculates, "I thought she might be Aztec" (20), a reference back to a fifteenth-century empire which hints at the layers of imperial history over a *longue durée* that are perhaps embedded in Lola (and in her coveted gold). This guess that Lola has Aztec ancestry perhaps participates in the early American romanticizing of Inca and Aztec peoples, as discussed by Eric Wertheimer. Wertheimer argues that in the late eighteenth and early nineteenth centuries, Aztecs and other Indian empires were seen as the originators of republican ideals of which contemporary Americans were the inheritors, and that these Indigenous peoples thus served as "the historiographic and literary site of a contest over American identity—over the ongoing positioning of Anglo-Americans in the North-South New World" (16). Dr. Norval denies Lola any claim to this romantic legacy of Anglo-American nativism, instead repositioning her within the American imaginary as the progeny of vilified European empires, explaining that she was born in Mexico to parents of Spanish and Austrian descent.

Later, when the dye on Lola's skin starts to fade, a member of the town guesses that "Lola must belong to a tribe of Mexican Indians called 'Pintos,' who are spotted," (78) and Mrs. Norval replies with paranoia, "But as the doctor says that she is not an Indian, then those ugly spots can't be accounted for, except on the theory that they are some disease" (78). Here, Ruiz de Burton critiques the pathologization of racial "others" and the way in which such pathologizing is used to excuse the extraction of resources from people of color. When Dr. Norval sees Lola after a long absence, he, too, demonizes Lola's racially ambiguous appearance, perhaps in an effort to delegitimize her claim to her own wealth, observing that

> The unfortunate spots had almost entirely disappeared; Lola's skin was white and smooth, and she was very pretty. Still, there were some spots yet on her neck and arms, though almost imperceptible, and he feared that Mrs. Norval would insist on regarding them as some sort of cutaneous disease. (79)

The confusion continues when Lola's skin lightens completely; when the Norvals' daughter Mattie remarks "talk of Spanish women being dark! Can anything be whiter than Lola's neck and shoulders?" their other daughter Ruth attempts to correct her and reassert what they see as Lola's lower status in nineteenth-century racial hierarchies, commenting: "Lola is not Spanish; she is Mexican" (232).[36]

Other critics have read the transformation in Lola's appearance as a strategy Ruiz de Burton employs to claim whiteness for Spanish-descended Mexicans and thus equal status with white Americans. For instance, Margaret Jacobs claims that because "many Yankees considered neither Californios nor Spaniards to be White, Ruiz de Burton made explicit that Lola and other elite Mexican and California women deserved to be considered White by virtue of their color" (222).[37] However, given the comparison of Lola to metals and gemstones—geological formations that also shift in appearance when the surface is scratched and similarly unearthed by Dr. Norval—I would read the mutability of Lola's skin color as Ruiz de Burton's rendering of the cumulative trauma of history in the *longue durée*, made visible on the body. Lola's liminal identity is the product of history, warring powers, alliances, varied intimacies forged by empire. Ruiz de Burton makes those layers of violence visible on her body, thus explaining the indeterminacy of her identity, despite the fact that characters are told many times where she is from. Because of these layered histories embedded in Lola's identity, it seems equally plausible to the Anglo-American New Englanders that Lola could be a "little girl very black indeed," or a member of the fifteenth-century Aztec empire, or a descendant of the very Spanish conquistadors who overthrew the Aztecs in a colonial quest for gold—but never a white American, because they can never see her as anything other than a member of a "conquered" race.

Who Would Have Thought It? takes some wild generic turns before reaching its conclusion, just as *Anne* does. The details of these turns are beyond the scope of this chapter, but they create a collage of historical fiction, mystery, romance, and even a didactic digression into political intrigue. The Civil War similarly serves as a rupture in the middle of the text, but here, the fissures in US national identity are overlaid on the fractures already created by the Mexican–American War of 1846–1848. Dr. Norval's son Julian and brother-in-law Isaac serve for the Union in the Civil War, and eventually show their disdain for the inefficacy of the US government during the war effort because of its lack of support for Union soldiers. In a searing indictment of the US government, Julian compares the "despotism" in America to that in Europe, concluding that it is

> despotism of a worse kind, because we pretend so loudly to the contrary. If we didn't say so much about freedom, the thing wouldn't be so bad. We are hypocrites and impostors besides . . . We are living on the credit of our fathers and squandering the inheritance of liberty left to us, but we want to humbug posterity by loudly insisting that we have greater riches, more freedom. (244)

Julian reverses the financial imagery of acquisition and speculation used by his parents, and instead insists that the US is borrowing on credit that it will be unable to repay. Rather than profiting from the interest paid on investments—as the Norvals hope to do through Lola—Julian suggests that the US will accumulate interest owed on the loan it took out on its values of liberty and freedom, until it is morally bankrupt. Through Julian's use of monetary language to discuss non-monetary ideals, Ruiz de Burton makes plain the deleterious moral consequences of unfettered capitalist and imperialist expansion.

Ruiz de Burton emphasizes just how destructive and distasteful the United States' expansionist greed is when the disillusioned Julian and Isaac depart for Mexico, seeing it as a favorable alternative to the US. A chance encounter between Isaac and Lola's long-lost father and grandfather reveals the truth about her heritage and rightful claim to the wealth Mrs. Norval has been hoarding. Further plot developments accompany this revelation, including the news that Dr. Norval is not dead after all, and the blossoming of Julian and Lola's romantic relationship. As the novel comes to a close,

Julian finishes out his service in the Civil War before moving permanently to Mexico to marry Lola, with whom he fell in love in spite of her spotted complexion. The novel holds up Lola and expatriates like Julian as exemplars of just moral values, and punishes Mrs. Norval for her unquenchable greed and lust in an unequivocal condemnation of US expansionist fervor.

The novel concludes with Lola blissfully married to Julian, living peacefully in Mexico, spots completely faded from her face. Although this conclusion, like Woolson's in *Anne*, resembles a conventional happy ending, Ruiz de Burton portends further trouble for Lola by implying a continuity between past and present in the "long succession of events" that perpetuate inter-imperial violence (Lyell 2). A conversation between Lola's father and grandfather alludes to the rumored crowning of the Austrian Archduke Maximilian to the throne of Mexico, with both men expressing approval of this European leader by connecting his campaign to historical imperial rule. Don Felipe, Lola's grandfather, comments,

> if it is positive and certain that the Archduke will accept the crown of Mexico, I shall be only too happy to be the most loyal of his subjects . . . I would consider it wrong to oppose the re-establishing of a monarch in Mexico under a Hapsburg, for the Hapsburgs were, and are, the legitimate and lawful heirs of the glorious Isabella and the great Charles V. (197)

Don Felipe's favorable opinion of Ferdinand Maximilian von Habsburg—who was eventually crowned the emperor of Mexico in 1864—aligns him historically with the conservative Monarchists of Mexico, who supported the establishment of a Mexican empire with a European-appointed ruler (McAllen xii). In her account of Maximilian's reign, Mary Margaret McAllen articulates the inter-imperial stakes of this debate over Mexican rule, explaining that in the mid-nineteenth-century, Mexico "became a microcosm of erupting European geopolitics" (xii), and the quest to establish Maximilian as emperor was motivated by European desires to curb further American expansionism. European powers, France and Austria in particular, "believed that it was only a matter of time before the United States annexed additional lands from its southern neighbor, as they had in 1848 and 1853, so they saw a race to grab territory" (McAllen xi). Conservative Mexicans like Don Felipe aligned themselves with these European interlopers because they thought the alliance could help them consolidate competing factions within Mexico and be better able to "withstand the rising power of the United States with its eyes on further territorial expansion" (McAllen 38). This historical allusion thus illuminates Ruiz de Burton's awareness of the strategic and fraught position Mexico held in a competitive inter-imperial field—a position not unlike that of Mackinac Island in the North American fur trade.

The historical competition for control over Mexico, alluded to in Don Felipe's remark about Archduke Maximilian, finds its analogue in the fictional competition for control over Ruiz de Burton's Lola, or Woolson's Anne. In their analysis of Don Felipe's comment, Rosaura Sánchez and Beatrice Pita use this historical context to situate Mexico as a liminal space in an inter-imperial field, explaining that

> through these characters, the novel acknowledges the French imperial threat to Mexico and sees it as an even more imminent and powerful threat from its northern neighbor, a U.S. in which—before and even after the Civil War—there were sectors favoring continued expansionism south. (lv)

The tenuousness of Mexico's position amid warring imperial rivals rings especially true, given my contention that Lola seems to play a similarly liminal role as an embodiment of Mexico's multivalent imperial past and a pawn in the Norvals' speculative gamble. However, these patriarchs' comments also point to the ways in which centuries of imperial rivalries continue to shape the present through their nostalgia for the fifteenth- and sixteenth-century Spanish monarchs Isabella and Charles V (an ancestor of Maximilian's), who orchestrated the colonial conquest and extraction of wealth from Mexico to Spain.[38]

The material effects of centuries of inter-imperial contests are alluded to once again in the novel's final pages. Just as Lola was once equated with gold, now she bears the signs of other networks of trade through Ruiz de Burton's description of her smile: "The coral lips parted in merry laughter again, showing the pearly teeth" (287). With this reference to coral and pearl, both luxury commodities that are the result of gradual accumulation over time and that are traded internationally through imperial networks of trade, Ruiz de Burton confronts readers with the reality that Lola cannot fully escape her imbrication in such global networks. Through the example of Lola's commodification, Ruiz de Burton uncovers the forces that ever-shifting networks of power exert on the bodies of those vulnerable to centuries of inter-imperial economic competition and violence.[39]

Set at the edges of empire, Ruiz de Burton's *Who Would Have Thought It?* and Woolson's *Anne* invoke centuries of inter-imperial conflict in ways more obvious than the oblique references in the works of quintessentially New England writers Alcott and Phelps discussed in the previous chapter. In focusing on the Northern and Southern territories at the periphery of the US empire, these authors more fully articulate the liminality of American national and racial identities. Furthermore, they allegorize inter-imperial jockeying through their female characters in order to exaggerate the violent effects of geopolitical conflict on women's domestic lives. Ruiz de Burton transposes inter-imperial histories onto her characters' relationships to show how the intimacies of empire played out in personal histories, much in the way that the centuries of rivalry over the fur trade structure characters' intimate relations in Woolson's *Anne*. Although influential, male writers like William Dean Howells and Mark Twain are known for writing explicitly against imperialism, novels by Constance Fenimore Woolson and María Amparo Ruiz de Burton give us insight into the ways in which women saw the discourses of empire saturating every aspect of their lives, and model how narrative plotting can critique this infiltration.

Notes

1. The fact that Irving was commissioned to write this report by John Jacob Astor perhaps accounts for its laudatory tone.
2. Asha Nadkarni traces the national and imperial stakes of the reproductive potential of women's bodies, examining nationalist feminist discourses in the US and India that participate in what she terms "eugenic feminism" by "launch[ing] their claims to feminist citizenship based on modernist constructions of the reproductive body as the origin of the nation" (5).
3. See José António Brandão, Ida Amanda Johnson, Eric Jay Dolin, Richard White, and Keith Widder for further history of the Mackinac region and the North American fur trade.
4. Exploring Woolson's investment in deconstructing Northern stereotypes about the Southern states, critics have interpreted the Reconstruction-era US South that she depicts as a kind of "postcolonial site" (Hall 178) because of its putative post-Civil War colonization by the North, and have located the global connections evident in her depictions of Florida. John Lowe, furthermore, uses Woolson's depiction of Florida as a "Creolized culture, where the peoples of the Caribbean jostle, interact, and create new hybrid forms of expression and material

culture" (37) as evidence for Woolson's status as a writer of "transatlantic fiction of the Global South basin" (39). See also Carolyn Hall and Annamaria Formichella Elsden.
5. See Brandão (xxiv), Eric Jay Dolin, and Richard White. Dolin notes that in addition to their settlements in Alaska, Russians established a trading post in northern California in 1812 to capitalize on its population of sea otters.
6. Richard White highlights the imperial stakes of the fur trade for the French in particular, noting that "the fur trade in its very organization could not be disentangled from political and imperial concerns" (115).
7. José António Brandão details the large volume of trade that took place at Michilimackinac, a fort at the Straits of Mackinac near Mackinac Island, noting that "at the height of the fur trade in 1755, Michilimackinac had eighteen licenses assigned to it. Detroit, established in 1701, had thirteen licenses in 1755, and post on the Saint Joseph river, operational since 1691, had four licenses assigned to it. All in all, these three forts shipped 1,950 packs of fur and hides, or about 195,000 pounds of furs/ hides (97 tons). This volume of trade represents 29.3 percent of all furs and hides traded in Canada, Louisiana, and Hudson's Bay districts, and about 38 percent of all furs from Canada. These forts, in the same order, ranked first, second, and fourth among all French forts in terms of volume of furs shipped through their gates" (xxvii).
8. See Widder (301).
9. See Johnson (107) and Widder (310).
10. See Dolin on changing fashions (281), overhunting (283), and the sale of Astor's company (280).
11. For more on the strategic silences and elisions of early American historiography, see Laura Doyle's chapter in *Freedom's Empire*, "Liberty's Historiography: James Harrington to Mercy Otis Warren" (57–78).
12. Doyle further characterizes this scene in Sedgwick's novel as "a scene of female resistance on this mountaintop that in the end enables Indian erasure" (*Freedom's Empire* 295), because of the way in which Hope Leslie allows her male companions to envision the Massachusetts territory as a site for future settlements, ignoring the Native Americans already living there.
13. See Malini Schueller and John Carlos Rowe for further discussion of the contradictions inherent in the American ethos that are brought to light by its practices of internal colonization.
14. "Saxonist discourse," according to Laura Doyle, was critical in establishing an Anglo-Atlantic racialized narrative of freedom: "The Protestant and Saxonist vocabularies of tender conscience and native birthright worked in this way to position liberty as an interior, racial inheritance, planted in the individual and constituting an irrevocable principle for the government of the state" (*Freedom's Empire* 4).

15. For instance, when caretaker Lois proclaims that "Tita is hideous" and "dwarfish, black, and sly," Anne rejoins "with heat" that "I do not think she is sly" (27). Similarly, Anne urges her father to see "what a remarkable child she is" (20).
16. See also Eric Wertheimer on early American assimilations of Columbus into the national mythos. Wertheimer describes the American "Black legend" that viewed the British Empire as superior to the Spanish, and that saw Columbus as a "heroic" missionary bringing Christianity to the New World, a noble mission that was corrupted by the greed of the Spanish empire. According to Wertheimer, in this legend, "Columbus, the Incas, and the Aztecs all stand as New World martyrs of corrupt empire" (20).
17. Commenting on the "implied readers of the early American sentimental novel," Cathy Davidson notes that many of these novels were addressed "to the 'daughters of United Columbia,' who are, implicitly or explicitly, young, white, of good New England stock, and for the most part unmarried" (*Revolution and the Word* 112).
18. See also Amy Kaplan and Don Pease's volume *Cultures of United States Imperialism*, which traces a "paradigm of denial" (13) in studies of American culture that "defines American exceptionalism as inherently anti-imperialist, in opposition to the empire-building of either the Old World or of communism and fascism" (12).
19. Jenny Heil identifies a similarly allegorical plot structure in Susanna Rowson's *Reuben and Rachel* (1798), explaining that Rowson "writes Anglo women into Columbian history by structuring the novel typologically so that Protestants redeem Catholic foundations in the New World" (626), repeating similar names for different characters as a form of "pedagogy whereby readers learned to associate Spanish, South American, British, and North American characters with an Anglicized past and future. Rowson uses typology in this way to highlight the importance of women to the development of this Anglicized Columbian-American history" (635). Rowson's typological plot thus offers a potential precedent for Woolson's international allegory in *Anne*.
20. Beam elaborates: "Miss Crief is not exactly a representative of Woolson's self, but an impersonation of a type, the social persona that Woolson understands to be imposed on the woman artist. This is where the story gets, not earnest, but funny. Woolson, I believe, is camping up her woman artist" (140).
21. See Brian Schoen and Sven Beckert.
22. Margaret Jacobs offers a succinct summary of Ruiz de Burton's biography (220–1), and Rosaura Sánchez and Beatrice Pita go into more depth about her personal history in their introduction to *Who Would Have Thought It?*

23. Ramirez, Jacobs, and Fisher also discuss Ruiz de Burton's desire to claim the mantle of white elite status.
24. Fisher explains that "in this contest, Lola Medina's endangered purity represents the political vulnerability of an elite, culturally superior Mexican civilization as it is incorporated into the greed-driven economy of the United States" (60), and it is through this contrast that Ruiz de Burton "draws attention to the terms through which the discourse of domesticity can translate expansionist desires into a language of womanly moral authority" (61).
25. Ramirez elaborates on the historical conditions shaping Ruiz de Burton's novel: "*Who Would Have Thought It?* was published when Americans, in emancipation's aftermath, were trying to shore up the value of whiteness. At the same time, they were trying to ascertain whether money should derive its value from gold (specie payment) or common trust (paper money). Just as Americans were trying to fix the value of metals and people, the novel untangles the intertwined discourses of gold, race, and worth" (155). Ultimately, according to Ramirez, Ruiz de Burton concludes that "only by disengaging themselves from a barbaric economy of plunder and reestablishing contractual relations with Mexicans can Anglo Americans restore a world of proper values—a world where gold and where white skin function as stable, universal standards" (144).
26. José Aranda notes that Ruiz de Burton fits uneasily in Chicano/a studies' models of postcolonial resistance because of the multidirectional nature of the colonial past that she engages with, noting that critics often overlook the importance of the novel's invocation of the "Spanish-Mexican colonial past" (572), and emphasizing that "the novel demands instead close attention to the multiple, and sometimes competing, colonial histories of peoples from Texas to California" (572).
27. Summarizing the critical consensus on the origins of gold working in the Pre-Columbian era of the Americas, Heidi King explains that "A commonly accepted theory is that gold working began in the Peruvian highlands in the mid-second millennium B.C. and that knowledge of the technology spread north to Ecuador and Colombia ... reaching Panama/Costa Rica by about the second century A.D. and Mexico by the ninth or tenth century. However, ongoing research argues for several points of origin for American metallurgy" (5).
28. It was also rumored that Cortés hoarded some of the gold for himself, possibly underreporting his acquisitions in order to avoid paying the full percentage he owed to the Spanish crown (Hartmann 50). Kwasi Kwarteng explains this mechanism through which the Spanish crown profited from gold-seeking ventures to the New World, describing the "*quinto real*, or royal fifth," which "was a 20 per cent royalty fee imposed on every ounce of gold and silver extracted from the New

World which came into Seville, the only permissible entry port into Europe for the Spanish treasures from further west" (18).

29. Peter Bernstein's cultural history of gold notes the scope of this process of exportation, calculating that "the total European stock of gold and silver at the end of the century was nearly five times its size in 1492" (135). As Carlos Marichal elucidates: "from the early sixteenth century to the early nineteenth, the Spanish crown controlled the territories with the richest mineral resources in precious metals" ("The Spanish-American Silver Peso" 27).

30. As Kwarteng explains, "Habsburg Spain was perpetually at war, and the resources of the New World were expended lavishly to pay for these campaigns" (18).

31. Marichal likewise notes the multiplying effects of Spanish extraction of gold and silver from the Americas, commenting that "there is no doubt that it was not until the New World exports of silver and gold began to generate large transatlantic and transpacific trade flows that the full circle of global commerce was joined, making world trade a reality" ("The Spanish-American Silver Peso" 26).

32. Janet Floyd similarly emphasizes the strike's larger effects in terms of migration and borders: "The gold and silver rushes and the mining industry and cultures that they created were harbingers of new conditions: they drove migration and created new cosmopolitan camps, towns, and cities; they made fortunes for companies and speculators; they had profound effects on the development and the demise of nations and communities" (8).

33. According to Malcolm Rohrbough, "the search for gold was uninhibited by institutional authority . . . Access to the rivers, streams, and valleys was, for all practical purposes, without limits" (12).

34. See TePaske 23, quoted previously in this chapter.

35. This moment is an example of what Elizabeth Maddock Dillon describes as "a long-standing trope that represents Native Americans as incapable of exercising proper judgment with respect to matters of value" ("Atlantic Aesthesis" 374).

36. In a similar moment in Woolson's novel, Anne clings to her half-sister Tita's European ancestry when her father warns about her "Indian blood," insisting, "Tita is French" (20).

37. Ramirez similarly interprets Lola's transformation as a narrative that "can be interpreted as stabilizing upper-class Mexicans' racial status by having a dignified Mexican woman's white skin become an object of intrinsic value. The fading of the stain emphasizes its nature as an extrinsic human mark that cannot destroy Lola's intrinsic value as a white woman. In other words, her whiteness may be misrepresented, but it cannot be destroyed" (161). See also John-Michael Rivera, who argues that "the tension between Lola's blood and her potential

economic wealth lies behind a body that 'deceives' Anglo perceptions, a body that renders her as racialized. The novel's question, then, is if blood or the body defines the rights and status of Mexicans in the United States" (460).
38. Mary Margaret McAllen observes that Maximilian himself perceived a continuity between his nineteenth-century rule of Mexico and the actions of fifteenth-century Spanish conquistadors: "To Maximilian, it all seemed magnificent in the land where his ancestor Charles V, Holy Roman Emperor, king of Castile and Aragón, ruler of Austrian lands, Flanders, Brabant, and Holland, Burgundy, and Naples, or roughly half of Europe, laid claim to the crown of Montezuma in 1519. Hernando Cortés referred to Charles as 'your Majesty to whom the whole world is subject'" (18).
39. The symbolic significance of the material history of pearls will be discussed at length in Chapter 4.

Chapter 3

Bouguereau is Best: Disentangling Economic and Aesthetic Values in Norris and Du Bois

By the early twentieth century, art itself becomes the commodity scrutinized by novelists. This chapter will focus on two examples of such work: Frank Norris's 1903 novel about the global wheat market *The Pit*, and W. E. B. Du Bois's 1911 novel about the global cotton market *The Quest of the Silver Fleece*. By juxtaposing these novels' shared economic concerns and strikingly similar aesthetic references, we can more clearly see Du Bois's revision of Norris's operatic drama, and his reflection on the gendered and raced conditions through which norms of taste are established and negotiated globally. If, as Simon Gikandi argues, the "signs of a black presence in the making of high culture often tended to slip away, not because of the invisibility of the enslaved but because the construction of the ideals of modern civilization demanded the repression of what it had introjected" (9), then Du Bois unearths the "black presence" lying dormant in economic narratives such as Norris's. Anticipating Gikandi's critical methodology, Du Bois, too, calls attention to "what was excluded from the discourse of taste and the series of omissions, repressions, and conceptual failures that were its condition of possibility" (Gikandi 35). The implicit iconography of women's bodies in Constance Fenimore Woolson's *Anne* and María Amparo Ruiz de Burton's *Who Would Have Thought It?*, as discussed in the previous chapter, becomes more self-referential in these novels by Norris and Du Bois, allowing these later writers to more fully question the way in which aesthetic values can shore up or disrupt economic values.

In this sense they anticipate Pierre Bourdieu's insights in his seminal sociological study *Distinction*, which argues that aesthetic values are not natural but socially constructed, operating in a system of coded knowledge that works to distinguish elites from those less educated or less privileged. Furthermore, the homogeneity of aesthetic taste among elites works to naturalize those distinctions so that they appear essential, rather than socially conditioned. This process of distinction relies on knowledge of a field of references that forms an "interminable circuit of inter-legitimation" (45), so that "to the socially recognized hierarchy of the arts, and within each of them, of genres, schools or periods, corresponds a social hierarchy of the consumers. This predisposes tastes to function as markers of 'class'" (xxv). In *The Pit* and *The Quest of the Silver Fleece*, Norris and Du Bois integrate allusions to the popular and wildly expensive art of William-Adolphe Bouguereau to excavate the way in which coded knowledge of these "hierarch[ies] of the arts" becomes assimilated and communicated among elites and those who aspire to join their ranks. Together, they ask: how does the transmission of these aesthetic values work to shore up economic and imperial hierarchies? How are narratives of capitalist imperialism naturalized through shared aesthetic norms? And what strategies can artists use to disrupt this unequal accumulation of economic and cultural capital?[1]

William J. Wilson's fictional sketch "Afric-American Picture Gallery" (1859), a literary precedent to Norris and Du Bois, offers an illustrative example of the role of visual art in re-narrativizing world historical events in the eyes of writers at this time. Wilson's short story imagines a gallery of exclusively African American art, and he describes a painting of Haitian Revolution leader Toussaint L'Ouverture by comparing him to leaders like George Washington and Thomas Jefferson. He writes:

> Pictures are teachings by example. From them we often derive our best lessons . . . A picture of a great man with whose acts we are familiar, calls up the whole history of his times. Our minds thus become reimpressed with the events and we arrive at the philosophy of them. A picture of Washington recalls to mind the American Revolution, and the early history of the Republic. A picture of Thomas Jefferson brings before the mind in all its scope and strength that inimitable document, the Declaration of Independence; and in addition, carries us forward to the times, when its broad and eternal principles, will be fully recognised by, and applied to the entire American people. I had these conclusions forced upon me by looking not upon either the picture of Washington or Jefferson in the gallery. Far from it; but by a most beautiful portrait of one of the greatest men the world ever saw—TOUISSANT L'OUVERTURE.

In his imagined gallery, William J. Wilson constructs a fictional, diasporic archive of African American art that he contrasts with traditional narratives of US history, explicitly drawing attention to the repressed "aura of blackness" (Gikandi 45) that looms over European discourses of taste and sensibility. While "a picture of Washington," according to Wilson's narrator, "recalls to mind the American Revolution, and the early history of the Republic," and a "picture of Thomas Jefferson brings before the mind in all its scope and strength that inimitable document, the Declaration of Independence," the portrait of the famed leader of the Haitian Revolution is noteworthy for how it conjures up the "long and interesting train of historical facts in relation to Hayti, that gem of the sea." Art, as Wilson's narrator understands it, is valuable not only for its aesthetic merit, but also for the historical knowledge and political orientation it can cultivate in the viewer. By centering Toussaint L'Ouverture as the exemplar of American democratic ideals, Wilson implies that the leader of the Haitian Revolution fulfilled the promise of liberty more completely than Washington or Jefferson (both of whom enslaved people) because he fought to extend that liberty to all people. By hanging L'Ouverture's portrait at the heart of this gallery, albeit a fictional one, Wilson leverages the currency of visual art to shape our perception of history, inviting readers to wonder how history would be different if works of art revered Black leaders like L'Ouverture in the same way they honor Washington and Jefferson.

Through this literary rendering of fictional visual art, Wilson presents metacommentary on the aura that artistic representation grants to political events, as well as art's indirect registering of economic disruptions. A successful uprising of enslaved people that produced ripples of hope globally about the possibility that liberty could be seized for all, the Haitian Revolution also threatened to upend the status quo of white supremacy, and along with it undermine one of the biggest global industries—cotton—and the coerced labor upon which the industry was predicated.[2] Du Bois shared Wilson's fascination with the history of Haiti, according to Robin Kelley, who notes that Du Bois "insisted on the world-historical importance of the Haitian Revolution in shaping United States policy toward slavery" (1054). Du Bois's incisive assessment of Haiti's global significance makes clear the inter-imperial stakes of L'Ouverture's revolt. As analysis by Elizabeth Maddock Dillon and Michael Drexler delineates, Haiti became a semi-peripheral actor amid warring empires at the time of its independence, since part of the reason Napoleon sold Louisiana cheaply to the US in the Louisiana Purchase was because of the Haitian Revolution and Napoleon's attendant fears of further antislavery rebellions that he might be unable to quash (7). For similar reasons, an embargo bill was passed in 1806 prohibiting trade with Haiti, "out of fear that an antislavery revolt might spread from Haiti to the southern United States" (8). Consequently, the "U.S. economy was propelled forward by global investment in the cotton industry," while "the economy of Haiti suffered from being cut off from trade with former partners such as the United States and France" (12).[3] While Haiti remained a symbol of Black liberation for William J. Wilson and others, it was also entangled in (and excluded from) the global cotton market, which would become a source of racial oppression, national fracture, and economic expansion for the US as the century went on.

Thus, the "long and interesting train of historical facts in relation to Hayti" that Wilson's portrait of L'Ouverture might conjure for the viewer includes not only the valorous fight for liberty that this leader strove for, but also the international economic upheavals and prejudices that resulted from the Revolution, the dramatic rise of the US cotton industry as a result, and the subsequent mid-nineteenth-century conflict over slavery that Wilson no doubt saw coming to a head. By highlighting the leader of the Haitian Revolution, Wilson's sketch demonstrates art's political potential, its entanglement in global economic shifts, and its role in reimagining dominant narratives of world history.

Decades after Wilson envisioned his fictional art gallery, after the Civil War had laid bare the international interdependencies wrought by cotton's role in the global economy, as US imports doubled and exports quadrupled, and as US culture became ever more stratified into hierarchies of class and taste, writers urgently sought to disentangle art, geopolitics, and economic uncertainty.[4] Frank Norris and W. E. B. Du Bois are representative of a larger contingent of writers at the turn of the century who investigated the relationship between economic and aesthetic values. For instance, in William Dean Howells' *The Rise of Silas Lapham*, the title character attempts to expand his paint manufacturing business into Central and South America while simultaneously upgrading his home furnishings and acquiring an affinity for fine art in order to align himself with bourgeois taste. The speculator depicted in Theodore Dreiser's *The Financier* uses his market gains to purchase carefully selected works by Harriet Hosmer and Hiram Powers, works that are auctioned off when he loses his fortune. Such novels depict an emerging class of nouveau riche men who took advantage of the increased infrastructure, industrialization, and expanded trade relationships across the globe in the decades after the Civil War to augment their personal wealth.[5]

These novels recognize the role that newly rich investors and entrepreneurs had in consuming and creating American culture, depicting the self-reinforcing cycle wherein the wealth these parvenus acquired speculating on commodities allowed them to in turn commodify works of fine art, which in turn raised the value of both the art and the collector through the gradual accumulation of greater cultural capital.[6] Novelists at the turn of the twentieth century document how art is conspicuously displayed in these efforts to shore up economic dominance, with writers like Du Bois viewing artistic expression as a way of resisting expansionist narratives, and writers like Norris depicting art's power to reify economic stratification by naturalizing norms of class and taste.

While commodities like gold and fur provide an ever-present backdrop for novels by María Amparo Ruiz de Burton and Constance Fenimore Woolson, the commodity exchanges of wheat and cotton drive the dramatic plots in fiction by Frank Norris and W. E. B. Du Bois. These writers make starkly visible the often unseen ties between economic hegemony and aesthetic taste. Norris's *The Pit* and Du Bois's *The Quest of the Silver Fleece* both portray the unfettered greed of those who speculate on globally traded commodities like wheat and cotton; they also share surprisingly specific art historical allusions. As I will demonstrate in this chapter, Norris and Du Bois juxtapose fictional art acquisitions with the instability of global commodities markets to probe the intertwined and arbitrary nature of economic and aesthetic value. In *The Pit*, Norris follows the wheat barons who profit from speculation on global markets, while in *The Quest of the Silver Fleece*, Du Bois depicts those who have been exploited through the inequities of the global cotton trade. Norris's ambivalent portrait of economic expansionism in *The Pit* can be attributed in part to criticism he received of his mostly well-received novel *The Octopus* that he "fashioned certain characters in *The Octopus* to serve as his spokespersons" in order to advance "a moralistic or didactic thesis" (McElrath and Crisler 399). Norris's biographers note that "one upshot of the drubbings administered to *The Octopus* is immediately apparent in *The Pit*: no character in that work is interpretable as Norris's spokesperson" (McElrath and Crisler 402). Yet Norris's ambivalence about the United States' imperial ventures is also evident in his reporting on the Spanish–American War that he did for *McClure's Magazine*, which vacillates from lively boosterism ("You want to see excitement, turmoil, activity, the marching and countermarching of troops" (qtd. in McElrath and Crisler 266)) to dismayed repulsion ("I want to get these things out of my mind and the fever out of my blood" (qtd. in McElrath and Crisler 316)). In contrast, Du Bois's sharper anti-expansionist critique in *The Quest of the Silver Fleece* is of a piece with his larger oeuvre and anti-imperialist politics. Four years after the publication of *Quest* in the midst of World War I, for instance, Du Bois published an essay for *The Atlantic* titled "The African Roots of War," which biographer David Levering Lewis calls "one of the analytical triumphs of the early twentieth century" into which Du Bois poured his "mature ideas about capitalism, class, and race" and presented the "novel proposition" that "Africa was the prime cause of the world war" (Lewis 327). In the 1915 essay, Du Bois decries the racist greed that incited nations to jockey for control over land in Africa and elsewhere, imploring, "How can love of humanity appeal as a motive to nations whose love of luxury is built on the inhuman exploitation of human beings, and who, especially in recent years, have been taught to regard these human beings as inhuman?... The doctrine of forcible economic expansion over subject people must go."

Using these politically divergent authors' allusions to the expensive works by the nineteenth-century French painter William-Adolphe Bouguereau as a comparative focus, I will elucidate Norris and Du Bois's commentary on the seductions and dangers of aestheticizing imperial economic ambition. Norris himself studied as an artist under Bouguereau, an experience that perhaps granted him inside knowledge of both Bouguereau's painterly techniques and his navigation of the business of art.[7] The common thread of art references illuminates the degree to which these authors saw questions of art and taste as central to maintaining or challenging international economic hierarchies. Read metafictionally, these references also show how Norris and Du Bois are themselves performing the "correct" attitude toward high art, to likewise claim a place for themselves in social hierarchies through their well-attuned "aesthetic dispositions" (Bourdieu 47).

In what follows, I compare Norris's dramatization of capitalism's seductive allure with Du Bois's vision of communal economic success, examining these writers' self-reflexive allusions to visual art as reflections on the similarly contingent nature of global economic status and international aesthetic ideals. My first section compares the remarkably similar language and style these authors use to describe wheat and cotton markets. In the subsequent section, I discuss

Du Bois's and Norris's shared references to art history—including works by Bouguereau—and the way they strategically juxtapose aesthetic and economic plot developments. In a section focused on an "all-Southern art exhibit" that takes place in *The Quest of the Silver Fleece*, I examine how Du Bois excavates the human agency driving seemingly insensate political and economic processes. Finally, I conclude by analyzing the visual strategies both authors use to frame their closing chapters, to contrast Norris's pessimistic vision with Du Bois's more optimistic one. Ultimately, while Norris sees high art as part of the invisible, inevitable, and self-reinforcing cycle of economic and cultural capital accumulation, Du Bois questions the aura granted to great works of art, imagining artistic reproduction and refraction as a means of resisting economic and aesthetic hegemony. Whereas Norris's characters turn paintings and sculptures into mere commodities that signify the owner's social status, Du Bois's characters elevate commodities like cotton into aesthetic objects, imagining a future in which laborers might not be alienated from their work and African American citizens might have more say in the political, economic, and aesthetic structures of their lives.

Global Wheat and Cotton Dramas

Early twentieth- and twenty-first-century critics alike have compared the similarities between Norris's *The Octopus* and *The Pit* and Du Bois's *The Quest of the Silver Fleece*, typically drawing parallels between their economic subject matter. In 1911, a reviewer in *The Crisis* magazine wrote:

> To Frank Norris' commercial epic of wheat and James Lane Allen's theological epic of hemp Dr. Du Bois now adds the spiritual epic of cotton. It becomes the woven texture in the hands of this poet, through which runs the pattern of a great problem, harmonized in its subtler details of human motives. (Braithwaite 77)

William L. Andrews echoes this early reviewer's words in his introduction to a 2007 edition of the novel, suggesting that if Norris subtitled his planned trilogy the "epic of wheat," then "*The Quest of the Silver Fleece* might be termed Du Bois's epic of cotton" (xxvi). In other recent criticism, Lawrence J. Oliver comments that *The Quest of the Silver Fleece* is "clearly influenced by Frank Norris' The Octopus and The Pit*" (32), and Gina Rossetti observes these novels' shared use of romance to critique "commodity fetishism and reification" (39). From large details—like their similarly epic narration of commodities markets—to small details—like similarly named characters, with Norris's Cressler and Du Bois's Cresswell—ample evidence exists that Du Bois was not merely influenced by Norris, but instead intentionally engages in an intertextual dialogue with Norris about white and Black Americans' disparate experiences of economic and cultural production.

The commonalities these critics observe become readily apparent when comparing the novels' descriptions of commodities markets. Norris's *The Pit* shines a spotlight on commodities trading in turn-of-the-century Chicago, following the dramatic financial rise and fall of social climber Laura Dearborn Jadwin and her real estate investor (and occasional commodities speculator) husband Curtis Jadwin. Norris apparently modeled Jadwin after real-life speculator Joseph Leiter, the heir of a dry goods fortune who initially profited from spiking wheat prices and international demand during the Spanish–American War but whose corner of the wheat market eventually failed (McElrath and Crisler 389–90). For most of the novel, Jadwin is so successful in his hobby as a speculator that other characters frequently call him "Napoleonic" (174, 229, 231, 291), a moniker that captures the inter-imperial nature of Jadwin's economic conquest, which likewise finds its echo in Leiter's nonfictional profiteering from historical inter-imperial battles. Though Jadwin is described as "unimaginative," the narrator attributes the novel's central recurring image of the trading pit to Jadwin's imagination, explaining that he had

> long since conceived the notion of some great, some resistless force within the Board of Trade Building that held the tide of the streets within its grip, alternately drawing it in and throwing it forth. Within there, a great whirlpool, a pit of roaring waters spun and thundered, sucking in the life tides of the city. (72)

This image of the Pit resurfaces throughout the novel, alternately referring to the physical trading floor in Chicago or the larger churning whirlpool of the global economy. The Pit is characterized in violent, vigorous, malevolent language—at times focalized through Jadwin, but more typically described by the narrator. Repeatedly termed a "maelstrom" (73), the Pit "spun and sucked, and guttered and disgorged" (294); it is "surcharged with a veritable electricity" (236); its "distant thunder" (295) creates a "centripetal convulsion"

(339); and it is "mad ... drunk and frenzied" (339), this "huge resistless Nourisher of the Nations" (368).

Not merely deterministic and irresistible, this swirling black hole of capitalism is also situated in a global and inter-imperial matrix of supply and demand. For example, Norris dwells upon the global interconnections forged by the economy in this description of the trading pit itself and the international wheat market:

> Because of some sudden eddy spinning outward from the middle of its turmoil, a dozen bourses of continental Europe clamoured with panic, a dozen Old-World banks, firm as the established hills, trembled and vibrated. Because of an unexpected caprice in the swirling of the inner current, some far-distant channel suddenly dried, and the pinch of famine made itself felt among the vine dressers of Northern Italy, the coal miners of Western Prussia. Or another channel filled, and the starved moujik of the steppes, and the hunger-shrunken coolie of the Ganges' watershed fed suddenly fat and made thank offerings before ikon and idol. There in the centre of the Nation, midmost of that continent that lay between the oceans of the New World and the Old, in the heart's heart of the affairs of men, roared and rumbled the Pit. (73)

Naturalizing the interconnectedness of man-made financial institutions by comparing them to geologic phenomena like a "sudden eddy" or hills that "tremble" and "vibrate" or the "swirling of the inner current," Norris's narrator dramatizes the destruction brought on by an interconnected global economic system, presenting an aesthetically compelling depiction of inter-imperial trade. Jason Puskar attributes Norris's aesthetic strategies here to neoclassical economics' "naturalizing of capitalism" (34), with this passage in particular relying on a "romantic and mystical" mode to capture what Puskar terms the "hypereconomy," a "massively distributed economic system that no longer has the clear boundaries, internal solidity, and ontological heft of a macroeconomy" (36).[8] While I concur with Puskar's assessment of how this passage naturalizes the workings of capitalism, I would also put even greater emphasis on Norris's self-conscious deployment of artistic allusions to make visible the processes through which such naturalization takes place. In Norris's aesthetic vision in the passage above, any human responsibility for the negative consequences of capitalist speculation is entirely deflected: the famine "made itself felt," rather than being the consequence of some human decision. Norris recognizes the human labor involved in the swirling whirlpool of capitalism—the "vine dressers," "coal miners," and "hunger-shrunken coolie." Yet the arbitrary feasts and famines these workers face come at the hand of an invisible force—the "roaring" and "rumbling" Pit—rather than from any individual speculators, investors, or colonizers.

Norris's ambitious portrait of wheat in his unfinished trilogy, of which *The Pit* was the second installment, speaks to the historical significance of this commodity in both the global economy and in the United States' trajectory in world history, especially during the nineteenth century. A domestic commodity that was crucial in establishing US power in the world economy, wheat served as an impetus for inter-imperial maneuvering from the beginning of the nation's history. Brooke Hunter documents the strategies that the newly formed American nation used to remain neutral and maintain trade relationships by supplying wheat to empires tied up in inter-imperial conflicts, including the Seven Years', French Revolutionary, and Napoleonic Wars, observing that although "cotton would quickly replace flour as America's top export commodity, wheat and flour together served as a cornerstone of America's newly independent transatlantic commerce" (506). The United States dominated the wheat export market by the end of the nineteenth century, as I described in Chapter 1.[9]

In *The Pit*, Norris imagines the multifarious repercussions that fluctuations in US wheat production might have for the rest of the world, personifying abstractions and entities like the "Old-World banks," famine, and the Pit itself in order to heighten the impact of global capitalism while minimizing the human forces driving these events and institutions. Jo March's concerns about the cost of flour in *Little Women* are expanded to a macroeconomic scale in *The Pit*, as Norris follows the international wheat crop failures and surpluses that create rippling economic effects for consumers and speculators. In assessing Norris's attitude toward US expansionism in his representation of the wheat, Kathryn Cornell Dolan argues that he depicts wheat "as a corrective against an excessive greed that could result from [economic] expansion" ("A 'Mighty World-Force'" 296) because as an ecocritical "example of interspecies interconnectedness" (295), wheat at times "acts directly against key figures of exploitive capitalism" (296). As much as Norris presents a warning against excessive expansionist greed, he also illustrates how easy it is to become entranced by the promise of imperial power—a seduction he himself at times seemed to succumb to, as evidenced by his operatic reporting of the deceptive calm in Key West during the Spanish–American War, which anticipates his later deterministic descriptions of The Pit: "Force is here, a vast, resistless, terrible Force, that a moment's warning may unleash in a wild red riot of fire and blood" (qtd. in McElrath and Crisler 273). Norris's narratological aestheticization of global capitalism in *The Pit*, I contend, tempts readers to be sucked into the pull of economic imperialism as much as his characters Laura and Jadwin are. Norris's metaphorical language makes visible the process through which unnatural financial transactions become imagined as natural through figurative comparisons to the physical world.

Norris also depicts the ease with which one can be seduced by economic power through the juxtaposition of cultural and economic events. In the opening chapter of the novel, for instance, Laura Dearborn (later Laura Jadwin) overhears brokers discussing a dramatic wheat corner during the intermission of a performance of the opera *Faust*.[10] Initially annoyed that the "jar of commerce" is "spoil[ing] all the harmony of this moment" (23), Laura suddenly realizes the parallel dramas unfolding before her:

> And abruptly, midway between two phases of that music-drama, of passion and romance, there came to Laura the swift and vivid impression of that other drama that simultaneously—even at that very moment—was working itself out close at hand, equally picturesque, equally romantic, equally passionate; but more than that, real, actual, modern, a thing in the very heart of that very life in which she moved. (33)

By perceiving the fictional opera about a man who sells his soul to the devil as "equally picturesque, equally romantic, equally passionate" as the international wheat trade, Laura falls into the trap of sentimentalizing the real-life Faustian bargains that may be happening before her very eyes. Although she is more perceptive than heroines like Phelps's Avis or Woolson's Anne of the economic transactions at the "very heart of that very life in which she moved," Laura accommodates the Faustian bargains necessitated by global capitalism in her process of climbing up the social ladder. Through moments like this that depict the entanglement of aesthetic and economic power, along with later metacommentary presented through his depictions of visual art, Norris alerts his readers to the dangers of unconsciously allowing aesthetics to reframe your vision of what is valuable, and of becoming oblivious to the way in which visually pleasing art can sentimentalize ugly inter-imperial economic realities. If Louisa May Alcott and Elizabeth Stuart Phelps taught artists to be wary of unconscious consumption of imperialist narratives lest these narratives seep into their art, Norris teaches readers to be suspicious of the imperialist values implicit in aesthetic forms.

In *The Quest of the Silver Fleece*, Du Bois crafts an image of the far reaches of the cotton markets that bears striking similarity to Norris's picture of the global flow of wheat. Set in post-Reconstruction Alabama, Du Bois's novel tracks the collusion between Northern capitalists, manufacturers, and Southern cotton growers as they attempt to corner the cotton market. Parallel to this plot is a bildungsroman tale of Bles and Zora, two African American children who come of age, move away to pursue careers, and return to their hometown of Toomsville, Alabama with the dream of developing a Black community supported by cooperative labor harvesting the precious cotton that Zora plants. The novel presents a possible strategy for undermining the power of mercenary white capitalists like Norris's Jadwin through the field of highly desirable cotton—the titular "silver fleece"—communally cultivated in secret by the impoverished Zora and Bles. Du Bois thus dramatizes the clash between Bles and Zora's utopic vision of communal cotton cultivation and the cotton barons' exploitative, greed-driven speculation.

Rather than rendering inevitable the global fluctuations in commodity values as Norris does with his depiction of wheat, Du Bois emphasizes the toll global capitalism takes on the primarily Black laborers who harvest and produce goods like cotton:

> The cry of the naked was sweeping the world. From the peasant toiling in Russia, the lady lolling in London, the chieftain burning in Africa, and the Esquimaux freezing in Alaska; from long lines of hungry men, from patient sad-eyed women, from old folk and creeping children went up the cry, 'Clothes, clothes!' Far away the wide black land that belts the South, where Miss Smith worked and Miss Taylor drudged and Bles and Zora dreamed, the dense black land sensed the cry and heard the bound of answering life within the vast dark breast. All that dark earth heaved in mighty travail with the bursting bolls of the cotton while black attendant earth spirits swarmed above, sweating and crooning to its birth pains. (25)

Whereas Norris imagines the Pit as a senseless force of nature, Du Bois draws attention to the human life of "all that dark earth" that animates the ebbs and flows of global exchange. Du Bois's language here is active and visceral, with verbs like "heaved," "swarmed," "sweating," and "crooning." While Norris's laborers seem to be the victims of arbitrary economic ebbs and flows, Du Bois's laborers drive this economic cycle with their "toiling," "drudging," and "dreaming." Importantly, Du Bois's vision of the global economy insists that workers have just as much a right to "dream" and develop their imagination as the speculators who purchase and hoard fine works of art. Unlike Norris, who problematically valorizes the traits of "Anglo-Saxons" in his journalistic writing but otherwise mostly evades the issue of race in *The Pit*, Du Bois explicitly acknowledges the exploitation of racial difference that divides the laborers and capitalists in the global economy through his image of the "dark earth."[11] The "dark earth" here refers on a literal level to the rich soil in which cotton seeds germinate, take root, and blossom. Yet it also indexes the typically Black labor required to work it, first in the form of enslaved labor, then later in the form of postbellum sharecroppers, indentured servants, and others bound by predatory labor arrangements—dynamics Du Bois likely knew well due to his work in Virginia, Georgia, and Alabama from 1898–1906 for the Bureau of Labor Statistics (Lewis 139–41). Du Bois's personification of this "dark earth" from which valuable cotton is extracted serves as a powerful metaphor for the people who are abused in order to supply clothes to the world.

Though some critics disparage *The Quest of the Silver Fleece* for bearing overly heavy traces of Du Bois's sociological training, such training granted Du Bois insight into the structural connections between US economic success and the exploitation of Black laborers, as is evident in the above passage.[12] Indeed, Robin Kelley claims that Du Bois "contributed more to 'internationalizing' American history than perhaps any other historian" (1054), noting that in *Black Reconstruction*, Du Bois "insisted on treating the question of emancipation within the context of industrial capitalism as a global matter," and "set out to establish slavery as a global system, one that was crucial to the development of capitalism in Europe and America" (1068). As Du Bois well knew, the cotton industry was almost singularly responsible for the United States' rapid rise to global power, and it succeeded in the US largely because slavery was instituted to ensure the availability of cheap labor. According to Sven Beckert, slavery

> was as essential to the new empire of cotton as a proper climate and good soil. It was slavery that allowed these planters to respond rapidly to rising prices and expanding markets. Slavery allowed not only for the mobilization of very large numbers of workers on very short notice, but also for a regime of violent supervision and virtually ceaseless exploitation that matched the needs of a crop that was, in the cold language of economists, "effort intensive." (91)[13]

Although *The Quest of the Silver Fleece* is set after the Civil War and the abolition of slavery, Du Bois recognizes the history of exploited Black people and the "dark earth" that fuels global capitalism, a phenomenon he also elaborates on elsewhere in essays like "The Color Line Belts the World" (1906). In the novel, cotton planters force Black sharecroppers into debt and prevent them from seeking education in order to coerce them into continuing to work the cotton fields—scenarios that likely mirror the historical reality.[14]

Likewise, Du Bois recognizes the global ripples that local labor can have. In the heart of the small Alabama town of Toomsville is a square, and "here pulsed the very life and being of the land," where "yonder great bales of cotton, yellow-white in its soiled sacking, piled in lofty, dusty mountains, lay listening for the train that, twice a day, ran out to the greater world" (16). Du Bois's characters themselves recognize the connection between the US South and the rest of the world that is woven through the ties of cotton. For example, Mary Taylor, a Northerner who moved south to teach at the rural Black school that Zora and Bles attend, forgets her reluctance about this teaching assignment when she romanticizes the cotton-flecked landscapes of her new home:

> For a moment something of the vision of Cotton was mirrored in her mind. The glimmering sea of delicate leaves whispered and murmured before her, stretching away to the Northward. She remembered that beyond this little world it stretched on and on—how far she did not know—but on and on in a great trembling sea, and the foam of its mighty waters would one time flood the ends of the earth. (10)

Mary envisions the "glimmering sea" of cotton spreading outward to the "ends of the earth" in an image that borrows from Norris's swirling currents of wheat. However, in reversing the flow of motion from centripetal inward force to an outward flood that "stretch[es] away to the Northward," Du Bois implies that the global capitalism driving cotton and wheat markets moves in every direction, sucking people in while also reaching out and grabbing them. Given the fact that Mary later ends up in an abusive marriage to one of the Cresswells, a Southern family who owns much of the cotton farming land in the area, Du Bois also presents Mary's sentimental vision of cotton as a warning of the dangers of aestheticizing the global spread of the fruits of exploitative labor practices.

Du Bois also exposes the wealthy speculators who benefit from the work of these laborers, describing them as "tense silent white-faced men" (25). Like Jadwin who is apparently "unimaginative" despite his vivid vision of the Pit, Du Bois's Wall Street broker John Taylor feels "no poetry and heard no song," and went into business "neither for his own health nor for the healing or clothing of the peoples but to apply his knowledge of the world's nakedness and of Black men's toil in such a way as to bring himself wealth" (25). Taylor's unromantic view of the world as described here perhaps underplays the naturalizing role that aesthetics can have in keeping men like him in power, because it is after all portraits of Washington and Jefferson, white men like him, that lined the walls of art galleries at the turn of the twentieth century, rather than Black revolutionaries like Toussaint L'Ouverture. In his vision of the globally connected economy, Norris is more interested in depicting the consequences of financial hubris for wealthy white men like Jadwin—and like Du Bois's John Taylor. Du Bois, however, heightens the white capitalists' villainy and instead makes two young African American entrepreneurs the heroes of his novel, in an intertextual revision of *The Pit* that recenters the narrative on Black voices, just as William J. Wilson does in his fictional gallery. Du Bois renders in great detail the effects the white speculators' political and economic maneuvers have on the individual people who toil to create value for them—maneuvers like thwarting the passage of child labor laws, influencing tariff legislation, shifting political control of schools in order to suppress the education of Black children in the South, and establishing putative monopolies. Focalized through different racial perspectives but linked through a shared vocabulary of visual art, which I discuss in more depth in the following section, *The Pit* and *The Quest of the Silver Fleece* meditate on ways in which norms of aesthetic taste can amplify economic and racial inequalities.

Bouguereau as Cultural, Economic, and Political Capital

When juxtaposed with their shared fascination with visual art, Du Bois and Norris's common concern with global commodities markets transforms into a metafictional dialogue about who has access to economic and cultural capital. *The Pit* and *The Quest of the Silver Fleece* are peppered with art historical allusions, feature key scenes set in art galleries, and reference the work of William-Adolphe Bouguereau. In *The Pit*, the Jadwins own a Bouguereau painting that they display in their home art gallery, while in *The Quest of the Silver Fleece*, Bles hangs a reproduction of a Bouguereau in the tree house he cobbles together for Zora. With his conservative style and sentimental subject matter, Bouguereau may seem like an odd choice for these writers to focus on, especially during a time when more avant-garde art movements like Expressionism, Fauvism, and Cubism were making a splash in the US and Europe. Although Norris himself studied under Bouguereau at his studio in Paris, he was somewhat ambivalent about the painter's work, according to Joseph R. McElrath Jr and Jesse S. Crisler's biography of Norris, where they suggest that in considering the relative merits of experimental impressionists and traditional Academic painters, "one might, without getting into a high dither, appreciate the strengths and acknowledge the limitations of both traditions and modes of representation, as was the habit of Frank Norris" (86). Norris's and Du Bois's use of Bouguereau as a cultural touchstone in their fiction reveals their divergent attitudes about the relationship between economic expansionism, aesthetic value, and taste. Norris critiques the venal attitude toward works of art that titans of industry hold, while Du Bois sees revisionist potential in reproducing, refracting, and reframing great works of art like Bouguereau's—just as he himself re-envisions Norris's literary art in his writing of *The Quest of the Silver Fleece*.

Comparatively little attention has been paid to these specific art historical allusions in Du Bois's and Norris's work, but scholars do recognize these authors' aesthetic investments more generally. In addressing Norris's representation of aesthetics in *The Pit*, critics have emphasized the role of opera and visual art in dramatizing the inner workings of the business world. Such critics have elucidated a variety of strategies employed by Norris to aestheticize market economics: Don Graham, for instance, uses a schema of "aesthetic documentation" to discuss Norris's work, and identifies opera and music as the primary motifs in *The Pit* that function as aesthetic opposites to the drama of commodity trading. David Zimmerman argues that Norris creates an "artist fable" through Jadwin, drawing a comparison between the invisible workings of Jadwin's organ and the invisible hand of the market—both of which Jadwin has uncanny control over (125). Turning his critical lens internationally, Russ Castronovo suggests that in *The Octopus*, the prequel to *The Pit*, Norris reflects a belief in a universal aesthetics located in global markets (*Beautiful Democracy* 180).[15] While they emphasize opera, music, and drama, these critics overlook the expressly visual language through which Norris asks us to read the novel—an important consideration, given not only Norris's training as a visual artist, but also the proliferation of art historical references throughout the novel.[16]

Likewise, critics have acknowledged Du Bois's political deployment of aesthetic strategies; rather than aestheticizing the workings of financial markets, Du Bois uses aesthetics to critique the problem of American racial prejudice and inequality.[17] Du Bois's famous words in "Criteria of Negro Art" that "all Art is propaganda" have led critics to focus heavily on his ideology while at times not fully accounting for his insistence that Black artists also commit themselves to "the creation of Beauty," "the preservation of Beauty," and "the realization of Beauty" (296). As Anne Carroll notes, in his essays for *The Crisis* magazine Du Bois "often discussed music, visual images, and performances, along with literature" (254), and developed aesthetic principles that aimed to accomplish "his goal of undermining American racism" (236). However, like Carroll, most scholars who discuss Du Bois's aesthetic commitments tend to focus on his nonfiction works such as "Criteria for Negro Art" (1926), or sections of *The Souls of Black Folk* (1903), rather than novels such as *The Quest of the Silver Fleece*.[18] Du Bois's mixing of genres in *The Quest of the Silver Fleece* particularly troubles critics in their efforts to assess the novel's aesthetic merits.[19] Even while demonstrating Du Bois's development of an "activist methodology out of aesthetic formalism" in his essays in *The Crisis* ("Color Line" 1445), Russ Castronovo undermines the artistic merit of Du Bois's novels such as *The Quest of the Silver Fleece* and *Dark Princess*, noting,

> While it is easy to see these novels as overtly, even blatantly, political, a lot of work—perhaps too much—must be done to claim these novels as artistic by conventional academic standards ... It may be wasted effort to claim these novels as artistic, but locating them as aesthetic interventions is another story. Aesthetics saturates these inartistic novels. ("Color Line" 1457)

Though he acknowledges Du Bois's aestheticized depiction of cotton, Castronovo neglects to discuss the pieces of visual art that punctuate the novel, and Keith Byerman similarly assesses Du Bois's literary efforts as "not of high quality in standard literary terms" (58).

By glossing over or ignoring Du Bois's art historical allusions, many critics underestimate his self-referential metacommentary about his own entrenchment in aesthetic battles and economic quandaries. Offering a dissenting view about the limited aesthetic value of Du Bois's fiction, Maurice Lee argues that by intentionally blurring the genres of romance and realism, *The Quest of the Silver Fleece* "engages and challenges major American texts; that, with careful, even subversive, attention to issues of language and form, Du Bois appropriates novelistic discourse for his own artistic and political ends," and that this supports the case for Du Bois as "a serious novelist with ambitious designs for the United States and its literatures" (389). Like Lee, who places Du Bois in revisionist dialogue with authors like Dreiser, Norris, and Hawthorne, among others, I believe that Du Bois saw his fiction as deeply artistic, and a vital rebuke to the limitations of the white American canon of literary and visual art. The pleasure of culture is an important piece of the liberatory vision that Du Bois paints in *The Quest of the Silver Fleece* and outlines in *The Souls of Black Folk*. In his essay "Of the Training of Black Men," Du Bois explores the "question of the permanent uplifting and civilization of black men in America," affirming that "we have a right . . . to ask gently, but in all sincerity, the ever-recurring query of the ages, Is not life more than meat, and the body more than raiment?" (114). Du Bois concludes this essay by claiming his place—as a reader, and implicitly, as a writer—among canonically great writers and philosophers, offering an earnest and compelling plea:

> I sit with Shakespeare and he winces not. Across the color line I move arm in arm with Balzac and Dumas, where smiling men and welcoming women glide in gilded halls. From out the caves of evening that swing between the strong-limbed earth and the tracery of the stars, I summon Aristotle and Aurelius and what soul I will, and they come all graciously with no scorn nor condescension. So, wed with Truth, I dwell above the Veil. Is this the life you grudge us, O knightly America? (130)

Du Bois's fictional allusions to art history contribute to his larger project of claiming Black Americans' right to aesthetic pleasure and knowledge. As if anticipating critics like Castronovo who would dismiss his work as "inartistic," Du Bois populates his writing with references to artwork by William-Adolphe Bouguereau and others to claim a place for himself in this aesthetic tradition. Much like later scholarship by Simon Gikandi, which aims "not to recover the figure of the black from the margins of the modern world picture," but rather "to recognize this marginalized figure, often denied even the status of the human, as occupying an essential and constitutive role in the construct of the interiority of modernity itself" (23), Du Bois's novel makes the case for the centrality of Black Americans' contributions to American culture. Engaging in an intertextual dialogue with Norris's *The Pit* through their common references to Bouguereau,

Du Bois relentlessly works to carve out recognition for the work of Black artists—both his characters and himself—in American high culture, because he understands the symbiotic relationship between cultural and economic power.

The many references to Bouguereau and other works of art illuminate these authors' deep understanding of aesthetic taste as entangled with global economic power. To look first at Norris's invocation of William-Adolphe Bouguereau in *The Pit*, Norris signals financial speculator Curtis Jadwin's acquisitive stature through Jadwin's response to paintings hanging in his home art gallery, collected by him and his wife Laura in Europe. In a scene set in this home art gallery, Jadwin shows off the collection to his friend and broker Samuel Gretry. Immediately preceding this moment in the art gallery, Jadwin explains his latest speculative venture to Gretry so that Gretry can purchase stocks on his behalf: he suspects an upcoming shortage in wheat and wants to buy up futures in September wheat so that he will have a stockpile to sell when the supply goes down and prices go up. The self-reinforcing relationship between economic and cultural capital that Norris observes is signaled by the immediate juxtaposition of this speculative financial plan and the speculative purchase and display of the works of art that cover the walls of Jadwin's home gallery. As Jadwin discusses his vast and expensive art collection, he makes little attempt to explain why the pieces were chosen, or to interpret the works' aesthetic value; the art seems to represent a larger project of accumulation. He comments, "'I don't know much about 'em myself . . . but Laura can tell you. We bought most of 'em while we were abroad, year before last. Laura says this is the best.' He indicated a large 'Bouguereau' that represented a group of nymphs bathing in a woodland pool" (175). Jadwin's dismissive description of the collection emphasizes how he acquired the pieces, referring to the works colloquially as "'em," as if they were a stack of postcards. Jadwin's flip appraisal is especially ironic given Norris's apprenticeship under Bouguereau—during which Norris even once earned high praise from the artist for a portrait of a cat—and Norris surely would have had the aesthetic vocabulary to speak to the specific merits of Bouguereau's work.[20] This ironic distance further underscores the philistinism of Jadwin's attitude toward his artistic acquisitions, and his emphasis that he and Laura purchased the paintings while "abroad" signals his mercenary-minded entry into the international art market.

Bouguereau, a nineteenth-century painter from the French Academic school, was popular among American collectors at the end of the nineteenth century, selling his paintings for as much as

$10,000 (Zafran 27). Norris's reference to the Bouguereau painting thus signals to readers that the painting is extraordinarily expensive, which provides a clue as to the scope of Jadwin's fortune and ambitions. Although Bouguereau had a reputation as outmoded and overly saccharine in France, his works were highly sought after by American collectors at the turn of the twentieth century because of their appealing, sentimental beauty and their reputation as a safe investment (Peck 12).[21] Norris's intentional juxtaposition of this artistic reference with the violent movements of commodity futures suggests a self-aware nod to the value of his own work as a literary artist, and an acknowledgment that art does not stand apart from the realities of global capitalism, but rather that artistic and economic value are co-constituted on an international scale.

Gretry's money-minded reaction to the Bouguereau painting and the art gallery as a whole underscores the fact that the gallery is a symbol of wealth, status, and acquisition. He remarks: "this certainly is the real thing, J. I suppose, now, it all represents a pretty big pot of money" (176). Norris's dialogue here describing the gallery as "the real thing" echoes the 1892 Henry James short story of the same name, a story similarly concerned with the mutability of class position.[22] This conversational turn reminds readers again of the cultural function that Jadwin's gallery serves in reifying Jadwin's economic status, financed as it was through his profits from real estate investment and wheat speculation, and thereby converting economic capital into cultural capital. As John Ingham explains, newly wealthy midwesterners such as Jadwin, not born with the same "cultural inheritance" (Bourdieu 69) as old-money elites, tried to prove themselves by "building huge mansions, by furnishing them with European antiquities, and by collecting art, especially the work of European painters" (3). Jadwin's gallery seems to produce this desired effect on visitors: Gretry's comment that the gallery is "the real thing" suggests that Jadwin and his wealth are "the real thing," as well.

The implicit status conferred by the Bouguereau painting becomes a topic of discussion again in a later scene when Jadwin's wife Laura gives a tour of the gallery to her artist friend Sheldon Corthell, a former suitor with whom she eventually has an emotional affair. The conversation between aspiring socialite Laura and the aesthetically sensitive Corthell, when contrasted with Jadwin's reaction to the painting, illuminates how visual art mediates men's and women's experiences of their disparate access to economic power. Norris's strategic choice to allude to Bouguereau creates a litmus test for the refinement of Laura's taste, given Bouguereau's immense popularity among Americans but passé reputation in France. The artist Corthell suggests snidely that Laura likes the painting because "it demands less of you than some others. I see what you mean. It pleases you because it satisfies you so easily. You can grasp it without any effort" (218). Clearly taken aback, Laura rattles off the qualities she appreciates in Bouguereau's work, stammering, "but . . . I thought that Bouguereau was considered the greatest—one of the greatest—his wonderful flesh-tints, the drawing, and colouring—" (218). Laura makes note of Bouguereau's technical prowess; the realistic rendering of the human figures that he often features speaks to his training in drawing from live models, and the luminous quality of the figures' flesh bears witness to his painstaking technical process of glazing layers of paint to create the effect.

Yet Laura's admiration of Bouguereau's "flesh-tints" seems to be a talking point she picked up from contemporary critics, rather than her own insight, a hint at her relatively recently acquired social status. In Bourdieu's analysis, those who have not naturally inherited cultural capital through family dynasties tend to have "more 'classical', safer cultural investments" because they "have acquired the bulk of their cultural capital in and for school" (58). Thus, Laura is drawn to the conservative and popular art of Bouguereau and offers a pedantic analysis of why she enjoys his work, which tips her hand that she has learned this appreciation rather than it coming to her "naturally." One reviewer writing in 1907 also points to Bouguereau's tints, but in a more disparaging context, writing, "he gives to his Madonnas and his nymphs the same smooth rosy tints, the same unreal universalised forms, until at last they become a *juste-milieu* between Raphael's *Galatea* and the wax models one sees in hairdressers' shops" (qtd. in Zafran 28). The critic's dismissal of Bouguereau's masterfully painted flesh tones represents a growing tendency at the time to see Bouguereau as overly idealized and conventional, a point of view expressed by Corthell when he tells Laura that "a fine hanging, a beautiful vase would have exactly the same value upon your wall" (218). Corthell's critique alludes to the painting's commodity status and expresses his distaste for art that serves a purely decorative function—yet, as McElrath and Crisler point out, Corthell's snide rejection of Bouguereau "reflects a dismissive point of view never expressed by Norris" (87), who saw the value of illustrators, Academic painters, and experimental avant-garde artists alike (88). That Norris's aesthetic judgments depart from Corthell's perhaps indicates his skepticism of such hierarchized views of art and taste more generally.

Whereas Jadwin is permitted to see the painting as a mere commodity because that acquisitive stance reinforces his masculine economic power, Laura experiences a greater urgency to experience art the "right" way because that is her only option for claiming cultural capital, since she is unable to invest in commodities herself the way her husband does. Laura's elite status is tenuous because she only recently married into it, and because it is contingent upon her successful performance as a beautiful object. The art gallery that allows Jadwin to display his conspicuous consumption becomes a training ground for Laura to learn the "proper" way to appreciate art; she learns to become a spectator of art, rather than imagining herself an object of it. But Corthell's disparagement of Laura's taste is also a way for him to perform his status as an elite by distinguishing his more refined taste from the more popular consensus. Such a truly refined aesthetic disposition, according to Bourdieu, refuses "any 'vulgar' surrender to easy seduction and collective enthusiasm" (27). In condescendingly observing that Laura likes the painting because it "demands less" of her and "satisfies [her] so easily," Corthell asserts his superior taste and thus social status, perhaps as a means of trying to put himself on an equal footing with her husband and his rival Jadwin, who has greater economic capital.

Jadwin's interruption of Laura and Corthell's encounter provides a dramatic reminder of the tension between economic and cultural capital that inheres in the painting and its potential fluctuation in value that makes it not unlike the wheat markets on which Jadwin speculates. As Corthell continues to denigrate the commodification of art in his attempt to educate Laura in proper aesthetic appreciation, Jadwin bursts into the room dramatically by throwing on the lights and announcing his conquest: he has made a huge profit in wheat by buying low and selling high. The narrator punctuates the drama of the scene with a strobing pulse of light: "the electrics all over the gallery flashed out in a sudden blaze, and Curtis Jadwin entered the room, crying out: 'Are you here, Laura? By George, my girl, we pulled it off, and I've cleaned up five—hundred—thousand—dollars'" (222). Suspecting there would soon be a wheat shortage because of various agricultural reports, Jadwin has bought a great deal of wheat at a low price and sold it for the five-hundred-thousand-dollar sum when word of a failed Argentinian crop leads to urgent European demand for wheat. This financial conquest was the result of a plan that Jadwin hatched with Gretry in the previous gallery scene, making this scene its structural mirror, with the moments of artistic appreciation bookended by moments of financial plotting.

This structural choice reflects the self-reinforcing cycle of economic and cultural capital that Norris identifies. Still coming to his senses after this enormous sale, Jadwin jovially compares the worth of art to the worth of commodities like wheat in a comment to Corthell, remarking, "take my advice. Buy May wheat. It'll beat art all hollow" (225). Jadwin's proclamation underscores the fact that there would be no gallery to muse over and contemplate if it were not for his involvement in risky global financial ventures. This intrusion also reminds readers of the stark contrast between the ways men and women of this era achieved social status. Though their means of acquiring cultural capital are different, the tenuousness of their standing is the same, dependent as it is on volatile markets of economic and aesthetic value. In an instant, Bouguereau could go out of style, the price of wheat could drop, and Laura could go back to being the parochial young woman she once was.

If for Norris Bouguereau represents crass conspicuous consumption, mercenary speculation, ambitious social climbing, and arbitrary valuation that ends up reinforcing itself, for Du Bois Bouguereau serves as a symbol of bourgeois norms that exclude African Americans from cultural and economic power. In an intertextual response to Norris's chiaroscuro-like rendering of the wheat trade, *The Quest of the Silver Fleece* brings to the forefront the economic and aesthetic contributions of Black Americans that Norris renders invisible. Du Bois's novel critiques cotton growers' devious machinations intended to limit their laborers' access to education and thereby ensure a continual supply of cheap labor. In one particularly explicit instance of such manipulation, landowner Harry Cresswell—who later marries Mary Taylor, a teacher in these schools—explains the downsides of a potential Black school to a fellow speculator, exclaiming, "See here! American cotton-spinning supremacy is built on cheap cotton," which, he observes, relies on cheap Black labor. If, Cresswell speculates, these Black laborers are educated, they will become "restless and discontented—that is, scarce and dear as workers" (85). Here, Cresswell's demeaning remarks reveal how he perceives education and expanded cultural capital as a serious threat to the "American cotton-spinning supremacy." Cresswell's logic connects aesthetic and economic power: if Black working- and middle-class people are able to participate more fully in the creation and consumption of American culture, then they might in turn become "restless and discontented" with their limited claim in the American economy. Furthermore, as Du Bois posits later in the novel, through art, literature, and music, Black artists could have more of a means to express that discontentment and enact change, because of the imaginative work that art can do to create empathy for victims of injustice. For Du Bois—and for many of his contemporaries who preached the politics of racial uplift—education promised a way to achieve independence, self-sufficiency, and dignity in the face of exploitative labor practices like those depicted in the above excerpt.[23] According to Maria Farland, Du Bois crafted *The Quest of the Silver Fleece* as a repudiation of racist scientific discourses that saw Black people as inherently culturally inferior, using the conventions of domestic fiction "to present genteel readers with evidence of blacks' capacity for self-control and self-mastery—the very mental aptitudes they were understood to lack" (1027). Because of its potential capacity to combat dehumanizing, racist stereotypes, cultural capital figures in Du Bois's work in many ways as prominently as economic capital.[24]

Du Bois's characters seek greater cultural capital by attempting to conform to norms of aesthetic appreciation, as is evident when Bles prepares an improvised home for Zora in an early scene in the novel. Significantly, this moment of ad hoc homemaking coincides with the pair's initial cultivation of their private crop of cotton. Planted on a seemingly undesirable piece of swampland, Bles and Zora's clandestine crop leaves them free to grow without becoming involved in an exploitative sharecropping agreement.[25] Bles arranges a little "nest" for Zora on a whim, to give her a comfortable spot from which to monitor the cotton. Just as Jadwin proudly displays his Bouguereau original in his home art gallery, so does Bles lovingly hang a Bouguereau reproduction in this tree house. Forming both an alternative means of production and an alternative model of domesticity, Bles improves the cozy tree house by "adding footrests to make the climbing easy, peep-holes east and west, a bit of carpet over the bark, and on the rough main trunk, a little picture in blue and gold of Bougereau's Madonna" (49). Bles's arrangements have their desired effect, as Zora is taken with the painting: "Zora sat hidden and alone in silent ecstasy. Bles peeped in—there was not room to enter: the girl was staring silently at the Madonna" (49).

Zora's instinctive posture of "silent ecstasy" conforms with late nineteenth-century attitudes about how to properly respond to a work of art, in the context of what Lawrence Levine calls the "sacralization of culture" that occurred in the United States in the second half of the nineteenth century. While shared cultural experiences like opera, symphony performances, or museum-going were widely popular and attended by Americans of all economic backgrounds early in the nineteenth century, these events became a more rarefied expression of cultural capital by the turn of the century that required a more reverential attitude from audiences: "audiences were to approach the masters and their works with proper respect and proper seriousness, for aesthetic and spiritual elevation rather than mere entertainment was the goal" (146). The rapt attention and moral enlightenment with which Zora approaches the Bouguereau print thus seems to emulate the requisite "proper respect" for culture that Levine argues audiences were expected to evince at the turn of the twentieth century.

Additionally, Bles's Bouguereau, unlike Jadwin's, is a reproduction, an allusion Du Bois makes to dramatize early twentieth-century Black Americans' aspirations to middle-class taste and their relative lack of access to the wealth that might enable them to purchase an original Bouguereau painting. The "little picture" reproduces and recontextualizes Bouguereau's work, just as Du Bois reproduces and reframes Norris's work in this intertextual dialogue about the role of art in determining economic power.[26] If a small reproduction of a painting can evoke the same response that the massive original can, then maybe in a way they are equally valuable forms of expression and appreciation—and, by extension, Du Bois's literary riff on Norris's epic of the wheat also deserves equal standing.

Further, Du Bois inserts Zora as a foil to Norris's Laura to claim equal or even superior status for his Black heroine. In contrast to Laura's studied response about Bouguereau, Zora evinces a seemingly "natural" appreciation for the artwork that aligns her with higher social status. The ostensible naturalness of taste is of course, as Bourdieu elucidates, a process of mystification that seeks to obscure the means by which class differences are established.[27] However, Du Bois taps into the presuppositions of his (likely well-educated) audience to position Zora as a possessor of this kind of "natural" taste, even as he deconstructs this ideology of taste elsewhere in the novel. In doing so, Du Bois makes visible and contradicts implicit assumptions about who can have "good" taste and who cannot. Like Laura Jadwin, Zora remarks on Bouguereau's rendering of skin tones, observing perhaps unwittingly the very "flesh-tints" that he was known for, again showing the aptness of her interpretation of the painting: "How white she is; she's as white as the lily, Bles; but—I'm sorry she's white—Bles, what's purity, just whiteness?" (49). The seemingly innocent, child-like nature of Zora's question masks the canniness of its insight into the power that aesthetic tropes have to essentialize socially constructed differences. Bouguereau's famed "flesh-tints" render exclusively white skin, and Du Bois calls out Norris's lack of commentary on the supremacy of whiteness in the aesthetic values of the time through Zora's response to the Madonna's whiteness. In recognizing the overwhelming whiteness of the painting, Zora's remarks observe how such images exclude people like her from being represented in art, but also function on a metafictional level to allow Du Bois to claim a space for Black artists and writers like himself to reframe norms of beauty and value.

Zora's question also pinpoints the insidious ways in which art produces and reinforces cultural associations of Blackness and whiteness with values like purity and impurity. Though Bles reassures Zora that purity is not just whiteness but rather "being good—just as good as a woman knows how" (49), in rejecting the cultural codes around whiteness, Bles simultaneously buys into gendered norms that require women to be pure and "good."[28] As we later find out, Zora's consternation about the question of purity is borne out of her anxiety that because she was raped by one of the powerful, white, cotton-growing patriarchs, she is no longer truly pure. Through Zora, Du Bois brings to life the damage that rigid ideology of "purity," "beauty," and "taste" can do. Visual coding in paintings like Bouguereau's, which implies that whiteness is equivalent to purity, further contributes to an unequal economic system that justifies the exploitation of "impure" Black bodies that worked the cotton fields and created unthinkable wealth for white planters and capitalists.[29] Du Bois shows the urgency of subverting white Eurocentric aesthetic and economic values, so that people like Zora will not look at a painting with "silent ecstasy" and feel as if they cannot live up to that standard, but rather will more frequently look at art and see themselves represented in it.[30]

By repeatedly juxtaposing these ekphrastic moments with economic and geopolitical uncertainties, Norris and Du Bois expose the ways in which art can alternately shore up or contest hegemonic power. Jadwin's expensive and ostentatious art collection represents his wealth, rising social status, and capacity to gamble on fluctuating economic and aesthetic values, while Zora and Bles's carefully guarded Bouguereau print represents the power of reproduction to democratize access to cultural capital. It is thus no coincidence that Zora's moment of reflection on the Bouguereau painting occurs just before Zora and Bles plant their first crop of monopoly-disrupting cotton. Recontextualizing the production of commodities like cotton, just as he reframes the Bouguereau painting, Du Bois implies that the means of production can be similarly democratized so that the profits do not accumulate exclusively in the hands of a few.

When Bles proposes the plan of planting a secret field of cotton to Zora, he frames this endeavor in terms of combating the pernicious inequality of the cotton industry, exclaiming,

> See! yonder lies the Silver Fleece spread across the brown back of the world; let's get a bit of it, and hide it here in the swamp, and comb it, and tend it, and make it the beautifullest bit of all. Then we can sell it, and send you to school. (23)

In mythologizing the humble cotton as comparable to the "golden fleece" sought by Jason and the Argonauts, Bles not only claims a place within a centuries-long literary tradition, but also reframes the actions of the landowning Cresswells. In their ecological approach to the novel that emphasizes the significance of land as offering "the possibility of freedom if it could be obtained" (465), Brett Clark and John Bellamy Foster point out that when Bles first associates the cotton with the myth of the Jason, his white teacher Mary Taylor corrects his assertion that "all yon golden fleece is Jason's now" by telling him the cotton belongs to the Cresswells.[31] However, this is precisely Bles's point because, as Clark and Foster explain, "Jason was a thief, just as the Cresswells were" (465). Here, Bles revises the Greek myth to position Jason as a villain rather than a hero, and the Cresswells as thieves of Indigenous land and Black labor, rather than entrepreneurial farmers. This revisionist mythology fits within Du Bois's larger project in the novel of recentering accepted aesthetic and economic narratives to question who and what is excluded and marginalized by cultural imperialism.

As Zora and Bles begin their planting, Du Bois reinforces the idea that whiteness is not a marker of inherent worth. The near-mythical heirloom seeds they plant come from a "big black chest," and the seeds themselves are "not the white-green seed which Bles had always known, but small, smooth black seeds" (50). Tellingly, the kernel of the promise of economic and cultural equality is not white but black, emphasizing the reproductive future potential of Blackness, if cultivated and cared for the same way that Bles and Zora lovingly tend their field. Like the seeds that promise to take root and grow, the field itself is a symbol of hope for Bles and Zora, a hope that is almost dashed when a week of rain nearly floods the newly planted cotton field. As it rains, Bles watches the weather "with leaden heart" because he anticipates the loss of "the fantasy, the hopes, the dreams" the cotton represents, wondering, "Was not this angry beating rain, this dull spiritless drizzle, this wild war of air and earth, but foretaste and prophecy of ruin and discouragement, of the utter futility of striving?" (80). However, Bles is surprised to discover that his agony is misplaced, because he finds that "the lagoon was dry," thanks to Zora's foresight in digging a trench to drain the excess water (81). Bles's vision of the cotton field rescued from the brink of disaster is anointed with beatific light, as if to emphasize the miraculous nature of the crop:

> A great sheet of dazzling sunlight swept the place, and beneath lay a mighty mass of olive green, thick, tall, wet, and willowy. The squares of cotton, sharp-edged, heavy, were just about to burst to bolls! And underneath, the land lay carefully drained and black! For one long moment he paused, stupid, agape with utter amazement, then leaned dizzily against a tree. (81)

Mimicking Zora's moment of "silent ecstasy" in front of Bouguereau's Madonna, Bles's "utter amazement" at the glorious crop of cotton that is "just about to burst to bolls" perpetuates the notion that this cotton crop is no mere commodity, but also an aesthetic object worthy of admiration and a symbol of future economic promise that disproves the "utter futility of striving."[32]

As the Silver Fleece grows into maturity and is harvested, Du Bois increasingly emphasizes its unusual beauty, aestheticizing this typically pragmatic commodity in order to transform it into a symbol of Black economic and cultural production that is inevitably exploited, appropriated, and exported globally by white people in positions of power. The visually lush description of the moment when the cotton bolls open and are ready for harvest typifies Du Bois's aestheticization of the commodity:

> A great white foam was spread upon its brown and green; the whole field was waving and shivering in the sunlight. A low cry of pleasure burst from [Zora's] lips; she forgot her weakness, and picking her way across the bridge, stood still amid the cotton that nestled about her shoulders, clasping it lovingly in her hands ... She stood on the island, ethereal, splendid, like some tall, dark, and gorgeous flower of the storied East. The green and white of the cotton billowed and foamed about her breasts; the red scarf burned upon her neck; the dark brown velvet of her skin pulsed warm and tremulous with the uprushing blood, and in the midnight depths of her great eyes flamed the mighty fires of long-concealed and new-born love. She did not move, but lifted both her dark hands, white with cotton; and then, as

he came, casting it suddenly to the winds, in tears and laughter she swayed and dropped quivering in his arms. And all the world was sunshine and peace. (83)

Du Bois renders the cotton in impressionistic patches of color, describing the striking effect of the "great white foam" against the "brown and green" of the field. As Zora takes in the scene, she becomes part of the tableau, "ethereal, splendid, like some tall, dark, and gorgeous flower of the storied East." Although Du Bois's allusion to the "storied East" here appears to veer into Orientalist territory, considered within his larger body of work, this remark seems more characteristic of the Pan-Africanism that he celebrates elsewhere, particularly in his novel *Dark Princess*. The rich beauty of Zora's "dark brown velvet" skin is contrasted with the whiteness of the cotton, as if a defiant rebuttal to the whiteness she identified in Bouguereau's Madonna. With the sunshine crowning Zora in a peaceful glow, she becomes a sort of Madonna herself, swept up in her "new-born love" for the metaphorical child she nurtured into life that offers a hope for the future, the Silver Fleece.

Of course, in Du Bois's post-Reconstruction-era Alabama, Zora is not permitted to retain ownership over her secret field of exceptionally beautiful cotton for long, and the aesthetically immaculate Silver Fleece is forcibly taken from her in a ruthless maneuver that signifies both the economic exploitation of Black labor and the cultural appropriation of Black artists' work. After harvesting the first crop of the Silver Fleece, Zora brings a sample of it to show to people in town. All are stunned by the cotton's striking quality: "The cotton lay in silken handfuls, clean and shimmering, with threads full two inches long. The idlers, black and white, clustered round, gazing at it, and fingering it with repeated exclamations of astonishment" (99). Echoing Bles's "utter amazement" with their "repeated exclamations of astonishment," the crowd's response to the almost sacred cotton reinforces its luminous aesthetic aura. Determined to buy Zora's fine cotton but unwilling to fairly compensate her for it, Harry Cresswell fabricates a debt that Zora owes because of her mother's back rent, even though neither she nor Zora has a sharecropping contract with the Cresswells. Cresswell then takes the two bales of the Silver Fleece to pay for the imagined debt in a chapter whose title captures the full weight of this violation: "The Rape of the Fleece."

Zora's reflection on this exploitation of her labor reverses the light-filled imagery that had characterized her first harvest and echoes Norris's vision of an unavoidable centripetal force dragging people in:

> They had stolen the Silver Fleece ... Somewhere in the world sat a great dim Injustice which had veiled the light before her young eyes, just as she raised them to the morning. With the veiling, death had come into her heart. And yet, they should not kill her; they should not enslave her. A desperate resolve to find some way up toward the light, if not to it, formed itself within her. She would not fall into the pit opening before her. (101)

Du Bois's characterization of the dark "pit" that Zora sees growing in front of her provides further evidence of the intertextuality between *The Quest of the Silver Fleece* and *The Pit*. While the "great dim Injustice" that Zora imagines calls to mind the deterministic themes of Norris's "resistless" Pit, she does not see her fall into this pit of capitalist exploitation as inevitable, but rather something that she feels a "desperate resolve" to fight against.[33] The motif of light and dark Du Bois establishes here—with the "veiling" of the light before her eyes and her desire to find "some way up toward the light"—again plays on the contrast between white and Black established when Zora took in the pure whiteness of Bouguereau's Madonna. Du Bois's "veiling" here invokes not a bridal accessory but rather a funeral shroud that threatens to put out the light of a future. While Zora here tries to fend off the darkness, Du Bois returns to this schema of light and shadow in his conclusion, as I will discuss at the end of this chapter, eventually lifting the ominous veil for good in order to symbolically distribute the light of economic and cultural promise to all.

Artistic Intrigues

Du Bois comments more overtly on art's political potential and its indirect connections with financial maneuvers later in the novel, when a Black woman's pseudonymously submitted sculpture wins the top prize at an "all-Southern art exhibit" at the Corcoran Art Gallery. A politician's wife organizes and judges the exhibit; by unwittingly granting the top award to a Black female artist, she becomes associated with desegregationist politics, and threatens her husband's conservative bona fides (187). This political intrigue mirrors the tensions Du Bois sees between his aesthetic project and Norris's and dramatizes the consequences of ignoring the political content of art. Art, Du Bois insists, is not politically neutral or purely concerned with aesthetics. Cultivating a reputation for the realistic nature of one's (exclusively white) "flesh-tints" is just as political as the work of a Black artist using the human form to create empathy for the disenfranchised. Whereas Norris depicts visual art as something to be consumed as a marker of imperial and economic power, here Du Bois imagines art's subversive political potential by giving readers a birds-eye view of the confluence of individual choices that erupt into political chaos. By switching the narrative point of view from politicians to philanthropists to artists to innocent bystanders, Du Bois pulls apart the currents that collide to create an economic and ideological whirlpool, emphasizing that it is human agency driving the downward pull of global capitalism, rather than merely the deterministic inanimate forces of nature, as Norris imagines.

The convoluted nature of this episode, which entangles several different plot threads and connects many of the novel's characters in unlikely ways, microcosmically represents the insidious entanglement that Du Bois sees between economic imperialism, political power, and artistic representation. The villainous episode begins with a battle between two cotton capitalists—Harry Cresswell and John Vanderpool—over a French ambassadorship. Prior to this moment, the well-meaning but ultimately self-serving New York philanthropist Mrs. Vanderpool makes morally compromising choices to win her husband the nomination that come at the expense of the grown-up, accomplished Bles specifically, and African American political representation more widely.[34] Upon the urging of Zora, who was working for her as a maid and travel companion, Mrs. Vanderpool had previously agreed to use her considerable political influence to back Bles's appointment as Register of the Treasury. When it became clear that supporting Bles's appointment would undermine John Vanderpool's nomination for ambassador, Mrs. Vanderpool conspired with Bles's former fiancée, Caroline Wynn, to indirectly sabotage his chances for the appointment—which subsequently goes to Samuel Stillings, whom Caroline then marries instead of Bles. Mrs. Vanderpool, whose name is suggestive of Miss Vanhorn's in Woolson's *Anne*, acts in surreptitious ways reminiscent of the allegorically geopolitical "maneuvering" of Anne Douglas's relatives and friends, as discussed in the previous chapter. Zora, who unlike Anne is aware of this maneuvering, feels rightfully betrayed by Mrs. Vanderpool's machinations. Zora resigns her job in disgust, protesting dejectedly to Mrs. Vanderpool, "I do not blame you ... I blame the world." In Mrs. Vanderpool's callous response, Du Bois emphasizes both the ubiquitousness of her cynical attitude as well as its wide-reaching, global consequences: "'I am the world,'

Mrs. Vanderpool uttered harshly, then suddenly laughed" (179). Perhaps as a form of penance, in a parting gesture Mrs. Vanderpool writes Zora a generous check to be used in furthering Black education in the South and gifts Zora the beautifully embroidered wedding dress that was made from the Silver Fleece and worn by Mary Cresswell.

Intent on winning this international political post for her husband after securing his nomination, Mrs. Vanderpool learns that his opponent has a strong edge with the Southern voters who might confirm his nomination, and thus determines that her "task was to discredit the Cresswells with the Southerners. It was not a work to her liking, but the die was cast and she refused to contemplate defeat" (187). Maneuvering not in the realm of politics or the economy but rather in the world of culture, Mrs. Vanderpool realizes in a "flash of inspiration" that she can undermine Mrs. Cresswell's work with an "all-Southern art exhibit" in DC's Corcoran Gallery by underhandedly politicizing the event. Mrs. Vanderpool plots to insert racial politics without Mrs. Cresswell's knowledge:

> None suspected a possible intrusion of the eternal race issue for no Negroes were allowed in the Corcoran exhibit or school. This Mrs. Vanderpool easily ascertained and a certain sense of justice combined in a curious way with her political intrigue to bring about the undoing of Mary Cresswell. (187)

Here, Du Bois presents wry commentary on the inadvertent way in which progress often gets made: the "certain sense of justice" that Mrs. Vanderpool feels when she integrates and elevates the work of a Black artist is secondary to her mission of "political intrigue."

Caught in the crosshairs of Mrs. Vanderpool's "political intrigue" is the talented Black sculptor Caroline Stillings, née Wynn, with whom Mrs. Vanderpool colluded in order to sink Bles's political appointment, and whom Mrs. Vanderpool recruits to covertly enter the all-white Southern art exhibit. Even before becoming a pawn in Mrs. Vanderpool's plot, Caroline Wynn Stillings faced exclusion from participation in US high culture because of her race, as the narrator describes: "The world had dealt cruelly with the young dreams and youthful ambitions of the girl; partly with its usual heartlessness, partly with that cynical and deadening reserve fund which it has today for its darker peoples" (137). In the economy of cruelty that Du Bois imagines here, he identifies a "cynical and deadening reserve fund" devoted to the demoralization and oppression of people of color, as if the economy that profits from their unpaid or underpaid labor in turn uses that surplus to further grind down those exploited by it. Although she was "brilliant and well-trained" and "had a real talent for sculpture," Caroline "found nearly all careers closed to her" (137). Such experiences surely color Mrs. Stillings's reticence to enter the Southern art exhibit when approached by the wily Mrs. Vanderpool:

> Mrs. Stillings did not intend to exhibit as she was sure she would not be welcome. She had had a bust accepted by the Corcoran Art Gallery once, and when they found out she was colored they returned it. But if she were especially invited? That would make a difference, although even then the line would be drawn somehow. (188)

In addition to the irony of an "all-Southern art exhibit" prohibiting participation from such a large portion of the Southern population that also fueled the region's economic growth, Mrs. Stillings's alienation from institutions of high art explains why William J. Wilson perhaps felt the need to create a fictional gallery of African American art, or why Zora and Bles resorted to gazing appreciatively at a reproduction of a Bouguereau painting, rather than an original in a gallery. By entangling Mrs. Stillings's exclusion with Mrs. Vanderpool's quest for political power, Du Bois again reminds readers that those whose images and cultural contributions are kept out of the halls of power are also excluded from shaping the narratives that drive political ideology—an exclusion with global consequences.

Despite Mrs. Stillings's resistance and fear of institutional racism, Mrs. Vanderpool convinces her to put up "a fight" and suggests submitting her artwork under her name before she was married, "Wynn"—the private purpose of which is, of course, to slip a piece of African American art past the organizer Mrs. Cresswell, undetected. This tactic proves successful, and Mrs. Vanderpool thus tricks Mrs. Cresswell, whose husband is known for his segregationist politics, into championing work by an African American artist:

> When Mrs. Vanderpool suggested the name of "Miss Wynn" to Mrs. Cresswell among a dozen others, for special invitation, there was nothing in its sound to distinguish it from the rest of the names, and the invitation went duly. As a result there came to the exhibit a little group called "The Outcasts," which was really a masterful thing and sent the director, Signor Alberti, into hysterical commendation ... Mrs. Cresswell was enthusiastic and voluble for the bit of sculpture, and it finally won the vote for the first prize. (188)

The title of "The Outcasts" that Caroline Wynn Stillings gives to her sculpture acknowledges her former exclusion from the halls of the

Corcoran Gallery, and also allows Du Bois to metaphorically put on a pedestal his central concern in speaking back to the work of white male naturalists like Norris. The statue embodies the way in which Black cultural production has been "outcast" from emerging artistic canons of literature and visual art.

The Southern art exhibit backfires on Mrs. Cresswell in exactly the way Mrs. Vanderpool intended, right at the moment of Harry Cresswell's potential confirmation as ambassador to France, a plot choice that stresses the international consequences of underestimating the political content of art and that ties Stillings's artistic exclusion to Bles's previous sidelining for the Treasury position. As the "boom for Cresswell as ambassador to France was almost visible in the air," a random woman rains on Mary Cresswell's parade by approaching her and whispering, "Mrs. Cresswell, have you heard the gossip?" She conveys the spreading rumor about Caroline Wynn's racial identity, further goading Mary Cresswell by adding that "Some are whispering that you brought her in purposely to force social equality" (188). Mary Cresswell immediately sees the repercussions of this rumor: "She saw ruin ahead—to think of a black girl taking a prize at an all-Southern art exhibit!" (188). And indeed, ruin comes for her. After her husband attends the "sub-committee on the cotton schedule" (191) and learns from his business partners about the infiltration of an African American artist into his wife's exhibit and the subsequent scandal over his presumed support of racial integration, he returns home and pronounces her fate. He states matter-of-factly,

> Of course, after your art exhibit and the scene of last night, Mary, it will be impossible for us to live longer together . . . I have seen the crisis approaching for some time, and the Negro business settles it . . . I have now decided to send you to my home in Alabama, to my father or your brother. I am sure you will be happier there. (193)

Thus, Du Bois illustrates how a political "crisis" that could seem inevitable or unpreventable was instead the result of many individual actions: Mary Cresswell's cynical organization of the all-Southern art exhibit to promote her husband's political future; Mrs. Vanderpool's underhanded plotting to undermine the exhibit; Mrs. Stillings's willingness to go along with the plan in spite of her reservations; the public's outcry at the racial integration of the show; and Harry Cresswell's repudiation of his wife in the face of political backlash. As Du Bois demonstrates, economic inequality is not just something that happens through the invisible hand of the free market, but rather is a hierarchy created and reinforced through hundreds of thousands of individual choices made in the realms of both the economy and culture. The consequences of these choices accrue and compound like interest. Sandwiched in between chapters that dramatize Washington DC machinations over economic policy and labor laws, this episode is structurally similar to the scenes in *The Pit* that are set in the Jadwins' home art gallery because of the way it punctuates the novel's more overtly political moments. Rather than serving as a brief diversion from the economic plots of these novels, both scenes prove their aesthetic topics to be inextricably linked to the larger global economic context. Jadwin's announcement about cornering the wheat market booms against the walls of their home art gallery, while whispers about a cotton baron's potential ambassadorship reverberate through the halls of the Corcoran Gallery, a metaphorical echo chamber that amplifies the role that artistic representation has in naturalizing the whiteness of imperial power. Ultimately, Mrs. Vanderpool's success in entering Mrs. Stillings's artwork in the all-Southern exhibit disrupts Harry Cresswell's appointment. While this maneuver somewhat stalls the expanding political power of this cotton magnate, it also inadvertently allows Cresswell to continue wielding control over the Farmers' League, to persist in cornering the cotton market, and to manipulate cotton prices for his own benefit.

Mrs. Stillings's modest sculptural collection of "The Outcasts" gives shape to the power of African American cultural production to identify injustice and threaten post-Reconstruction white supremacy, but, as this incident shows, voicing such inequities carries economic and political risks. Thus, Du Bois dramatizes both the ways in which African Americans have been systematically excluded from US high culture and the political and economic consequences of such exclusion. The "cynical and deadening reserve fund" mentioned earlier here seems to strike all of Du Bois's lead Black characters with indiscriminate cruelty in one swirling blow (137). Bles loses out on a prominent political appointment, Zora is forced to recognize the blithely self-serving ethos of the white people she is surrounded by and loses her job over it, and Caroline gets caught up in political maneuvering in which she turns out to be a mere pawn in the white political elites' game, and she is humiliated by being asked to withdraw her sculpture from the exhibition when it is discovered she is a woman of color. Whereas for Norris such damage is wrought by the random, faceless, insurmountable force of "some sudden eddy spinning outward" (73), for Du Bois human actions drive the churning cycle of imperial conquest and economic inequality. The "cynical and deadening reserve fund" lines the pockets of opportunists like Mrs. Vanderpool.

Concluding Studies in Contrast

Both *The Pit* and *The Quest of the Silver Fleece* end with visually evocative scenes that rely on light and contrast to create two different concluding silhouettes: financial institutions and human figures. These images frame these authors' responses to the capitalist cycle; Norris presents a haunting image of the looming inanimate presence of a financial monolith that will suck everyone into a narrowly defined path, while Du Bois captures the warmth of human connection and communal labor that promises to bring light to formerly dark places. At the end of *The Pit*, the Jadwins find themselves financially ruined and headed west for a new start after Curtis's hubristic corner on wheat fails. *The Quest of the Silver Fleece* ends with Zora and Bles reunited in the fateful swamp where they first grew the Silver Fleece, both having been battered by the political and economic schemes of white cotton growers and speculators. With their verbal, thematic, and visual echoes of earlier scenes, in these concluding scenes Du Bois and Norris formally replicate the spinning centripetal force of global capitalism, forcing readers to experience the difficulty of escaping its pull. Du Bois and Norris confront readers with the reality that our role as consumers of art makes us complicit in the process by which dominant narratives are reproduced and popularized.

In *The Pit*'s conclusion, Norris integrates repetitious language and structural elements to imply that the Jadwins will not be able to escape capitalism's gravitational pull, despite their best efforts. This closing scene of the novel follows a climactic chapter depicting the failure of Jadwin's corner on wheat. Prior to this, Jadwin bought nearly all available supplies of wheat to corner the market and drive prices up. However, in order to maintain these high prices and be able to make a profit when he eventually sells, Jadwin must continue buying up wheat, taking out heavy mortgages on all of his real estate holdings to finance this speculation. When news of ample good wheat harvests breaks, indicating a sharp increase in the available supply, Jadwin is unable to maintain the unusually high prices, and his corner busts in a dramatic battle on the trading floor, witnessed as avidly as an opera by a packed visitors' gallery.[35] As the novel draws to a close and Laura and Jadwin prepare to move out west to start their lives anew after this financial failure, they appear to have been suitably chastened: Jadwin, for his greed, and Laura, for her vanity. Norris introduces an echo motif, as Laura reflects on the rippling effects of Jadwin's failed corner of the wheat:

> The great failure had precipitated smaller failures, and the aggregate of smaller failures had pulled down one business house after another. For weeks afterward, the successive crashes were like the shock and reverberation of undermined buildings toppling to their ruin. An important bank had suspended payment, and hundreds of depositors had found their little fortunes swept away. (367)

Recalling a passage from earlier in the novel in which "an unexpected caprice" from the "swirling inner current" (73) of the Pit resulted in disastrous repercussions all over Europe and Asia, here Norris alludes to the fact that Jadwin's greedy speculation on wheat is indeed one such "unexpected caprice."

Nonetheless, Laura persists in deflecting any responsibility for these disruptions, relying on the same passive tone to characterize the global economy that Norris used previously:

> But Laura would not admit her husband was in any way to blame. He had suffered, too. She repeated to herself his words, again and again: "The wheat cornered itself. I simply stood between two sets of circumstances. The wheat cornered me, not I the wheat." And all those millions and millions of bushels of Wheat were gone now ... the Wheat that had intervened like a great torrent to drag her husband from her side and drown him in the roaring vortices of the Pit, had passed on, resistless, along its ordered and predetermined courses from West to East. (368)

Personifying the wheat in order to justify her husband's actions, Laura situates Jadwin as helpless and drowning in the "resistless" "great torrent" of wheat in order to naturalize the very unnatural fissures in the economy caused by men like him.[36] Cressler, Laura's family friend and a reformed speculator who eventually fatally succumbs to his former speculation addiction, warned of such dangers earlier in the novel, pinning the poisonous and wide-reaching effects of speculation directly on men like Jadwin:

> Those fellows in the Pit don't own the wheat; never even see it. Wouldn't know what to do with it if they had it. They don't care in the least about the grain. But there are thousands upon thousands of farmers out here in Iowa and Kansas or Dakota who do,

and hundreds of thousands of poor devils in Europe who care even more than the farmer. I mean the fellows who raise the grain, and the other fellows who eat it. It's life or death for either of them. And right between these two comes the Chicago speculator, who raises or lowers the price out of all reason, for the benefit of his pocket. (115)

Without deflection or passive voice, Cressler does not mystify the Pit in the way that Jadwin and Laura do, but instead states clearly that it is the "Chicago speculator" who "raises or lowers the price" of wheat, with deleterious consequences for American farmers and European consumers.

While at that earlier moment in the novel, before her marriage to Jadwin, Laura was "immensely interested" in Cressler's lesson on the "workings of political economy" (116), at the end of the novel she seems to have forgotten or rejected this interpretation in favor of Jadwin's vision of the global economy. Continuing to contemplate the wheat corner, she faces a question that Cressler once gave her the answer to:

For a moment, vague, dark perplexities assailed her, questionings as to the elemental forces, the forces of demand and supply that ruled the world. This huge resistless Nourisher of the Nations—why was it that it could not reach the People, could not fulfil its destiny, unmarred by all this suffering, unattended by all this misery? She did not know. (368)

Because Jadwin's image of the Pit as a "huge resistless Nourisher of Nations" is a more compelling narrative to Laura, she forgets or ignores the competing narrative once told to her by Cressler—that "all this misery" could be avoided if speculators would just stop trying to over- or under-inflate the price of commodities, and instead "keep wheat at an average, legitimate value" (115). As Norris articulates, the narratives we create and choose to believe have real, global, financial consequences. Aestheticizing the Pit as a system of "elemental forces" and "roaring vortices," almost invoking the aesthetic of the sublime characteristic of nineteenth-century Romantic painters, makes it easier to deny responsibility for the damage wrought by capitalism and imperialism, and easier to repeat the same greed-driven mistakes over and over again.[37]

Norris draws attention to the recursive nature of Laura's line of thinking by putting her face to face with an image she saw in the first chapter of the novel, the "monstrous sphinx" of the Board of Trade building (39, 369). Immediately following her questioning about the misery inflicted by global capitalism, Laura has the "strange sense of having lived through this scene, these circumstances, once before" (368). What follows is a visually and thematically evocative passage: two paragraphs replicated almost verbatim from the first chapter, a haunting conclusion that emphasizes the cyclical nature of economic power's seduction. Laura looks out of her carriage window and sees the Chicago skyline receding behind her:

> On either side of the vista in converging lines stretched the tall office buildings, lights burning in a few of their windows even yet. Over the end of the street the lead-coloured sky was broken by a pale faint haze of light, and silhouetted against this rose a sombre mass, unbroken by any glimmer, rearing a black and formidable façade against the blur of the sky behind it.

> And this was the last impression of the part of her life that that day brought to a close; the tall gray office buildings, the murk of rain, the haze of light in the heavens, and raised against it, the pile of the Board of Trade building, black, monolithic, crouching on its foundations like a monstrous sphinx with blind eyes, silent, grave—crouching there without a sound, without sign of life, under the night and the drifting veil of rain. (368–9)[38]

Norris's description of the Board of Trade Building combines the artistic technique of aerial or atmospheric perspective, in which depth is rendered through sharpening of the foreground and blurring of the background, with one-point perspective, a drawing technique that uses a central vanishing point where parallel lines converge to create a sense of three-dimensionality.[39] The "pale faint haze of light" and the "blur of the sky" invokes atmospheric perspective, while the "converging lines" of the office building invoke one-point perspective. Both of these artistic strategies serve to emphasize the object in the foreground, the "black and formidable façade" of the Board of Trade Building that is "silhouetted" against the hazy sky, capturing just how large the global financial markets that the building metonymically represents still loom in the Jadwins' lives.

Norris's visual vocabulary here anticipates cityscapes of modernist painters like Georgia O'Keeffe and Charles Sheeler, who two decades after *The Pit* was published used the "haze of light" and strong "converging lines" to depict that very contemporary subject matter, the urban skyscraper.[40] It is telling that in the closing image of his novel, the former painter Norris draws on modern, forward-thinking aesthetic strategies to capture this scene, rather than, say, the sentimental and nostalgic "flesh-tints" of Bouguereau's genre paintings. In doing so, Norris aligns his own aesthetic vision with artists who are concerned with the future and recognize the danger of being sucked into repeating the past perpetually. Norris's self-aware artistic intervention replaces Jadwin's image of the senseless, faceless, yet vitality-filled Pit with this image of the silent, powerful sphinx that crouches inert "without sign of life." A potent symbol of exotic mystery and hidden wisdom, the sphinx is a symbol that has been invoked by centuries of writers—including Elizabeth Stuart Phelps, who repurposes the sphinx as an image of feminine power and sacrifice, as discussed in Chapter 1. Situated as it is so close to Laura's unanswerable question of why it was that the globally circulating wheat "could not fulfil its destiny, unmarred by all this suffering, unattended by all this misery?" (368), the sphinx almost seems to hold silently within it the answer to this riddle. However, since the sphinx remains "blind" and "silent," and recedes on the horizon away from Laura as well as readers, Norris implies that we are not getting any closer to resolving the economic and cultural inequalities that are established and exacerbated through the global flow of capital. The answer to the riddle will always be obscured by the aesthetic techniques—in this case, narrowing perspective—implemented to depict it.

Structurally similar to *The Pit*, *The Quest of the Silver Fleece* ends where it began: in the swamp where Bles and Zora planted their precious cotton crop. In contrast to Norris's overpowering, back-lit urban landscape, Du Bois constructs a rural tableau diffuse with life-affirming light that signals a more optimistic path forward for his characters than Norris envisions. Much has transpired at this point since the all-Southern art exhibit escapades: Zora, armed with the treasured gown made from the first crop of the Silver Fleece and a ten-thousand-dollar check from the philanthropic and remorseful Mrs. Vanderpool, returns to Alabama from New York. There, she decides to buy the swamp and surrounding land from the Cresswells to establish a farm sustained by communal Black labor, and to secure the future of the school for Black sharecroppers' children, the very school that she and Bles once attended. Zora is temporarily successful in her endeavor, much to the chagrin of white landowners like the Cresswells who lose Black laborers to Zora's more equitable and independent farming arrangement. However, in a brutally violent episode, the school is burned down by an angry white mob, irate that the school accepted poor white students and thus became racially integrated. Meanwhile, Bles becomes thoroughly disenchanted with the insincere nature of DC politics, and, stung by his failure to win the Registry of the Treasury appointment, also returns to Alabama. Thus, the closing of the novel leaves its protagonists even more bruised and battered by the world than the broke and westward-bound Jadwins.

In her grief at her quashed vision for the future, Zora nearly surrenders to deterministic imagery reminiscent of the language that Norris uses to describe the "resistless" force of the Pit, a deliberate warning from Du Bois of the dangers of indulging in narratives that encourage the ceding of one's agency to ostensibly immovable societal structures. Moved by some silent, insistent urging, Zora is drawn to don the gown made from the Silver Fleece and wander her way to the ravaged and recovering swamp:

> With trembling hands she drew the Silver Fleece round her . . . She heard a calling in the swamp, and the shadow of Elspeth seemed to hover over her, claiming her for her own, dragging her down, down . . . She rushed through the swamp. The lagoon lay there before her presently, gleaming in the darkness—cold and still, and in it swam an awful shape. (237)

Like the "great torrent" that Laura imagines worked to "drag" Jadwin down until it could "drown him in the roaring vortices of the Pit" (368), the swamp and the memory of Zora's mother Elspeth "hover over her, claiming her for her own, dragging her down, down." Using identical language of "dragging," Du Bois revises Norris's image of a dark, indiscriminate, ever-hungry void with a similarly haunting image of a dark, life-filled yet inert presence, in which swims "an awful shape"—perhaps Zora's own reflection mirrored back at her, a figure ready to emerge redeemed and reborn.

Like Norris, Du Bois reverts to earlier themes in his novel to conclude on a recursive note. When Bles appears almost mystically by Zora's side, their dialogue recycles the previous conversation they had initiated by the Bouguereau reproduction, on the topic of purity. Stunned to see Bles appear by her side in this almost spiritual moment, but unable to fully trust the hope of a romantic reunion, Zora insists to Bles that she knows, based on rumors she has heard, that he is going to marry a young woman named Emma. When Bles informs Zora that he is in fact in love with someone else, Zora immediately inquires, "'Who is it? . . . And is'—she struggled at the word madly—'is she pure?'" (238). In a reclamation of the painful conversation in their youth when Zora asked, "what's purity, just whiteness?" (49), Bles assures Zora that the woman he loves is "more than pure" and that he "is not worthy of her" (238). In an outpouring of natural forces that ends the novel on a visually exuberant note, the swamp seems to effervesce with the love between Zora and Bles, and Zora responds to Bles's confession with a proposal:

> Then at last illumination dawned upon her blindness. She stood very still and lifted up her eyes. The swamp was living, vibrant, tremulous. There where the first long note of night lay shot with burning crimson, burst in sudden radiance the wide beauty of the moon. There pulsed a glory in the air. Her little hands groped and wandered over his close-curled hair, and she sobbed, deep voiced: "Will you—marry me, Bles?" (238)

Whereas Norris's closing image repeats earlier language with almost no difference in a formal gesture to the repetitive determinism of *The Pit*'s plot, Du Bois calls back to Zora's inquiry about purity and adjusts the narrative. Maria Farland observes the way in which Du Bois challenges the discourses of colorism and purity in this conclusion, suggesting, "The restoration of Zora's 'purity' (despite her impure past), and the elevation of the dark-skinned Zora over the virginal, pale-faced Emma, departed markedly from the sentimental novels of Du Bois's contemporaries," in effect turning "the cultural hierarchies of his racist opponents on their heads" (1032). No longer trusting in the norms and standards defined by self-serving white politicians and businessmen, Bles now understands that the purity of Zora's love was in front of him all along.

Furthermore, the imagery of this scene reflects the dissolution of the definition of purity that associates it exclusively with whiteness, to suggest a more equitable distribution of goodness, truth, and beauty.[41] Unlike the foreboding "lead-coloured sky" that is only faintly illuminated by a "haze of light" nearly stanched out by the "sombre mass" of the Board of Trade building, the night sky hovering over Du Bois's swamp is "shot with burning crimson," bursting with the "sudden radiance" of the "wide beauty of the moon." Whereas Norris's sphinx-like building crouches "without sign of life," the swamp is "living, vibrant, tremulous," with a pulsing "glory in the air."[42] Du Bois lifts the veil that Zora once imagined lowering down on her, and rather than shining a singular beam of light on the reunited couple, the moon disperses a celebratory glow, evenly distributed over the whole swath of land. Anointing Zora as a Black Madonna in contrast to Bouguereau's white Madonna, Du Bois crowns her with light that spreads beyond her immediate vicinity to softly illuminate everything around her, a variation on typical Bouguereau iconography such as *The Madonna of the Lilies*, in which only the Madonna and her sacred child are granted the light of a thin, sharply defined, neatly contained halo. Aesthetically reiterating Du Bois's thematic message of equality and community with such widely diffuse illumination, this final image offers hope in the promise of the future, with Bles and Zora preparing to marry, and the swamp once again bursting forth with the fruits of Black self-determination.

In conclusion, through their visually rich narratives about wheat and cotton that strategically juxtapose financial and aesthetic events, Norris and Du Bois make the case for the inextricability of economic and cultural capital. When commodities like wheat and cotton travel globally, they carry with them images of power and value that are likewise bought and sold, consumed and reconstituted. Literature, as both these authors recognize, is entangled in this capitalist cycle as both a commodity that is exchanged and a reference point in the "interminable circuit of inter-legitimation" (Bourdieu 45) that functions to establish hierarchies of taste and class. In these closing scenes, Norris's and Du Bois's visual strategies for capturing their characters' struggles self-consciously point to their own artistic contributions in depicting the whirling cycle of capitalist exploitation. Du Bois and Norris thus make visible the artistic strategies through which narratives of economic success or failure are variously constructed, dramatized, vilified, or valorized. Inserting himself deliberately in the "circuit of inter-legitimation" through his intertextual dialogue with Norris, Du Bois presents a possible way out of the soul-sucking cycle of capitalist acquisition and competition through the refraction, revision, and democratization of more established works of art, centering Black cultural and economic production as crucial to the United States' future as a world power.

Notes

1. As Edward Said writes, "the enterprise of empire depends upon the *idea* of *having an empire* . . . and all kinds of preparations are made for it within a culture; then in turn imperialism acquires a kind of coherence, a set of experiences, and a presence of ruler and ruled alike within a culture" (*Culture and Imperialism* 11).

2. According to Robin Kelley, Haiti has long served as a central coordinate in the Black diasporic imaginary because of its "heroic history of becoming the first black republic as well as the first nation in the Western Hemisphere to abolish slavery" (1064).
3. As Sven Beckert explains, cotton prices spiked after the 1791 Haitian Revolution, which "all but halt[ed] production of commodities for world markets, including cotton" (96), had serious economic and political consequences for the European manufacturers who relied on the Haitian supply of cotton, and indirectly led to increased cotton production in the US to assure an alternative supply (102). Beckert elucidates the connection between the 1791 Revolution in Haiti and the beginnings of the US cotton industry: "Revolution [in Haiti] thus in one stroke both brought needed growing expertise to the United States and increased the financial incentive for American planters to grow cotton" (102).
4. According to David Pletcher, "between 1865 and 1898 U.S. exports increased from $281 million to $1,231 million, imports from $239 million to $616 million" (9).
5. While these extremely wealthy few were often denigrated as "robber barons," historically they also made sizeable contributions to American cultural institutions. As historian John Gordon explains, "the United States in its early days had been a cultural backwater, and artists and writers routinely went to Europe to study. By the turn of the twentieth century, the United States was as great a cultural and intellectual power as it was an economic one, largely thanks to the often poorly educated men who are remembered today as robber barons" (262). Gordon notes that during this time, exponential growth in railroads, steel, and other manufacturing meant that wealth accumulated rapidly in the hands of an elite few who were propelled into the upper classes of society, creating a new class of nouveau riche Americans with "enormous new personal fortunes, of an order of magnitude quite undreamed of before" (260).
6. Some of these so-called robber barons included: "George Peabody (the Peabody Museums at Harvard and Yale, among much else), Peter Cooper (the Cooper Union, still the only major college in the United States not to charge tuition), and John Jacob Astor, whose Astor Library is today the core of the New York Public Library, the second largest library in the country and the largest privately financed library in the world" (Gordon 261).
7. See David Teague for more about Norris's artistic career.
8. Peter Collins concurs with this assessment of Norris's work of naturalizing the economy, comparing Norris with Dreiser in order to conclude that "one of Norris and Dreiser's most important contributions to economic discourse is their drawing attention to the terrifying inhumanity of Darwinian nature, and its indifference to the individual. Even as they represent the free market as natural, they suggest that nature is not

always nurturing—that a commitment to a 'natural' marketplace might clash with a commitment to the value of the individual" (577).

9. Richard Perren attributes the increase in US exports to Britain to an early adoption of roller milling technology (423). Hunter suggests that inter-imperial conflict had a role in the United States' adoption of these new wheat-milling technologies: "Imperial warfare accelerated economic developments in the mid-Atlantic region, particularly the adoption of new technologies and regional specialization" (526). See also Sharp and Weisdorf, who argue for a longer history of integrated wheat markets between the US and Britain than is typically accounted for. Ejrnæs et al. note that "wheat from the Americas and India gained an increasing share of the market, crowding out most of the European wheat by the end of the nineteenth century" (146).

10. Although Norris does not mention the opera by name in the text of the novel, editors Joseph R. McElrath, Jr. and Gwendolyn Jones mention in their footnotes that "Norris cited *Faust*" in a manuscript version of *The Pit*, but later "canceled the reference, possibly because his subsequent descriptions of the opera were derived from memory rather than the libretto and not accurate in all cases" (371).

11. Biographers McElrath and Crisler quote what they call Norris's "politically incorrect" writing from Cuba during the Spanish–American War, where he describes "Anglo-Saxons" approvingly as "the race whose blood instinct is the acquiring of land," elaborating that "it was impossible not to know their feeling, glorying, arrogant, the fine brutal arrogance of the Anglo-Saxon" (313).

12. Keith Byerman deems Du Bois's fiction and other literary work as "not of high quality in standard literary terms," even though it asks "key questions about the nature of African-American writing" (58). On the other hand, Maurice Lee defends Du Bois's sociological influence as a necessary pairing with the more Romantic elements of his fiction in order to articulate the "*Realpolitik* of power and difference that affected African Americans" (393). Furthermore, Maria Farland argues that Du Bois applies contemporary scientific discourse in a literary context in a process of "transvaluation" that "employ[s] the categories of the dominant scientific discourse, but work[s] to change the valuations attached to them." In *The Quest of the Silver Fleece*, Du Bois transforms "racialist concepts and categories," "putting them to unanticipated use in a domestic fiction of racial uplift" (Farland 1020).

13. Beckert further comments on the United States' unique position in the global cotton economy: "What distinguished the United States from virtually every other cotton-growing area in the world was planters' command of nearly unlimited supplies of land, labor, and capital, and their unparalleled political power" (105).

14. See Beckert for more on these kinds of sharecropping agreements (280–92).

15. For further discussion of the aestheticization of business in Norris's work, see Kim Savelson, and Clare Eby, "Big Business as Art."
16. For more on Norris's training as an artist, see David Teague.
17. Claudia Tate suggests that Du Bois combines art, ideology, and erotics in his nonfiction and fiction, noting his "complex association of propaganda with erotic delight" in "Criteria of Negro Art" and *Dark Princess* ("Race and Desire" 153).
18. As Maurice Lee observes, "although the presence of Du Bois in literary journals no longer requires justification, and though valuable scholarship has recently treated the question of Du Bois and other minds, we pay his novels scant attention, despite our current occupation with racial politics, intellectual influence, and popular narrative form" (389). While Lee's comments in 1999 are perhaps somewhat out of date now, nonetheless the critical tendency to focus primarily on Du Bois's nonfiction remains.
19. While Maurice Lee defends Du Bois's "mediation of romance and realism" as "skillful and strategic" (389), Mark Van Wienen and Julie Kraft draw on Du Bois's "consistent blurring of the lines between fiction and nonfiction, fantasy and polemic" to support their effort to use the novel as "historical evidence" of the early genesis of Du Bois's "socialist commitment" (68), and Keith Byerman denigrates Du Bois's use of literary romance to present a political message because it "generates a text whose message is rendered problematic by the necessity of creating a coherent narrative" (70).
20. Joseph McElrath and Jesse Crisler write that because Norris's portrait of a cat was "hung on the line," during the next Monday's class, Norris was honored as "one of the ten upon whom Bouguereau had bestowed a front-row seat from which to observe the model" (94).
21. As Thérèse Burollet explains, Academic artists were "eminently aware of the importance of form and technique," sometimes seen as conventional, and often (though perhaps unfairly, according to her) contrasted with the more avant-garde style of Impressionists (32).
22. Miles Orvell distinguishes between the modernist search for authenticity through formal experimentation and the authenticity sought by realist and naturalist writers like Norris: "Frank Norris and the other realist writers around the turn of the century had said what sounds like the same thing: we want life not literature. But what they in fact meant was blood, sex, grime, garbage, immigrants, and killing snowstorms—a recognition of areas of experience previously excluded from polite literature" (240). Despite its thematic propensity to capture the gritty aspects of daily life, this kind of realism, according to Orvell, "had itself grown conventional" by the time modernists like William Carlos Williams were writing (240).
23. See Kevin Gaines for the history of and contradictions within racial uplift ideology. As he explains, elite educated Black Americans who

believed "that the improvement of African Americans' material and moral condition through self-help would diminish white racism" ... "sought to rehabilitate the race's image by embodying respectability, enacted through an ethos of service to the masses. Through racial uplift ideology, elite blacks sought the cooperation of white political and business elites in the pursuit of race progress" (xiv). Some of the problems with racial uplift ideology, as Gaines points out, include the fact that it is grounded in a kind of "unconscious internalized racism" because it implicitly accepts the false, racist premises that it reacts to, and that it is reliant on class differences to establish racial equality (6).

24. Bles Alwyn in particular finds himself regularly in need of education as to the "correct" ways to present oneself in the world, especially later in the novel as he moves to Washington DC and seeks to advance his career. A DC socialite discreetly sends him to a tailor so that he will fit in with the city's dapper norms, and gently suggests trying a different tie when the one he wears simply will not do.

25. Elsewhere the novel describes the consequences such sharecroppers face from cotton growers' manipulations: "When cotton rose, the tenants had already sold their cotton; when cotton fell the landlords squeezed the rations and lowered the wages. When cotton rose up again, up went the new Spring rent contracts. So it was that the bewildered black serf dawdled in listless inability to understand" (182).

26. Bles's treasuring of this fragmentary reproduction of Bouguereau's work perhaps aligns him with an African American tradition of valuing the absences marked by fragments of artistic culture. As Simon Gikandi suggests about earlier historical periods, "Within the reigning ideologies of culture, slaves were systematically excluded from the realm of beauty and taste; their relationship to objects that would be considered beautiful was hence tenuous; and given the regimen of labor and control, their notions of pleasure were radically different from those of their masters." Thus, "slaves would come to value works of art as ruins and fragments—broken bowls, jars and quilts, and half-remembered African dances—because only the fragmentary and incomplete had the capacity to denote the doubleness that was the mark of African identities in the new world, the sign of a presence and absence both in time and space" (199).

27. Bourdieu writes, "The ideology of natural taste owes its plausibility and its efficacy to the fact that, like all the ideological strategies generated in the everyday class struggle, it *naturalizes* real differences, converting differences in the mode of acquisition of culture into differences of nature; it only recognizes as legitimate the relation to culture (or language) which least bears the visible marks of its genesis, which has nothing 'academic', 'scholastic', 'bookish', 'affected' or 'studied' about it, but manifests by its ease and naturalness that true culture is nature—a new mystery of immaculate conception" (61).

28. See Hazel Carby on the gendered limitations of Du Bois's work. Carby argues that Du Bois's framework of racial advancement in *The Souls of Black Folk* is flawed because of its "complete failure to imagine black women as intellectuals and race leaders" (235).
29. Art historian Martin Berger argues that in late nineteenth-century art the "acceptance of whiteness conditions the sight, beliefs, and actions of European-Americans, thus naturalizing their sense of entitlement" and that "this racialized value system led European-Americans to interpret their art in decidedly racial terms" (7). In this passage, Zora seems to identify the "racialized value system" in Western art that contributes to the "economic, political, and judicial inequities suffered by non-white peoples" (Berger 14).
30. In a 1914 letter to his daughter, Du Bois likewise affirms the beauty of Blackness, asserting, "You must know that brown is as pretty as white or prettier and crinkly hair as straight even though it is harder to comb" (qtd. in Lewis 298).
31. Scott Hicks likewise emphasizes the importance of the physical environment in Du Bois's work, placing him in a reconstructed "genealogy of African American ecocriticism" (203).
32. However, as Russ Castronovo notes, the discourses of beauty in *Quest of the Silver Fleece* are never far removed from the threat of violence because beauty is a topic that "momentarily unites black men and white women" in the novel, thus provoking white paranoia around "the myth of the white woman's vulnerability to black male physicality" ("Color Line" 1458).
33. Maurice Lee similarly perceives Du Bois as more optimistic than his contemporaries, claiming that "like Norris and (for the most part) Dreiser, Du Bois bemoans the relentless materialism his novel sets in play; but unlike them, he does not depict a world of grim determinism" (391).
34. The name "Vanderpool" also seems to imply Dutch heritage and thus Old New York money.
35. For more on the novel's operatic resonances, see Don Graham.
36. Peter Collins interprets Norris's conclusion as his way of "affirm[ing] the free market, naturalizing it, and in particular naturalizing the laws of supply and demand. Furthermore, he suggests that nature will rebalance any temporary aberrations that hinder the functioning of those laws. Whatever local difficulties might arise—cornered markets or local disputes between farmers and railroads—the market eventually smoothes them over" (569).
37. Comparing the wheat market with Jadwin's organ playing, David Zimmerman proposes a theory of the "mesmeric sublime" in *The Pit*, which he describes as "the entranced mind's fatal surrender to automatistic forces at once within and without" (142). Jason Puskar also frequently characterizes Norris's descriptions as invoking the sublime.

38. For comparison, the similar passage in the first chapter of the novel reads: "On either side of the vista in converging lines stretched the blazing office buildings. But over the end of the street the lead-coloured sky was rifted a little. A long, faint bar of light stretched across the prospect, and silhouetted against this rose a sombre mass, unbroken by any lights, rearing a black and formidable façade against the blur of light behind it. And this was her last impression of the evening. The lighted office buildings, the murk of rain, the haze of light in the heavens, and raised against it the pile of the Board of Trade Building, black, grave, monolithic, crouching on its foundations, like a monstrous sphinx with blind eyes, silent, grave,—crouching there without a sound, without sign of life under the night and the drifting veil of rain" (38–9).
39. See "Aerial Perspective" and "Perspective (Art)" for more specific definitions of these terms.
40. Norris's imagery of a stark black building against a hazy sky specifically calls to mind O'Keeffe's 1926 painting *The Shelton with Sunspots, N.Y.*
41. In "Criteria of Negro Art," Du Bois in fact specifically names the aspects of goodness, truth, and beauty as the necessary methods for creating great works of art (296).
42. Du Bois's vibrant swamp recalls Avis Dobell's carmine shawl, which she imagines "throb[s] with the life that has been yielded to make [it]" (133). Perhaps the Du Bois swamp likewise throbs with the lives yielded to the production of cotton across the globe, including Zora's mother, who reappears here in Zora's imagination.

Chapter 4

Orientalist Consumption of Pearls and Blue Chinese Porcelain in Wharton and Larsen

> "To have things had always seemed to her the first essential of existence, and as she listened to him the vision of the things he could have unrolled itself before her like the long triumph of an Asiatic conqueror" (Wharton, *The Custom of the Country* 329).

> "She took to luxury as the proverbial duck to water ... Always she had wanted, not money, but the things which money could give, leisure, attention, beautiful surroundings. Things. Things. Things" (Larsen, *Quicksand* 67).

Nella Larsen's repetition quoted above aptly captures the consumerist concerns that structure many novels at the turn of the twentieth century: "Things. Things. Things." During this era of increasingly widely available consumer goods, women's material desires forcefully drive the plots of novels by female writers. Although fantasies of consumption took root in much earlier fiction—such as Meg March's coveting of expensive violet silk in *Little Women*—in early twentieth-century works by Edith Wharton and Nella Larsen characters' material ambitions are essential rather than incidental to each novel's action. And as evidenced by the vision of the "Asiatic conqueror" imagined by Wharton's character Undine Spragg in the epigraph, the discourse of consumption was often a vehicle for symbolically flaunting ownership over the riches of other regions.

Wharton and Larsen's obsession with things has not gone unnoticed; scholars have discussed their responses to shifting standards of fashion in an era of mass production, often focusing on the way in which gender inflects the issues of consumption, commodification, taste, and display tackled in their novels. Women in the early twentieth century were active consumers of goods that in turn amplified their own commodification, like clothes and jewelry, contributing to what Lori Merish describes as women's "unstable construction as both subjects and objects of exchange." She elaborates that "this instability is especially apparent in the fashion system, a symbolic structure that historically has entangled signs of liberation and oppression—of feminine pleasure and autonomy, and masculine power and domination—within the image of the fashionable female body" ("Engendering Naturalism" 322).

Tracing the material history of the fashion system that Merish describes can lend further complexity to early twentieth-century American women's efforts toward economic liberation and self-actualization. If Spanish, Portuguese, and French competition over carmine dye can allow us to see the questions about ethical consumption raised by the crimson curtains in Elizabeth Stuart Phelps's *The Story of Avis*, and if French, British, and Dutch jockeying over control of the North American fur trade enables us to see Constance Fenimore Woolson's ironic critique of US economic expansionism in *Anne*, what else might we be able to see if we were to investigate the global material history of the things within the fiction of Edith Wharton and Nella Larsen?

Because their plots mirror each other in their focus on acquisitive female protagonists who alternately pursue or escape their own commodification, Wharton's 1913 novel *The Custom of the Country* and Larsen's 1928 novel *Quicksand* exemplify how a global material history of objects recasts stories of female consumption.[1] While both novels are stuffed with things—endless dresses, all manner of bric-a-brac, lavish carpets, historic tapestries, gilt, lacquered tables—I will focus on just two kinds of objects: those made of pearls in *Custom* and those described as "blue Chinese" in color in *Quicksand*. In *The Custom of the Country*, social climber Undine Spragg lusts after pearls and gradually acquires and trades up for increasingly valuable sets of them. Likewise in *Quicksand*, perpetually dissatisfied and dislocated Helga Crane grounds her ambitions in the "blue Chinese" objects with which she surrounds herself. With attention to the histories of these commodities, my analysis reveals the connection between their structural function in both the novels and the gendered inter-imperial capitalist economy. As Malini Schueller documents when discussing the opening of trade between the US and Asia in the nineteenth century, the mania to trade with Asia and the Near East "both created and satisfied the demands of the public," who acquired silks, pearls, and china as symbols of their status and cultural dominance (28).

Wharton's early Orientalist sensibility is evident in her 1897 guide *The Decoration of Houses*, co-written with Ogden Codman, and which emphasizes the importance of being a knowledgeable consumer of foreign goods:

> no one should venture to buy works of art who cannot at least draw such obvious distinctions as those between old and new Saxe, between an old Italian and a modern French bronze, or between Chinese peach-bloom porcelain of the Khang-hi period and the Japanese imitations to be found in every "Oriental emporium." (184)

Anticipating language later used by Pierre Bourdieu to describe the way aesthetic taste is performed and aligned along class lines, yet without his critical angle, Wharton and Codman write that "Good objects of art give to a room its crowning touch of distinction. Their intrinsic beauty is hardly more valuable than their suggestion of a mellower civilization" (184). In their characterization of the "distinction" and "suggestion of a mellower civilization" granted by well-chosen bibelots, Wharton and Codman convey the idea that the objects decorating one's home are both a way of imagining yourself in geographic relation to the rest of the world and of distinguishing your hierarchical status within that world.[2]

In Wharton's fiction, the inter-imperial resonances of internationally traded goods like the ones she describes in *The Decoration of Houses* are underscored through her widespread language of conquest and allusions to historical imperial leaders. In the opening pages of *The Custom of the Country*, for example, Undine's mother is "enthroned" beneath "oval portraits of Marie Antoinette and the Princess de Lamballe" (3). Later, Undine's husband Ralph Marvell imagines nouveaux riches as "the Invaders" who emulate "indigenous" New York aristocrats in order to acquire "the speech of the conquered race" (48). Undine's understanding of her social rivalries perhaps unwittingly mirrors Ralph's combative characterization; when announcing to a friend her intention to annul her marriage to Ralph, she perceives it as "virtually a declaration of war" (250). Likewise, Undine's third husband, Raymond de Chelles, also views Undine as an invading colonizer, especially when she attempts to sell his family tapestries, which were, significantly, a gift from Louis XV to his "great-great grandfather" (326). The typically reserved Raymond lashes out at Undine, exclaiming,

> You come among us from a country we don't know, and can't imagine, a country you care for so little that before you've been a day in

ours you've forgotten the very house you were born in—if it wasn't torn down before you knew it! (334)

In the face of criticism from her second and third husbands, Undine actively participates in the construction of her image as an imperial conqueror, planning to dress up for a ball as "the Empress Josephine, after the Prudhon portrait in the Louvre" (121), and later her fantasies of imperial spoils are realized when her wealthy fourth husband buys her "a necklace and tiara of pigeon-blood rubies belonging to Queen Marie Antoinette" (358). Alan Ackerman interrogates the source of Undine's conquering impulses, commenting, "Whether Undine, who is 'fiercely independent and yet passionately imitative,' is beyond good and evil or has most fully internalized conventional morality, with its colonizing approach to material resources, remains open to question" (934). Whereas in *Custom* Undine is depicted as the leader of an encroaching army, in *Quicksand* Helga is perpetually in retreat from the forces that threaten to commodify her sexuality. Drawing on language of Orientalist mystique rather than of imperial conquest, Larsen instead highlights Asian commodities for the fantasies of flight they enable.

Despite the at times pointed language in their novels, Wharton's and Larsen's critiques are couched in the use of third-person subjective narration focalized primarily through Undine and Helga, which encourages identification with these characters' morally complicated journeys to achieve economic and social stability. While Larsen narrates *Quicksand* almost entirely from Helga's perspective, Wharton's narration shifts between several different characters' points of view, making her authorial assessment of her characters' actions even more ambiguous. As I argue in this chapter, these writers' ambivalence about their heroines' attempts to affiliate with global power allows readers to vacillate between the thrilling escapism of imagined material conquest, the moral superiority of judging up-and-comers like Undine and Helga for their ostensibly avaricious desires, and empathy for the impossibility of their circumstances. In tenuous social positions themselves—Wharton for her divorce in 1913, which turned her into "something of a social outcast" (Wagner-Martin xiii), and Larsen for her uneasy relationship with her social milieu of Harlem Renaissance artists, intellectuals, and activists—these writers capture the ever-hovering uncertainty of social and economic position. As George Hutchinson elaborates in his biography *In Search of Nella Larsen*, after being accused of plagiarizing her short story "Sanctuary" in 1930, Larsen's "general reputation in

Harlem plummeted" (346). In subsequent years she became more and more isolated as she suffered from ongoing depression (418), experienced an even more dramatic mental decline concurrent with the demise of her marriage because of her husband's affair (420), battled addiction and drinking problems (448), and confronted shifting literary tastes that made her fiction seem outdated (450). Wharton and Larsen knew how easy it is to fall from grace, and they captured that perilousness in their portraits of Undine and Helga. Navigating their fraught and contradictory positions as simultaneously consumers and commodities, Undine and Helga commodify a more distant "other"—the "East"—as an attempt to claim their own status as active agents in a world that limits their access to wealth and capital.

Posing for portraits, as Undine and Helga both do, further dramatizes their precarious positions. As they enact their dual roles as objects and subjects, participating in the reproduction of their own images while purchasing representations of global wealth and status in the form of Asian luxury goods, these characters make visible the limits of their own control. Although the Asian commodities they acquire and admire symbolically involve them in the US economic conquest of the "Orient," the only way these women can access wealth is by selling themselves off, either as *objets d'art* by posing for portraits, or as objects on the marriage market. Through their fetishization of Asian luxuries, Undine and Helga symbolically attempt to triangulate access to the United States' economic dominance in global trade relationships, thus seeking a position of relative power because of their nationality, even though their subject positions disempower them in other ways. Thus, I would argue that it is not a mere offhand comparison when the promise of the great spoils her suitor might offer calls to Undine's mind the image of an "Asiatic conqueror," as quoted in the epigraph to this chapter. In depicting the acquisition of luxury foreign goods as a kind of international conquest, Wharton and Larsen highlight how women like Undine and Helga must perpetuate the fiction that they are indeed conquerors in order to maneuver successfully in the marriage market—the only arena in which they can gamble, speculate, and express economic agency in the way white male characters can.

Although Wharton's and Larsen's heroines follow strikingly similar paths, the novels' plot arcs reveal the divergent limitations faced by white and Black aspiring social climbers at the turn of the twentieth century. Undine Spragg is the daughter of a financier from the provincial midwestern town of Apex, while Helga Crane is the daughter of a white Danish immigrant mother and a Black father who was a gambler and abandoned them. Undine and Helga perpetually seek to transcend the social circumstances in which they were born. Yet while Undine is as absorbent as a sponge in her perception, imitation, and assimilation of elite manners, Helga is both a more incisive and more critical observer, suspicious of conformity and desirous of a social status that would allow her freedom of movement from the restrictive codes of conduct modeled by her Black middle-class acquaintances' adherence to the ideology of "racial uplift." Obsessed with clothes, especially "elaborate ones" (*Quicksand* 18), Undine and Helga possess finely tuned aesthetic sensibilities; while the conventional Undine wants what everyone else has, Helga is drawn to vivid colors that distinguish her attire from the crowd. In a society in which women had few opportunities to amass wealth independently, Undine and Helga likewise leverage their sexuality as a means of climbing the social ladder: while Undine speculates on her marriage prospects the way one would bet on commodities futures, Helga finds herself a subject of fascination in Copenhagen as a sort of "curio," (73) accepting the objectifying gaze of the fascinated Danes in exchange for greater freedom of movement than she had in the segregated United States.

These novels also share a certain circularity in plot structure, a similarity that serves to contrast the ostensible success of Wharton's insatiably selfish Undine with the unrelenting longing felt by Larsen's Helga. After years of maneuvering in an attempt to solidify her unsteady social position, Undine ultimately remarries her secret first husband once his career unexpectedly takes off, just as Helga ends up back in the same place where she started, miserable in the deeply segregated South. The cyclical nature of Wharton's and Larsen's plots reveal the recurring economic barriers faced by white women and women of color in this period. Whereas Undine experiences a market-like cycle of booms and busts as she speculates on her marital future and attempts to "cash in" when most advantageous, Helga finds herself constantly on the run as she flees the material, social, and emotional limitations placed on her because of her race and seeks material possessions in a futile attempt to soothe her sense of internal conflict and displacement. In the end, Wharton and Larsen reveal that it is not greed that drives these characters to continually consume more and more, but rather the perpetual precarity of their positions, which remain unstable regardless of the amount of wealth or power they acquire.

Recognizing the similarities between Wharton's and Larsen's work, scholars typically situate these authors on a continuum of literary influence, with Larsen's fiction throwing into relief the overwhelmingly white vision of US racial politics that Wharton depicts. Though

Wharton's commentary on race in *The Custom of the Country* is primarily limited to the glorification of Undine's whiteness (as I will discuss in a later section), her private writings reveal more explicit prejudice, according to biographer Hermione Lee: "Wharton's snobbery, racism, anti-Semitism and anti-feminism are much more crudely voiced (as is almost always the case with the bigotry of intelligent people) in her private letters than in her fiction" (612). In contrast, *Quicksand* provides "a critical rereading of the Whartonian plot," according to Meredith Goldsmith, that "problematizes class and racial categories" (3), while Emily Orlando argues that Larsen "irreverently and deliberately appropriated and revised Wharton's work" in order to present a modernist critique of Wharton's purported realism for not accurately capturing the racial dynamics of the early twentieth-century US ("Irreverent Intimacy" 33).[3] These critics quite rightly articulate Larsen's reframing of Wharton's tales of social ambition in light of the additional barriers faced by people of color.

White and Black Americans' divergent historical relationships to commodification can be further extrapolated by looking more narrowly at the specific objects that populate early twentieth-century fiction. If we focus our attention on the materiality of the goods that characters desire and consume, a comparison of Wharton and Larsen demonstrates how race drastically alters one's relationship to commodification. Perhaps Undine is more comfortable commodifying herself because, as a white woman, she has not had to face the not-so-distant threat of one's ancestors literally being bought and sold. Larsen, on the other hand, is keenly aware of the danger such commodification presents to women of color, especially since her mother's country of origin, Denmark, continued to exert colonial control of the Danish West Indies within Larsen's lifetime. Yet through Helga, Larsen simultaneously observes the pleasures of material goods that are often intensified because they had so recently been denied to African Americans. Embedded within Wharton's pearls and Larsen's blue Chinese decor are rich histories of interimperial competition and conquest, entangled with gender and sexuality as well as race and class, of which Undine and Helga perform a simulacrum through their marital and social ventures.

Violent Desires for Pearls in *The Custom of the Country*

The opalescent luster of pearls catches Undine's eye from the early chapters of Wharton's *The Custom of the Country*, setting into motion a chain reaction of desire that escalates until the end of the novel. The novel first mentions pearls in a scene in an art gallery, when Undine spies a woman wearing an enviable pearl chain attached to an eye-glass. Immediately the treasures tint Undine's vision, as we learn through Wharton's third-person narration focalized through Undine: "It seemed suddenly plebeian and promiscuous to look at the world with a naked eye, and all her floating desires were merged in the wish for a jewelled eye-glass and chain" (30). While I discuss this scene at greater length later in this section, for now I would like to emphasize the seductive lure of the pearls, which narrows our gaze as readers along with Undine's as she fixates on the pricey gems. The sight of the pearlescent accessories changes the way Undine looks at the world, as her "floating desires" become embodied in the lustrous Asian commodities adorning the woman's neck. No incidental plot accoutrement, pearls structure Undine's ambitions, triggering an acquisitive imagination increasingly driven by conquest.

Undine's acquisition of pearls tracks closely her acquisition of husbands and lovers, from her secret first husband Elmer Moffatt, to her second husband Ralph Marvell, to her illicit lover Peter Van Degen, to her third husband Raymond de Chelles, and finally back to Moffatt, whom she remarries at the end of the novel. Ticien Marie Sassoubre succinctly summarizes the way in which Undine's acquisition of paramours corresponds to her accumulation of pearl jewelry: "Undine owns three different sets of pearls over the course of the novel: the pearls Ralph gives her ... Van Degen's, and the pearls Moffatt gives her (which the papers identify as having belonged to 'an Austrian Archduchess')" (702). The subtle striations of social classes are rendered through Undine's succession of husbands and lovers, as she "trades in" each one in turn for gradually more powerful men. Undine's suitors indicate their social status through their pearl accoutrements. Whereas Moffatt the upstart fastens his shirt with an artificial pearl, Ralph Marvell's deep connections to old New York elites are reflected in the family heirlooms that he gifts to Undine, and Peter Van Degen displays his much deeper pockets by perpetually donning a giant real pearl tie pin.

In addition to its shrewd observations about well-to-do New Yorkers at the turn of the twentieth century, Wharton's novel simultaneously protests the limited economic and political opportunities available to women at the time, and slyly celebrates the way in which women leveraged what power they did have to participate adjacently in the United States' imperial economic ventures. Undine, presumably like many women of Wharton's era, uses her beauty and body as currency, exchanging all that is available to her to claim part of the economic imperial vision to which the men in her life have more direct access. Seductive symbols of Eastern mystique and luxury, the pearls that Undine practically harvests from these men signify her second-hand claim to imperial and economic power.

Wharton's complex and shifting narrative techniques in *The Custom of the Country* mediate readers' potentially contradictory responses to Undine's gendered imperial conquest, allowing critique and catharsis to coexist through her pervasive use of free indirect discourse. Undine's actions and their consequences provoke readers' judgment; her marriages are almost entirely mercenary, her extortion of custody of her son from her second husband Ralph Marvell leads to his suicide, she manipulates her parents, and she neglects her son when she gains full custody. Wharton herself wrote in her memoir *A Backward Glance* (1934) that in her depiction of Undine, "to whatever hemisphere her fortunes carried her, my task was to record her ravages and pass on to her next phase" (182). Wharton's characterization of Undine here is laden with the language of conquest, as she imagines Undine traveling to various "hemispheres" to "ravage" the people and resources therein. Yet while Wharton's description of her character is full of judgment, her assessment of her own writerly task is neutral: she sought to "record" Undine's actions, not critique them, nor celebrate them. Wharton's paradoxical vision of her authorial mission here offers a preview of her narrative evasion and ambiguity throughout *The Custom of the Country*. In the novel, the possibility of any unequivocal condemnation of Undine is further undercut by the permissive observations other characters make about her—judgments presented in subjective third-person narration, which allows readers to slip almost unconsciously into each character's point of view. The opening pages of the novel, for instance, begin with the narrator's birds-eye view of a moment when Undine receives a letter that her mother and their masseuse Mrs. Heeny presume to be from a suitor. Though Mrs. Spragg admonishes Undine in the novel's opening line, exclaiming, "Undine Spragg—how *can* you?", the narrator observes that her protest was "feeble," and that she actually looks upon her daughter's flirtatiousness with "deprecating pride" (3). Mrs. Heeny follows Mrs. Spragg's lead in looking at Undine with "good-humoured approval" (3).

Soon we slip into Mrs. Spragg's consciousness, as if we, too, might share in her "deprecating pride" of Undine. Mrs. Spragg reflects on Undine's difficulty transitioning into New York society, considering, "she seemed as yet—poor child!—too small for New York: actually imperceptible to its heedless multitudes; and her mother trembled for the day when her invisibility should be borne in on her" (9). Wharton drops the interjection "poor child!" seamlessly into this narration that is focalized through Mrs. Spragg, inviting readers to move from their omniscient view of the scene to Mrs. Spragg's subjective assessment of her daughter's success. Additionally, this insight into Mrs. Spragg's consciousness ironizes the apparent approbation she and Mrs. Heeny expressed pages earlier, because it reveals the underlying worries behind her performative admiration of Undine—in turn subverting trust in the ostensibly objective narration at the chapter's opening.

Later narrative moments echo Mrs. Spragg's sympathy for Undine. Undine's husband Ralph, again rendered in subjective third person, feels a pang at the "sense of inevitableness" about their entanglement as husband and wife:

> Poor Undine! She was what the gods had made her—a creature of skin-deep reactions, a mote in the beam of pleasure. He had no desire to "preach down" such heart as she had—he felt only a stronger wish to reach it, teach it, move it to something of the pity that filled his own. (136)

A more detached observer of Undine's actions than Ralph, his sister's friend Charles Bowen takes a structural view of the "sense of inevitableness" that Ralph feels. In a conversation with Ralph's sister bemoaning the fact that Undine forgot to attend her son's birthday party, Bowen speculates aloud about how the romance of business often replaces the romance of marriage, and elaborates on the limited options women can choose from in such a scenario, concluding,

> All my sympathy's with them, poor deluded dears, when I see their fallacious little attempts to trick out the leavings tossed them by the preoccupied male—the money and the motors and the clothes—and pretend to themselves and to each other that *that's* what really constitutes life! (126)

Because three different characters express their sympathy for "poor Undine," however problematic, enabling, and ambivalent that sympathy is, their evaluation of the obstacles Undine faces undermines any sense of straightforward critique of Undine's "ravages," and instead acknowledges how the world is organized to disempower women.

Furthermore, though Wharton's narration shifts variously between the perspectives of Undine's parents, Ralph, Charles Bowen, and Undine's young son Paul, the majority of the novel is focalized through Undine, which further encourages identification with her quest for social ascendancy, as well as the frustration and confusion she encounters along the way. Although a careful student of social manners, Undine does not have a sufficient framework to discern the subtle mores of the elites, as her reaction to a dinner party early in the novel attests: "All was blurred and puzzling to the girl in this world of half-lights, half-tones, eliminations and abbreviations; and she felt a violent longing to brush away the cobwebs and assert herself as the dominant figure of the scene" (23). Wharton establishes Undine's unreliability as a narrator through her inability to parse the "half-lights, half-tones, eliminations and abbreviations" that her more well-established peers are fluent in. In turn, she demonstrates how Undine fashions herself as a "violent" and "dominant" conqueror in order to combat her feelings of helplessness. Though not an outright celebration of Undine's imperialist imagination, *The Custom of the Country* explicates the structural conditions that lead Undine to envision herself in this way.[4]

A wealthy cosmopolite who lived and traveled a great deal abroad, Wharton surely had opinions about globalization, economic power, and US efforts to jockey for position on a world stage. Detailing the wide range of Wharton's Parisian acquaintances who were sympathetic to French colonialism, along with Wharton's tongue-in-cheek comment in a letter averring that she was a "rabid imperialist" (784), Frederick Wegener makes the case that these attitudes pervade Wharton's fiction, contributing to an "imperial sensibility" that manifests itself not only "thematically or polemically but also informing her aesthetic lexicon" (803). He suggests that Wharton's fiction evinces an ambivalence about social climbers and their contribution to the United States' "drift into empire," noting that these kinds of characters "tend to be vilified in terms that nonetheless salute their all-conquering power" (794). Analyzing the symbolic function that pearl jewelry plays in *The Custom of the Country* allows us to see the intersection of Wharton's gendered critique and her apparent ambivalence about imperialism that Wegener describes. As I elaborate, Wharton's characters attempt to assert such "all-conquering power" through their consumption of internationally sourced jewelry, and they are frequently well aware of the direct connection between their social status and their gems' geography. Characters in other fiction by Wharton are keenly attuned to the international provenance of their jewelry, as Jenny Glennon notes in her discussion of Asian gems in Wharton's novel *Twilight Sleep*. Glennon contends that because Wharton's female characters are "largely precluded from earning money in their own right," they "come to rely on jewelry as an alternative form of currency" (17). Furthermore, Wharton's own preoccupation with fashion and design suggests some of her sympathies might be more aligned with Undine's than her harsh language of invasion and battle implies. As Hermione Lee notes, Wharton's evening dress was often accessorized with a "choker of pearls, the long pendants" and "the bracelets and pearl-drop earrings she liked" (308). If we pay attention to histories of the commodities that women in Wharton's fiction interact with, we see her subtle portrait of early twentieth-century women's vexed participation in imperial economic conquest—through consumption, rather than through adventuring.

Focusing on pearls allows for a more global reading of *The Custom of the Country* because of their peripatetic material history, which merits attention here. Sought after by Columbus, imported by Spain to finance its expansionist ventures, hunted by explorers and capitalists drawn to India and Bahrain to establish trade relationships, and targeted by Japan for competitive innovations in production processes, the accreted layers of calcium carbonate in pearls represent centuries of inter-imperial trade, conquest, and imagining. Stephen Bloom elucidates the expansionist origins of the pearl trade in *Tears of Mermaids: The Secret Story of Pearls*, explaining that Columbus was commanded by the Spanish monarchy to acquire a range of valuable commodities during his trip to the New World, chief among them pearls. Columbus and other explorers were so successful in harvesting pearls from the New World, particularly in the waters near Venezuela, that in the early sixteenth century, "Spain's coffers so swelled that pearls helped underwrite a series of expansionist battles to seize lands belonging to France and Brittany," and thus, "in less than thirty years, pearls had become a prime symbol of Spanish colonial dominance in the New World" (Bloom 15). While in the sixteenth and seventeenth centuries Venice served as a cultural hub for the pearl trade (Bloom 21), in the mid-nineteenth century Paris rose to prominence as "the world's pearl-trading epicenter" because of "its proximity to what were then three of the world's richest natural pearl beds: the Persian Gulf . . . the Red Sea; and the Gulf of Mannar . . . Once strung in Bombay, pearls would be shipped to Paris, where they'd fetch top prices, to be transported worldwide" (Bloom 22).

Because of the way they have long linked distant countries through global trade, for centuries pearls have represented not only luxury and social status, but also imperial power. At the time *The Custom of the Country* was published, jewelers like Cartier (a designer whom

Wharton herself frequented) purchased their finest pearls from traders in India, who imported the gems from the Persian Gulf, especially Bahrain. Although freshwater pearls were cultivated in the US in places like Ohio and Wisconsin, these pearls were "normally confined to the American market," presumably because they were perceived to be lower in quality (Nadelhoffer 134). An 1854 article from *Godey's Lady's Book* offers evidence that women would have been aware of the international origins of their jewelry. Titled "History of Pearls, Natural and Artificial," the article details the process by which pearls are cultivated, naming the geographic origins of the gem:

> Pearl fisheries exist in Ceylon, on the Coromandel coast, and in the Persian Gulf, the last named being the most productive. Fisheries of less importance also exist in Algiers, and in the Zooloo Islands. Two thousand years ago, the Romans found pearls in Britain, and within modern times the rivers of Scotland have afforded considerable quantities, though not of the best quality. Several rivers of Saxony, Silesia, Bavaria, and Bohemia afford pearls, and they are also found in two or three Russian provinces. There are also pearl fisheries in the western hemisphere. The coast of Columbia and the Bay of Panama have furnished considerable quantities, but they are not considered equal to the pearls of the East in shape or color. (533)

Here, as in much of the writing about pearls at the time, pearls from "the East" are explicitly favored over "Western" pearls, revealing both the exotic cachet of these pearls as well as the implicit knowledge about geography that a discerning jewelry purchaser would be assumed to have. By donning the visible evidence of the treasures of "the East" that their wealth could acquire, Westerners flaunted their symbolic ownership over the riches of distant regions in a competition for status, just as Undine competes for a favorable position in the marriage market, and just as the United States competed for economic dominance in an inter-imperial field.

The Orientalist mystification of Asian pearls is laid bare in much more obvious terms in an ambitious 1908 book by George Frederick Kunz and Charles Hugh Stevenson with the self-serious title *The Book of the Pearl: The History, Art, Science, and Industry of the Queen of Gems*. Describing the long-running imaginative link between pearls and "the East," Kunz and Stevenson write:

> Pearls seem to be peculiarly suggestive of oriental luxury and magnificence. It is in the East that they have been especially loved, enhancing the charms of Asiatic beauty and adding splendor to the barbaric

courts celebrated for their display of costume. From their possession of the rich pearl resources it is natural that the people of India and Persia should have early found beauty and value in these jewels, and should have been among the first to collect them in large quantities. (3)

Kunz and Stevenson's paean to Asian pearls reveals common *fin-de-siècle* Orientalist fantasies and assumptions about "the East" as a place of luxury, excess, and mysterious beauty, and suggests how strongly these images were associated with pearls at the time. Malini Schueller affirms that this exoticizing was common in writing at the time, noting that "in many U.S. Orientalist works, Asia was simply a place of unlimited wealth," with writers often using "the metonymy of the Orient as riches" (154). Exoticizing "the East" as foreign, distant, and other allowed Americans to imagine their dominance and superiority over powers like the Chinese, Japanese, and Ottoman empires, symbolizing their global economic power through the extraction of precious resources from these regions.

For some, the Orientalist fantasies triggered by the allure of pearls moved into the realm of reality; at the beginning of the twentieth century, Jacques Cartier made several trips to India and the Persian Gulf to take stock of the market, establish relationships with traders, see oyster beds in person, and hunt down the finest pearls. During a 1911 trip, Cartier dined with maharajas, attempted to learn to speak "Hindustani," bought valuable gems and sought commissions, and drew design inspiration from Indian jewelry and decor (Brickell 104). Upon his return, Cartier put on exhibits in London and New York of "Oriental Jewels and Objets d'Art recently collected in India" (Brickell 109), and the Cartier brand long capitalized on the Orientalist inspiration of its designs and jewels. A review of a similar 1928 exhibit in Paris illustrates the way in which Cartier captivated Western consumers by importing Eastern goods and designs: "This is a dream world, the incarnation of a fugitive Oriental dream ... At Cartier's, dreams take shape, we are in the world of One Thousand and One Nights, and the beauty, and the extent of this collection surpasses the imagination" (Brickell 114). Pearls, as Cartier's example demonstrates, had the imaginative potential to spur on actual "Oriental" ventures. Knowledge of Cartier's travels to acquire pearls perhaps conjured up romanticized images of the East similar to those described by the reviewer above, images that in turn reenacted and justified imperial conquest for the women who wore these gems.

Thus, although this history of imperialist speculation and exploitation remains implicit throughout *The Custom of the Country*, the pearls referred to so frequently in the novel have an "oriental" origin that people at the time were likely well aware of and understood as a signifier of imperial dominance. To return to one of the novel's first mentions of pearl jewelry, during the episode in the art gallery, Wharton establishes a relationship between visual art, the commodification of women's appearances, and the cultural and economic currency of luxury Asian goods. Still new to the New York social scene, Undine attends a dinner party and feels embarrassed at her lack of cultural knowledge and conversation material, forced to answer "questions as to what pictures interested Undine at the various exhibitions of the moment" entirely "in the negative," privately considering to herself that she "did not even know that there were any pictures to be seen, much less that 'people' went to see them" (24). As Bourdieu suggests, "Taste classifies, and it classifies the classifier" (xxix). Undine's inability to classify works of art leaves her incapable of signaling her concomitant social status (unlike Laura Jadwin in Chapter 3, who knows enough to comment on Bouguereau's "flesh-tints"). Undine quickly discovers that her lack of cultural capital contributes to her lack of capital on the marriage market, and she seeks to amend her ignorance so that she can be a better party guest in the future. Ever the socialite rather than the intellectual, when Undine rectifies the gap in her conversational repertoire by attending one of the art galleries mentioned by her host, she is drawn much more strongly to the people in the gallery than to the paintings on the wall.

Immediately Undine's gaze is caught by a woman with an elaborate pearl chain, an accessory that becomes a symbol of calculated self-presentation as Undine scrutinizes the woman's gestures:

> Presently her attention was drawn to a lady in black who was examining the pictures through a tortoise-shell eye-glass adorned with diamonds and hanging from a long pearl chain. Undine was instantly struck by the opportunities which this toy presented for graceful wrist movements and supercilious turns of the head. It seemed suddenly plebeian and promiscuous to look at the world with a naked eye, and all her floating desires were merged in the wish for a jewelled eye-glass and chain. So violent was this wish that, drawn on in the wake of the owner of the eye-glass, she found herself inadvertently bumping against a stout tight-coated young man whose impact knocked her catalogue from her hand. (30)

As an aspirational image of social status, the woman in the gallery represents the height of fashion for the still parochial Undine, donning one of the most the popular and pricey early twentieth-century accessories worn by Wharton herself and other elites, the pearl chain. According to Katherine Joslin, Wharton herself had a "chain with diamonds and pearls designed by Cartier" that she "wore in nearly every photograph taken of her" (2). For Jenny Glennon, this item of jewelry communicates a great deal about Wharton's values and ideals: "The necklace was everything Wharton most revered: French, stylish, unobtrusive, and clearly of impeccable quality" (18). If fashion "functions as hieroglyph," as Joslin suggests, "clearly setting limits on those included and excluded from its web of meaning" (Joslin 6), then the pearl necklace signifies Wharton's status as a fashionable elite—much like the woman in the art gallery whom Undine envies—who was well attuned to current jewelry trends, knowledgeable about the "best" jewelers, and wealthy enough to purchase brand-name luxuries.

Perhaps foreshadowing Ralph Marvell's later critical description of up-and-comers like Undine as "the Invaders" (48), Undine's "floating desires" for these bejeweled accessories are "so violent" that she literally invades the space of other gallery patrons. Undine's glimpse at the pearl chain becomes instinctively competitive, as she begins to feel "plebeian" next to this sophisticate when "look[ing] at the world with a naked eye." At this moment, Undine's gaze becomes clouded by her singular focus on the acquisition of expensive international gems and the relative status that she might achieve through them. Because this scene is focalized through Undine, readers are encouraged to share the escapist fantasy that pearls signify for her, yet Wharton also hints at Undine's crassness through her clumsy collision and her materialistic focus on the gallery attendees' jewelry rather than on the paintings.

Furthermore, the eye-glass on the pearl chain gains its value from both the precious materials used to create it and the material worth it can add to Undine's appearance. In a gallery full of art objects, Undine imagines herself one of them, fantasizing about how she might look in others' eyes when able to use the eye-glass to make "graceful wrist movements and supercilious turns of the head." Undine's self-conscious presentation of her body here recalls Lori Merish's articulation of the way in which nineteenth-century women struggled to navigate the tension between claiming power through self-presentation and being subject to objectification because of their legal relationship to men. As Merish explains, "In a legal and socio-economic context in which women were collectively defined as men's sexual property, and in which men controlled much of the wealth women spent, women's self-presentation as public subjects, Wharton suggests, inevitably competed with their objectification by men and their status as men's (sexual) objects" ("Engendering Naturalism" 326). I would suggest that in her depiction of pearl jewelry,

Wharton articulates how Undine (and women like her) attempts to tip the balance of power in her favor through her fetishization of imported objects like the eye-glass and pearl chain here, which function as talismans of American imperial conquest and economic expansionism that symbolically grant the wearer an aura of that power. In concert with Mrs. Spragg's solicitous narrative interjection in the first chapter, "poor child!", a structural analysis of Undine's limited economic circumstances allows more room for sympathy for her "floating desires."

This early moment in the novel teaches Undine how to take advantage of global goods to bolster her own value. Wharton makes the connection between Undine's consumer desires and her marital prospects clear when immediately after this covetous moment Undine collides with the wealthy Peter Van Degen, the "stout tight-coated young man" described in the quote above. Later in the novel, Van Degen buys Undine costly pearls in a bid for her affection, and at the moment of their encounter is in fact wearing a "huge pearl" for a tie pin. At first put off by Van Degen's "unpleasant-looking" appearance with his "grotesque saurian head, with eye-lids as thick as lips and lips as thick as ear-lobes," Undine changes her attitude when she realizes who this man is, recalling having seen "innumerable newspaper portraits, all, like the original before her, tightly coated, with a huge pearl transfixing a silken tie" (31). Again, pearls are closely associated with social status in Undine's mind. The "unpleasant-looking" appearance that initially devalued the man's worth is superseded by his prominence in New York social circles, as signaled by his frequent appearance in newspapers—his image always accompanied by the ostentatious pearl pin. Undine is able to swiftly sort Van Degen into a more rarefied social category, all because of the implicit knowledge coded in the "huge pearl." Furthermore, in characterizing Van Degen as "the original" here to distinguish from the newspaper replicas, Undine's focalized narration employs a moniker that confers authenticity much like a work of art, or even a valuable and unique pearl. As I elaborate in the following section, Wharton plays with the taxonomy of pearls to create a metaphor that reinforces implicit social hierarchies.

The "Real Thing" and the Copy

In addition to being a symbol of consumer conquest of the "East," pearls can also be read as a metaphor for the deeply embedded social hierarchies and class prejudices that Wharton catalogues throughout the novel. In the early twentieth century, several kinds of pearls were integrated in fashion and jewelry: natural, artificial, and cultured. Natural pearls were those harvested off the coast of Bahrain, Ceylon, and elsewhere that were collected by the painstaking process of diving, grabbing a bunch of oysters, and hoping to find a few pearls when opening them. Today natural pearls of this kind are "exceedingly rare" (Bloom 22) because of overfishing, pollution, and the relative market share of cultured pearls. Techniques for creating cultured pearls were developed starting in the late nineteenth century in Japan, and drove down the price of expensive natural pearls when cultured pearls became popularized by Mikimoto in the early twentieth century. Despite their disparate production processes, natural and cultured pearls look very similar and even experts "can distinguish only slight differences" between them (Bloom 25). Artificial pearls, on the other hand, are simply beads made from glass to resemble pearls. The distinctions between natural, cultured, and artificial pearls present an apt metaphor for the social rankings of Wharton's characters. Like "natural" pearls, characters like Peter Van Degen, Ralph Marvell, and Raymond de Chelles were born into their position, and "naturally" exhibit the social graces implicitly expected of the upper class because they never knew otherwise. Thus, they are seen as more valuable because their social status is "natural" and inherited. To refer again to the moment when Peter Van Degen wears his "huge pearl" tie pin at the art gallery, Undine is able to identify him as the "original" after which so many newspaper portraits were taken precisely because of that (likely natural) pearl. The characterization of Van Degen as an "original" likewise nods at his status as an "original" New Yorker, and thus a more powerful one.

In spite of his relative lack of wealth, Ralph Marvell is similarly an "original" due to his family connections, an authenticity he celebrates and ironizes through a tongue-in-cheek comparison between his family and Indigenous peoples: he "sometimes called his mother and grandfather the Aborigines, and likened them to those vanishing denizens of the American continent doomed to rapid extinction with the advance of the invading race" (45). In framing his family members as the "vanishing denizens" of America, Ralph's analogy blithely underplays the real genocidal violence toward actual Native Americans wrought by Anglo-American families like his, while at the same time reflecting his woundedness at the violence that social climbers like Undine do to New York's aristocratic traditions. Undine in turn views Ralph's worth through the lens of invasion when reflecting on their engagement, pondering,

> Now at last she was having what she wanted—she was in conscious possession of the "real thing"; and through her other, more diffused, sensations of Ralph's adoration gave her such a last refinement of pleasure as might have come to some warrior Queen borne in triumph by captive princes. (60)

Wharton, like Norris in the previous chapter, alludes here to Henry James's 1892 story "The Real Thing," which features a formerly affluent couple who are forced to pose for portraits when they find themselves in reduced circumstances. The portrait artist nonetheless notices an indefinable quality in the couple that he deems "the real thing," a quality he does not see in his typical models. "The Real Thing" thus posits an essentialized cultural superiority that cannot be taken away even with economic hardship. Wharton's allusion to this story suggests that Undine perceives Ralph Marvell as possessing a similar quality that makes him inherently superior—much in the way natural pearls are valued over cultured pearls. Wharton thus makes visible a process of distinction that was critical for achieving social standing in this era, according to Miles Orvell, who notes that "Learning to tell the true from the false, the lie from the truth, learning trust and mistrust, was part of an acculturation process that shows up again and again in nineteenth-century culture" (58). Significantly, Undine is satisfied that she is in "conscious possession" of the "real thing"; she is happy because she is *conscious* of the worth of what she possesses, not unlike the satisfaction that a pearl connoisseur might take from being able to assess a gem's color, luster, and orient. Finally, Wharton's characterization of Undine's triumph as like that of "some warrior Queen" renders her perspective through the language of conquest, recalling the acquisitive imagination set into motion previously by the sight of the woman's pearl chain in the art gallery. Undine envisions herself as a warrior queen to maintain the guise of control over her marital and economic prospects.

The unsteadiness of Undine's navigation of New York society becomes evident when she receives a set of family jewels upon marrying Ralph and determines to have the jewels reset more in keeping with recent fashions. After discovering an unexpected bill from the jeweler, Ralph feels betrayed by Undine's dissimulation. Taking full note of the bill, Ralph observes,

> The bill was not large, but two of its items stood out sharply. "Resetting pearl and diamond pendant. Resetting sapphire and diamond ring." The pearl and diamond pendant was his mother's wedding present; the ring was the one he had given Undine on their engagement. That they were

both family relics, kept unchanged through several generations, scarcely mattered to him at the time: he felt only the stab of his wife's deception. She had assured him in Paris that she had not had the jewels reset. (130)

Notably, the jewels reset by Undine include a "pearl and diamond pendant," pointing once again to the importance of pearls as a signifier for social status and the allure they hold for "Invaders" or "warrior Queens" like Undine. Both pieces of jewelry are described as "family relics," granting them the gravitas and sense of authentic provenance that one might associate with religious reliquaries, or with artifacts recovered from the ruins of an ancient civilization. Implicit in Ralph's sense of attachment to the jewels is the material reality of intergenerational family wealth, through which power accretes like so many layers of a pearl—accumulation for which Wharton expresses a hint of nostalgia, given Ralph's sympathetic depiction and her own family history of affluence.

Although Ralph imagines his pique to be directed at Undine's deception, a later passage reveals the degree to which his family legacy provokes his ire. Considering Undine's affront, Ralph acknowledges,

> He no longer minded her having lied about the jeweller; what pained him was that she had been unconscious of the wound she inflicted in destroying the identity of the jewels. He saw that, even after their explanation, she still supposed he was angry only because she had deceived him; and the discovery that she was completely unconscious of states of feeling on which so much of his inner life depended marked a new stage in their relation. (130)

Whereas Undine previously prided herself on being in "conscious possession" of the "real thing," here, Ralph faults her for being "unconscious"—both of the "wound she inflicted" and of the "states of feeling" Ralph experiences. The shift in narrative perspective in this chapter from Undine's point of view to Ralph's emphasizes this difference. Ticien Marie Sassoubre comments on the contrast between Undine's sentiments toward the gems and Ralph's, explaining that "the pang he feels upon discovering they have been reset involves the realization that they have no emotional or aesthetic value for Undine" (695). Wharton's repetition of the word "unconscious" in this excerpt implies that even though Undine appreciates the monetary value of the pearls and the status they confer, she blatantly disregards the family legacy of the pearls so important to Ralph in her single-minded quest for ownership over them. Here, Wharton seems to remind readers of how much damage can be inflicted by "unconscious" conquerors who are so drawn to wealth and power that other values are abandoned, even while she also allows Undine to continue undaunted in her quest for money and power and recognizes the gendered limitations that govern that quest.

If the "identity" of Ralph's jewels does not matter to Undine, the size of them certainly does, and Undine's dissatisfaction with the string of pearls bought by Ralph early in the novel becomes the impetus for an illicit flirtation and her eventual divorce, as Undine markets her sexual wares in order to trade up to a larger set of pearls. Undine's insatiable quest for increasingly larger and more valuable pearls is also a quest for social status, and she recognizes the competitive advantage achieved through access to a foreign luxury good. While pearls accentuate Undine's status as economically dominant, they also amplify her whiteness, a feature emphasized frequently in descriptions of her appearance—much like the Anglo-Saxon whiteness of Woolson's Anne, or the whiteness of Bouguereau's Madonna that Du Bois's Zora reveres. Undine's complexion is described as a "pure red and white" so vivid that "she might have been some fabled creature whose home was in a beam of light" (14), her "white shoulders" are mentioned favorably several times (53, 135), and she frequently dons an attractive white dress (168, 288). By creating an association between the beautiful white pallor of Undine's complexion and the luminous opalescence of her pearls, Wharton comments on the global value of both, alluding to the way in which whiteness is used to construct otherness in order to devalue and exploit it. As we will see later, the darkness of Helga's skin in Larsen's *Quicksand* presents the inverse of Undine's valuable whiteness, devaluing her currency on the marriage market because of others' damaging exoticization of her sexuality. In *The Custom of the Country*, however, Undine increasingly employs the language of global commodities markets, ever aware of her current worth and how she might maximize it through strategic self-presentation.

The social power of pearls is amplified by their representation in art, and the society portraits so popular among those in Undine's crowd present the opportunity to flaunt wealth in the form of jewelry. Indeed, the fictional painter Claud Popple serves as the designated portrait artist among Undine's social acquaintances not because of his exceptional talent, but because of his ability to adequately render the trappings of wealth that are so important to his affluent clientele. Wharton's narrator explains Popple's specific set of skills:

> his reputation had been permanently established by the verdict of a wealthy patron who, returning from an excursion into other fields of

portraiture, had given it as the final fruit of his expertise that Popple was the only man who could "do pearls." To sitters for whom this was of the first consequence it was another of the artist's merits that he always subordinated art to elegance. (114)

Wharton's emphasis on Popple's ability to "do pearls" not only signals the commodification of his art, but also links his work to the international luxury trade. The fact that Popple is secretly derided by the more aristocratic members of Undine's milieu—Ralph thinks of him as "the egregious Popple" (44)—suggests his loss of status because of his commercial hawking of his artistic wares.

When Undine's pearls are scrutinized in Popple's portrait of her, this derision spurs her into action to negotiate for a better set of pearls, and relatedly, a more favorable social position. At a gathering in Popple's studio, Undine and some friends assess Popple's recent portrait of Undine. Peter Van Degen, the same man with whom Undine had collided at the art gallery with the "huge pearl" tie pin, ribs good-humoredly about the portrait: "Yes, it's good—it's damn good, Popp; you've hit the hair off rippingly; but the pearls ain't big enough" (115). Cannily seeing Van Degen's comment as an opportunity to deploy her feminine wiles, Undine jokes about the pearls, "Of course they're not! But it's not *his* fault, poor man; *he* didn't give them to me!" Undine's strategic negotiation for increasingly valuable sets of pearls echoes contemporaneous discourses comparing the origins of various grades of pearls. A 1913 text by Herbert Vertrees envisions pearls as a signifier of international status, noting the distinction between "oriental" pearls, which are available only from Asian, Pacific, and Caribbean fisheries, and "fresh-water" pearls, which are found throughout the US. He comments that despite long-standing prejudice from "the European aristocracy," US pearls "have nearly reached their deserved economic position among the gems of the world" (18). Vertrees casts pearls as an indicator of global economic standing, and substituting "the United States" for "fresh-water pearls" reveals his inter-imperial rhetoric: implicitly, it is not just the pearls, but also the US that has nearly reached its deserved economic position among the gems of the world. In Undine's analogous maneuvering, Wharton illuminates how pearls offer a tangible piece of the United States' jockeying for global power—power that women at this time primarily accessed through their husbands, or their inherited material wealth. But again, Wharton's shifting narrative perspective reserves explicit judgment of her characters' actions. While Undine's contempt for the pearls from sympathetic

Ralph makes her appear villainous and mercenary, Wharton's subjective third-person narration presented from Undine's point of view encourages identification with the steps she takes to make the most of what she has. Wharton thus reveals Undine's unsteady navigation between the competing forces of her own ambition and the social mores that would cast that ambition as tacky or unfeminine.

The subtle body language that follows Undine's remark about her diminutive pearls, as described by the narrator, reveals Van Degen's and Undine's unspoken intentions, as Van Degen "transfer[s] his bulging stare from the counterfeit to the original. His eyes rested on Mrs. Marvell's in what seemed a quick exchange of understanding; then they passed on to a critical inspection of her person" (115). Just as Undine previously compared "the original" Van Degen with his portraits she had seen in the papers, so here is Undine characterized as an "original" in comparison to her "counterfeit" image in the portrait. Because the narrator's characterization of Undine as an "original" is so closely juxtaposed with Van Degen's "bulging stare," there seems to be some implicit valuation in his gaze, as he assesses Undine's worth, silently makes an offer based on that valuation, and makes a "quick exchange" with Undine. The double entendre in the description of Van Degen's stare as "bulging" hints at the sexual nature of their transaction. Furthermore, part of Undine's value seems to be generated by her whiteness, a quality emphasized in the description immediately following their "exchange": "She was dressed for the sitting in something faint and shining, above which the long curves of her neck looked dead white in the cold light of the studio; and her hair all a shadowless rosy gold, was starred with a hard glitter of diamonds" (115). Undine's appearance is layered with whiteness: her "faint and shining" dress, her ominously "dead white" complexion, and of course the pearls described previously. Whereas here Wharton alludes to the valuable currency of Undine's white skin, in *Quicksand* Larsen will reflect on the dehumanizing commodification of Helga's dark skin and the way Asian commodities facilitate her escape from her own exoticization. For Undine, pearls secure her position in the elite society that Helga flees—both Undine's modest strand from Ralph Marvell that she wears in the portrait and the large, showy necklace that she later solicits from Van Degen as the price of their unspoken arrangement in this studio scene.

Undine and Van Degen's tacit exchange in the studio later escalates to an explicit exchange, as Van Degen gives Undine a string of expensive pearls with the expectation that she will reciprocate with sexual favors. In this venture, Undine must reconcile her vision of herself as a conqueror who extracts wealth with the reality that she is an object of exchange whose cost is a set of pearls. On the one hand, because of the international trade routes the pearls have traversed, they register cultural mastery of the "Orient" through economic expansionism, and Undine attempts to lay claim to a piece of that mastery. On the other hand, she is only able to do so by putting herself on the market of global exchange because her economic opportunities are circumscribed by her gender. When Van Degen comes to collect his fees, he frames their exchange in expressly transactional terms, and Undine expresses her understandable reluctance to completely give up her position of dominance by surrendering her body as yet another pearl on a strand. Wharton draws attention to the limits of Undine's power with Van Degen's impatience at her perpetual deferral of physical consummation of their affair, as he confronts her with frustration: "Look here—the installment plan's all right; but ain't you a bit behind even on that?. . . Anyhow, I think I'd rather let the interest accumulate for a while. This is good-bye till I get back from Europe" (140). Van Degen's overtly economic language here—seeing their affair as an "installment plan" that accumulates interest—highlights the commodification of Undine's body, as well as the equivocation between her and the pearls. Undine instinctively recognizes this equivocation; in response to Van Degen's veiled threat, she subconsciously turns to the symbol of her indebtedness to him, with "her hand absently occupied with the twist of pearls he had given her" (140). Simultaneously Undine recognizes the potential fluctuation in her "market value" that might come with Van Degen's departure to Europe: "In a flash she saw the peril of this departure. Once off on the Sorceress, he was lost to her—the power of old associations would prevail. Yet if she were as 'nice' to him as he asked—'nice' enough to keep him—the end might not be much more to her advantage" (140).

In a speculative gamble calculated to best preserve her strategic advantage, Undine decides to run off to Dakota to secure a divorce so that she can marry Van Degen and thus climb further up the social ladder. Undine convinces her father to break the news of their divorce to Ralph, who is shocked to learn that Undine has gone to Dakota when he thought she was in Europe, exclaiming, "Do you mean to say Undine's in the United States?" Mr. Spragg's dry rejoinder acknowledges the geopolitical history of the divorce destination, musing, "Why, let me see: hasn't Dakota been a state a year or two now?" (203). A territory that was acquired from the French as part of the Louisiana Purchase in 1803, gradually wrested away from the Sioux people who long inhabited it, populated by Anglo-American settlers thanks in part to the Homestead Act in 1862, became the states of North and South Dakota in 1889, and played a critical role in the US fur, gold, and wheat export trades, Dakota signifies the expanding frontier, as well as the frontier of Undine's marital conquests.[5] Yet Wharton again reminds readers of the limitations to Undine's expansionist fantasy when Van Degen reneges on their agreement after pressure from his wife. Consequently, Undine's gamble is a bust, and she frames her poorly timed divorce in explicitly economic terms: "Her one desire was to get back an equivalent of the precise value she had lost in ceasing to be Ralph Marvell's wife. Her new visiting-card, bearing her Christian name in place of her husband's, was like the coin of a debased currency testifying to her diminished trading capacity" (221). Wharton was well acquainted with the risk of debasing one's cultural capital through divorce, as she herself was in the process of divorcing her husband while writing *The Custom of the Country*, after both partners had committed infidelities and she learned of her husband's secret speculation with $50,000 of her inherited money (Lee 399, 373). But unlike Wharton who was at least somewhat shielded by her literary success, Undine cannot participate in global financial markets in the way that her male peers do because of women's restricted public roles in the early twentieth century, so instead she speculates on her own worth, at this moment in the novel so unsuccessfully that she sees herself as a "debased currency."

By contrasting Undine's romantic maneuvers with Mr. Spragg's financial ones, Wharton acknowledges women's economic limitations and the creative steps they must take if they desire power: "She had done this incredible thing, and she had done it from a motive that seemed, at the time, as clear, as logical, as free from the distorting mists of sentimentality, as any of her father's financial enterprises. It had been a bold move, but it had been as carefully calculated as the happiest Wall Street 'stroke'" (223). Though Curtis Jadwin's attempt to short the wheat market in *The Pit* ends in financial ruin for him, his loss is not nearly so personal as Undine's because it is not his bodily autonomy that is at stake. Undine takes "bold moves" to acquire power in global economic context, but because the commodity is herself and not, say, pearls, or cotton, or wheat, Undine feels the weight of her mistimed bet much more intimately.

Luckily for Undine, even after her divorce and break with Van Degen, she still owns some collateral: the expensive pearls that

Van Degen had bought for her. These pearls reaffirm Undine's image of herself as a "warrior Queen" (60) despite evidence to the contrary and become an important means for her to reinvest in her social and marital future. Undine is reminded of the connection between the value of pearls and the value of a marriage (or divorce) when she confers with her recently divorced and remarried friend Indiana Rolliver. As Indiana advises Undine that she should have gotten her divorce "first thing" because "divorce is always a good thing to have: you never can tell when you may want it," she twirls her meretriciously long strands of pearls under Undine's fascinated gaze: "she wound her big bejewelled hand through her pearls—there were ropes and ropes of them" (212). The narrator interjects an aside as Undine stares at the pearls, and Wharton's use of free indirect discourse makes it unclear if the ironic commentary originates from the narrator or from Undine: "Undine . . . continued to gaze at the pearls. They were real; there was no doubt about that. And so was Indiana's marriage—if she kept out of certain states" (212). Although Indiana Rolliver's excessively long strands of pearls here are undoubtedly "real," the mockery of Indiana's quickie divorce seems to undercut the pearls' value as a signifier of "real" social status, and Wharton's blurring of the narrator's and Undine's perspective here allows readers to slip unthinkingly into adopting this competitive attitude of judgment toward Indiana. Wharton's language also hints at the geopolitical implications of marital ties through the narrator's suggestion that the authenticity of Indiana's marriage is determined by the jurisdiction of "certain states," raising the question of states' sovereignty and their ability to legislate intimate relationships.

Despite the back-handed criticism from the narrator that perhaps also reflects Undine's judgment of Indiana, Undine simultaneously seems to express a twinge of admiration for Indiana's ruthless pursuit of riches, and seeks to follow her example as the novel progresses. Wharton again draws attention to the double bind women face in leveraging their limited economic options, yet her ambiguous narration resists any definitive sense of judgment. Frederick Wegener claims such ambivalence is typical of Wharton's depiction of American social climbers, observing that "however sharply Wharton might have satirized uncultivated arrivistes" and "the nouveaux riches whose financial and social rise attended (and helped accelerate) America's drift into empire," she simultaneously seems to valorize these characters' unabashed thirst for power (794). In Undine's admiration for Indiana Rolliver's "ropes and ropes" of pearls, she buys into the "imperialist sensibility" (Wegener 803) that drives Wharton's characters to increasingly greater conquests. Yet at the same time Wharton points to the societal conditions that drive women like Undine to attempt to see themselves as powerful conquerors to combat the lack of actual economic and social power they have.

Thus, when Undine's father chastises her indiscretion in continuing to wear the expensive pearls that Van Degen bought her, Undine stubbornly resists his insistence that she return the pearls and instead devises a scheme to exchange the value of her pearls for a better position in the marriage market. When her father catches a glimpse of "the string of pearls she always wore" and asks where they came from, Undine is reminded of their affiliation with her affair: "She really had not thought about the pearls, except in so far as she consciously enjoyed the pleasure of possessing them; and her father, habitually so unobservant, had seemed the last person likely to raise the awkward question of their origin" (229). Just as Undine previously enjoyed the "conscious possession of the 'real thing'" when married to Ralph, here she "consciously" enjoys "the pleasure of possessing" Van Degen's pearls, all the while striving to be unconscious of the "awkward question of their origin." It is telling that it is Undine's father who makes her feel the discomfort of the "awkward question" of where the pearls came from; in his role as a moral arbiter of Undine's transgressions, his judgment is also a reminder of the determinant power of patriarchy over women's lives. Implicitly perhaps an element of the "pleasure of possessing" the pearls for Undine is the danger of knowing of their "awkward origin" (an extramarital affair) and wearing them anyway, as a reminder of how much or how little it is possible for women to flout societal norms. And because it is pearls that are the symbol of Undine's defiance, they also subtextually allude to their inter-imperial material history of dominance over cultural and economic Others.

After the Spraggs' masseuse and manicurist Mrs. Heeny exclaims upon sight of the pearls that Undine has "got a fortune right round your neck whenever you wear them," Undine has a realization: "for the first time she saw what they might be converted into, and what they might rescue her from; and suddenly she brought out: 'Do you suppose I could get anything for them?... They cost a lot of money: they came from the biggest place in Paris.'" (231). Undine recognizes the multiple levels of value that the pearls have: economic, social, symbolic, and pragmatic. The international provenance of the pearls, having come from the "the biggest place in Paris" along with being sourced from Asia, signals their relative status, but also a way for Undine to lay claim to participation in global markets and triangulate access to imperial power through her possession of these gems. Perhaps, in Undine's mind, she might be able to elevate her "debased currency" into something more valuable by converting the exotic lure of the pearls into economic and bodily freedom.

Undine dispatches Mrs. Heeny to sell the pearls in order to finance a trip to Europe to recover from the losses she suffered in her failed venture with Van Degen, and to burnish her reputation through European influence. Selling the pearls enables Undine to circulate more widely, traveling to Europe to seek better conditions for her current valuation by entering a market overseas. By equivocating between the value of the pearls and the value of Undine's beauty and status, Wharton emphasizes the inevitability of women's commodification regardless of their best efforts to maintain an illusion of power through imperial consumption. In spite of her attempts to claim power through her possession of pearls and vision of herself as a combative "warrior Queen," here any tenuous empowerment slips through her fingers as easily as Van Degen's necklace.

Undine's Royal Pearls and Global Vision of Conquest

Even when Undine acquires some actual international power through her calculated marriage to the French count Raymond de Chelles, she is not satisfied because his wealth does not finance her visions of luxury, as it is tied up in family land and heirlooms. Undine eventually expands her quest for economic dominance elsewhere, and the imperialist discourse that underwrote her previous actions finally rises to the surface of her self-conception when she reunites with her ex-husband Elmer Moffatt. When Undine attempts to surreptitiously sell de Chelles's family tapestries to a wealthy American art collector in an effort to convert them into a more liquid currency, she discovers the collector is none other than Moffatt, her first husband from her midwestern hometown whom she divorced because of his lack of economic prospects, but who now has made a fortune through shady but shrewd financial speculation, and has a reputation as "the greatest American collector" who "buys only the best" (325). Through Moffatt's collecting and Undine's final ensconcing in an imperial-like portrait, Wharton underscores the intertwined relationship between art and global financial dealings. One's image and reputation, she implies, circulate globally just as the commodities one speculates upon. Further, the power acquired through the purchase of art enables the purchaser to exert control over what kinds of visual narratives have value in a global market—a power to determine the narrative of one's relative social position that Undine has sought throughout the novel.

Moffatt's wealth and power tempts the opportunistic Undine, and she listens to his tales of conquest with a vision of him as an "Asiatic conqueror," seemingly almost a modern-day Genghis Khan with whom she might be able to enjoy the spoils of plunder. To cite again the quote included in the epigraph to this chapter, Undine's thoughts turn to things: "To have things had always seemed to her the first essential of existence, and as she listened to him the vision of the things he could have unrolled itself before her like the long triumph of an Asiatic conqueror" (329). The simile here "like the long triumph of an Asiatic conqueror" situates Undine's fantasy of consumption specifically in Asia, this time explicitly linking her vision to the stereotypical and racialized images of the "Orient" as resplendent with luxury and riches available for the taking. The phrasing of the comparison is also somewhat ambiguous here, leaving open the possibility that either she sees Moffatt as an "Asiatic conqueror" because of his material wealth, or perhaps that she herself is the "Asiatic conqueror" who will soon lay claim to these "things" by conquering Moffatt himself. Regardless, Undine's vision of power is framed in global, imperial terms, and her body is still currency in this nexus of exchange.

The image of Moffatt as an imperial conqueror through whom Undine gains access to wealth is reinforced by the novel's conclusion, in which pearls return as a symbol of imperial status that Undine can access only through marriage. After ending her brief marriage to de Chelles, Undine hastily remarries Moffatt, who is now in drastically different economic circumstances than when she first met him. Indulging her love for international travel, Undine neglects her son at home in New York, a son who knows his mother better through news clippings than through personal interaction. Mrs. Heeny, charged with caring for the boy, reads him some of these newspaper accounts of his mother's social conquests, pointing out one article that details a pearl necklace owned by Undine. Mrs. Heeny observes,

> Here's one about her last portrait—no, here's a better one about her pearl necklace, the one Mr. Moffatt gave her last Christmas. "The necklace, which was formerly the property of an Austrian Archduchess, is composed of five hundred perfectly matched pearls that took thirty years to collect. It is estimated among dealers in precious stones that since Mr. Moffatt began to buy the price of pearls has gone up over fifty per cent." (357)

Whereas Undine once attended a ball dressed as Empress Josephine "after the Prudhon portrait in the Louvre" (121), here she steps into a genuinely imperial role, signifying her power through the pearls once owned by an "Austrian Archduchess." Further, the newspaper notes that as a wedding gift, Moffatt gave Undine "a necklace and tiara of pigeon-blood rubies belonging to Queen Marie Antoinette" (358). Similarly, whereas Moffatt once wore a "large imitation pearl" (61), now he can buy "five hundred perfectly matched pearls" with a royal pedigree; his pearls are finally the "real thing."

In his historical account of Cartier jewelry, Hans Nadelhoffer notes that jewelry with a royal heritage (whether real or apocryphal) was highly sought after at the beginning of the twentieth century, and that "the greatest demand of all was for pearl necklaces which, despite their nebulous origins, were invariably attributed to Catherine the Great, Marie Antoinette or Empress Eugenie" (125). These jewels granted an air of legitimacy to nouveau riche Americans: "the purchase of foreign family jewels whose age and provenance gave their new owners a spurious pedigree" was "intended to legitimize their vast wealth in the eyes of the world and to establish them firmly within the desired cultural context" (Nadelhoffer 125). Undine's pearls are invested with the trappings of empire through the supposed "Austrian Archduchess" who once owned them, and they confer that symbolic status on Undine. In her discussion of Undine's jewelry and attire, Katherine Joslin even compares Undine to the famously avaricious Marie Antoinette—herself once an "Austrian Archduchess" before she became Queen of France. Joslin observes, "Undine Spragg works to display her clothes and jewels as Marie Antoinette would have done before the mirrors of Versailles. The tragic French queen stands as the iconic image of luxurious fashion in Western culture, and we see in Wharton's novel Undine's desire to define herself in Marie's image" (103). Undine's self-conscious fashioning of herself after this monarch reveals the global and imperial scope of her ambitions, given Marie Antoinette's leadership during a period of inter-imperial conflict between France, Great Britain, Austria, Russia, and the soon-to-be-independent American colonies. Wharton dissects the pleasures and perils of such affinities with imperial rulers: given women's limited paths to wealth and power, it can perhaps feel cathartic to align oneself with ruthless monarchs, and in this final triumphant image of Undine, we see the protagonist of the novel get what she has always wanted. Yet because this final chapter is focalized primarily through Undine's pitiable son Paul, who is reduced to reading about his mother's conquests in newspapers,

Wharton also establishes distance between readers and Undine. Perhaps Paul, like his father Ralph before him, sees Undine as one of "the Invaders" (48) who leave endless destruction in their wake.

The novel's conclusion implies that the access to economic power provided by Undine's marriage to Elmer Moffatt will never satisfy her expansionist vision, no matter how many royal gems she accumulates, because her social status will always be vulnerable and mutable. Upon arriving home one evening, Elmer casually mentions that one of their friends was recently appointed Ambassador to England. Undine expresses her skepticism that the newly appointed ambassador's wife would want to go to the "banquets and ceremonies and precedences" required of the position because of her lack of finery, speculating, "I shouldn't say she'd want to, with so few jewels" (363). In this moment, Undine makes explicit the connection between jewels and power that has been implicit for most of the text: in her mind, pearls and other gems grant the possessor entry to geopolitical negotiations. And yet no amount of pearls will be enough to secure Undine such a coveted and influential position, because, as Elmer points out, "they won't have divorced Ambassadresses" (363). Here Wharton makes even more overt the challenge that Undine has confronted for much of the novel: the entanglement of marital status and imperial power. The novel's final words voice Undine's frustration that this piece of global influence will be forever out of reach because of her divorce:

> But under all the dazzle a tiny black cloud remained. She had learned that there was something she could never get, something that neither beauty nor influence nor millions could ever buy for her. She could never be an Ambassador's wife; and as she advanced to welcome her first guests she said to herself that it was the one part she was really made for. (364)

Undine has internalized the message of empire, forever seeking to extend her power, yet in her dismay is also perhaps an embedded gendered protest, because her access to power will forever be determined by her past and present relationships with men. Although she is fairly successful at conquest in the limited ways that she can be, because she is a woman, her conquest is limited to trafficking in her own image to facilitate her consumption of Asian luxuries. As a woman in the early twentieth century, she can never be a geopolitical leader herself, nor even the wife of a global ambassador.

Compared to characters discussed in previous chapters, Undine seems uniquely bent on participating in the United States' expansionist economic mission, and uniquely unchastened for her symbolic participation in empire. In *Little Women,* Jo March comes to regret her imperialist imaginings that she sells in her potboiler fiction. Elizabeth Stuart Phelps's *Avis* is punished for her unconsciousness of the uglier aspects of global trade by losing her husband and her artistic vision. Woolson's *Anne* learns the dangers of inter-imperial competition and the way in which nostalgia for a more violent time can allow such violence to creep back in and structure one's life. Frank Norris's character Laura Jadwin is perhaps the closest analogue to Undine because of her performative self-fashioning as an art object and her dependence on her husband's wealth. But none of these characters acts as single-mindedly in search of power as Undine, nor do any of these authors seem quite so ambivalent about their moral judgment of their characters. With her portrait of Undine, a woman desperate to see herself as a "warrior Queen," the "Empress Josephine," or Marie Antoinette in the face of a world determined to diminish her value to the cost of a set of pearls, Wharton reveals the at times empowering symbolism of imperial conquest, even while detailing the "ravages" that such a mindset can wreak. However, as we will see in Nella Larsen's *Quicksand*, when one descends from colonized peoples, it is much more difficult to take lightly the fantasy of becoming an "Invader."

Shuttling Toward Orientalist "Things" in Larsen's *Quicksand*

The foreign incursion of Asian imports carries different associations for Wharton's Undine Spragg—a white middle-class social climber—than it does for Helga Crane, the protagonist of Nella Larsen's novel *Quicksand*—a mixed-race woman seeking to understand her place in a post-Reconstruction United States. Helga Crane's consumerist desires in Larsen's *Quicksand* mirror Undine's; however, the class and gender barriers to wealth and power that Helga faces are compounded because of her race. A manifestation of her deeper discontent with her conflicted identity, Helga's desire for "things" permeates Larsen's novel. We are told that "all her life Helga Crane had loved and longed for nice things" (6), Helga constantly chafes against a "ruthless force" in her life that keeps her "from getting the things she had wanted" (11), she wants "not money, but the things which money could give" (67), and though later in the novel Helga realizes that "things ... weren't enough for her" (116), she is nonetheless driven by the allure of consumption from the novel's first words to its last because of the perpetual precarity of her position that she continually seeks to stabilize. Though Helga loves clothes as much as Undine does, it is what Larsen describes as "blue Chinese" decor that recurs as a symbol of Helga's displaced longing, rather than the pearls that motivate Undine. Yet I suggest that these objects with "Oriental" associations serve a similar function in both Wharton's and Larsen's fiction. Larsen, like Wharton, dramatizes the consumer strategies women employ to reap some of the benefits of imperial power. In Helga, Larsen illustrates how much more tenuous the control over their own commodification is for women with hybrid, transnational, racially indeterminate identities, especially insofar as imperial power is racialized. If Undine's whiteness works as currency that she exchanges for greater access to luxury goods and economic power, Helga's Blackness holds value only if she gives in to the dehumanizing exotification of her image. Since nearly the entire novel is focalized through Helga, other than the final paragraph that hints at her death in childbirth, *Quicksand* makes it difficult to disentangle oneself from Helga's point of view, making readers fully feel the pain of her internalized "sense of shame" (7), "ironical disillusion" (7), a "feeling of smallness which had hedged her in" (46), and a recurring sense of "indefinite discontent" (81).

Through the geographic distance and inter-imperial movement they represent, objects like a "blue Chinese carpet" (1), or "blue Chinese jars of great age" (56), or even a "Chinese blue sky" (120) enable Helga to figure her escape from the restrictive structures of race, gender, and sexuality that "hedge her in." Helga rejects the exoticism projected onto her by fixating on the more concretely embodied exoticism of "blue Chinese" goods. The distant origins of these objects also allow Helga to imagine solidarity with peoples of color from around the world and the potential of forming a shared racial identity that could give her solace from her feelings of not belonging—a possibility that never comes to fruition. In *Quicksand*, Larsen offers a contrasting example to ambitious white heroines like Wharton's Undine Spragg, painfully detailing the more fraught and limited set of choices women of color like Helga must make in order to survive in a system that relentlessly works to disempower them.

In analyzing Helga's reluctance and even disdain toward her male suitors, Johanna M. Wagner comments that "she has stronger feelings about her wardrobe than about the men in her life" (131). Larsen critics have tended to focus more on what that calculus tells us about Helga's sexuality, rather than what it tells us about Helga's habits of consumption. Certainly there is much to be said about Larsen's complex depiction of early twentieth-century Black queer female sexuality. In her influential introduction to the Rutgers University Press edition of *Quicksand*, Deborah E. McDowell makes the case for the centrality of Black female sexuality in Larsen's novel, while Cheryl Wall elucidates the novel's dramatization of the psychic tolls of racism and sexism, and Claudia Tate carefully extracts the narrative strategies that Larsen crafts to first encourage and then subvert readerly identification with Helga's tormented subjectivity. Critics have observed not only the significance of the intersection of race and sexuality in *Quicksand*, but also the subtextual presence of Helga's queer desires, which, they variously argue, challenge the racial legacy of Atlantic modernity, the nativist undercurrents of twentieth-century African American culture and politics, and heteronormative structures of kinship.[6] In a world in which Black women's sexuality was "sensationalized" and literature often "pandered to the stereotype of the primitive exotic," *Quicksand*, according to McDowell, raises the question of "how to give a black female character the right to healthy sexual expression and pleasure without offending the proprieties established by the spokespersons of the black middle class" (xvi). In order to navigate this threat of the commodification of her sexuality, I suggest, Helga engages in a repetitive, insistent exoticization of the goods she consumes to maintain her dominant status over these objects, with even more desperation than Undine's reflexive envisioning of herself as some form of conqueror.

The urgency of Helga's consumption is driven by her perpetual sense of not belonging, a feeling rooted in her biracial identity and disconnection from her family. Abandoned by her Black father and ostracized by her deceased white mother's relatives, Helga reflects on their mutual animus: "They feared and hated her. She pitied and despised them" (6). If Helga is shunned by her white family "because of her Negro blood" (6), she is similarly cast out from the middle- and upper-class ranks of African American society because of lack of family connections: "Negro society, she had learned, was as complicated and as rigid in its ramifications as the highest strata of white society. If you couldn't prove your ancestry and connections, you were tolerated, but you didn't 'belong'" (8). Haunted throughout the novel by her sense of "a lack somewhere" (7), "some peculiar lack in her" (81), or a "formless and undesignated" feeling of "incompleteness" (92), Helga feels dismayed that "she could neither conform, nor be happy in her unconformity" (7). When she confronts her former desire to contribute to the racial uplift mission of the Naxos school where she works, Helga frames her current disgust with the school's hypocrisy in a materialist metaphor: "It was as if she had deliberately planned to steal an ugly thing, for which she had no desire, and had been found out" (7). For Helga, the acquisition of tangible "things" becomes a substitute for finding the nameless thing inside her that is always lacking. Although Helga's vague but persistent sense of dissatisfaction seems to originate from her alienation from her family and her search for a racial solidarity that affirms her identity, she struggles to name the source of her "indefinite longings" (51) and instead attempts to placate her desires with imported material objects that allow her to imagine her flight from the limitations of her current circumstances.

The exotic allure of Helga's possessions has not gone unnoticed by critics, though they primarily discuss the generalized aura of foreignness of the objects that Helga is so fond of, without exploring their specific material history. Cherene Sherrard-Johnson, for instance, identifies how Larsen "situates [Helga] within a modern setting saturated with Orientalist motifs" (841) as a way of "modernizing the mulatta figure" (836) by tapping into the primitivist trends in modernist literature and art. Both Sherrard-Johnson and Debra Silverman see Larsen as critical of the racist stereotypes of Black female sexuality as exotic implied in modernist primitivism. However, critics frequently see Helga as a passive, languid object of the gaze within a larger Orientalist tableau rather than an active consumer of foreign goods participating in a symbolic "act of imperial buy-in" (Hoganson 11). In doing so, they overlook the way Helga aims to use her consumption to tip the scales in her favor as she balances on the edge of subject and object, as well as the way these objects allow her to expand her imaginative vista to further-off horizons.

Transnational and imperial readings of *Quicksand* enable readers to identify the connection between Helga's self-protective movement throughout the novel and the global and inter-imperial origins of the "things" that propel her around the world. By linking Helga's "racially indeterminate" identity with her frequent geographic movement, scholars such as Laura Doyle, George Hutchinson, Karsten Piep, and Arne Lunde and Anna Westerstahl Stenport shed light on the global frame of Larsen's concerns about sexuality, commodification, and self-presentation through art, seeing Helga not as a passive figure in an Orientalist fantasy, but rather an active example of "the African-American's construction and self-construction as art object abroad" (Gray 258). Laura Doyle reveals that it is not only gender and race but also sexuality that threatens to constrict Helga, identifying a connection between Helga's "Atlantic crisscrossing" and her queer rejection of the "heterosexually captained mission of race" (394). As I argue, Helga deflects the exoticization of her racial, gender, and sexual identities onto Asian commodities, allowing her to imagine the escape that Doyle describes. The shared imperial history between the US and Denmark that Arne Lunde and Anna Westerstahl Stenport identify provides historical evidence of the inter-imperial subtext for Larsen's depiction of "Oriental" goods. Lunde and Stenport point to *Quicksand*'s silences about Danish colonialism, and contend that

> Denmark's own vexed attitudes (pride, glorification, shame, and amnesia) toward its colonial heritage in the Danish West Indies (which was sold to the United States in 1917) and the nation's role in the black Atlantic slave trade haunt the text in ways that have not been sufficiently interrogated. (229)

The US and Denmark shared not only a colonial history, but also, as I will illustrate, a history of imperial trade with China. The material history of "blue Chinese" porcelain that both empires imported—and that Larsen repeatedly invokes throughout *Quicksand*—reveals the hybridity and inter-imperial exchange that marked the production of these porcelain objects. As John Cullen Gruesser suggests, Black writers at the turn of the twentieth century were critical of US imperial expansion because of its damaging implications for Black Americans, but they also "often did not adopt and maintain a fixed position on the subject of imperialism" (6). This is certainly the case for Larsen's ambivalent depiction of the consumption of goods that signify imperial control. Helga's longing for "Oriental" goods figures her desire to lay claim to the United States' dominance in inter-imperial trade, her effort to shore up her sense of self in the face of the psychological wounds that threaten to undo her, and her attempt to resist the ever-looming threat of commodification in a system that once bought and sold women like her.

The Inter-Imperial Hybridity of "Blue Chinese" Porcelain

Larsen peppers *Quicksand* with references to Asian-inspired decor, and her mentions of "blue Chinese" objects occur at three important turning points in the text: the "blue Chinese carpet" (1) in the opening scene, where Helga voices her discontent with her life at the restrictive Naxos school; the "blue Chinese jars of great age" (56) in a scene at the New York house of her friend Anne Grey immediately before Helga leaves for Copenhagen; and the "Chinese blue sky" (120) that Helga sees toward the end of the novel after her unexpected religious conversion and return to the South with her new husband Reverend Mr. Pleasant Green. The opening of the novel, where Larsen first refers to "blue Chinese" goods, instigates the cyclical and transnational movement of the rest of the novel. Here, Helga sits in her room, surrounded by an exotic array of objects, and feeling "unnerved" (2). Larsen writes:

> Helga Crane sat alone in her room, which at that hour, eight in the evening, was in soft gloom. Only a single reading lamp, dimmed by a great black and red shade, made a pool of light on the blue Chinese carpet, on the bright covers of the books which she had taken down from their long shelves, on the white pages of the opened one selected, on the shining brass bowl crowded with many-colored nasturtiums beside her on the low table, and on the oriental silk which covered the stool at her slim feet. It was a comfortable room, furnished with rare and intensely personal taste, flooded with Southern sun in the day, but shadowy just then with the drawn curtains and single shaded light. (1)

Helga's "rare and intensely personal taste" attracts her to vibrant objects with distant associations, including a "blue Chinese carpet" and an "Oriental silk." Describing this scene as an "'oriental' portrait" of Helga (Wagner 134) that resembles "a chamber in an Arabian harem" (Tate 248), scholars often read it as a tableau that gives an "illusion of aesthetic harmony" (Hostetler 37) in which Helga is one colorful object among many.

Instead of perceiving Helga as a passive object in an Orientalist scene, I see Helga's active consumption as an acquisitive gesture toward the United States' power in inter-imperial trade. As critics such as Kevin Gaines, Lauren M. Rosenblum, and Keguro Macharia have described, the substantial Black middle-class population in the early twentieth century employed various strategies, including consumption, to legitimize their class status in defiance of racial prejudice. Helga participates in such legitimization efforts through her enthusiastic consumption of sophisticated goods, and yet she also resists the didactic ideology of "racial uplift" promulgated by the Black middle-class population of the Naxos school, developing "a deep hatred for the trivial hypocrisies and careless cruelties which were, unintentionally perhaps, a part of the Naxos policy of uplift" (5). Rosenblum emphasizes the class status signaled by Helga's consumption in the opening scene, explaining that early twentieth-century magazines written by and for Black audiences

> referred to similar material items that also helped to counteract the negative stereotype of Blacks as poor and rural by focusing on items that represent sophistication and wealth. A 1918 advertisement from *The Messenger* ... offers "Frank R. Smith Furniture of the Better Kind" and "Oriental and Domestic Rugs" perhaps not unlike the "blue Chinese carpet" Helga has in her room. (51)

If the purchase of foreign goods was a way for Black consumers to defy demeaning stereotypes, it was also a way for some to project their superiority over immigrants and other marginalized groups, according to Keguro Macharia. Macharia notes that the juxtaposition of Helga's "high yellow" skin color with her immersion among "orientalist motifs" reframes "the contemporary African American designation 'high yellow' by refracting it through anti-immigrant, specifically anti-Asian, discourses" (261).[7]

Given this context of Black middle-class status signaling that, as Macharia describes, at times worked in concert with anti-immigrant rhetoric, I interpret Helga's desire for "blue Chinese" goods as yet another example of the conflicted consumption that allowed Undine Spragg, Avis Dobell, and Zora Cresswell to navigate their varied positions in relation to US empire and economic expansion. In the following paragraphs, I will briefly outline the history of "blue Chinese" pigments and porcelain to argue for Helga's "blue Chinese" objects as symbols of hybridity, cultural exchange, and imperial economic power.

Although Larsen uses the descriptor "blue Chinese" in reference to a variety of objects in *Quicksand*, historically the term has typically been used to describe the blue-glazed Chinese porcelain that was first produced on a large scale during the Yuan dynasty (1280–1368 CE) and sold throughout the world well into the nineteenth and twentieth centuries (Juan, Leung, and Jiazhi 188). From its earliest years, the trade in Chinese blue porcelain was international and inter-imperial; according to Wu Juan, Pau L. Leung, and Li Jiazhi, "in the Yuan dynasty, porcelain was exported to Japan, Korea, the Philippines, Thailand, India, Turkey, Iran and some European countries" (188). The anachronistic names used here belie the full inter-imperial history of these regions that were involved in the porcelain trade: during the Yuan dynasty, Turkey was part of the Ottoman Empire, Iran would have been known as "Persia" and was under attack by the Mongols led by Genghis Khan, and the Philippines would not yet have been known by its current colonial name given by the Spanish in the sixteenth century, after King Philip.[8] The process and materials for producing Chinese blue porcelain were international, as well. Some of the cobalt used to create the blue glaze was likely imported from Persia (Juan et al. 195), and the chemistry techniques for stabilizing these blue pigments were likely passed on from Egyptian sources through the exchanges along the Silk Road (Berke 2486). Chinese porcelain was coveted globally for centuries, and by the eighteenth century, it was exported to "Holland, England, France, Sweden, Denmark, Portugal, and Spain" (Le Corbeiller and Frelinghuysen 28).

Though the Chinese blue porcelain that draws Helga in *Quicksand* would have been available in her mother's home of Denmark before it was available in the US, it took on uniquely American imperial and patriotic connotations once the US established direct trade with China after the American Revolution. Indeed, one of the more economically enticing benefits of the US achieving independence from England was the ability to engage in direct trade with China for lucrative and desired goods like porcelain, tea, and silks. Clare Le Corbeiller and Alice Cooney Frelinghuysen explain that

> shortly after the United States signed the Treaty of Paris in 1783, signaling the country's ultimate independence, a group of four enterprising businessmen from Philadelphia and New York formed a syndicate that would embark on direct trade with China for the first time. (40)

In its first voyage to trade directly with China, the US vessel the *Empress of China* was packed full of American commodities—including some discussed previously in this book—ready to exchange for porcelain and other Chinese goods popular with American consumers: "The *Empress of China*, with a cargo of ginseng from Maryland and Virginia, furs from the northern states and Canada, and lead, wine, tar, and silver dollars, sailed from New York Harbor on February 22, 1784, bound for Canton (Guangzhou)" (40).

As imported goods like Chinese blue porcelain became more widely available to American consumers, they grew to symbolize US independence and economic power, according to Jessica Lanier, who notes that "trade with China and its products had enormous symbolic as well as practical value for the new nation's aspirations. Commerce, patriotism, and the future of America as 'a free and independent nation' were bound up in the U.S.-China trade from its inception" (100), and that "the acquisition of Chinese porcelain, in particular, allowed people of all classes to secure a piece of America's new global identity" (101). The purchasing power of American and European customers influenced the designs that decorated Chinese export porcelain, becoming "an artistic hybrid, subsuming ever-shifting balances between East and West as well as interactions within each culture" (Le Corbeiller and Frelinghuysen 28) because of the way that American requests for their coats of arms and patriotic imagery were integrated together with more traditional designs by Chinese artisans. This intermingling of cultural forms shifted the symbolism of Chinese blue porcelain by the end of the nineteenth century, as it came to represent "not China but rather American patriotism, its peaceful harbors and prosperity, perhaps a good bowl of punch, and a toast to the success of a rising empire" (Lanier 113).

Thus, "blue Chinese" objects in *Quicksand* can signify not just Helga's "exotic" aesthetic taste, but also this centuries-long history of inter-imperial material and cultural exchange, the rise of the US as an independent nation and empire, an American consumer power so strong that it could bend international designs to conform to its own taste, and US patriotism grounded in imperial economic expansion. This geographically expansive and geopolitically fraught history draws our attention to the fantasies of flight and movement that almost always immediately follow Helga's appreciations of Asian imports. In the first chapter of *Quicksand*, for instance, shortly after gazing down at the blue Chinese rug, Helga picks up a book with even more explicit Orientalist associations, and dreams of leaving Naxos to go on a vacation. The narrative, focalized through Helga, explains her rationale for her reading material: "Of the books which she had taken from their places she had decided on Marmaduke Pickthall's *Saïd the Fisherman*. She wanted forgetfulness, complete mental relaxation, rest from thought of any kind" (2). Deborah McDowell's footnote about Helga's reading material explains that Pickthall was an "English Orientalist novelist. *Saïd the Fisherman* (1903) has Eastern color, movement, and sharp authenticity. Perhaps Larsen intends an ironic contrast to the dull sobriety and sterility of Naxos" (243). With her Orientalist imagination triggered by the blue carpet—which is the color of the aesthetically hybrid, globe-crossing symbol of US patriotic imperialism, Chinese export porcelain—Helga turns to an overt narrative of "Eastern" exoticism and otherness. I suggest that this is not merely Larsen's way of creating an "ironic contrast" to Naxos, as McDowell writes, but also Larsen's strategy for making the Orientalist subtext of the carpet into text. Larsen deconstructs the process by which the cultural dominance symbolized by consuming "Oriental" goods enters the consumer's imagination and is reinforced through literary discourse. Similar to Jo March's unthinking internalization of the Orientalist message of the pyramids lecture, Larsen has Helga move subconsciously from Asian object to Orientalist narrative.

Helga subsequently gives up on her reading, determining that even *Saïd the Fisherman* cannot offer enough of an escape, because "in such a mood even *Saïd* and his audacious villainy could not charm her, she wanted an even more soothing darkness" (3). The hint of erotic imagery in the idea that *Saïd* "could not charm her" suggests that the culturally dominant heterosexual script does not fully seduce Helga, a glimpse at her psychological turmoil about her sexual identity. Perhaps inspired by the symbolically distant origins of the blue Chinese carpet and the far-off caper recounted in *Saïd*, and seeking to escape the confinement of the heteronormative world she lives in, Helga yearns for similar geographic distance: "She wished it were vacation, so she could get away for a time. 'No, forever!' she said aloud" (3). As if Helga's Orientalist projection does not suffice as a salve for her inner wounds around her conflicted racial, gender, and sexual identity, she seeks a physical displacement of her problems through movement. Orientalist discourses of otherness like the ones Helga consumes here were prevalent in the nineteenth-century Black press, according to Helen Jun. Discussing what she terms "black Orientalism," Jun analyzes how "Orientalist discourses of Asian cultural difference ambiguously facilitated the assimilation of black Americans to ideologies of political modernity and consolidated black identification as U.S. national subjects" (1048). Yet at the same time, early twentieth-century African American activists sought to align themselves in solidarity with peoples of color from around the globe, including in the "East." For instance, in a fictional international summit that includes representatives from China, Japan, Egypt, India, and the US, W. E. B. Du Bois's 1928 novel *Dark Princess* forwards the notion that "Pan-Africa belongs logically with Pan-Asia" (20). Thus, Helga's fetishization of Asian goods facilitates her ambivalent jockeying among intersecting and competing imperial dynamics—perhaps triangulating power over a distant region to elevate herself, or perhaps expressing a shared feeling of marginalization.

Larsen thus forges a connection between Asian-inspired goods and Helga's desired or actual movement across the globe throughout the novel. This connection represents her mutable status as active consumer and decorative object to be consumed. Larsen calls attention to Helga's balancing act when a colleague at Naxos makes a comment that is intended as a compliment, but which further reinforces Helga's commodification. When the colleague hears that Helga might be leaving Naxos, she implores her not to, saying, "we need a few decorations to brighten our sad lives" (14). Helga responds by turning her gaze once again to objects that figure both her ability to escape and her claim to "a piece of America's new global identity" (Lanier 101):

> Helga was unmoved. She was no longer concerned with what anyone in Naxos might think of her, for she was now in love with the piquancy of leaving. Automatically her fingers adjusted the Chinese-looking pillows in the low couch that served for her bed. Her mind was busy with plans for departure. (15)

Reflexively, upon being diminished into a mere object and boxed in by her circumstances, Helga reaches "automatically" for the "Chinese-looking pillows," rooting her plan for "departure" in the distance they represent.

Larsen establishes Helga's "automatic" grasping for imported goods as a repeated ritual through which Helga reaches for imperial consumer power in defiance of her own commodification. When Dr. Robert Anderson, like Helga's colleague, urges her not to leave Naxos because of her unique "appreciation of the rarer things in life" and her "dignity and breeding" (21), Helga again grounds her revolt in the objects around her. Before defiantly quitting for good, Helga's mind swirls with Dr. Anderson's assumption of her refined family history in his comment that she has "breeding," an observation she knows is contradicted by the fact that her "father was a gambler who deserted my mother, a white immigrant," and that "it is even uncertain that they were married" (21). Dr. Anderson's mischaracterization of her family history torments Helga, and she turns her gaze to his rug to escape her feeling of shame: "At these words turmoil rose again in Helga Crane. The intricate pattern of the rug which she had been studying escaped her. The shamed feeling which had been her penance evaporated. Only a lacerated pride remained" (21). The carpet in Dr. Anderson's office offers a visual echo of the "blue Chinese carpet" in the opening scene that led Helga to realize that she wanted to get away, not for a vacation, but "forever!" (3). Looking carefully at the "intricate pattern of the rug" until it "escaped her," Helga soon follows the disappearing trail of the rug by insisting on her departure and developing a plan to move to Chicago. Larsen thus illustrates the intervening forces that cause women like Helga to waver in their resolve and sense of identity, yet also spurs them on to buy into and challenge the competitive system that determines status. In this system, foreign goods can offer a quick recentering of power, because they reinforce the possessor's position of dominance over cultural Others in an inter-imperial field.

As Helga's travel transforms from imagined to actual, Larsen threads references to Asian goods at various places along her journey, as if their exotic allure and imaginative distance propel Helga away from the psychic wounds that haunt her. When Helga settles in New York after an ill-fated stint in Chicago, the narrative that is again focalized through Helga frames her newfound good luck in stereotyped imagery of Chinese good luck. Helga reflects, "having finally turned her attention to Helga Crane, Fortune now seemed determine to smile, to make amends for her shameful neglect. One had, Helga decided, only to touch the right button, to press the right spring, in order to attract the jade's notice" (37). Helga links her good fortune with an imaginary jade talisman—a stone mined in China and often carved into intricate sculptures—as if implicitly recognizing the connection between her ability to move geographically and flee her intractable sense of alienation and her consumption of Asian commodities. More symbols of good fortune greet Helga when she arrives at the home of Anne Grey, where she lodges in New York. Anne and Helga soon bond over the unanimity of their "aesthetic sense" (44), which, significantly, is characterized by a judicious sprinkling of Asian decorative objects. Upon entering Anne's home, Helga notes the way Anne's European furniture "mingled harmoniously" with decor from Asia—much in the way nineteenth-century Chinese blue export porcelain mixed traditional Asian designs with American or European motifs. Anne's tastefully decorated home features "brass-bound Chinese tea-chests . . . a lacquered jade-green settee with gleaming black satin cushions, lustrous Eastern rugs, ancient copper, Japanese prints, some fine etchings, a profusion of precious bric-a-brac, and endless shelves filled with books" (44). As if fulfilling Helga's prediction that she might "attract the jade's notice," Anne's home includes a "lacquered jade-green settee"; these new circumstances seem to offer Helga an escape from her previous feelings of confinement because of their novelty, because of the many objects that offer outlets for her imaginative travel to places like China and Japan, and because of the empowering association with these places and ownership of their products. Perhaps subtextually, the objects for which Anne and Helga have a shared affinity also signal a potential connection between them that could assuage Helga's lack of family and connections.

However, Larsen demonstrates how the consumption and admiration of foreign objects offers only a temporary escape, especially if the world conspires to close off one's movements and identity, as it does for Helga. Anne's fixation on the question of race especially troubles Helga: "It stirred memories, probed hidden wounds, whose poignant ache bred in her surprising oppression and corroded the fabric of her quietism" (49). Anne proves to be an irritant rather than a balm for Helga's "hidden wounds" about her identity. In her discomfort with Anne's insistent focus on race, Helga imagines herself as a piece of fabric slowly fraying away, just as the carpet in Dr. Anderson's office began to escape her vision when she felt limited by his assessment of her "dignity and breeding."

To manage this feeling of turning back into an object, Helga looks again to blue Chinese goods to envision the distance she will soon travel to escape Anne's constricting views on race. Helga thus lays claim to rightful participation as a full citizen in the "success of a rising empire" (Lanier 113) represented by the hybridity of Chinese export porcelain. Just before leaving for Copenhagen to stay with her mother's relatives, Helga attempts to do penance for her abrupt abandonment of Anne by arranging the decor in her house:

> She busied herself with some absurdly expensive roses which she had ordered in, spending an interminable time in their arrangement. At last she was satisfied with their appropriateness in some blue Chinese jars of great age. Anne *did* have such lovely things, she thought. (56)

To underscore the tie between Anne's "blue Chinese jars of great age" and Helga's imminent journey, Larsen immediately follows this detail with Helga's fantasy of travel: "With rapture almost, she let herself drop into the blissful sensation of visualizing herself in different, strange places, among approving and admiring people, where she would be appreciated, and understood" (56). Larsen's juxtaposition here suggests that Anne's "blue Chinese jars of great age" are the conduit for Helga's "blissful sensation of visualizing herself in different, strange places" and her subsequent departure for Copenhagen. Helga's reverie about an array of "approving and admiring people" also alludes to the possibility of an internationalist, Pan-African, and

Pan-Asian solidarity to be found in the "different, strange places" where the blue Chinese jars came from, a solidarity that might finally soothe the "poignant ache" of her "hidden wounds."

Weaving an Integrated Selfhood

As Helga attempts to resolve the feelings that "corroded the fabric of her quietism" by turning her gaze to Chinese goods and the possibility of both dominance and solidarity that they represent, Larsen introduces an image that competes against Helga's disintegrating fabric of self-worth: the shuttle. Larsen repeats this shuttle simile twice in the novel to characterize Helga's desire for psychological and physical movement. When she eventually finds herself in Copenhagen, Helga cannot help thinking back to the world she left behind in New York, to the point where Helga "caricatured herself moving shuttle-like from continent to continent" (96). Later, after Helga has returned to New York and had an uncomfortable conversation with Dr. Anderson about an unplanned kiss between them, Larsen describes Helga's flustered thoughts: "back and forth in her staggered brain, wavering, incoherent thoughts shot shuttle-like" (109). Given Helga's movement throughout the novel from Naxos, to Chicago, to New York, to Copenhagen, back to New York, and then to Alabama—movement often imaginatively instigated by the foreign goods surrounding her—the shuttle is an apt metaphor for Helga's transnational crisscrossing. As Jeffrey Gray observes, "This shuttling movement is the controlling figure of *Quicksand*" (259). Yet embedded within the geographic image of Helga's "shuttle-like" thoughts identified by critics like Gray is a second, more material, symbol: the shuttle as a tool to weave thread back and forth in a loom to create fabric. The shuttle's dual meaning brings together images of movement, entanglement, and commodity production, thus aptly capturing the competing forces that Helga negotiates. The shuttle image also reintroduces the question of Helga's indeterminate agency: if she and her thoughts move "shuttle-like," is Helga the weaver in this scenario, or the tool that is moved and manipulated by someone else, or the fabric that is in the process of formation? In this image, Larsen continues to unravel the tension Helga experiences between acting as an agent and an object, and as a commodity and a consumer.

Joined together with the movement of Helga's shuttle-like thoughts is the metaphorical fabric created as Helga attempts to weave her identity together into an integrated whole. Larsen frequently compares the natural world above and below Helga to various fabrics, as if to signify the ever-looming and slightly out-of-reach hope of achieving a coherent sense of self-worth that threads together the pleasure of consumption with freedom from the threat of objectification. Like the recurring appearance of "blue Chinese" goods, a cloth-like sky follows moments when Helga feels the vulnerability of her subject position, and when she consequently reaffirms her agency through imaginative and physical movement. For instance, when Helga's gazing at Dr. Anderson's intricate rug gives her the fortitude to quit her position at Naxos, following her resignation she sees "Long, soft white clouds, clouds like shreds of incredibly fine cotton, streaked the blue of the early evening sky" (22). On Helga's ocean journey to Copenhagen, she enjoys "the serene calm of the lingering September summer, under whose sky the sea was smooth, like a length of watered silk, unruffled by the stir of any wind" (64). The visual harmony of the sky and the sea represent the tightly woven rather than antagonistic sense of identity and integrity that Helga seeks through her shuttle-like movements, the empowering possession of foreign goods propelling her forward. Larsen makes Helga's feeling of self-possession explicit immediately following her description of the sea as a "length of watered silk," writing that on this journey Helga has a renewed feeling of "that blessed sense of belonging to herself and not to a race" (64). In contrast to the way in which Anne Grey's concern about race "corroded the fabric of her quietism" (49), here the movement of Helga's shuttle restores the frayed edges of her sense of self into a luxurious length of silk—tellingly another commodity frequently imported from China.

Yet Larsen illustrates how readily the fabric of Helga's self-worth can be undone by the exoticization of her image, a danger made dramatically clear during her time in Copenhagen. Much has been written about the way Helga's Danish aunt and uncle capitalize on her seemingly exotic appearance by dressing her in brightly colored clothes and putting her on display at social gatherings. Lunde and Stenport analyze how the history of Danish colonialism frames the actions of Helga's aunt and uncle, even as they are oblivious to their implicit reenactment of imperial history:

> The Dahls themselves are obtuse about and indifferent to the social, political, and historical ramifications of Denmark's own historical involvement in the slave trade and its still fresh imperial memories of the Danish West Indies. Nor do they ever acknowledge their own ambivalent relationship to racial and ethnic differences. (233)

These geopolitical echoes resound in the portrait that artist Axel Olsen paints of Helga. Steeped in racist stereotypes of Black female sexuality, the painting alienates Helga from her perception of herself:

> The picture—she had never quite, in spite of her deep interest in him, and her desire for his admiration and approval, forgiven Olsen for that portrait. It wasn't, she contended, herself at all, but some disgusting sensual creature with her features . . . Yes, anyone with half an eye could see that it wasn't she. (89)

Critics agree about the degrading aesthetics of Olsen's painting: Anthony Dawahare suggests that Olsen "replicates the racist fantasy about black women as jezebels" (27); Claudia Tate argues that the painting forces Helga to recognize "the sexuality that she has so carefully sublimated or adamantly rejected" ("Desire and Death in *Quicksand*" 249); and Cherene Sherrard-Johnson interprets the painting as "a purchasable version of Helga as a sexualized, primitive objet d'art" (846).

Though Helga, like Undine, poses for paintings as a way of harnessing the currency of her image, she is unwilling to cash in the way that Undine does because the vision of herself in another's eyes degrades her humanity. Recalling Du Bois's theory of "double consciousness," Helga sees herself through the eyes of this white Danish male artist, and his vision contrasts sharply with her own. While Undine's whiteness is emphasized and celebrated in her portrait, Helga's Blackness is exaggerated and fetishized, pigeonholing her into the limited visual vocabulary available to early twentieth-century artists to represent Black female subjectivity. Cherene Sherrard-Johnson argues that *Quicksand* is a direct rebuke to nineteenth-century visual tropes of the mulatta figure as "pathetic victim or tragic symbol" (836), suggesting that Larsen's novel "is anchored in a critique of the visual images of African American women then circulating throughout the culture and limiting the mobility of the New Negro woman in the intellectual and artistic communities of the 'talented tenth.'" (836). Here, Larsen critiques the deterministic iconography of Black women's bodies created and perpetuated by white patriarchal imperial culture, which threatens to dismantle the sense of self that Helga shored up in her journey across the Atlantic.

Thus, adding another length of weft to the fabric of her identity, Helga shuttles back to the US in search of a greater sense of belonging. Feeling adrift after an unplanned kiss with Robert Anderson—who at this point in the novel is married to Anne Grey—Helga stumbles forlornly into the church service of a visiting preacher from the

South. After a feverish conversion, Helga wakes up the next morning feeling an urgency for existential and spiritual fulfillment, reflecting, "all I've ever had in life has been things—except just this one time. At that she closed her eyes, for even remembrance caused her to shiver a little. Things, she realized, hadn't been, weren't enough for her. She'd have to have something else besides" (116). In this moment, the sky appears in her vision, untethered from the images of cotton and silk it had been associated with previously, as if to symbolize Helga's desire for "something else besides" things: "Just for a fleeting moment Helga Crane, her eyes watching the wind scattering the gray-white clouds and so clearing a speck of blue sky, questioned her ability to retain, to bear, this happiness at such cost as she must pay for it" (116).

The cost that Helga must pay for this happiness apparently entails both a renouncement of her consumerist desires and a self-sacrificing marriage to Reverend Mr. Pleasant Green, which requires a move to Alabama and a seemingly perpetual state of child-bearing. Though Helga seems to experience a brief glimmer of happiness in her early moments of living in the South and serving as a pastor's wife, the reappearance of blue Chinese goods in her imagination suggest Helga's subconscious resistance to the self-abnegation required by religious devotion. The symbolism of blue Chinese porcelain returns, this time sublimated in the sky, as Helga's final gesture to solidify her status as an agent of empire instead of an object of it:

> Here, she had found, she was sure, the intangible thing for which, indefinitely, always she had craved. It had received embodiment... Everything contributed to her gladness in living. And so for a time she loved everything and everyone. Or thought she did. Even the weather. And it was truly lovely. By day a glittering gold sun was set in an unbelievably bright sky. In the evening silver buds sprouted in a Chinese blue sky, and the warm day was softly soothed by a slight, cool breeze. (120)

Helga's hope that she has finally found the "intangible thing" that she had always "craved" locates the source of her consumer desires in her ineffable woundedness for which she has not yet found a tangible treatment. While expressing an apparent appreciation for non-material things like the weather and the sun, Helga's language here also associates the sky's hue with the Chinese imports that once decorated her room. Bringing Helga's fantasies about blue Chinese goods together with the sky as a fabric woven through her shuttle-like movement, Larsen offers a brief glimpse at the peace Helga might achieve by reconciling her zig-zagging desires. However, the fact that Helga's sense of satisfaction is reliant on the distance implicit in the far-off, foreign sky suggests that it is impossible for Helga to remain suspended in this moment of harmony for long.

In her repeated references to "blue Chinese" goods that culminate in Helga's final vision of this "Chinese blue sky," Larsen dramatizes the constant temptation to triangulate one's identity in relation to notions of "domestic" and "foreign" goods and spaces, illustrating the conflictedness faced by US racial minorities when engaging in forms of Orientalist consumption that were once available only to white consumers. In spite of Helga's daydream earlier in the novel that she might meet "approving and admiring people" in her international travels, a latent wish for Afro-Asian solidarity, she never actively expresses or enacts such affinities, which in turn become problematically mingled with Orientalist consumer desire. Although Helga strives to find herself through imaginative and physical displacement, projection, and fantasy, the fact that she can never find lasting fulfillment shows the emptiness of Orientalism as a strategy for self-actualization.

In the conclusion of the novel, which ends with the birth of Helga's fifth child and, implicitly, her death as a result of the physical and psychic trauma of these births, Larsen illustrates the fatal damages wrought by the constant management of the forces threatening to undo Helga's identity. Indeed, even in the penultimate paragraph of the novel, delirious from lack of sleep and ill from her pregnancy, Helga continues to reach for foreign "things" that might ground her identity once more in the dominance of imperial consumption:

> It was so easy and so pleasant to think about freedom and cities, about clothes and books, about the sweet mingled smell of Houbigant and cigarettes in softly lighted rooms filled with inconsequential chatter and laughter and sophisticated tuneless music. It was so hard to think out a feasible way of retrieving all these agreeable, desired things. Just then. Later. When she got up. By and by. (135)

Dreaming of French perfume and cigarettes made from globally traded tobacco, Helga drifts off thinking about the difficulty of envisioning "a feasible way of retrieving all these agreeable, desired things." Though Helga aspires to acquire these things "when she got up," again associating the consumption of commodities with physical and imaginative movement, Larsen hints that Helga's shuttle-like journeys have finally come to a close.

As their protagonists cycle through the ups and downs of social status, Wharton and Larsen furnish them with physical touchstones that ground their ambitions. With their repeated references to pearls and "blue Chinese" bric-a-brac, Wharton and Larsen walk the tenuous tightrope balancing women's status as consumer and commodity, carefully observing how women use foreign goods in their attempts to more firmly establish their dominant status as consumers in an inter-imperially contested economy. Though Undine appears to achieve success in her quest for wealth and status and Helga's journey concludes in failure and death, both characters remain dissatisfied to the very end. This perpetual unfulfillment presents Wharton and Larsen's final protest against the gendered, racialized, and heteronormative limitations placed on women at the turn of the twentieth century. Undine and Helga continue grasping for more because class, race, and gender barriers to power persist, and because their status remains uncertain no matter how rich or desirable they become. In Undine's relentless drive to acquire more and Helga's constant longing for some "intangible thing" that might resolve the tensions in her identity, Larsen's and Wharton's plots are structured by their protagonists' continual attempts to outrun the precarity of their positions. Along the way these characters confront endless mechanisms that reinforce the status quo: the objectification of women's bodies and sexuality; the limited opportunities women have to support themselves; the social and political ostracizing of divorcees; the regressive and heterosexist gender roles that relegate childcare and household duties to women; the segregated society that presents women of color with limited options for achieving middle-class stability; and the competitive geopolitical conditions that pit empires—and women—against each other. Narrating their novels through Undine's and Helga's embattled perspectives, Wharton and Larsen force us to feel their triumphs and torments.

In their emphasis on capturing the complexity of subjectivity and human consciousness, novels like Wharton's and Larsen's align readers' gazes with those of their characters to encourage identification with their psychological struggles, all while presenting a realistic and unromantic dissection of contemporary social problems. Early twentieth-century realist and modernist fiction thus names and dramatizes the psychological desires that structure economic forces, affirming the fantasies and frustrations of this rapidly growing global consumer culture that would only become more efficient and widespread by the end of the century and into the twenty-first.

Notes

1. While I focus here on Wharton's depiction of pearls, Alan Ackerman focuses on the global life of oil in his analysis of consumption in Wharton's work, arguing that "her novels critique a society that takes for granted high-volume, nonrenewable energy, and specifically revolutionary new kinds of energy: petroleum, natural gas, and the fossil-fueled power stations necessary for the large-scale, continuous production of electricity" (925).
2. In characterizing the tone of Wharton and Codman's book, Miles Orvell likewise notes that it "wove the language of social distinctions into their judgments and warnings" (61). For more on Victorian decoration and material culture, see Kenneth Ames.
3. See also Kedon Willis, who analyzes *Quicksand* and *Custom of the Country* in particular, arguing that "given the overlooked similarities existing between *Custom* and *Quicksand*, Larsen's focus on race in both the US and Europe serves as a crucial rebuttal of racial erasure in both the United States and Europe" (65).
4. Further muddying readers' perception of Undine's imperial self-image are the nonfiction articles that were published in the same pages of *Scribner's Magazine* in the months that *The Custom of the Country* debuted. With essays celebrating the recent completion of the Panama Canal (Bishop, "A Benevolent Despotism"), or the North American conquests of seventeenth-century French settler-colonialism (Finley, "The French in the Heart of America"), *Scribner's* provided additional imaginative fodder for the readers who followed Undine's plight alongside such favorable depictions of imperial expansion.
5. See Norman K. Risjord, "North Dakota" and "South Dakota" in *Dakota: The Story of the Northern Plains*.
6. See Laura Doyle's chapter on Larsen in *Freedom's Empire*, Keguro Macharia, and Johanna Wagner, respectively.
7. Conversely, Larsen's reappropriation of European Orientalist discourses could be a strategy for speaking back to the conditions of oppression that they represent. This kind of imitation with a difference has long been a strategy for Black artists to defy the hegemony of white Western culture, according to Simon Gikandi (234).
8. See bibliographical entries for "Turkey," "Iran," and "Philippines."

Conclusion

A 2014 deconstruction of James McNeill Whistler's 1876 Gilded-Age *Peacock Room*, Darren Waterston's installation *Filthy Lucre* captures the persistent, dangerous allure of international trade from the nineteenth century to today. The walls of Waterston's room drip with gold paint, the floors are strewn with the detritus of smashed porcelain, and the shelves that once held ceramic vessels sag under the weight of the history they carried. In a replica of Whistler's painting *La Princesse du Pays de la Porcelaine* that hangs on the wall, Waterston covers the face of a kimono-clad woman with a swath of black paint, taking the objectification of the original painting to its extreme by removing any possibility of subjectivity from the woman depicted, while simultaneously creating an unsettling and uncanny picture of the black void of Orientalist desire. Waterston's refracted recreation of the *Peacock Room* thus offers a visual metaphor for the decay wrought by centuries of inter-imperial violence over global trade—damage still being felt and wrought well into the twenty-first century.

Whistler's original *Peacock Room* is a gilt-edged, richly saturated composition in blue and gold. Influenced by Asian designs with its intricately drawn peacocks, Whistler's room features walls full of nooks and crannies that eventually displayed his patron Frederick Richards Leyland's extensive collection of blue and white Chinese porcelain.[1] Curator Susan Cross observes that Waterston's piece "manifests visually and physically the ugliness embedded in the story of [the *Peacock Room*'s] creation"—a story that includes both a contentious dispute between Leyland and Whistler over the direction and scope of the project, and "the commodity culture that Leyland's collecting represents for Waterston" (13).[2] Characterizing *Filthy Lucre* as "a scab from a wound that will never truly heal," art historian John Ott suggests that the piece reminds viewers that "we cannot fathom a work of art without also looking at its complex web of economic and social relationships" (114). Though Waterston and his critics focus their attention primarily on the economic relationship between artist and patron, the history of the room's imported

Chinese porcelain, as detailed in the previous chapter, makes it impossible to look at this artwork without thinking about the economic relationships between empires that fought to secure favorable trade conditions, as well as the inter-imperial cultural exchange that led to the artistically hybrid blue and white porcelain. *Filthy Lucre* oozes with the ferocious competition over trade named and negotiated by the nineteenth- and twentieth-century writers in this book, an inter-imperial history that continues to shape contemporary geopolitics and culture. The twenty-first century, like the nineteenth, is confronted with questions about international trade policies, the ethical implications of consumption, and the consequences of economic inequality—questions that reveal the ongoing relevance of the cultural work begun by writers like Louisa May Alcott, Elizabeth Stuart Phelps, Constance Fenimore Woolson, María Amparo Ruiz de Burton, Frank Norris, W. E. B. Du Bois, Edith Wharton, and Nella Larsen.

During the same cultural moment in which Waterston envisions the destructive legacy of Orientalism, China continues to play an outsized role in the discourse of America's global trade relationships. More than a century after debates about tariffs raged in Congress and dominated election concerns, tariffs returned to the American political consciousness as a symbol of global economic power. In March 2018 President Donald Trump announced "punishing tariffs" on steel and aluminum in what reporters David J. Lynch and Caitlin Dewey call "a major escalation of his 'America First' trade offensive."[3] In September 2018, Trump enacted further tariffs that impacted as much as half of all imports from China, and he also expressed interest in placing tariffs on *all* Chinese goods.[4] Though during his presidency Trump battled with the United States' long-standing allies over trade policy—including Canada, Mexico, and the European Union—seemingly the greatest object of his consternation was China. Repeatedly characterizing Chinese trade policies as "unfair," Trump's rhetoric often constructed an opposition between American farmers—whom he claimed were "patriots, remember that"—with "China's very abusive trade practices," emphasizing that "we will not let anyone bully our wonderful American farmers."[5] Trump cast American farmers in a similarly sentimental light in a tweet posted on July 25, 2018, writing,

> China is targeting our farmers, who they know I love & respect, as a way of getting me to continue allowing them to take advantage of the U.S. They are being vicious in what will be their failed attempt. We were being nice—until now! China made $517 Billion on us last year.

Trump's narrative imagines the US and China in a competitive, zero-sum battle over economic dominance in which China is the "vicious" villain in contrast to the noble and innocent American farmers "who they know I love & respect." The consistent ire with which Trump has decried China's surging economic status betrays the fact that his trade penalties were at heart an expression of anxiety about the imagined threat that China poses to American imperial power, a reversal of the balance of power that has existed between the US and China since at least the nineteenth century.[6]

The history of trade with China, as we learned in Chapter 4 with Edith Wharton and Nella Larsen's depiction of pearls and porcelain, has carried imperial and patriotic weight since the years of American independence, when US entrepreneurs sought direct trade with China.[7] Indeed, in an essay on Trump's tariff policies for *Jacobin Magazine*, University of Massachusetts Amherst economics professor David M. Kotz connects twenty-first century trade policy with nineteenth-century desires, noting that "US big business has long felt conflicted about China," especially because "access to the storied China market—which has exerted a pull on the imagination of US businesses since the nineteenth century—has allowed them to make hefty profits." As the global balance of economic power has shifted and China has become an increasingly formidable leader, its relation to the US has become "one of rivalry," according to Kotz, who sees the "role of capitalist imperialism com[ing] into play" in the United States' twenty-first-century tariff policies with China, because "the biggest capitalist states, responding to the profit drive of capitalism, always seek to dominate markets, to control sources of raw materials, and to secure locations for profitable investment of capital. That impels such states to exercise political dominance over as much of the world as possible." To those familiar with the United States' historical participation in inter-imperial trade—as dramatized in novels by Norris, Ruiz de Burton, Woolson, and other writers at the turn of the twentieth century—this recent reassertion of economic power should be seen as no surprise, but rather a continuation of the US imperial economic project dating back to the eighteenth century. The disproportionate role that China has played in American consumers' imagination for centuries, including in fiction by Alcott and Larsen, contextualizes why China's economic position looms so large in politicians' minds today.

As the novels in this book have demonstrated, commodities and internationally traded goods have the power to conjure up narratives of imperial dominance. For Trump and the economic nationalists who have supported him, goods like steel and aluminum signify an ideological battleground over the United States' status as a world power and its self-sufficiency in supplying domestic products. In this way, the current rhetoric of "made in the USA" and "make America great again" echoes that of the 1861 article quoted in the introduction to this book, which argued that the United States' self-sufficiency in trade and lack of reliance on foreign imports demonstrated its superiority "over all other nations, in its commercial position or strength" ("Our Civil War").

Yet the United States' balance of trade has shifted dramatically since the Civil War era, when the country's global economic influence was rooted in its extensive exportation of natural resources like cotton and wheat.[8] While in the early years of its history the United States imported more goods than it exported, beginning in the 1870s it became a net exporter (Lipsey 690, 692), a trend that persisted for over a century until "the dramatic reversal of the 1980s" (Lindert 409).[9] Beginning in the late 1970s, the balance of trade turned negative, with the US importing far more than it exported; as of 2017, the total imports were approximately 1.5 times total exports.[10] For writers like Phelps and Du Bois, the United States' powerful export trade raised ethical questions about capitalism, imperialism, and consumers' involvement in the exploitation of a domestic labor force. However, twenty-first century American writers and artists must grapple additionally with a relatively recent shift in the United States' economic identity, as a nation and an empire increasingly dependent on imported goods just as it was during the early years of its history. Seeing the continuities between the United States' past and present economic ties to the globe, Waterston's *Filthy Lucre* offers a model for how contemporary artists might begin to reckon with the country's evolving position in a globally connected economy, as well as the increasingly urgent issue of climate disaster brought on by unbridled human consumption.

For literary scholars, there is a great deal more material to be mined in nineteenth- and twentieth-century American fiction that responds to the United States' economic position through the representation of commodities. Linking texts based on their places along temporally and geographically expansive commodity chains offers a methodology for comparing literature from different periods, genres, and national traditions. One might not imagine an author of sentimental children's fiction like Alcott to have much in common with a cynical naturalist writer like Norris, and yet, as this book has shown, they share a vision of a world interconnected by the materials and messages of inter-imperial trade. Further investigation of commodities in nineteenth- and twentieth-century fiction promises to reveal more unexpected pairings—perhaps articulating common economic concerns between Herman Melville's canonical epic tale of the whaling industry *Moby Dick* (1851) and the shipping business and climactic shipwreck at the center of Elizabeth Stoddard's much more obscure *The Morgesons* (1862). The United States' powerful international export trade recontextualizes a regional novel like Willa Cather's *My Ántonia* (1918), as the narrator's grandfather envisions how Nebraska's cornfields would one day become "the world's cornfields; that their yield would be one of the great economic facts, like the wheat crop of Russia, which underlie all the activities of men, in peace or war" (104). While best known for his muckraking novel about Chicago's meat industry, Upton Sinclair might also be understood as a critic of the global entanglement of business and empire, as dramatized in his novel *Oil!* (1926). Sinclair vilifies American oil tycoons' exertion of political pressure in the midst of World War I, as they express dissatisfaction with President Woodrow Wilson "not because he wasn't making the world safe for democracy, but because he wasn't making it safe for oil operators" (253).[11]

Many more American novels—canonical and not—come into contact with global commodities at some point along the chain, and thus have the potential to offer additional voices of dissent, celebration, or ambivalence about US participation in the gendered economies of inter-imperial trade. One thinks of Lydia Maria Child's *Hobomok* (1824), which is haunted by US timber, fur, and tobacco export industries, or iron korl in Rebecca Harding Davis's *Life in the Iron Mills* (1861), the titular amber beads in Harriet Prescott Spofford's "The Amber Gods" (1863), gemstones in Helen Hunt Jackson's *Ramona* (1884), curios of sea travel in Sarah Orne Jewett's *The Country of the Pointed Firs* (1896), the Western gold and silver prospecting in Mark Twain's *Roughing It* (1872), or the successful timber company of Angela Murray's morally dubious suitor in Jessie Fauset's *Plum Bun* (1929). A novel like Henry James's *The Spoils of Poynton* (1897) might be seen as an allegory for inter-imperial cultural and economic jockeying for power, as its characters competitively navigate family and marriage relationships to secure ownership over the titular Poynton. A home filled with an artfully curated collection of global bric-a-brac, Poynton is ruled over by matriarch Adela Gereth, for whom "the sum of the world was rare French furniture and oriental china" (49). James's violent and ambiguous conclusion that finds Poynton mysteriously burned to the ground anticipates the implosion of imperial fantasies spawned by global trade as figured in Waterston's *Filthy Lucre*.

The study of commodities in fiction presents a strategy for globally oriented literary scholarship not only through the international economic histories represented in American literature, but also through possible future comparative study with literature from around the world. Writers like Claude McKay and Amitav Ghosh present harsh critiques of imperial trade through the eyes of the laborers, farmers, and merchants who merely skirt the margins of most nineteenth- and twentieth-century American novels. McKay's *Banana Bottom* (1933) repudiates the destructive influence of Western international trade that forces the small Jamaican town of Banana Bottom to supply the desires of the international market. Closing the novel with a hurricane that wipes out the banana crop, McKay depicts the damages inflicted on the local population because of their lack of crop diversification. More recently, Ghosh's *Ibis Trilogy*, which includes the historical fiction novels *Sea of Poppies* (2008), *River of Smoke* (2011), and *Flood of Fire* (2015), narrates the nineteenth-century opium trade from the perspective of the multinational cast of characters brought together by the journey of a former slave ship turned opium export vessel from Baltimore, to Mauritius, to India, to China. While Alcott's *Eight Cousins* (1875) travels on an imaginative journey to China through a tour of a ship recently docked in Boston from China, Ghosh's trilogy depicts the voyage of a similar vessel bound for India and China, telling the story of the ship's treacherous trip through Indian farmers, American, Chinese, and African sailors, British merchants, and indentured laborers from around the globe—figures mostly invisible from Alcott's tale.[12] Decentering American consumers and capitalists in the story of inter-imperial trade offers an important way to expand the scope of literary critique represented here, critique that cannot be fully achieved by wealthy and influential American "insiders" like Wharton.

As climate change and the threat it poses to the Anthropocene has moved to the forefront of nineteenth-century Americanists' scholarly concerns, objects like coal, gold, cobalt, amber, coral, and diamonds offer future points of focus for analyzing writers' visions of their place in the world over a *longue durée*.[13] Such minerals, whose life span extends far beyond that of humans, can serve as symbols for the limitations of human existence, as the treasure and detritus that outlasts the imperial battles fought over them. If commodities like cotton and wheat allowed nineteenth- and twentieth-century writers to navigate their relationship to the inter-imperial economy in which these goods circulated, then minerals, metals, and other slowly accruing organic matter might present further opportunities for writers to concretize the geographical, geological, and temporal layers of empire in which their current literary and historical moment is but a speck.[14] As Wai Chee Dimock contends, genres like the novel "unfold against long durations, requiring scale enlargement for their analysis" (5). By connecting novels through their common engagement with long international histories of commodity chains, we can see affinities across chronologies, geographies, genres, and fields. Something as minuscule as a cochineal beetle, or a grain of wheat, or a seed of cotton becomes a prism through which to view the gendered and racialized conditions of writers' entanglement in the United States' imperial economic ventures, in the nineteenth century and beyond.

Notes

1. Lee Glazer, the Associate Curator of American Art at the Freer Gallery, gives some context about Leyland, who was a British shipping magnate, writing: "A self-made man with a taste for Old Masters, Leyland aspired to make his house into a palace of art and affirm his place in London society" (67).
2. Cross explains that while Leyland originally envisioned a relatively modest decorative project, Whistler "took dramatic liberties" in an undertaking that spanned months rather than days, and Leyland would only pay half of what Whistler charged for the "unsolicited work" (13).
3. This announcement included a 25% tariff on steel and 10% on aluminum. See Annie Lowrey on the various ways in which Trump's tariffs on steel would actually hurt many of the demographics he promised to support. Lowrey writes, "It is true that American steel producers would benefit from higher prices, and steel stocks are already up considerably on the prospect. But there are far more manufacturing workers in industries buying steel than selling it, businesses that would suffer from higher input costs."
4. See Katie Lobosco, who writes for CNN on September 5, 2018 that "The United States could impose tariffs on roughly half of all Chinese goods entering the country by the end of the week." Alan Rappeport reports in the *New York Times* on September 7, 2018: "President Trump threatened China with another round of punishing tariffs on Friday, saying he was prepared to tax essentially all Chinese goods imported into the United States if Beijing did not change its trade practices. The threat comes as the administration prepares to move forward with another round of tariffs on $200 billion worth of Chinese imports, including many everyday consumer products like electronics and housewares."

5. Trump made these particular remarks on July 26, 2018 at a steel mill in Granite City, Illinois, as if to further underscore the competition he perceived between American and Chinese industries. Trump's theme of unfairness can be seen again in a tweet he posted on April 6, 2018: "China, which is a great economic power, is considered a Developing Nation within the World Trade Organization. They therefore get tremendous perks and advantages, especially over the U.S. Does anybody think this is fair."
6. See Teemu Ruskola on the United States' enforcement of extraterritorial jurisdiction in China in the 1840s.
7. See Jessica Lanier, and Clare Le Corbeiller and Alice Cooney Frelinghuysen.
8. See Brooke Hunter on wheat and Sven Beckert on cotton. Economist Robert E. Lipsey writes that "The composition of American exports in the late eighteenth century and the beginning of the nineteenth century reflected the fact that American comparative advantage was based on the exploitation of abundant natural resources" (699).
9. Lipsey explains, "For most of the period from the inauguration of George Washington to the end of the nineteenth century, the United States imported more merchandise than it exported. Only in the last three decades of the century did exports exceed imports, and that export surplus continued into the twentieth century" (692).
10. See two publications from the U.S. Census Bureau: "U.S. Trade in Goods and Services—Balance of Payments (BOP) Basis," which tracks the balance of trade from 1960 to 2017, and "International Transactions and Foreign Commerce," which tracks the balance of trade from 1790 to 1970 (see especially pages 884–6).
11. Stephanie LeMenager offers a more thorough reading of Sinclair's novel through the lens of petrofiction, arguing that "Sinclair's *Oil!* is a type of peak oil fiction, since it was written as a warning against global petromodernity from around the moment of peak oil *discovery* in the United States—again, the late 1920s. The novel strives to imagine curtailing petromodern development in a manner complementary to the fictional post-petrol futures offered by twenty-first-century peak oilers. In both cases, imaginative thinkers struggle to break out of media environments already sustained by petroleum infrastructure" (70).
12. See Lorinda B. Cohoon for more on the Orientalism of this chapter of *Eight Cousins*. Though the chapter features "two genuine Chinamen" (75), these Chinese laborers are treated as foreign curiosities and are largely silent during the young American girl's tour of the ship.
13. This trend is exemplified by the 2018 C19 conference in Albuquerque, New Mexico on "Climate." The C19 conference website argues that "the urgency of 'Climate' today is simultaneously a nineteenth-century topic, as well," as "the nineteenth century witnessed the coinage of such terms as 'ecology' and 'climatology,' and it grappled with questions

of agency and environment by asking whether human behavior had a collective impact on climate, or whether climate shaped human temperament and culture." See also Robert Levine, "American Studies in an Age of Extinction," Tobias Menely and Jesse O. Taylor, Timothy Sweet, Bob Johnson, and Cody Marrs.

14. Indeed, Laura Doyle employs geologically inspired language when she makes the case for a *longue durée* approach to literature, suggesting that a framework of inter-imperiality "opens up new backstories about the sedimented political conditions of culture" ("Inter-imperiality and Literary Studies" 337).

Bibliography

Ackerman, Alan. "Edith Wharton's Resource Aesthetics and the Dawn of the American Energy Crisis." *Journal of American Studies* 53.4 (2019): 925–52.

Adams, Cyrus C. *An Elementary Commercial Geography*. New York: D. Appleton and Company, 1919.

Adams, Sean Patrick. *Old Dominion, Industrial Commonwealth: Coal, Politics, and Economy in Antebellum America*. Baltimore, MD: Johns Hopkins UP, 2004.

"Aerial Perspective." *Encyclopedia Britannica*. 2012.

Alberghene, Janice M., and Beverly Lyon Clark, eds. *Little Women and the Feminist Imagination: Criticism, Controversy, Personal Essays*. New York: Garland, 1999.

Alcott, Louisa May. *A Double Life: Newly Discovered Thrillers of Louisa May Alcott*. Eds. Madeleine B. Stern, Joel Myerson, and Daniel Shealy. Boston: Little, Brown, 1988.

—. *Eight Cousins, or, The Aunt-Hill*. London: Sampson Low, Marston, Low, & Searle, 1875.

—. *Little Women*. Eds. Anne K. Phillips and Gregory Eiselein. New York: Norton, 2004.

—. *Moods*. Ed. Sarah Elbert. New Brunswick, NJ: Rutgers UP, 1999.

—. *The Journals of Louisa May Alcott*. Eds. Joel Myerson, Daniel Shealy, and Madeleine B. Stern. Boston: Little, Brown, 1989.

Alexandre, Sandy. "'[The] Things What Happened with Our Family': Property and Inheritance in August Wilson's *The Piano Lesson*." *Modern Drama* 52.1 (2009): 73–98.

"American Manufactures: Letter to the Editress." *Godey's Lady's Book*. Oct. 1865: 359.

Ames, Kenneth L. *Death in the Dining Room and Other Tales of Victorian Culture*. Philadelphia, PA: Temple UP, 1992.

Andrews, William L. Introduction. *The Quest of the Silver Fleece*. W. E. B. Du Bois. Oxford: Oxford UP, 2007. xi–xxvii.

Appadurai, Arjun, ed. *The Social Life of Things: Commodities in Cultural Perspective*. Cambridge: Cambridge UP, 1986.

Arabindan-Kesson, Anna. *Black Bodies, White Gold: Art, Cotton, and Commerce in the Atlantic World*. Durham, NC: Duke UP, 2021.

Arac, Jonathan, and Harriet Ritvo, eds. *Macropolitics of Nineteenth-Century Literature: Nationalism, Exoticism, Imperialism*. Philadelphia: U of Pennsylvania P, 1991.

Aranda, José F., Jr. "Contradictory Impulses: María Amparo Ruiz de Burton, Resistance Theory, and the Politics of Chicano/a Studies." *American Literature* 70.3 (1998): 551–79.

Araújo, Ana Cristina. "The Lisbon Earthquake of 1755: Public Distress and Political Propaganda." *E-Journal of Portuguese History* 4.1 (2006): N.P.

Bair, Jennifer, ed. *Frontiers of Commodity Chain Research*. Stanford, CA: Stanford UP, 2009.

Bannet, Eve Tavor. *Transatlantic Stories and the History of Reading 1720–1810*. Cambridge: Cambridge UP, 2011.

Banta, Martha. *Imaging American Women: Ideas and Ideals in Cultural History*. New York: Columbia UP, 1987.

Barker, Deborah. *Aesthetics and Gender in American Literature: Portraits of the Woman Artist*. Lewisburg, PA: Bucknell UP, 2000.

Beam, Dorri. "Henry James, Constance Fenimore Woolson, and the Figure in the Carpet." *American Literature's Aesthetic Dimensions*. Eds. Cindy Weinstein and Christopher Looby. New York: Columbia UP, 2012. 137–55.

—. *Style, Gender, and Fantasy in Nineteenth-Century American Women's Writing*. Cambridge: Cambridge UP, 2010.

Beckert, Sven. "Emancipation and Empire: Reconstructing the Worldwide Web of Cotton Production in the Age of the American Civil War." *American Historical Review* (2004): 1405–38.

—. *Empire of Cotton: A Global History*. New York: Knopf, 2014.

Beecher, Catharine. *The American Woman's Home*. 1869. Hartford, CT: Stowe-Day Foundation, 1987.

Bender, Thomas. *A Nation Among Nations: America's Place in World History*. New York: Hill and Wang, 2006.

Bennett, Jane. *Vibrant Matter: A Political Ecology of Things*. Durham, NC: Duke UP, 2010.

Berger, Martin. *Sight Unseen: Whiteness and American Visual Culture*. Berkeley: U of California P, 2005.

Berke, Heinz. "Chemistry in Ancient Times: The Development of Blue and Purple Pigments." *Angewandte Chemie-International Edition* 41.14 (2002): 2483–7.

Bernstein, Peter L. *The Power of Gold*. Hoboken, NJ: Wiley, 2000.

Bernstein, Susan Naomi. "Writing And *Little Women*: Alcott's Rhetoric Of Subversion." *American Transcendental Quarterly* 7.1 (1993): 25–43.

Berry, Kate. "How Can an American Woman Serve Her Country?" *Godey's Lady's Book*. Dec. 1851: 362–5.

Bishop, Joseph Bucklin. "A Benevolent Despotism." *Scribner's Magazine*. 53 (Jan. 1913): 303–18.

Blackford, Holly Virginia. "Vital Signs at Play: Objects as Vessels of Mother-Daughter Discourse in Louisa May Alcott's *Little Women.*" *Children's Literature* 34 (2006): 1–36.
Bloom, Stephen G. *Tears of Mermaids: The Secret Story of Pearls.* New York: St. Martin's, 2009.
Boston Board of Trade. *Annual Report.* Vol. 9. Boston: Alfred Mudge, 1863.
Bourdieu, Pierre. *Distinction: A Social Critique of the Judgement of Taste.* Cambridge, MA: Harvard UP, 1984.
Boyd, Anne E. (*see also* Rioux, Anne E. Boyd). "Tourism, Imperialism, and Hybridity in the Reconstruction South: Woolson's *Rodman the Keeper: Southern Sketches.*" *Witness to Reconstruction: Constance Fenimore Woolson and the Postbellum South, 1873–1894.* Ed. Kathleen E. Diffley. Jackson: UP of Mississippi, 2011. 56–72.
—. *Writing for Immortality: Women and the Emergence of High Literary Culture in America.* Baltimore, MD: Johns Hopkins UP, 2004.
Boyle, T. "The Venezuela Crisis and the Liberal Opposition, 1895–96." *The Journal of Modern History* 50.3 (1978): D1185–D1212.
Braithwaite, William Stanley. "What to Read: Du Bois, W. E. B. 'The Quest of the Silver Fleece.'" *The Crisis.* Dec. 1911: 77–8.
Brandão, José António. Introduction. *Edge of Empire: Documents of Michilimackinac, 1671–1716.* Eds. Joseph L. Peyser and José António Brandão. East Lansing: Michigan State UP, 2008.
Brehm, Victoria, ed. *Constance Fenimore Woolson's Nineteenth Century: Essays.* Detroit, MI: Wayne State UP, 2001.
Brickell, Francesca Cartier. "Maharajas, Pearls and Oriental Influences: Jacques Cartier's Voyages to the East in the Early Twentieth Century." *Jewellery Studies* 12 (2012): 103–16.
Brickhouse, Anna. "Nella Larsen and the Intertextual Geography of *Quicksand.*" *African American Review* 35.4 (2001): 533–60.
Brodhead, Richard. "Starting out in the 1860s: Alcott, Authorship, and the Postbellum Literary Field." *Cultures of Letters: Scenes of Reading and Writing in Nineteenth-Century America.* Chicago: U of Chicago P, 1993. 69–106.
Bromell, Nick. "Reading Democratically: Pedagogies of Difference and Practices of Listening in *The House of Mirth* and *Passing.*" *American Literature* 81.2 (2009): 281–303.
Brown, Bill. *A Sense of Things: The Object Matter of American Literature.* Chicago: U of Chicago P, 2003.
Brown, Gillian. *Domestic Individualism: Imagining Self in Nineteenth-Century America.* Berkeley: U of California P, 1990.
Buell, Frederick. "A Short History of Oil Cultures: Or, the Marriage of Catastrophe and Exuberance." *Journal of American Studies* 46.2 (2012): 273–93.
Burollet, Thérèse. "Pompier Art." *William Bouguereau: 1825–1905.* Montreal: Montreal Museum of Fine Arts, 1984. 31–7.

Byerman, Keith. "*The Quest of the Silver Fleece* as Utopian Narrative." *American Literary Realism* 24.3 (1992): 58–71.

"C19 2018 Conference: Climate." *C19: The Society of Nineteenth-Century Americanists*, <https://www.c19society.org/_files/ugd/ca9039_43c7f5355 ceb43289f00f6c76ebc2b2e.pdf>. Accessed 23 September 2018.

Calhoun, Ricky-Dale. "Seeds of Destruction: The Globalization of Cotton as a Result of the American Civil War." Dissertation. Kansas State University, 2012.

Carby, Hazel V. "The Souls of Black Men." *Next to the Color Line: Gender, Sexuality, and W. E. B. Du Bois*. Eds. Susan Gillman and Alys Eve Weinbaum. Minneapolis: U of Minnesota P, 2007. 234–68.

Carrión, María Dolores Narbona. "19th-Century American Women Writers' European Connections: The Case of Elizabeth Stuart Phelps." *New Perspectives in Transatlantic Studies*. Eds. Heidi Slettedahl Macpherson and Will Kaufman. Lanham, MD: UP of America, 2002. 117–30.

Carroll, Anne E. "Du Bois and Art Theory: *The Souls of Black Folk* as a 'Total Work of Art.'" *Public Culture* 17.2 (2005): 235–54.

Cass, Jeffrey. "Elizabeth Stuart Phelps and the American Sphinx: Commercial Orientalism in *The Story of Avis*." *Auto-Poetica: Representations of the Creative Process in Nineteenth-Century British and American Fiction*. Ed. Darby Lewes. Lanham, MD: Lexington Books, 2006. 53–66.

Castronovo, Russ. *Beautiful Democracy: Aesthetics and Anarchy in a Global Era*. Chicago: U of Chicago P, 2007.

—. "Beauty along the Color Line: Lynching, Aesthetics, and the *Crisis*." *PMLA* 121.5 (2006): 1443–59.

Cather, Willa. *My Ántonia*. 1918. New York: Vintage, 1994.

Chester, David, and Olivia Chester. "The Impact of Eighteenth Century Earthquakes on the Algarve Region, Southern Portugal." *The Geographic Journal* 176.4 (2010): 350–70.

Child, Lydia Maria. *Hobomok and Other Writings on Indians*. Ed. Carolyn L. Karcher. New Brunswick, NJ: Rutgers UP, 1995.

Chow, Rey. *Entanglements: Or Transmedial Thinking About Capture*. Durham, NC: Duke UP, 2012.

Clark, Brett, and John Bellamy Foster. "Land, the Color Line, and the Quest of the Golden Fleece." *Organization & Environment* 16.4 (2003): 459–69.

Cognard-Black, Jennifer. *Narrative in the Professional Age: Transatlantic Readings of Harriet Beecher Stowe, George Eliot, and Elizabeth Stuart Phelps*. New York: Routledge, 2004.

Cohen, Joanna. *Luxurious Citizens: The Politics of Consumption in Nineteenth-Century America*. Philadelphia: U of Pennsylvania P, 2017.

Cohoon, Lorinda B. "'A Highly Satisfactory Chinaman': Orientalism and American Girlhood in Louisa May Alcott's *Eight Cousins*." *Children's Literature* 36 (2008): 49–71.

Collins, Peter E. "Nature, the Individual, and the Market in Norris and Dreiser." *Twentieth-Century Literature* 58.4 (2012): 556–81.

Coronado, Raúl. "The Aesthetics of Our America: A Response to Susan Gillman." *American Literary History* 20.1/2 (2008): 210–16.

Cross, Susan. "Beauty and Bile: Darren Waterston's *Filthy Lucre*." *Darren Waterston: Filthy Lucre*. Ed. Cross. New York: Skira Rizzoli, 2014. 11–25.

Daly, Suzanne. *The Empire Inside: Indian Commodities in Victorian Domestic Novels*. Ann Arbor: U of Michigan P, 2011.

Davidson, Cathy. "No More Separate Spheres." *American Literature* 70.3 (1998): 443–63.

—. *Revolution and the Word: The Rise of the Novel in America*. New York: Oxford UP, 1988.

Davis, Rebecca Harding. *Life in the Iron Mills and Other Stories*. 1861. New York: Feminist Press, 1993.

Dawahare, Anthony. "The Gold Standard of Racial Identity in Nella Larsen's *Quicksand* and *Passing*." *Twentieth Century Literature* 52.1 (2006): 22–41.

De Grazia, Victoria. *Irresistible Empire: America's Advance through Twentieth-Century Europe*. Cambridge, MA: Harvard UP, 2005.

Diamanti, Jeff. "From Fields of Wheat to Fields of Value: The Energy Unconscious of *The Octopus*." *Western American Literature* 51.4 (2017): 391–407. JSTOR, <https://www.jstor.org/stable/44668494>. Accessed June 18 2021.

Dillon, Elizabeth Maddock. "Atlantic Aesthesis: Books and *Sensus Communis* in the New World." *Early American Literature* 51.2 (2016): 367–95.

—. *New World Drama: The Performative Commons in the Atlantic World, 1649–1849*. Durham, NC: Duke UP, 2014.

Dillon, Elizabeth Maddock, and Michael J. Drexler. "The Haitian Revolution and the Early United States, Entwined." *The Haitian Revolution and the Early United States: Histories, Textualities, Geographies*. Eds. Dillon and Drexler. Philadelphia: U of Pennsylvania P, 2016. 1–15.

Dimock, Wai Chee. *Through Other Continents: American Literature Across Deep Time*. Princeton, NJ: Princeton UP, 2008.

Dolan, Kathryn Cornell. *Beyond the Fruited Plain: Food and Agriculture in U.S. Literature, 1850–1905*. Lincoln: U of Nebraska P, 2014.

—. "A 'Mighty World-Force': Wheat as Natural Corrective in Norris." *Interdisciplinary Studies in Literature and Environment* 19.2 (2012): 295–316.

Dolin, Eric Jay. *Fur, Fortune, and Empire: The Epic History of the Fur Trade in America*. New York: Norton, 2010.

Domosh, Mona. *American Commodities in an Age of Empire*. New York: Routledge, 2006.

Donaldson, Susan V. "Elizabeth Stuart Phelps, Realism, and Literary Debates on Changing Gender Roles." *Realism and Its Discontents*. Eds. Danuta Fjellestad and Elizabeth Kella. Karlskrona, Sweden: Blekinge Institute of Technology, 2003. 87–111.

Douglas, Ann. *The Feminization of American Culture*. New York: Farrar, Straus and Giroux, 1977.

—. "Introduction to *Little Women*." *Little Women and the Feminist Imagination: Criticism, Controversy, Personal Essays*. Eds. Janice M. Alberghene and Beverly Lyon Clark. New York: Garland, 1999. 43–62.

Doyle, Laura. *Freedom's Empire: Race and the Rise of the Novel in Atlantic Modernity, 1640–1940*. Durham, NC: Duke UP, 2008.

—. "Inter-Imperiality: Dialectics in a Postcolonial World History." *Interventions* 16.2 (2014): 159–96.

—. "Inter-Imperiality and Literary Studies in the Longer *Durée*." *PMLA* 130.2 (2015): 336–47.

—. *Inter-Imperiality: Vying Empires, Gendered Labor, and the Literary Arts of Alliance*. Durham, NC: Duke UP, 2020.

Du Bois, W. E. B. "The African Roots of War." *The Atlantic*. May 1915.

—. "The Color Line Belts the World." *Collier's*. 20 Oct. 1906: 30.

—. "Criteria of Negro Art." *The Crisis*. 32 (Oct. 1926): 290–7.

—. *Dark Princess*. 1928. Jackson: UP of Mississippi, 1995.

—. *The Quest of the Silver Fleece*. 1911. Ed. William L. Andrews. Oxford: Oxford UP, 2007.

—. *The Souls of Black Folk*. Gildan Media, 2019.

Dwight, Nathaniel. *A Short But Comprehensive System of the Geography of the World: By Way of Question and Answer. Principally Designed for Children and Common Schools*. Boston: West & Greenleaf, 1801.

Eby, Clare Virginia. "Domesticating Naturalism: The Example of *The Pit*." *Studies in American Fiction* 22.2 (1994): 149–68.

—. "*The Octopus*: Big Business as Art." *American Literary Realism* 26.3 (1994): 33–51.

Eckes, Alfred E. *Opening America's Market: U.S. Foreign Trade Policy Since 1776*. Chapel Hill: U of North Carolina P, 1995.

Edelstein, Sari. "Louisa May Alcott's Age," *American Literature* 87.3 (2015): 517–45.

Ejrnæs, Mette, Karl Gunnar Persson, and Søren Rich. "Feeding the British: Convergence and Market Efficiency in the Nineteenth-Century Grain Trade." *Economic History Review* 61.S1 (2008): 140–71.

Elbert, Sarah. *A Hunger for Home: Louisa May Alcott and* Little Women. Philadelphia, PA: Temple UP, 1984.

Elsden, Annamaria Formichella. "'A Modern and a Model Pioneer': Civilizing the Frontier in Woolson's 'A Pink Villa.'" *Witness to Reconstruction: Constance Fenimore Woolson and the Postbellum South, 1873–1894*. Ed. Kathleen E. Diffley. Jackson: UP of Mississippi, 2011. 285–92.

Farland, Maria. "W. E. B. Du Bois, Anthropometric Science, and the Limits of Racial Uplift." *American Quarterly* 58.4 (2006): 1017–44.

Fauset, Jessie Redmon. *Plum Bun: A Novel Without a Moral*. 1929. Boston: Beacon, 1990.

Felski, Rita. *The Limits of Critique*. Chicago: Chicago UP, 2015.

Finley, John. "The French in the Heart of America." *Scribner's Magazine*. 53 (Jan. 1913): 115–29.

Fisher, Beth. "The Captive Mexicana and the Desiring Bourgeois Woman: Domesticity and Expansionism in Ruiz de Burton's *Who Would Have Thought It?*" *Legacy* 16.1 (1999): 59–69.

Fishkin, Shelley Fisher. "Crossroads of Cultures: The Transnational Turn in American Studies—Presidential Address to the American Studies Association, November 12, 2004." *American Quarterly* 57.1 (2005): 17–57.

Fitzpatrick, Tara. "Love's Labor's Reward: The Sentimental Economy of Louisa May Alcott's *Work*." *NWSA Journal* 5.1 (1993): 28–44.

Fleming, E. McClung. "From Indian Princess to Greek Goddess: The American Image, 1783–1815." *Winterthur Portfolio* 3 (1967): 37–66.

Floyd, Janet. *Claims and Speculations: Mining and Writing in the Gilded Age*. Albuquerque: U of New Mexico P, 2012.

Fluck, Winfried. "A New Beginning?: Transnationalisms." *New Literary History* 42.3 (2011): 365–84.

Foote, Stephanie. "Resentful *Little Women*: Gender and Class Feeling in Louisa May Alcott." *College Literature* 32.1 (2005): 63–85.

Freedgood, Elaine. *The Ideas in Things: Fugitive Meaning in the Victorian Novel*. Chicago: U of Chicago P, 2006.

Freese, Barbara. *Coal: A Human History*. Cambridge: Perseus, 2003.

"Furs for the Ladies; and Where They Come From." *Godey's Lady's Book*. Mar. 1855: 203–5.

Gaines, Kevin. *Uplifting the Race: Black Leadership, Politics, and Culture in the Twentieth Century*. Chapel Hill: U of North Carolina P, 1996.

Gerritsen, Anne, and Giorgio Riello, eds. *The Global Lives of Things: The Material Culture of Connections in the Early Modern World*. London: Routledge, 2016.

Ghosh, Amitav. "Petrofiction." *New Republic* 2 Mar. 1992: 29–34.

—. *Sea of Poppies*. New York: Picador, 2008.

Gikandi, Simon. *Slavery and the Culture of Taste*. Princeton, NJ: Princeton UP, 2011.

Giles, Paul. *Transatlantic Insurrections: British Culture and the Formation of American Literature, 1730–1860*. Philadelphia: U of Pennsylvania P, 2001.

Gillman, Susan. "The New, Newest Thing: Have American Studies Gone Imperial?" *American Literary History* 17.1 (2005): 196–214.

Gilroy, Paul. *The Black Atlantic: Modernity and Double Consciousness*. Cambridge, MA: Harvard UP, 1993.

Glazer, Lee. "A Story of the Beautiful: Whistler's Peacock Room." *Darren Waterston: Filthy Lucre*. Ed. Susan Cross. New York: Skira Rizzoli, 2014. 67–83.

Glennon, Jenny. "The Big Bribes: Jewelry, American Taste, and Globalization in Wharton's Twenties Novels." *Edith Wharton Review* 27.1 (2011): 17–23.

Glickman, Lawrence B. "'Buy for the Sake of the Slave': Abolitionism and the Origins of American Consumer Activism." *American Quarterly* 56.4 (2004): 889–912.

Goldsmith, Meredith. "Wharton's Gift to Nella Larsen: *The House of Mirth* and *Quicksand.*" *Edith Wharton Review* 11.2 (1994): 3–5, 15.

Gordon, John Steele. *An Empire of Wealth: The Epic History of American Economic Power*. New York: HarperCollins, 2004.

Graham, Don. *The Fiction of Frank Norris: The Aesthetic Context*. Columbia: U of Missouri P, 1978.

Gray, Jeffrey. "Essence and the Mulatto Traveler: Europe as Embodiment in Nella Larsen's *Quicksand*." *Novel* 27.3 (1994): 257–70.

Greenfield, Amy Butler. *A Perfect Red: Empire, Espionage, and the Quest for the Color of Desire*. New York: HarperCollins, 2005.

Griffith, George V. "An Epistolary Friendship: The Letters of Elizabeth Stuart Phelps to George Eliot." *Legacy* 18.1 (2001): 94–100.

Gruesser, John Cullen. *The Empire Abroad and the Empire at Home: African American Literature and the Era of Overseas Expansion*. Athens: U of Georgia P, 2012.

"The Guilty Press." *The United Opinion*. 4 Mar. 1898.

Hager, Christopher, and Cody Marrs. "Against 1865: Reperiodizing the Nineteenth Century." *J19: The Journal of Nineteenth-Century Americanists* 1.2 (2013): 259–84.

Hall, Carolyn. "Poking King David in His Imperial Eye/'I': Woolson Takes on the White Man's Burden in the Postbellum United States." *Witness to Reconstruction: Constance Fenimore Woolson and the Postbellum South, 1873–1894*. Ed. Kathleen E. Diffley. Jackson: UP of Mississippi, 2011. 177–93.

Harde, Roxanne. "'One—hundred—hours': Elizabeth Stuart Phelps' Dress Reform Writing." *Styling Texts: Dress and Fashion in Literature*. Eds. Cynthia Kuhn and Cindy Carlson. Youngstown, NY: Cambria, 2007. 167–87.

Hardt, Michael, and Antonio Negri. *Empire*. Cambridge, MA: Harvard UP, 2000.

Hartmann, William K. *Searching for Golden Empires: Epic Cultural Collisions in Sixteenth-Century America*. Tucson: U of Arizona P, 2014.

Harvey, David. *The New Imperialism*. Oxford: Oxford UP, 2003.

Hazareesingh, Sandip, and Jonathan Curry-Machado. "Commodities, Empires, and Global History." *Journal of Global History* 4.1 (2009): 1–5.

Hebard, Andrew. *The Poetics of Sovereignty in American Literature, 1885–1910*. New York: Cambridge UP, 2013.

Heil, Jenny. "Imperial Pedagogy: Susanna Rowson's Columbus for Young Ladies." *Early American Literature* 47.3 (2012): 623–48.

Hellman, Caroline Chamberlin. *Domesticity and Design in American Women's Lives and Literature: Stowe, Alcott, Cather, and Wharton Writing Home*. New York: Routledge, 2011.

Hendel, Erin. "'Work and Wait': Louisa May Alcott's Female Artists." *Women and Work: The Labors of Self-Fashioning*. Eds. Christine Leiren Mower and Susanne Weil. Cambridge: Cambridge Scholars, 2011.

Hicks, Elias. "Observations on the Slavery of the Africans and their Descendants, and on the Use of the Produce of their Labor." *Letter of Elias Hicks: Including Also a Few Short Essays Written on Several Occasions, Mostly Illustrative of his Doctrinal Views*. New York: Isaac T. Hopper, 1834. 9–20.

Hicks, Scott. "W. E. B. Du Bois, Booker T. Washington, and Richard Wright: Toward an Ecocriticism of Color." *Callaloo* 29.1 (2006): 202–22.

Hinckley, C. T. "The Manufacture of Silk." *Godey's Lady's Book*. Sept. 1857: 204–6.

"History of Pearls, Natural and Artificial." *Godey's Lady's Book and Magazine* 48 (June 1854): 533–7.

Ho, Fred Wei-han, and Bill Mullen. *Afro Asia: Revolutionary Political and Cultural Connections between African Americans and Asian Americans*. Durham, NC: Duke UP, 2008.

Hodgson, Louisa Jayne. "Transatlantic *Little Women*: Louisa May Alcott, the Woman Writer and Literary Community." *49th Parallel* 23 (2009): 1–14.

Hody, Cynthia A. *The Politics of Trade: American Political Development and Foreign Economic Policy*. Hanover, NH: UP of New England, 1996.

Hoeller, Hildegard. *From Gift to Commodity: Capitalism and Sacrifice in Nineteenth-Century American Fiction*. Durham: U of New Hampshire P, 2012.

Hoganson, Kristin L. *Consumers' Imperium: The Global Production of American Domesticity, 1865–1920*. Chapel Hill: U of North Carolina P, 2007.

Honour, Hugh. *The Image of the Black in Western Art*. Vol. IV. Cambridge, MA: Harvard UP, 1989.

Horne, Gerald. *The White Pacific: US Imperialism and Black Slavery in the South Seas after the Civil War*. Honolulu: U of Hawaii P, 2007.

Horsman, Reginald. *Race and Manifest Destiny: Origins of American Racial Anglo-Saxonism*. Cambridge, MA: Harvard UP, 1981.

Hostetler, Ann E. "The Aesthetics of Race and Gender in Nella Larsen's *Quicksand*." *PMLA* 105.1 (1990): 35–46.

Hsu, Hsuan. "Circa 1898: Overseas Empire and Transnational American Studies." *Journal of Transnational American Studies* 3.2 (2011): 1–6.

Hume, Ivor Noël. *Belzoni: The Giant Archaeologists Love to Hate*. Charlottesville: U of Virginia P, 2011.

Humphreys, R. A. "Presidential Address: Anglo-American Rivalries and the Venezuela Crisis of 1895." *Transactions of the Royal Historical Society* 17 (1967): 131–64.

Hunter, Brooke. "Wheat, War, and the American Economy during the Age of Revolution." *The William and Mary Quarterly* 62.3 (2005): 505–26.

Hutchinson, George. "An End to the Family Romance: Nella Larsen, Black Transnationalism, and American Racial Ideology." *Race, Nation, and Empire in American History*. Eds. James T. Campbell, Matthew Pratt Guterl, and Robert G. Lee. Chapel Hill: U of North Carolina P, 2007. 55–72.

—. *In Search of Nella Larsen: A Biography of the Color Line*. Cambridge, MA: Harvard UP, 2009.

—. "*Quicksand* and the Racial Labyrinth." *Soundings* 80.4 (1997): 543–71.

Immerwahr, Daniel. *How to Hide an Empire: A History of the Greater United States*. New York: Picador, 2019.

"India Rubber; or, Caoutchouc." *Godey's Lady's Book*. Dec. 1835: 283.

Ingham, John N. "Reaching for Respectability: The Pittsburgh Industrial Elite at the Turn of the Century." *Collecting in the Gilded Age: Art Patronage in Pittsburgh, 1890–1910*. Eds. Gabriel P. Weisberg, DeCourcy E. McIntosh, and Alison McQueen. Hanover, NH: UP of New England, 1997. 3–51.

Innis, Harold. *The Fur Trade in Canada: An Introduction to Canadian Economic History*. 1930. Toronto: U of Toronto P, 1999.

Insko, Jeffrey. "Anachronistic Imaginings: *Hope Leslie*'s Challenge to Historicism." *American Literary History* 16.2 (2004): 179–207.

"Iran." *Worldmark Encyclopedia of the Nations*. Eds. Timothy L. Gall and Jeneen M. Hobby, 12th ed., vol. 4: Asia and Oceania: Gale, 2007. 259–77. *Gale Virtual Reference Library*, <http://link.galegroup.com/apps/doc/CX2586700201/GVRL?u=mlin_w_umassamh&sid=GVRL&xid=052eaed6>. Accessed 10 November 2018.

Irving, Washington. *Astoria; Or, Anecdotes of an Enterprise Beyond the Rocky Mountains*. Philadelphia: Carey, Lea, & Blanchard, 1836.

Irwin, Douglas A. "Tariffs and Growth in Late Nineteenth Century America." *World Economy London* 24 (2001): 15–30.

Isaacson, Walter. *Benjamin Franklin: An American Life*. New York: Simon & Schuster, 2003.

Jackson, Helen Hunt. *Ramona*. 1884. New York: Modern Library, 2005.

Jacobs, Margaret D. "Mixed-Bloods, Mestizas, and Pintos: Race, Gender, and Claims to Whiteness in Helen Hunt Jackson's *Ramona* and María Amparo Ruiz de Burton's *Who Would Have Thought It?*" *Western American Literature* 36.3 (2001): 212–31.

James, Henry. "The Real Thing." 1892. *Henry James: Collected Stories 1892–1898*. New York: Library of America, 1996. 32–57.

—. *The Spoils of Poynton*. 1897. Ed. David Lodge. New York: Penguin, 1987.
Jay, Paul. "Beyond Discipline? Globalization and the Future of English." *PMLA* 116:1 (2001): 32–47.
Jennings, Francis. *The Invasion of America: Indians, Colonialism, and the Cant of Conquest*. Chapel Hill: U of North Carolina P, 1975.
Jewett, Sarah Orne. *The Country of the Pointed Firs*. 1896. Oxford: Oxford UP, 1996.
Johnson, Bob. "Energy Slaves: Carbon Technologies, Climate Change, and the Stratified History of the Fossil Economy." *American Quarterly* 68.4 (2016): 955–79.
Johnson, Ida Amanda. *The Michigan Fur Trade*. Lansing: Michigan Historical Commission, 1919.
Johnston, Patricia, and Caroline Frank, eds. *Global Trade and Visual Arts in Federal New England*. Durham: U of New Hampshire P, 2014.
Joslin, Katherine. *Edith Wharton and the Making of Fashion*. Durham: U of New Hampshire P, 2009.
Juan, Wu, Pau L. Leung, and Li Jiazhi. "A Study of Chinese Blue and White Porcelain." *Studies in Conservation* 52.3 (2007): 188–98.
Jun, Helen H. "Black Orientalism: Nineteenth-century Narratives of Race and U.S. Citizenship." *American Quarterly* 58.4 (2006): 1047–66.
Kaplan, Amy. *The Anarchy of Empire in the Making of US Culture*. Cambridge, MA: Harvard UP, 2005.
Kaplan, Amy, and Don Pease, eds. *Cultures of United States Imperialism*. Durham, NC: Duke UP, 1993.
Kelley, Robin D. G. "But a Local Phase of a World Problem: Black History's Global Vision, 1883–1950." *The Journal of American History* 86.3 (1999): 1045–77.
Kelly, Lori Duin. "Elizabeth Stuart Phelps, *Trixy*, and the Vivisection Question." *Legacy* 27.1 (2010): 61–82.
King, Heidi. "Gold in Ancient America." *The Metropolitan Museum of Art Bulletin* 59.4 (2002): 5–55.
Klein, Shana. *The Fruits of Empire: Art, Food, and the Politics of Race in the Age of American Expansion*. Oakland: U of California P, 2020.
Knoper, Randall. *Acting Naturally: Mark Twain in the Culture of Performance*. Berkeley: U of California P, 1995.
Kopytoff, Igor. "The Cultural Biography of Things: Commoditization as Process." *The Social Life of Things: Commodities in Cultural Perspective*. Ed. Arjun Appadurai. Cambridge: Cambridge UP, 1986. 64–91.
Kotz, David M. "What's Behind the Trade War?" *Jacobin Magazine*. 28 June 2018, <https://www.jacobinmag.com/2018/06/donald-trump-trade-war-china-tariffs>. Accessed 23 September 2018.
Kunz, George Frederick, and Charles Hugh Stevenson. *The Book of the Pearl: The History, Art, Science, and Industry of the Queen of Gems*. New York: The Century Co., 1908.

Kurlansky, Mark. *Cod: A Biography of the Fish that Changed the World*. New York: Penguin, 1997.

Kwarteng, Kwasi. *War and Gold: A 500-Year History of Empires, Adventures, and Debt*. New York: PublicAffairs, 2014.

LaFeber, Walter. *The New Empire: An Interpretation of American Expansion, 1860–1898*. Ithaca, NY: Cornell UP, 1963.

Lahey, Sarah T. "Honeybees and Discontented Workers: A Critique of Labor in Louisa May Alcott." *American Literary Realism* 44.2 (2012): 133–56.

Lanier, Jessica. "Salem's China Trade: 'Pretty Presents' and Private Adventures." *Global Trade and Visual Arts in Federal New England*. Eds. Patricia Johnston and Caroline Frank. Durham: U of New Hampshire P, 2014. 99–118.

Larsen, Nella. *Quicksand* and *Passing*. Ed. Deborah E. McDowell. New Brunswick, NJ: Rutgers UP, 1986.

Le Corbeiller, Clare, and Alice Cooney Frelinghuysen. "Chinese Export Porcelain." *The Metropolitan Museum of Art Bulletin* 60.3 (2003): 1–60.

Lears, T. J. Jackson. *No Place of Grace: Antimodernism and the Transformation of American Culture, 1880–1920*. Chicago: U of Chicago P, 1981.

Lee, Hermione. *Edith Wharton*. New York: Vintage, 2008.

Lee, Maurice. "Du Bois the Novelist: White Influence, Black Spirit, and *The Quest of the Silver Fleece*." *African American Review* 33.3 (1999): 389–400.

LeMenager, Stephanie. *Living Oil: Petroleum Culture in the American Century*. Oxford: Oxford UP, 2014.

Levander, Caroline Field, and Robert S. Levine, eds. *Hemispheric American Studies*. New Brunswick, NJ: Rutgers UP, 2008.

Levine, Lawrence W. *Highbrow/Lowbrow: The Emergence of Cultural Hierarchy in America*. Cambridge, MA: Harvard UP, 1988.

Levine, Robert S. "American Studies in an Age of Extinction." *Race, Transnationalism, and Nineteenth-Century American Literary Studies*. Cambridge: Cambridge UP, 2017. 46–62.

Lewis, Becky Wingard. "'That idyl of the June, that girls' gospel': Elizabeth Stuart Phelps and Browning's *Aurora Leigh*." *Womanhood in Anglophone Literary Culture: Nineteenth and Twentieth Century Perspectives*. Newcastle: Cambridge Scholars, 2007. 123–35.

Lewis, David Levering. *W. E. B. Du Bois: A Biography*. New York: Holt, 2009.

Lindert, Peter H. "U.S. Foreign Trade and Trade Policy in the Twentieth Century." *The Cambridge Economic History of the United States*. Vol. 3. Eds. Stanley L. Engerman and Robert E. Gallman. Cambridge: Cambridge UP, 2008. 407–62.

Lionnet, Françoise and Shu-mei Shih, eds. *Minor Transnationalism*. Durham, NC: Duke UP, 2005.

Lipsey, Robert E. "U.S. Foreign Trade and the Balance of Payments, 1800–1913." *The Cambridge Economic History of the United States*. Vol. 2. Eds. Stanley L. Engerman and Robert E. Gallman. Cambridge: Cambridge UP, 2008. 685–732.

Lobosco, Katie. "Trump's tariffs could hit $200 billion of Chinese goods this week." *CNN*. 5 Sept. 2018, <https://www.cnn.com/2018/09/04/politics/china-200-billion-tariffs/index.html>. Accessed 23 September 2018.

Long, Lisa A. "The Postbellum Reform Writings of Rebecca Harding Davis and Elizabeth Stuart Phelps." *The Cambridge Companion to Nineteenth-Century American Women's Writing*. Eds. Dale M. Bauer and Philip Gould. Cambridge: Cambridge UP, 2001. 262–83.

Lowe, John. "Constance Fenimore Woolson and the Origins of the Global South." *Witness to Reconstruction: Constance Fenimore Woolson and the Postbellum South, 1873–1894*. Ed. Kathleen E. Diffley. Jackson: UP of Mississippi, 2011. 37–55.

Lowe, Lisa. *The Intimacies of Four Continents*. Durham, NC: Duke UP, 2015.

Lowrey, Annie. "The Limits of 'Made in America' Economics." *The Atlantic*. 20 July 2017, <https://www.theatlantic.com/business/archive/2017/07/made-in-america/534339>. Accessed 23 September 2018.

Lunde, Arne, and Anna Westerstahl Stenport. "Helga Crane's Copenhagen: Denmark, Colonialism, and Transnational Identity in Nella Larsen's *Quicksand*." *Comparative Literature* 60.3 (2008): 228–43.

Lyell, Charles. *Principles of Geology: or, The Modern Changes of the Earth and its Inhabitants, Considered as Illustrative of Geology*. 9th ed. Boston: Little, Brown, and Company, 1853 (originally published 1830–1833).

Lynch, David J., and Caitlin Dewey. "Trump finally gets his tariffs—and much of the world recoils." *Washington Post*. 2 Mar. 2018, <https://www.washingtonpost.com/business/economy/trump-finally-gets-his-tariffs--and-much-of-the-world-recoils/2018/03/01/ee277bd8-1d89-11e8-9de1-147dd2df3829_story.html?utm_term=.e303fb8e5dcc>. Accessed 23 September 2018.

McAllen, Mary Margaret. *Maximilian and Carlota: Europe's Last Empire in Mexico*. San Antonio, TX: Trinity UP, 2014.

McDowell, Deborah E. "Introduction to *Quicksand and Passing* by Nella Larsen." Ed. McDowell. New Brunswick, NJ: Rutgers UP, 1986. ix–xxxi.

McElrath, Joseph R., Jr, and Jesse S. Crisler. *Frank Norris: A Life*. Urbana: U of Illinois P, 2006.

McEntee, Grace. "'Have You Not Heard of Baptiste?': Educating the Reader in Constance Fenimore Woolson's 'Jeannette.'" *American Literary Realism* 47.2 (2015): 151–68.

Macharia, Keguro. "Queering Helga Crane: Black Nativism in Nella Larsen's *Quicksand*." *Modern Fiction Studies* 57.2 (2011): 254–75.

McKay, Claude. *Banana Bottom*. New York: Harper & Brothers, 1933.

Macleod, Dianne Sachko. *Enchanted Lives, Enchanted Objects: American Women Collectors and the Making of Culture, 1800–1940*. Berkeley: U of California P, 2008.

McPhee, John. *Oranges*. New York: Farrar, Straus and Giroux, 1967.

Macpherson, C. B. *The Political Theory of Possessive Individualism*. 1962. New York: Oxford UP, 2011.

Madsen, Deborah L. *Feminist Theory and Literary Practice*. London: Pluto Press, 2000.

Maibor, Carolyn. "Upstairs, Downstairs, and In-Between: Louisa May Alcott on Domestic Service," *The New England Quarterly* 79.1 (2006): 65–91.

Makdisi, Saree. "Empire and Human Energy." *PMLA* 126.2 (2011): 318–20.

Marichal, Carlos. "Mexican Cochineal and the European Demand for American Dyes, 1550–1850." *From Silver to Cocaine: Latin American Commodity Chains and the Building of the World Economy, 1500–2000*. Eds. Steven Topik, Carlos Marichal, and Zephyr Frank. Durham, NC: Duke UP, 2006. 76–92.

—. "The Spanish-American Silver Peso: Export Commodity and Global Money of the Ancien Regime, 1550–1800." *From Silver to Cocaine: Latin American Commodity Chains and the Building of the World Economy, 1500–2000*. Eds. Steven Topik, Carlos Marichal, and Zephyr Frank. Durham, NC: Duke UP, 2006. 25–52.

Marrs, Cody. "Dickinson in the Anthropocene." *ESQ: A Journal of Nineteenth-Century American Literature and Culture* 2.247 (2017): 201–25.

Marx, Karl. *Capital: A Critique of Political Economy*. Vol. I. 1867. New York: Penguin, 1990.

Melville, Herman. *Moby Dick*. 1851. New York: Barnes and Noble, 2003.

Menely, Tobias, and Jesse O. Taylor. *Anthropocene Reading: Literary History in Geologic Times*. University Park: The Pennsylvania State UP, 2017.

Merish, Lori. "Engendering Naturalism: Narrative Form and Commodity Spectacle in US Naturalist Fiction." *NOVEL: A Forum on Fiction* 29.3 (1996): 319–45.

—. *Sentimental Materialism: Gender, Commodity Culture, and Nineteenth-Century American Literature*. Durham, NC: Duke UP, 2000.

Michaels, Walter Benn. *The Gold Standard and the Logic of Naturalism: American Literature at the Turn of the Century*. Berkeley: U of California P, 1987.

Mitchener, Kris James, and Marc Weidenmier. "Trade and Empire." *The Economic Journal* 118 (2008): 1805–34.

Miller, Andrew H. *Novels Behind Glass: Commodity Culture and Victorian Narrative*. Cambridge: Cambridge UP, 1995.

Miller, David C., ed. *American Iconology: New Approaches to Nineteenth-Century Art and Literature*. New Haven, CT: Yale UP, 1993.

Miller, Marla. *The Needle's Eye: Women and Work in the Age of Revolution.* Amherst: U of Massachusetts P, 2006.

Mintz, Sidney. *Sweetness and Power: The Place of Sugar in Modern History.* New York: Penguin, 1986.

Montgomery, Maureen E. *Displaying Women: Spectacles of Leisure in Edith Wharton's New York.* New York: Routledge, 1998.

Mullen, Bill. *Afro-Orientalism.* Minneapolis: U of Minnesota P, 2004.

Murphy, Ann B. "The Borders of Ethical, Erotic, and Artistic Possibilities in *Little Women*." *Signs* 15.3 (1990): 562–85.

Muthyala, John. "Reworlding America: The Globalization of American Studies." *Cultural Critique* 47 (2001): 91–119.

Nadelhoffer, Hans. "Pearls." *Cartier: Jewelers Extraordinary.* 1984. 125–39.

Nadkarni, Asha. *Eugenic Feminism: Reproductive Nationalism in the United States and India.* Minneapolis: U of Minnesota P, 2014.

Norris, Frank. *The Pit.* 1903. New York: Penguin, 1994.

"North Dakota." *Gale Encyclopedia of U.S. Economic History.* Eds. Thomas Carson and Mary Bonk. Gale, 1999. *U.S. History in Context*, <http://link.galegroup.com/apps/doc/EJ1667500476/UHIC?u=mlin_w_umassamh&sid=UHIC&xid=d965d1a9>. Accessed 10 November 2018.

Nugent, Walter. *Habits of Empire: A History of American Expansion.* New York: Knopf, 2008.

Nwankwo, Ifeoma Kiddoe. *Black Cosmopolitanism: Racial Consciousness and Transnational Identity in the Nineteenth-Century Americas.* Philadelphia: U of Pennsylvania P, 2005.

O'Donnell, Elizabeth. "'There's Death in the Pot!' The British Free Produce Movement and the Religious Society of Friends, with Particular Reference to the North-east of England." *Quaker Studies* 13.2 (2009): 184–204.

Oliver, Lawrence J. "W. E. B. Du Bois' *The Quest of the Silver Fleece* and Contract Realism." *American Literary Realism* 38.1 (2005): 32–46.

Orlando, Emily J. *Edith Wharton and the Visual Arts.* Tuscaloosa: U of Alabama P, 2007.

—. "Irreverent Intimacy: Nella Larsen's Revisions of Edith Wharton." *Twentieth-Century Literature* 61.1 (2015): 32–62.

Orvell, Miles. *The Real Thing: Imitation and Authenticity in American Culture, 1880–1940.* Chapel Hill: U of North Carolina P, 1989.

Ott, John. "Eruptions in Art and Money." *Darren Waterston: Filthy Lucre.* Ed. Susan Cross. New York: Skira Rizzoli, 2014. 107–15.

"Our Civil War and European Trade." *New York Times.* 2 October 1861: 2.

Peck, Amelia. *Interwoven Globe: The Worldwide Textile Trade, 1500–1800.* New Haven, CT: Yale UP, 2013.

Pereira, Alvaro. "The Opportunity of a Disaster: The Economic Impact of the 1755 Lisbon Earthquake." *The Journal of Economic History* 69.2 (2009): 466–99.

Perren, Richard. "Structural Change and Market Growth in the Food Industry: Flour Milling in Britain, Europe, and America, 1850–1914." *The Economic History Review* 43.3 (1990): 420–37.

"Perspective (Art)." *Encyclopedia Britannica*. 2012, <https://www.britannica.com/art/perspective-art>. Accessed 8 September 2022.

Phelps, Elizabeth Stuart. *Chapters from a Life*. Boston: Houghton Mifflin, 1897.

—. *Doctor Zay*. 1882. New York: The Feminist Press, 1987.

—. "The Greatest Crime in Modern History." *The Advocate of Peace* 58.1 (Jan. 1896): 16.

—. *Hedged In*. Boston: Fields, Osgood, & Co., 1870.

—. "Is War Ever Justifiable from a Woman's Point of View?" *The Boston Sunday Globe*. 13 Mar. 1898: 30.

—. "A Protest Against the Possible War." *The American Advocate of Peace and Arbitration* 54.2 (Mar.–Apr. 1892): 52.

—. *The Silent Partner*. 1871. New York: The Feminist Press, 1983.

—. *The Story of Avis*. 1877. Ed. Carol Farley Kessler. New Brunswick, NJ: Rutgers UP, 2001.

—. *Three Spiritualist Novels by Elizabeth Stuart Phelps: The Gates Ajar, Beyond the Gates, and The Gates Between*. Ed. Nina Baym. Chicago: U of Illinois P, 2000.

—. *Trixy*. Boston: Houghton Mifflin, 1904.

—. *What to Wear?* Boston: James R. Osgood and Company, 1873.

"Philippines." *Worldmark Encyclopedia of the Nations*. Eds. Timothy L. Gall and Jeneen M. Hobby, 11th ed., vol. 4: Asia & Oceania: Gale, 2004: 547–65. *Gale Virtual Reference Library*, <http://link.galegroup.com/apps/doc/CX3410200233/GVRL?u=mlin_w_umassamh&sid=GVRL&xid=5bef7b83>. Accessed 10 November 2018.

Piep, Karsten H. "'Home to Harlem, Away from Harlem': Transnational Subtexts in Nella Larsen's *Quicksand* and Claude McKay's *Home to Harlem*." *Brno Studies in English* 40.2 (2014): 109–21.

Pletcher, David. *The Diplomacy of Trade and Investment: American Economic Expansion in the Hemisphere, 1865–1900*. Columbia: U of Missouri P, 1998.

Pomeranz, Kenneth. *Great Divergence: China, Europe, and the Making of the Modern World Economy*. Princeton, NJ: Princeton UP, 2000.

Proceedings of the Convention of the American Bankers' Association. New York: American Bankers' Association, 1877.

Puskar, Jason. "Hypereconomics: Frank Norris, Thomas Piketty, and Neoclassical Economic Romance." *Studies in American Naturalism* 12.1 (2017): 28–49.

Ramirez, Pablo A. "Conquest's Child: Gold, Contracts, and American Imperialism in María Amparo Ruiz de Burton's *Who Would Have Thought It?*" *Arizona Quarterly* 70.4 (2014): 143–65.

Rappeport, Alan. "Trump, Escalating Trade Feud, Threatens Tariffs on All Chinese Imports." *New York Times*. 7 Sept. 2018: B3.

@realDonaldTrump. "China is targeting our farmers, who they know I love & respect, as a way of getting me to continue allowing them to take advantage of the U.S. They are being vicious in what will be their failed attempt. We were being nice - until now! China made $517 Billion on us last year." *Twitter*. 25 July 2018, 4:20 a.m.

@realDonaldTrump. "China, which is a great economic power, is considered a Developing Nation within the World Trade Organization. They therefore get tremendous perks and advantages, especially over the U.S. Does anybody think this is fair. We were badly represented. The WTO is unfair to U.S." *Twitter*. 6 Apr. 2018, 7:32am.

Reitano, Joanne R. *The Tariff Question in the Gilded Age: The Great Debate of 1888*. University Park: Pennsylvania State UP, 1994.

Riello, Giorgio. *Cotton: The Fabric that Made the Modern World*. Cambridge: Cambridge UP, 2013.

Rioux, Anne E. Boyd. (*see also* Boyd, Anne E.). *Constance Fenimore Woolson: Portrait of a Lady Novelist*. New York: Norton, 2016.

Risjord, Norman K. *Dakota: The Story of the Northern Plains*. Lincoln: U of Nebraska P, 2013.

Rivera, John-Michael. "Embodying Greater Mexico: María Amparo Ruiz de Burton and the Reconstruction of the Mexican Question." *Look Away!: The U.S. South in New World Studies*. Eds. Jon Smith and Deborah N. Cohn. Durham, NC: Duke UP, 2004. 451–70.

Robbins, Bruce. "Commodity Histories." *PMLA* 120.2 (2005): 454–63.

Roberts, Kimberley. "The Clothes Make the Woman: The Symbolics of Prostitution in Nella Larsen's *Quicksand* and Claude McKay's *Home to Harlem*. *Tulsa Studies in Women's Literature* 16.1 (1997): 107–30.

Rohrbough, Malcolm J. *Days of Gold: The California Gold Rush and the American Nation*. Berkeley: U of California P, 1997.

Rosenblum, Lauren M. "'Things, Things, Things': Nella Larsen's *Quicksand* and the Beauty of Magazine Culture." *Communal Modernisms: Teaching Twentieth-Century Literature and Culture in the Twenty-First Century Classroom*. Eds. Emily H. Hinnov, Laurel Harris, and Lauren M. Rosenblum. New York: Palgrave Macmillan, 2013. 50–61.

Rossetti, Gina M. "Turning the Corner: Romance as Economic Critique in Norris's Trilogy of Wheat and Du Bois's *The Quest of the Silver Fleece*." *Studies in American Naturalism* 7.1 (2012): 39–49.

Rowe, John Carlos. *Literary Culture and U.S. Imperialism: From the Revolution to World War II*. Oxford: Oxford UP, 2000.

Ruiz de Burton, María Amparo. *Who Would Have Thought It?* 1872. Eds. Rosaura Sánchez and Beatrice Pita. Houston: Arte Público Press, 1995.

Ruskola, Teemu. "Canton Is Not Boston: The Invention of American Imperial Sovereignty." *American Quarterly* 57.3 (2005): 859–84.

Rust, Marion. *Prodigal Daughters: Susanna Rowson's Early American Women.* Chapel Hill: U of North Carolina P, 2008.
Said, Edward. *Culture and Imperialism.* New York: Vintage, 1994.
—. *Orientalism.* New York: Vintage, 1979.
Samson, Jane. *Imperial Benevolence: Making British Authority in the Pacific Islands.* Honolulu: U of Hawaii P, 1998.
Sassoubre, Ticien Marie. "Property and Identity in *The Custom of the Country.*" *Modern Fiction Studies* 49.4 (2003): 687–713.
Savelson, Kim. "The Romance of Process: Means Meets Ends in Frank Norris's *McTeague.*" *Where the World Is Not: Cultural Authority and Democratic Desire in Modern American Literature.* Columbus: Ohio State UP, 2009. 41–59.
Schoen, Brian. *Fabric of Union: Cotton, Federal Politics, and the Global Origins of the Civil War.* Baltimore: Johns Hopkins UP, 2009.
Schueller, Malini Johar. *U.S. Orientalisms: Race, Nation, and Gender in Literature, 1790–1890.* Ann Arbor: U of Michigan P, 1998.
Schweitzer, Ivy. "Most Pleasurable Reading We're Not Doing: Louisa May Alcott's *Little Women.*" *J19: The Journal of Nineteenth-Century Americanists* 2.1 (2014): 13–24.
Sedgwick, Catharine Maria. *Hope Leslie, or, Early Times in Massachusetts.* 1827. Ed. Carolyn L. Karcher. New York: Penguin, 1998.
Seltzer, Mark. *Bodies and Machines.* New York: Routledge, 1992.
Shannon, Laurie, et al. "Editor's Column: Literature in the Ages of Wood, Tallow, Coal, Whale Oil, Gasoline, Atomic Power, and Other Energy Sources." *PMLA* 126.2 (2011): 305–26. *JSTOR,* <www.jstor.org/stable/41414106>. Accessed 17 August 2021.
Shapiro, Stephen. *The Culture and Commerce of the Early American Novel: Reading the Atlantic World-System.* University Park: Pennsylvania State UP, 2008.
Sharp, Paul, and Jacob Weisdorf. "Globalization Revisited: Market Integration and the Wheat Trade between North America and Britain from the Eighteenth Century." *Explorations in Economic History* 50 (2013): 88–98.
Sherman, Sarah Way. *Sacramental Shopping: Louisa May Alcott, Edith Wharton, and the Spirit of Modern Consumerism.* Durham: U of New Hampshire P, 2013.
Sherrard-Johnson, Cherene. "'A Plea For Color': Nella Larsen's Iconography of the Mulatta." *American Literature* 76.4 (2004): 833–69.
Sigourney, Lydia. "To a Fragment of Cotton." 1841. *Lydia Sigourney: Selected Poetry and Prose.* Ed. Gary Kelly. Peterborough, Ontario: Broadview, 2008. 183–5.
Silverman, Debra B. "Nella Larsen's *Quicksand*: Untangling the Webs of Exoticism." *African American Review* 27.4 (1993): 599–614.
Sinclair, Upton. *Oil!.* 1926. New York: Penguin, 2007.

Slotkin, Richard. *Regeneration through Violence: The Mythology of the American Frontier*. Norman: Oklahoma UP, 1973.

Smith, Laura A. "Textile Mills and the Political Economy of Domestic Womanhood in Elizabeth Stuart Phelps's *The Silent Partner*." *Women and the Material Culture of Needlework and Textiles, 1750–1950*. Eds. Maureen Daly Goggin and Beth Fowes Tobin. Burlington, VT: Ashgate, 2009. 185–201.

Smith-Rosenberg, Carroll. *Disorderly Conduct: Visions of Gender in Victorian America*. New York: Oxford UP, 1986.

—. *This Violent Empire: The Birth of an American National Identity*. Chapel Hill: U of North Carolina P, 2012.

Spofford, Harriet Prescott. *Art Decoration Applied to Furniture*. New York: Harper and Brothers, 1878.

—. *"The Amber Gods" and Other Stories*. 1863. Ed. Alfred Bendixen. New Brunswick, NJ: Rutgers UP, 1989.

Sofer, Naomi. *Making the "America of Art": Cultural Nationalism and Nineteenth-Century Women Writers*. Columbus: Ohio State UP, 2005.

"South Dakota." *Worldmark Encyclopedia of the States*, 8th ed., vol. 2. Gale, 2016: 807–20. *U.S. History in Context*, <http://link.galegroup.com/apps/doc/CX3632200051/UHIC?u=mlin_w_umassamh&sid=UHIC&xid=396769ab>. Accessed 10 November 2018.

Stephens, Michelle Ann. *Black Empire: The Masculine Global Imaginary of Caribbean Intellectuals in the United States, 1914–1962*. Durham, NC: Duke UP, 2005.

Stern, Madeleine B. *Louisa May Alcott*. Norman: U of Oklahoma P, 1950.

Stoddard, Elizabeth. *The Morgesons*. 1862. Philadelphia: U of Pennsylvania P, 1984.

Stoler, Ann Laura, ed. *Haunted by Empire: Geographies of Intimacy in North American History*. Durham, NC: Duke UP, 2006.

—. "Tense and Tender Ties: The Politics of Comparison in North American History and (Post) Colonial Studies." Stoler, ed. *Haunted by Empire*. Durham, NC: Duke UP, 2006. 23–67.

Streeby, Shelley. *American Sensations: Class, Empire, and the Production of Popular Culture*. Berkeley: U of California P, 2002.

Sussman, Charlotte. *Consuming Anxieties: Consumer Protest, Gender & British Slavery, 1713–1833*. Stanford, CA: Stanford UP, 2000.

Sweet, Timothy. *American Georgics: Economy and Environment in American Literature, 1580–1864*. Philadelphia: U of Pennsylvania P, 2011.

Swinton, William. *Elementary Course in Geography: Designed for Primary and Intermediate Grades, and as a Complete Shorter Course*. New York: Ivison, Blakeman, Taylor, and Company, 1875.

Szeman, Imre. *On Petrocultures: Globalization, Culture, and Energy*. Morgantown: West Virginia UP, 2019.

Tate, Claudia. "Desire and Death in *Quicksand*, by Nella Larsen." *American Literary History* 7.2 (1995): 234–60.

—. "Race and Desire: *Dark Princess: A Romance*." *Next to the Color Line: Gender, Sexuality, and W. E. B. Du Bois*. Eds. Susan Gillman and Alys Eve Weinbaum. Minneapolis: U of Minnesota P, 2007. 150–208.

Taylor, George Rogers, ed. *The Turner Thesis: Concerning the Role of the Frontier in American History*. Lexington, MA: D. C. Heath and Company, 1972.

"Tea for the Ladies, and Where it Comes From," *Godey's Lady's Book*. Apr. 1860: 302–6.

Teague, David. "Frank Norris and the Visual Arts." *Frank Norris Studies* 19 (1994): 4–8.

TePaske, John J. *A New World of Gold and Silver*. Leiden: Brill, 2010.

Tompkins, Jane P. *Sensational Designs: The Cultural Work of American Fiction, 1790–1860*. New York: Oxford UP, 1985.

Tonkovich, Nicole. "Of Compass Bearing and Reorientations in the Study of American Women Writers." *Legacy* 26.2 (2009): 242–61.

Trachtenberg, Alan. *The Incorporation of America: Culture and Society in the Gilded Age*. New York: Hill and Wang, 1982.

Trafton, Scott. *Egypt Land: Race and Nineteenth-Century American Egyptomania*. Durham, NC: Duke UP, 2004.

Trentmann, Frank. *Empire of Things: How We Became a World of Consumers, from the Fifteenth Century to the Twenty-First*. New York: Harper Perennial, 2016.

Trump, Donald. Speech on Trade at Illinois Steel Plant. 26 July 2018, Granite City Works, Granite City, Ill.

"Turkey." *Worldmark Encyclopedia of the Nations*. Eds. Timothy L. Gall and Jeneen M. Hobby, 12th ed., vol. 4. Asia and Oceania: Gale, 2007: 849–70. *Gale Virtual Reference Library*, <http://link.galegroup.com/apps/doc/CX2586700239/GVRL?u=mlin_w_umassamh&sid=GVRL&xid=a88dfd4f>. Accessed 10 November 2018.

Twain, Mark. *Roughing It*. 1872. Ed. Hamlin Hill. New York: Penguin, 1985.

US Bureau of the Census, Economic Indicator Division. "US. Trade in Goods and Services—Balance of Payments (BOP) Basis." 6 June 2018, <https://www.census.gov/foreign-trade/statistics/historical/gands.pdf>. Accessed 23 September 2018.

—. "International Transactions and Foreign Commerce." *Bicentennial Edition: Historical Statistics of the United States, Colonial Times to 1970*. Washington, D.C.: US Bureau of the Census, 1975. 858–907.

Van Hook, Bailey. *Angels of Art: Women and Art in American Society, 1876–1914*. University Park: Penn State UP, 1996.

Van Wienen, Mark, and Julie Kraft. "How the Socialism of W. E. B. Du Bois Still Matters: Black Socialism in *The Quest of the Silver Fleece*—and Beyond." *African American Review* 41.1 (2007): 67–85.

Veblen, Thorstein. *The Theory of the Leisure Class: An Economic Study of Institutions*. Ed. Stuart Chase. New York: Modern Library, 1934.

Vertrees, Herbert. *Pearls and Pearling*. New York: Fur News Publishing, 1913.

Volo, Dorothy Denneen, and James M. Volo. *Daily Life in Civil War America*. Westport, CT: Greenwood, 1998.

Voltaire, *Candide*. Trans. Lowell Bair. New York: Bantam, 1981.

Vucetic, Srdjan. "A Racialized Peace? How Britain and the US Made Their Relationship Special." *Foreign Policy Analysis* 7.4 (2011): 403–22.

Wagner, Johanna M. "(Be)Longing in *Quicksand:* Framing Kinship and Desire more Queerly." *College Literature* 39.3 (2012): 129–59.

Wagner-Martin, Linda. Introduction. *The Custom of the Country*, by Edith Wharton. New York: Penguin, 2006. vii–xvii.

Wall, Cheryl A. "Passing for what? Aspects of Identity in Nella Larsen's Novels." *Black American Literature Forum* 20.1/2 (1986): 97–111.

Wallach, Alan. "The Birth of the American Art Museum." *The American Bourgeoisie: Distinction and Identity in the Nineteenth Century*. Eds. Sven Beckert and Julia B. Rosenbaum. New York: Palgrave, 2010. 245–56.

Warhol, Robyn. "'Reader, Can You Imagine? No, You Cannot': The Narratee as Other in Harriet Jacobs's Text." *Narrative* 3.1 (1995): 57–72.

Waterston, Darren. *Filthy Lucre*. 2014. Mixed media. Massachusetts Museum of Contemporary Art, North Adams.

Wegener, Frederick. "'Rabid Imperialist': Edith Wharton and the Obligations of Empire in Modern American Fiction." *American Literature* 72.4 (2000): 783–812.

Wertheimer, Eric. *Imagined Empires: Incas, Aztecs, and the New World of American Literature, 1771–1876*. New York: Cambridge UP, 1999.

West, Patricia. "Gender Politics and the Orchard House Museum." *Domesticating History: The Political Origins of America's House Museums*. Washington: Smithsonian Institution Press, 1999. 39–91.

Wexler, Laura. *Tender Violence: Domestic Visions in an Age of U.S. Imperialism*. Chapel Hill: U of North Carolina P, 2000.

Wharton, Edith. *A Backward Glance*. Ed. Louis Auchincloss. New York: Simon and Schuster, 1998.

—. *The Custom of the Country*. 1913. New York: Penguin, 2006.

Wharton, Edith, and Ogden Codman, Jr. *The Decoration of Houses*. 1897. New York: Norton, 1997.

White, Richard. *The Middle Ground: Indians, Empires, and Republics in the Great Lakes Region, 1650–1815*. 1991. New York: Cambridge UP, 2011.

Widder, Keith R. "Effects of the American Revolution on Fur-Trade Society at Michilimackinac." *The Fur Trade Revisited: Selected Papers of the Sixth North American Fur Trade Conference, Mackinac Island, Michigan*. Eds. Jennifer S. H. Brown, W. J. Eccles, and Donald P. Heldman. East Lansing: Michigan State UP, 1994. 299–316.

Wilhelm Julie. "'Don't laugh! Act as if it was all right!' And Other Comical Interruptions in *Little Women*." *Studies in American Humor* 3.19 (2009): 63–82.

Williams, William Appleman. *Empire As A Way of Life: An Essay on the Causes and Character of America's Present Predicament Along with a Few Thoughts about an Alternative*. New York: Oxford UP, 1980.

Willis, Kedon. "Unsettled Intimacies: Revisiting Edith Wharton's *The Custom of the Country* through Nella Larsen's *Quicksand*." *Tydskrif vir Letterkunde* 56.1 (2019): 62–73.

Wilson, Sheena, Adam Carlson, and Imre Szeman, eds. *Petrocultures: Oil, Energy, and Culture*. Montreal: McGill-Queen's UP, 2017.

Wilson, William J. "Afric-American Picture Gallery." *Anglo-African Magazine* 1.3 (March 1859): 87–90. Eds. Leif Eckstrom and Britt Rusert. <http://jtoaa.common-place.org/welcome-to-just-teach-one-african-american/introduction-afric-american-picture-gallery>. Accessed 17 September 2015.

Winders, Jamie. "Imperfectly Imperial: Northern Travel Writers in the Postbellum U.S. South, 1865–1880." *Annals of the Association of American Geographers* 95.2 (June 2005): 40.

Woolson, Constance Fenimore. *Anne*. New York: Harper & Brothers, 1882.

Wry, Joan R. "Lydia Sigourney's 'To a Shred of Linen': Lineaments of the Domestic and the Sublime." *American Transcendental Quarterly* 22.2 (2008): 403–14.

Zafran, Eric M. "William Bouguereau in America: A Roller-Coaster Reputation." *In the Studios of Paris: William Bouguereau and his American Students*. Ed. James F. Peck. New Haven, CT: Yale UP, 2006. 17–44.

Zimmerman, David A. *Panic! Markets, Crises, and Crowds in American Fiction*. Chapel Hill: U of North Carolina P, 2006.

Ziser, Michael. "Oil Spills." *PMLA* 126.2 (2011): 321–3.

Index

Note: 'n' indicates chapter note number.

Ackerman, Alan, 187, 233n1
Adams, Sean Patrick, 48
Advocate of Peace, The, 58, 59
aesthetic taste, 5, 6, 9–10, 19–20, 23, 36n46
  and Du Bois's *The Quest of the Silver Fleece*, 135–6, 138, 139, 148–57, 160, 177, 181nn26–7
  and Larsen's *Quicksand*, 189, 220, 223, 226
  and Norris's *The Pit*, 135–6, 138, 139, 143, 145–6, 149–57, 177
  and Phelps's *The Story of Avis*, 58, 65–7, 69, 72–3, 75, 77, 81n38
  and Wharton's *The Custom of the Country*, 184, 186, 189, 198, 203
African Americans, 10, 12, 13, 20, 33nn27–8, 136–7, 141, 142, 146, 149, 152, 157, 159, 165, 167–9, 179n12, 180n23, 181n26; see also Blackness
Alcott, Louisa May, 2, 6, 7, 20, 237
  Eight Cousins, 79n18, 240, 242n12
  journals, 46, 48–9, 52, 54, 79nn21–2, 81n34
  Little Women, 40–1, 43–55, 76–7
  Moods, 54
  "The Fate of the Forrests," 54
  Work, 52
Alexandre, Sandy, 13
allegory, 42, 71–2, 75, 88, 91, 98, 100–1, 103, 107, 112, 115, 119, 122, 129, 131n19, 239
American Civil War *see* Civil War, US
American Revolution, 17, 88, 91, 93, 137, 222
American Studies, 7–8, 12, 14

Andrews, William L., 141
Anglo-Saxons, 90, 94, 98–104, 147, 179n11, 204
Appadurai, Arjun, 3, 30n5, 71
Arabindan-Kesson, Anna, 12
Arac, Jonathan, 11
Aranda, José, 115, 132n26
art, 2, 5, 12, 19–20, 35–6nn44–45, 235–6
  and Alcott's *Little Women*, 40, 41, 52–3, 77
  and Du Bois's *The Quest of the Silver Fleece*, 135–41, 145–60, 163–70, 174, 177, 178n5, 180n17, 181n26, 182n29, 183n41
  and Larsen's *Quicksand*, 218, 229, 230
  and Norris's *The Pit*, 135–41, 145–60, 163–70, 174, 177, 178n5
  and Phelps's *The Story of Avis*, 40, 41, 42, 44, 57, 60–4, 73–7
  and Wharton's *The Custom of the Country*, 186, 191, 198–205, 211–12, 215
  and Woolson's *Anne*, 99, 112
Astor, John Jacob, American Fur Company, 86–7, 93, 94, 96, 129n1
Atlantic, The, 140

Banta, Martha, 99
Barker, Deborah, 65, 81n38, 82n50
Barrett, Ross, 14
Beam, Dorri, 112, 131n20
beauty, 67, 100, 109, 151, 154, 160, 162, 163, 176, 182n30, 211
Beckert, Sven, 16, 47, 64, 78n6, 79n23, 147, 178n3, 179n13

Beecher, Catharine, *A Treatise on Domestic Economy*, 37n51, 84n60
Belzoni, Giovanni Battista, 29, 50, 51, 80n30
Bennett, Jane, 18
Berger, Martin, 182n29
Bernstein, Peter, 119, 133n29
Bernstein, Susan Naomi, 54
Berry, Kate, 37n55
bildungsroman structure, 7, 101, 105, 146
Black Americans *see* African Americans
Blackford, Holly, 53
Blackness, 12, 33n26
  and Du Bois's *The Quest of the Silver Fleece*, 135, 137, 138, 146–9, 151–3, 157–66, 174, 177, 182n30
  and Larsen's *Quicksand*, 188–90, 216–21, 224, 229, 234n7
Blake, William, 34n31
Bloom, Stephen, 195, 201
Bonaparte, Napoleon, 82n47, 103, 137–8, 142
Boston Herald, The, 59
Bouguereau, William-Adolphe, 136, 140, 149–64, 177, 180n20
Bourdieu, Pierre, 135–6, 140, 155, 156, 177, 181n27, 186, 198
Brandão, José António, 92, 93, 130n7
Brehm, Victoria, 89–90
Brodhead, Richard, 50
Brontë, Emily, *Wuthering Heights*, 105, 110
Brown, Bill, 16
Brown, Gillian, 17
Buell, Frederick, 38n58
Burollet, Thérèse, 180n21
Byerman, Keith, 151, 179n12, 180n19

capital, cultural/economic/political, 6, 20, 40, 42, 44, 136, 139, 141, 149–64, 177, 198, 208, 237
capitalism, 4, 5, 17, 31n14, 32n16, 237, 238, 240
  and Alcott's *Little Women*, 42, 52
  and Du Bois's *The Quest of the Silver Fleece*, 136, 140, 143–9, 154, 160, 164, 165, 170, 172–3, 177
  and Larsen's *Quicksand*, 185, 223

  and Norris's *The Pit*, 136, 140, 143–9, 154, 160, 164, 165, 170, 172–3, 177
  and Phelps's *The Story of Avis*, 56, 60, 61, 76
  and Wharton's *The Custom of the Country*, 185, 195
Carby, Hazel, 182n28
carmine dye, 3, 14, 18, 21, 57–8, 66–73, 83–4nn56–60
Carroll, Anne, 151
Cartier, Jacques, 195, 197, 199, 213
Cass, Jeffrey, 63, 82n48, 82n50
Castronovo, Russ, 150, 151, 182n32
Cather, Willa, *My Ántonia*, 239
China, 9, 21, 22, 30n9, 32n21, 48, 79n18, 219, 222–4, 226, 229, 236–7, 240, 241n4, 242n5; *see also* porcelain, Chinese blue
Civil War, US, 2–3, 5, 6, 24–5, 31n11, 35n44, 42, 43, 51, 64, 65, 88, 105, 106, 111, 112, 115, 116, 126, 127, 138–9, 148, 238
Clark, Brett, 161
class, 19
  and Alcott's *Little Women*, 48, 50, 54
  and Du Bois's *The Quest of the Silver Fleece*, 136, 138–9, 154, 157, 159, 177, 178n5, 181n27
  and Larsen's *Quicksand*, 189, 215, 217, 220, 221, 233
  and Norris's *The Pit*, 136, 138–9, 154, 157, 159, 177, 178n5, 181n27
  and Phelps's *The Story of Avis*, 61, 74, 84nn61–2
  and Wharton's *The Custom of the Country*, 186, 190, 191, 200, 201
  see also aesthetic taste; hierarchies, social
climate change, 240–1, 242n13
coal, 3, 13, 24, 38n58, 40, 47, 48, 49, 52, 77, 80n26, 143, 240
cochineal *see* carmine dye
Codman, Ogden *see* Wharton, Edith
coffee, 3, 21
Cohen, Joanna, 37n55
Collins, Peter, 178n8, 182n36
Columbus, Christopher, 36n48, 55, 99, 118, 131n16, 195

commodities, 1–26, 235, 237–41
  as term, 30n5
  see also art; carmine dye; coal; coffee; consumption of commodities; cotton; flour; fur; gold; India shawls; linen; oil; oranges; pearls; porcelain, Chinese blue; sugar; wheat; women, commodification of
complicity in economic systems, 5, 15, 45, 53, 56, 76, 170
connections/interconnectedness, global, 2, 15, 16, 40, 44, 47, 61, 85n66, 143–4, 238–9
conquest, imperial, 2, 5, 41, 42, 44, 61
  and Larsen's *Quicksand*, 186–8, 190, 217
  and Norris's *The Pit*, 142, 156
  and Ruiz de Burton's *Who Would Have Thought It?*, 87, 116–18, 121, 122, 123, 128
  and Wharton's *The Custom of the Country*, 184, 186–8, 190–2, 194, 195, 197, 200, 202, 203, 207, 208, 210, 211–15, 234n4
  and Woolson's *Anne*, 87, 92, 106–8, 113, 114
consumption of commodities, 2, 4, 6, 10–13, 16–17, 20–6, 238, 240
  and Alcott's *Little Women*, 40–1, 44, 46, 55
  and Larsen's *Quicksand*, 184–90, 215–28, 231–3
  and Phelps's *The Story of Avis*, 40–1, 43, 44, 57–8, 60–1, 67, 76, 83n56
  and Wharton's *The Custom of the Country*, 184–90, 194, 195, 197, 200, 211–14, 232–3, 233n1
Coronado, Raúl, 8
Cortés, Hernán, 118, 132n28
cotton, 1–3, 6, 7, 9, 10, 12, 13, 16, 24, 238
  and Alcott's *Little Women*, 40, 41, 46–8, 78n6, 78n14, 79n23
  and Du Bois's *The Quest of the Silver Fleece*, 135, 137–9, 140, 141–9, 151, 157, 158, 160–3, 165, 170, 174, 177, 178n3, 179n13, 181n25, 183n42
  and Phelps's *The Story of Avis*, 40, 41–4, 57, 58, 60, 61, 64–5, 76
Crisis, The, 141, 151

Crisler, Jesse S., 150, 155, 180n20
Cross, Susan, 235, 241n2
Curry-Machado, Jonathan, 15

Daly, Suzanne, 16, 113
David, Jacques-Louis, *Portrait of Madame Récamier*, 99
Davidson, Cathy, 10, 131n17
Dawahare, Anthony, 230
debt, national, 46, 65, 79n17
Declaration of Independence, 10, 137
decoration, home, 20, 23, 37n52, 83n56, 185–6, 226
detritus of empire, 93, 116, 235, 240
Dewey, Caitlin, 236
Dillon, Elizabeth Maddock, 36n46, 133n35, 137
Dimock, Wai Chee, 241
Dolan, Kathryn Cornell, 84n64, 144
domestic guides, 22–3, 37n51, 185–6
domesticity, 2, 4–5, 6, 11, 17–18, 23, 30n7, 40–7, 55, 71–2, 76–7, 88, 96, 108, 114, 123, 158; *see also* consumption of commodities; decoration, home
Douglas, Ann, 35n40
Doyle, Laura, 3–4, 6, 10, 14, 25, 29n3, 31n13, 33n24, 44, 85n65, 97, 113, 130n12, 130n14, 218, 243n14; *see also* inter-imperiality
Dreiser, Theodore, *The Financier*, 138, 178n8
Drexler, Michael, 137
Du Bois, W. E. B., 2, 6, 7, 12–13, 20, 238
  Black Reconstruction, 147
  "Criteria of Negro Art," 151, 183n41
  Dark Princess, 151, 163, 224
  letters, 182n30
  "Of the Training of Black Men," 152
  The Quest of the Silver Fleece, 16, 135, 139–42, 146–77
  The Souls of Black Folk, 152, 182n28
  "The African Roots of War," 140
  "The Color Line Belts the World," 11, 148
Dwight, Nathaniel, 21

Eckes, Alfred, 38n56
Egypt, 3, 43, 47, 52–3, 61, 64–5, 82n47
"Egytpomania," 46–7, 49, 62, 65

Ejrnæs, Mette, 80n25
Elbert, Sarah, 78n15
empowerment, 56, 188, 193, 211, 215, 216, 226, 229
enslavement/slavery, 2, 5, 10, 19, 23–4, 33n28, 43, 46, 48, 98, 135, 137–8, 147–8, 181n26; *see also* exploitation
ethics, 2, 3, 4, 17, 18, 24, 26, 40, 44, 46, 50, 56–7, 58, 64, 73, 238
exceptionalism, US, 8, 10, 83n54, 85n65, 104, 131n18
exoticism/exoticization, 11, 55, 196, 197, 204, 206, 211, 216, 217, 218, 220, 223, 226, 229; *see also* Orientalism
expansionism, US, 2, 3, 5–6, 9, 10, 11, 13, 22, 30n10, 32n20, 45, 49, 58, 76, 77, 139, 144, 150
exploitation of labor, 4, 6, 16, 18–19, 22, 43, 44, 45, 46, 53, 56, 58, 60, 61, 66, 70–1, 73, 238
exports, 2, 3, 5, 9, 21–2, 24–5, 42, 43, 48, 60, 64, 74, 79n23, 80n25, 113, 118–19, 133n29, 133n31, 138, 144, 179n9, 208, 238–9; *see also* imports

Farland, Maria, 158, 176, 179n12
feminism, 4, 17, 35n41, 45, 56–7, 89, 129n2
Fiji, 42–3, 77n4
Fisher, Beth, 115, 123, 132n24
Fitzpatrick, Tara, 78n11
Fleming, E. McClung, 99
Florida, 5–6, 60, 69, 73–4
flour, 47–8, 49, 52, 77, 144
Floyd, Janet, 133n32
Foster, John Bellamy, 161
Frank, Caroline, 30n9
Franklin, Benjamin, 91–2, 93
Freedgood, Elaine, 16
Frelinghuysen, Alice Cooney, 222
fur, 3, 13, 86–98, 112–14, 128, 129, 130nn6–7

Gaines, Kevin, 180n23, 220
gender, 20, 45, 54, 56, 59, 65, 66, 73, 98, 99, 112, 115, 117, 135, 160, 182n28, 184, 190, 192, 194, 204, 207, 214, 215, 216, 218, 224, 233, 239

genre, 7, 13, 41, 50, 54, 105, 151, 241
geography textbooks, 21–2, 36nn48–9
Ghosh, Amitav, 14, 33n29
  Ibis Trilogy, 240
Gikandi, Simon, 18–20, 33n28, 135, 152, 181n26
Gillman, Susan, 7
Gilroy, Paul, 33n26
Glazer, Lee, 241n1
Glennon, Jenny, 194, 199
Glickman, Lawrence, 23
Godey's Lady's Book, 22–3, 24, 37n51, 196
gold, 3, 86, 87, 88, 111, 115–22, 128, 132–3nn27–29, 132n25, 133nn31–3, 235, 240
Goldsmith, Meredith, 190
Gordon, John Steele, 31n11, 178n5
Graham, Don, 150
Gray, Jeffrey, 228
Greenfield, Amy, 68, 83n57
Gruesser, John Cullen, 12, 219

Habsburg, Ferdinand Maximilian von, 127–8, 134n38
Hager, Christopher, 8
Haitian Revolution, 136–8, 178nn2–3
Harde, Roxanne, 58
Harvey, David, 31n14
Hazareesingh, Sandip, 15
Heil, Jenny, 21, 36n48, 131n19
Hendel, Erin, 45
Hicks, Elias, 23
Hicks, Scott, 182n31
hierarchies
  imperial, 136, 140, 169, 186
  racial, 49–50, 94, 115–17, 120–1, 125
  social, 11, 19, 136, 138, 140, 155, 177, 186, 200
  see also class
historiography, 85n65, 96, 124, 130n11
Hodgson, Louisa Jane, 46
Hoganson, Kristin, 5, 41
home/household *see* decoration, home; domesticity
Hopkins, Pauline, 12
Howells, William Dean, *The Rise of Silas Lapham*, 138
Hsu, Hsuan, 8

Hunter, Brooke, 47, 80n25, 144, 179n9
Hutchinson, George, 187, 218

iconography, 42, 99, 135, 177, 230
identity/ies, US national, 10, 16, 19, 25–6, 31n12, 32nn22–3, 33n28
and Ruiz de Burton's *Who Would Have Thought It?*, 122, 124, 125, 126, 129
and Woolson's *Anne*, 90, 91, 93, 96, 98, 99, 101, 104, 107, 129
ideology/ies, 17, 21, 38n57, 52, 56, 94, 189, 220, 238
imaginary/imaginings, imperial, 2, 3, 26, 41–4, 63, 75
Immerwahr, Daniel, 32n22
imports, 3, 5, 11, 20, 24–6, 37nn54–5, 38n58, 40, 48, 74, 138, 178n4, 196, 197, 200, 238
Asian, 215, 218, 222–3, 225, 229, 231, 236–8, 241n4; *see also* exports
India, 1–2, 3, 43, 47, 55, 64, 195–7, 240
India shawls, 113–14
Indigenous/Native Americans, 5–6, 49, 60, 73, 87, 90, 92, 93, 97–8, 106, 117–21, 122, 124, 133n35, 201
individualism, 17, 34n37
industrialization, 48, 80n25, 184
inequality/inequity, 33n24, 69, 78n11, 90, 139, 149, 151, 161, 168, 169, 174, 236
Ingham, John, 154
Innis, Harold, 13, 92
Insko, Jeffrey, 95–6
inter-imperiality, 2, 3–4, 7–20, 25–6, 29n3, 36n45, 235–7, 243n14
and Alcott's *Little Women*, 41–2
and Du Bois's *The Quest of the Silver Fleece*, 137
and Larsen's *Quicksand*, 185, 215, 216, 218, 219–27, 233
and Norris's *The Pit*, 142, 143, 144, 145, 179n9
and Phelps's *The Story of Avis*, 43, 44, 59, 60–9, 71–2, 73
and Ruiz de Burton's *Who Would Have Thought It?*, 87–8, 114–17, 119, 127, 129
and Wharton's *The Custom of the Country*, 185, 186, 195, 196, 205, 210, 213, 215, 233

and Woolson's *Anne*, 87–8, 89–93, 98, 102, 106, 108, 112
intertextuality, 13, 46, 97, 113, 142, 149, 152, 157, 159, 164, 177
intimacies, 41, 44, 77n2
Irving, Washington, *Astoria; Or, Anecdotes of an Enterprise Beyond the Rocky Mountains*, 86–7, 129n1
Isaacson, Walter, 92

Jacobin Magazine, 237
Jacobs, Margaret, 115, 125, 131n22
James, Henry
The Spoils of Poynton, 239–40
"The Figure in the Carpet," 112
"The Real Thing," 154, 202
Johnston, Patricia, 30n9
Joslin, Katherine, 199, 213
Jun, Helen, 224

Kaplan, Amy, 4–5, 7, 22, 30n7, 37n51, 38n60, 41, 49, 74, 85n65, 131n18
Kelley, Robin D. G., 8, 12, 33n27, 147, 178n2
Kelly, Lori Duin, 70, 84n61
Kessler, Carol Farley, 67, 82n48
King, Heidi, 117, 122, 132n27
Klein, Shana, 74
Knoper, Randall, 34n37, 36n44
Kotz, David M., 237
Kraft, Julie, 180n19
Kunz, George Frederick, 196–7
Kwarteng, Kwasi, 132n28, 133n30

labor *see* enslavement/slavery; exploitation of labor
Lahey, Sarah, 81n34
Lanier, Jessica, 222
Larsen, Nella, 6, 12–13, 237
Quicksand, 184, 185, 187–90, 215–33
"Sanctuary," 187
Le Corbeiller, Clare, 222
Lee, Hermione, 190, 195
Lee, Maurice, 151–2, 179n12, 180n18, 182n33
Leiter, Joseph, 142
LeMenager, Stephanie, 15, 33n29, 35n43, 242n11
Levine, Lawrence, 19, 158–9

Lewis, David Levering, 140
Leyland, Frederick Richards, 235, 241nn1–2
liberty, 10, 99–100, 109, 126, 130n14, 185
linen, 29n2, 46, 78n14
Lipsey, Robert E., 242nn8–9
Lisbon earthquake (1755), 51–3, 80nn32–3
Louisiana Purchase, 5, 137–8, 208
Lowe, John, 90, 129n4
Lowe, Lisa, 18, 77n2
Lowrey, Annie, 241n3
Lunde, Arne, 218–19, 229
Lyell, Charles, *The Principles of Geology*, 116
Lynch, David J., 236

McAllen, Mary Margaret, 127, 134n38
McClure's Magazine, 139–40
McDowell, Deborah E., 217, 223
McElrath, Joseph R. Jr, 150, 155, 180n20
McEntee, Grace, 111
Macharia, Keguro, 220–1
McKay, Claude, *Banana Bottom*, 240
Mackinac Island, Michigan, 88–95, 102, 112, 120, 128, 130n7
Macpherson, C. B., 17
Makdisi, Saree, 34n31
marginalization, 11, 114, 124, 152, 161, 221, 224
Marichal, Carlos, 84n59, 133n29, 133n31
Marrs, Cody, 8
Marx, Karl/Marxism, 4, 30n5
material culture, 2, 3, 18
material objects/goods, 41, 44, 46, 54–5, 76–7, 218
Melville, Herman, *Moby Dick*, 239
Merish, Lori, 17, 185, 199
Mexican-American War, 5, 87, 115, 119, 122, 126
Miller, Andrew H., 16
Miller, David C., 36n45
Miller, Marla, 37n54
morality, 18, 70, 75–6
mythology, 91, 99, 100, 161, 182n32

Nadelhoffer, Hans, 213
Nadkarni, Asha, 129n2

narration, 187, 191, 192, 193, 200, 206, 209
national identity/ies *see* identity/ies, US national
Native Americans *see* Indigenous/Native Americans
New York Times, The, 24–5
Norris, Frank, 6, 7, 237
  The Octopus, 139–42, 150
  The Pit, 135, 139–46, 147, 149–77
oil, 9, 13–15, 33n29, 35n43, 233n1, 239, 242n11
O'Keeffe, Georgia, 173, 183n40
Oliver, Lawrence J., 141
oranges, 3, 13, 40, 60–1, 73–7
Orientalism, 11, 46–7, 49, 54, 60–6, 75, 79n18, 82n47, 82n51, 185–6, 187, 196–8, 205, 215–21, 223–4, 232, 234n7, 235, 236; *see also* exoticism/exoticization
Orlando, Emily, 190
Orvell, Miles, 180n22, 202, 234n2
"other"/otherness, 11, 106, 114, 124, 125, 204, 223, 224
Ott, John, 235

Pan-Africanism, 163, 224, 227
pearls, 3, 11, 13, 185, 190–215, 232
Pease, Don, 7, 131n18
Pereira, Alvaro, 80n33
Perren, Richard, 80n25, 179n9
Phelps, Elizabeth Stuart, 6, 7, 20, 238
  Chapters of a Life, 56, 84n62
  Dr. Zay, 57
  essays, 58–9
  The Gates Ajar, 57
  Hedged In, 57
  The Silent Partner, 57, 61, 84n61
  The Story of Avis, 16, 18, 40, 42–4, 55–77, 106–7, 115, 123, 174, 183n42
  Trixy, 70, 84n61
Pickthall, Marmaduke, *Saïd the Fisherman*, 223–4
Piep, Karsten, 218
Pita, Beatrice, 117, 128, 131n22
Pletcher, David, 31n11, 38n57, 178n4
political engagement, 17–18, 23, 76–7
Pomeranz, Kenneth, 48

porcelain, Chinese blue, 3, 11, 21, 219–27, 231, 235–6
postcolonialism, 4, 6, 90, 129n4, 132n26
purity, 110, 159–60, 175–6
Puskar, Jason, 143, 182n37

queerness, 217, 218

race, 11–13, 16, 20, 115, 122, 124–6, 129, 130n14, 133n37, 135, 138, 140, 147, 149, 158, 166, 168, 179n11, 180n23, 182nn28–9, 189–90, 215–18, 226–7, 229, 233, 234n3
  skin color/tone, 124–9, 155, 159, 165, 174
  see also Blackness; whiteness
racial hierarchies, 49–50
racism, 11, 49–50, 54, 121, 140, 158, 176, 180n23
Ramirez, Pablo, 116, 123, 132n25, 133n37
Rioux, Anne Boyd, 89, 90
Ritvo, Harriet, 11
rivalry/ies, 89, 90–1, 98, 101–10, 114, 128, 129, 186
Rivera, John-Michael, 133n37
Robbins, Bruce, 13
Rosenblum, Lauren M., 220
Rossetti, Gina, 141–2
Rowe, John Carlos, 38n60, 101
Rowson, Susanna
  Abridgment of Universal Geography, 21, 36n48
  Reuben and Rachel, 131n19
Ruiz de Burton, María Amparo, *Who Would Have Thought It?*, 6, 20, 87–8, 114–29, 135, 237

Said, Edward, 11, 19, 62, 82n47, 82n51, 177n1
Sánchez, Rosaura, 117, 128, 131n22
Sassoubre, Ticien Marie, 191, 203
Schueller, Malini, 11, 185, 197
Schweitzer, Ivy, 45, 81n36
Scribner's Magazine, 234n4
Sedgwick, Catharine Maria, *Hope Leslie*, 95, 97, 113, 130n12
self-actualization, 45, 61, 185, 232
self-fashioning, 92, 215

selfhood, 5, 16–17, 227–33
self-presentation, 198, 199, 204, 218
self-reflexivity, 15, 19, 40, 135, 140, 151
self-sufficiency, 10, 24–5, 53, 158, 238
Seltzer, Mark, 34n37
sensationalist fiction, 49–54
sentimental fiction, 7, 35n40, 41, 44, 55–6
Seven Years' War, 52, 144
sexuality, 187, 189, 190, 204, 216–18, 229–30, 233
Shapiro, Stephen, 30n8
Sheeler, Charles, 173
Sherrard-Johnson, Cherene, 218, 230
Sigourney, Lydia
  "To a Fragment of Cotton," 1–2
  "To A Shred of Linen," 29n2
Silverman, Debra, 218
Sinclair, Upton, *Oil!*, 35n43, 239, 242n11
slavery *see* enslavement/slavery
Smith, Adam, 81n35
Smith, Laura A., 84n61
Smith-Rosenberg, Carroll, 5, 10, 32n23
social status *see* class; hierarchies
Sofer, Naomi, 81n44, 82n50
Southworth, E.D.E.N., *The Hidden Hand*, 50, 81n35
Spanish-American War, 22, 139, 142, 144, 179n11
Spenser, Edmund, *The Faerie Queene*, 67–8
sphinx, 62–6, 72–3, 75–6, 82n50, 172, 174, 176
Spofford, Harriet Prescott, *Art Decoration Applied to Furniture*, 23, 83n56
Stenport, Anna Westerstahl, 218–19, 229
Stern, Madeleine, 78n14
Stevenson, Charles Hugh, 196–7
Stoddard, Elizabeth, *The Morgesons*, 239
Stoler, Ann Laura, 8, 18, 77n2
Stowe, Harriet Beecher, 23, 74, 84n64
Streeby, Shelley, 85n65
sugar, 5, 13, 21
supply and demand, 47, 143, 182n36
Swinton, William, *Elementary Course in Geography*, 21, 70

tariffs, 3, 20, 24, 26, 38nn56–7, 236–7, 241n3
taste *see* aesthetic taste
Tate, Claudia, 180n17, 217, 230
TePaske, John, 117–19
Tompkins, Jane, 35n40
trade *see* exports; imports; tariffs; self-sufficiency
Trafton, Scott, 62, 82n46
transnationalism, 8, 12, 31n12, 41, 48, 90, 218, 219, 228
Trump, Donald, 236–8, 241n3, 242n5
Turner, Frederick Jackson, 30n10, 32n20
Twain, Mark, 34n37, 129, 239

United Opinion, The, 59

Veblen, Thorstein, *The Theory of the Leisure Class*, 19
Vedder, Elihu, *The Questioner of the Sphinx*, 63, 82n48
Venezuelan Crisis (1895), 59
Vertrees, Herbert, 205
violence, imperial, 4, 235
　and Alcott's *Little Women*, 49–50, 55
　and Phelps's *The Story of Avis*, 43, 71
　and Ruiz de Burton's *Who Would Have Thought It?*, 117, 121, 122, 125, 127, 128, 129
　and Wharton's *The Custom of the Country*, 190–200, 201, 215
　and Woolson's *Anne*, 88–9, 91, 93, 94, 96, 98, 100, 104, 107–8, 113, 114
Voltaire, *Candide*, 52, 80n32

Wagner, Johanna M., 216
Wall, Cheryl, 217
Wallach, Alan, 35n44
War of 1812, 5, 88, 93, 94, 112
Waterston, Darren, *Filthy Lucre*, 235–6, 238
Wegener, Frederick, 194, 209
Wertheimer, Eric, 124, 131n16
West, Patricia, 37n52, 78n12
Wharton, Edith, 6, 20, 237
　A Backward Glance, 192
　The Custom of the Country, 184, 185, 186–215, 232–3
　and Ogden Codman, *The Decoration of Houses*, 23, 186
　Twilight Sleep, 194–5
wheat, 3, 9, 24, 40, 47–8, 52, 80n25, 135, 139, 140, 141–9, 153, 154, 156–7, 169, 170–2, 174, 177, 179n9, 182n37, 238
　flour, 47–8, 49, 52, 77, 144
Whistler, James McNeill, *Peacock Room*, 235, 241n2
White, Richard, 93, 130n6
whiteness, 12, 13, 20
　and Du Bois's *The Quest of the Silver Fleece*, 149, 152, 159–63, 164, 169, 176, 182n29
　and Larsen's *Quicksand*, 188, 217, 230, 232, 234n7
　and Norris's *The Pit*, 149, 159–61, 164, 168, 169, 176
　and Ruiz de Burton's *Who Would Have Thought It?*, 115, 123, 124, 133n37
　and Wharton's *The Custom of the Country*, 188, 189–90, 204, 206, 216
　and Woolson's *Anne*, 90, 94, 98, 100, 109–10
Wienen, Mark Van, 180n19
Wilhelm, Julie, 48, 80n28
Wilson, William J., "Afric-American Picture Gallery," 136–8, 149, 167
Winders, Jamie, 84n63
women, commodification of
　and Larsen's *Quicksand*, 184–5, 187–8, 216, 217, 218, 219, 224, 225
　and Phelps's *The Story of Avis*, 67, 72
　and Ruiz de Burton's *Who Would Have Thought It?*, 119, 120, 121, 128
　and Wharton's *The Custom of the Country*, 184–5, 187–8, 190, 198, 206, 207, 211
women writers, 17–18, 35nn40–5, 49–54, 77
women's bodies, 88, 99, 100, 119–20, 124–5, 128, 129n2, 133n37, 135, 160, 185, 191, 199, 207, 211, 212, 230, 233

women's magazines, 22, 24, 37n51, 196
Woolson, Constance Fenimore, 6, 20, 237
   Anne, 87–114, 115, 120, 122, 124, 129, 135, 165
   "Jeannette," 111
   "Miss Grief," 112
Worden, Daniel, 14
World War I, 6, 239
Wry, Joan R., 29n2

Yaeger, Patricia, 14

Zimmerman, David, 150, 182n37
Ziser, Michael, 80n26

EU representative:
Easy Access System Europe
Mustamäe tee 50, 10621 Tallinn, Estonia
Gpsr.requests@easproject.com

www.ingramcontent.com/pod-product-compliance
Lightning Source LLC
Chambersburg PA
CBHW050211240426
43671CB00013B/2291